JOURNAL
As Ambassador to Great Britain.

HERBERT HOOVER

JOURNAL

AS AMBASSADOR
TO GREAT BRITAIN

by Charles G. Dawes

Foreword by Herbert Hoover

WITH ILLUSTRATIONS

GREENWOOD PRESS, PUBLISHERS
WESTPORT, CONNECTICUT

Originally published in 1939
by The Macmillan Company, New York

First Greenwood Reprinting 1970

Library of Congress Catalogue Card Number 72-109728

SBN 8371-4218-0

Printed in the United States of America

FOREWORD

General Dawes in writing his impressions and experiences over these fateful years is performing two services. He is giving the invaluable guidance of experience to this generation. He is making the accurate backgrounds of written history when the distant time comes that this period can be truly appraised. The history of the gigantic forces which dominate national and international life can never be written from the current newspapers, magazines, or even the Congressional Record. They record such public knowledge as there may be of these incidents at the time. But what lies behind those incidents will be appraised from such contributions as this book. General Dawes has seen as few Americans have seen the struggles of men in these vital years, and he has seen as few men have seen the forces which make the destiny of nations.

HERBERT HOOVER

ILLUSTRATIONS

Illustrations

Illustrations

JOURNAL

As Ambassador to Great Britain

I was appointed Ambassador to Great Britain last month when I was in the Dominican Republic, engaged in the formation of a plan of business reorganization for that Government, as chairman of a commission of Americans of my own selection. To this task I had been invited by President Vasquez. It was completed in four weeks—three of which were spent in Santo Domingo. The Dominican Congress has already enacted into law our suggested legislation, and the plan is now in operation.

On returning to Chicago, preparations for my new work were added to the work incident to arranging my business and personal affairs for a long absence.

My recent visit at Washington, however, should be outlined while it is fresh in my recollection. At President Hoover's invitation, I arrived at Washington last Wednesday morning, May 15th. Before leaving Chicago, and knowing that I was expected to deal with the naval disarmament problem, I had prepared a speech upon that subject to be delivered before the Society of the Pilgrims of Great Britain in London at the inception of my work in London. This address I took with me to Washington to submit to the President and to Secretary Stimson, as tending toward "limiting debate" upon the matter, since the discussion then would naturally be as to modifications in the address, rather than in generalities.

Was met at the depot and taken to the White House where I was given an office room adjoining my bedroom. After paying my respects to the President, I went to the State Department, where I met the Secretary of State, Henry L. Stimson, and we plunged into the subject of naval disarmament.

In the afternoon, after lunch, the President and I went to his library office where I read him my address.

1

Journal as Ambassador to Great Britain

What I write of this visit will largely revolve around a definition of a proper method of arriving at naval equality. I had written my speech with care, and in my remarks about a definition of abstract naval equality I had followed exactly the definition of Hugh Gibson at Geneva, knowing that it then represented our Government's attitude.

My two sentences which were the starting point of our discussion were: "At the beginning of the work, the contribution of naval experts to the problem should be the definition of abstract equality. It is certainly possible for naval experts to arrive at some abstract definition of what constitutes this equality, either by limitation by tonnage, by category as suggested by Ambassador Gibson in his speech at Geneva, or otherwise."

The President, approving of the rest of the speech, discussed the Gibson formula at length. He finally suggested for my sentence containing Gibson's suggestion the following sentence: "It is certainly possible for the naval experts to arrive at some abstract definition for evaluation of fighting strength of ships."

On the following morning when I showed Stimson this change, he felt that instead of abandoning the Gibson definition it would be well to substitute an extension of it. This, by the way, was much easier to say than to do. The President had explained in detail to us the exact method he thought ought to be followed, and the problem was to outline it in some way which would be satisfactory to him and be "water tight," so to speak, when the naval experts started their search for leaks.

I asked Theodore Marriner, of the State Department, who is thoroughly conversant with the problem to try his hand. He evolved the following in place of the second sentence: "Thus, for instance, one might compare mathematically the military value of individual ships within a given category. These ships might differ in displacement, size of guns, age, speed and other characteristics. The total of the comparison, ship by ship, would amount to the equivalent value of any given category (such as cruisers, destroyers or submarines) of one navy as compared with the same category of another."

In the afternoon, Stimson and I held another session over the sentence. This—chiefly Stimson's—was the result: "Thus, for in-

2

HENRY L. STIMSON

stance, one might compare mathematically the military value of individual ships. These ships might differ in displacement, size of guns, age, speed and other characteristics, and yet such a weighted value might be given to each of these differing characteristics as to make it possible to compare the cruiser fleets of two navies and establish a parity between them."

When I took this formula to the President in the evening, he suggested in place of the words "compare mathematically," the words "find a yardstick with which to determine." He also added the words "for example" between the words "compare" and "the cruiser fleets"; and the words "or combined fleets," after the words "the cruiser fleets."

Thus the sentence stood on the evening of May 16th, and I thought it completed; but on Friday morning when I called on my friend, Sir Esme Howard, the British Ambassador in Washington, I inserted the words: "an agreed properly weighted."

Accordingly the sentence on this particular point finally read as follows: "At the beginning of the work, the contribution of the naval experts to the problem should be a definition of abstract equality. It is certainly possible for naval experts to arrive at a definition of fighting strength of ships. Thus, for instance, one might find a yardstick with which to determine the military value of individual ships. These ships might differ in displacement, size of guns, age, speed and other characteristics, and yet such an agreed properly weighted value might be given to each of these differing characteristics as to make it possible to compare, for example, the cruiser fleets or combined fleets of two navies, and establish a parity between them."

If it does nothing else, all the above will indicate with what care any serious expression on this subject must be prepared.

Evanston, Illinois,
May 20, 1929.

There are still a number of things to note in connection with my Washington visit. Sumner Welles spent considerable time with me in re the aftermath of our Dominican Commission work, as did also Henry P. Seidemann, of the Institute for Government Research (Brookings Institution). The latter is going to Santo Domingo later in the year to aid in establishing our new system of governmental accounting, provided for by the law we recommended. I left Lieut.-Colonel J. Clawson Roop in Santo Domingo to help them institute the budget operations and system. He is sending us his reports as to progress.

I have never lost an opportunity to urge the establishment of a proper accounting system in our own Government. Realizing its necessity when Director of the Bureau of the Budget, I instituted at that time an effort to provide one, only to have it condemned by the Comptroller General's organization. This matter I took up again with Hoover at Washington and found that he has it in mind. He is thinking of recommending to Congress the establishment by law of a separate accounting office, thus relieving John R. McCarl of this line of work, while continuing his functions of passing upon the legality of payments. As soon as McCarl, capable as a lawyer but who is not an expert in accounting and is under the advice of subordinates wedded to our present archaic and ridiculous system of government accounting, is relieved of this part of his present responsibilities, the proper system should be promptly instituted. For eight years, off and on, I have been urging this necessary reform.

On Thursday evening with the statement that "we might do a little team work on naval disarmament," the President read me an address which he had prepared that day to be delivered at Arlington on May 30th. In it he had kept away from the grounds of my address, as he explained, but had most powerfully presented the cause of naval disarmament, linking it to the Kellogg Peace Pact. It should make a good impression everywhere and, while still to be revised, seems in its present form to me to be the best plea for the cause yet made.

He asked me about the vacancy in the office of the Director of the Budget. I recommended Roop for the place. The President said he was afraid he had gone too far with another man, but took his name down in a note book.*

* Colonel Roop was afterwards appointed by President Hoover as Director of the Bureau of the Budget.

Journal as Ambassador to Great Britain

S.S. Olympic,
en route to England,
June 10, 1929.

From May 24th to noon of June 5th, when I left Chicago for Washington, was a period of activity in my life, more exacting than any I remember except some during critical times in France during the war. As I look back upon it now I see better the risks which I assumed, and the penalties which would have been attached to failure to reach my objective.

On May 23rd (Thursday), I realized that Chicago's second World's Fair enterprise, ably conducted to its present well-organized state by my brother Rufus C. Dawes, was doomed, owing to the inability of those who had assumed that responsibility, to raise the necessary funds. This was no fault on their part, but because of the illness of the Chairman of the Finance Committee, their leader. The delayed moving in this work of fund-raising had demoralized the friends of the Fair, and the attitude of Chicago civic leaders—the most of them—was indifferent and in some cases extremely adverse.

The sudden realization of this led me on Friday, May 24th, of my own initiative, to assume full responsibility for the financing of the Fair under a plan which had been suggested by Mr. George Woodruff. In doing this, the first step in which was to assure $10,000,000 for the Fair from private sources, before I sailed for England, June 7th, a date which could not be deferred, I can see now that I was wholly actuated by a sense of loyalty to my brother and indignation at the position in which he had been left in a great civic enterprise, without fault of his own.

My first step was to call peremptorily to my office, and without explanation, certain civic leaders of our city whose friendly attitude I regarded as essential to unify the different elements which should be behind the Fair. These were mostly friends whose unselfish, constructive, exacting and unremunerated work for Chicago in the past had placed every loyal citizen of our city in their debt, and with whom for years I had cooperated, and at times followed, as a worker under them.

5

Journal as Ambassador to Great Britain

But I met them now as enemies. To me their indifference to this civic enterprise was inexcusable, and I addressed them somewhat as I once did a war-time Congressional committee. But I knew my men. Behind my harsh language was a call to duty for their city in a crisis and from a friend, and to that kind of a call no one of them during a lifetime had ever failed to respond. After the three hours we remained together, the World's Fair, its name changed by our agreement to "A Century of Progress," had a united civic sponsorship behind it.

I shall never forget their kindness and loyal offer of help in time of need. In their presence I dictated the following memorandum, to which all agreed:

May 24, 1929.

At a meeting held this afternoon in connection with the proposed celebration of the One Hundredth Anniversary of the Incorporation of the City of Chicago, at which were present:

Rufus C. Dawes	Melvin A. Traylor
James Simpson	George Woodruff
Silas H. Strawn	John W. O'Leary
Colonel R. R. McCormick	C. Howard Marfield
Walter A. Strong	Charles G. Dawes

it was unanimously agreed to recommend to the Board of Trustees of the World's Fair the following:

(1) That the name of the Celebration be "A Century of Progress."
(2) That the scope of the Celebration should be enlarged to embrace, not only a central exhibition located out on the lake front, but should include an arrangement for the cooperation of the important industries and institutions in and contiguous to Chicago, which will make accessible to the inspection of visitors, their various processes, methods and products and the organization of pageants, contests in sports and social activities in all parts of the city and in the parks and forest preserves;
(3) That a sum of not less than $10,000,000 be underwritten for the commencement and carrying on of the work.

S.S. Olympic,
June 11, 1929.

A meeting of the Board of Trustees of the Fair having been arranged for Monday morning, I devoted Saturday to securing guarantees. By night time, guarantees for over three million dollars had been secured.

* This name was suggested by James Simpson.

6

Journal as Ambassador to Great Britain

In these notes, I will not go into details—indeed I cannot remember them. From this time, until I took the train on June 5, from early in the morning until late in the evening every day, I was engaged in strenuous endeavor—in one personal interview after another—and in meetings and conferences of various kinds.

Although I varied the method of approach according to the individual from that of the inspiring to that of the insidious, in all this time—and our final list showed over one hundred guarantors—I did not meet with a refusal. My three best cooperators were my brother Rufus C. Dawes, Melvin A. Traylor and George Woodruff. But there were many others who did fine work in solicitation. Some of them I name in my last Address to the Citizens of Chicago, which I will append.

On Monday, I addressed the Board of Trustees of the Fair. They took immediate action along the line of our recommendations as to the change of name and adoption of the plan of financing.

On the morning of May 27, in the Chicago papers, I issued the following statement to the Citizens of Chicago:

Although I sail for London June 7, I have accepted the chairmanship of the Finance Committee of the Chicago Centennial Celebration and, under the authority of the Board of Trustees, expect to have accomplished during the next week the completion of the first and most important step in the financial program of that great enterprise. I do this in response to what I believe to be a call to duty to this great city, so dear to us all.

It is a duty not only to the City of Chicago, but to the President and Board of Trustees of the Celebration Association. By hard work, and without beating of drums, they have carried this enterprise through its difficult preliminary stages. They have been recognized and sponsored by the National Research Council, supported by cash contributions of over 125,000 of the every day citizens of Chicago and endorsed by the Congress of the United States. They have secured the services of eminent architects who now, after laborious effort and many conferences, present a plan of striking interest and promise. They have now earned the right to demand the financial support which had been promised to them at the beginning of their exacting effort.

I found that the absence from the country for necessary rest of the Chairman of the Finance Committee, whose name and promise have always been a guaranty of the success of civic enterprise, imposed a moral obligation upon me as Vice Chairman to take his place, which I propose to meet. Before doing this I sounded the call of Chicago to her most heavily laden civil leadership. To James Simpson and Silas Strawn I called, and to Julius

7

Journal as Ambassador to Great Britain

Rosenwald, to Col. R. R. McCormick, to Walter A. Strong, Charles F. Glore, Roy D. Keehn, J. C. Shaffer, S. E. Thomasen, Herman Black, Melvin A. Traylor, Glenn Griswold, John W. O'Leary, and others of the bone and sinew of our strenuous civic life.

In conference with the President of the Board of Trustees, and with his approval, a number of us joined with him in recommending to the Board of Trustees that the original program of the Celebration be so enlarged in its definition as to remove all the doubts which some of the best of our leading citizens formerly had as to the proper objective of the great enterprise. This enlargement of scope will not restrict the activities of the National Research Council nor dim the glamour of the collective exhibit by industries of the progress brought about by the discoveries of science, but will widen the field for participation by the people of Chicago in the display of its industries and contests in sports in all parks and all sections of the city.

In view of this enlargement of scope, if the legislature will respond to the demands of Chicago and give to it, without further delay, the opportunity to make a final solution of its traction problem, this Centennial Celebration of a Century of Progress would be greatly advanced.

The Board of Trustees, having accepted in principle the recommendations for enlargement of scope and reconsideration of name, as Chairman of the Finance Committee and with my associates, I now undertake to assure to this enterprise the sum of $10,000,000.

It was the expressed judgment of Congress that $5,000,000 at the outset would be an assurance of success, but we will provide this greater sum. There should be no loss to the purchasers of the bonds to be offered. They will be secured by a lien upon and transfer of the first 40 cents of every dollar of gate receipts. But, in addition to this, I am asking prominent and wealthy individuals and corporations to guarantee severally to the extent of their respective underwriting the payment of these bonds already thus secured. The purchaser of these bonds will, therefore, have unquestionable security and a fair interest return. The guarantors should have no loss and they will have the satisfaction of having made the success of this world commitment of our city as certain as the passage of time. Later on there will be opportunity for the industries to make their contribution. The burden will then be carefully spread and no one will be asked to give or subscribe more than he can reasonably afford.

Within the last two days, I have managed to see only a few of the thousands to whom this enterprise appeals but, to start with, I have already secured guarantees in excess of $4,000,000 with almost as much more in immediate prospect.

There are prophets of evil here who say that, notwithstanding the years of hard work and steady progress in this enterprise, committed as we are to the world for its completion, this city—our pride—dear to us as having made each one of us what we are—will lie down like a dog on its back with its feet in the air and change its motto from "I will" to "I quit."

Let there be no mistake, we are not less courageous than our forebears, who have found no past crisis unsurmountable and have given us by their civic devotion the imperial city in which we live. The City of Chicago is

8

young, as measured in terms of municipal life. In its heart is youth, vitality, energy, hope and determination. It is in the name of Chicago that I call for cooperation from its citizens.

On the morning of June 5th, after having secured signed guarantees of over $10,000,000 the following statement by me was printed:

To the Citizens of Chicago:

I have now secured signed and executed guarantees for the "Century of Progress" exposition celebrating the 100th anniversary of the City of Chicago, amounting to over $10,000,000. Large additional guarantees have been promised and will be reduced to writing, but I make this announcement as I must leave for London today. Additional guarantees which have been promised but not yet signed may be handed to Mr. Charles F. Glore, of Field, Glore & Company, or Melvin A. Traylor, of the First National Bank. I attach hereto an alphabetical list of those who have already signed the guaranty.

The $10,000,000 of bonds of the "Century of Progress," which will soon be issued, will be secured by the first forty cents of every dollar of gate receipts and this impregnable list of loyal citizens of Chicago.

The Finance Committee, of which I shall remain Chairman, will include Mr. Charles F. Glore, Rufus C. Dawes, Melvin A. Traylor, Charles A. Schweppe and other leading financiers of the city. Of the Executive Committee of the Finance Committee, Mr. Charles F. Glore will be chairman.*

The reading of the list of guarantors indicates the complete consolidation of the civic leadership and financial strength of Chicago behind this great celebration of world import. We are going to show Chicago to the world as it is—young, virile, progressive, hopeful and determined.

I cannot refrain here from a tribute to one of the great figures which this celebration has brought to the fore—a modest man, a loyal Chicagoan, a great organizer—Mr. Stuyvesant Peabody, who performed a service to the city incomparably greater in the burdens it entailed than mine, and who secured $5 each from 118,773 of the citizens of our commonwealth in support of the "Century of Progress."

It was the wonderful foundation he laid, showing how the masses stand as regards their confidence in civic leadership when behind any enterprise looking to the betterment of Chicago, which gave me confidence to assume my task. To Rufus C. Dawes, President, and the Board of Trustees who quietly, without ostentation and with continuing and well-directed effort, have brought this great enterprise to its present well-organized position—to the National Research Council, cooperating for the last year with them, who have brought behind it a large group of the most distinguished of industrial and scientific leaders in the United States—to the architects who have their plans nearing completion, I wish I had space to pay proper tribute.

To Rufus C. Dawes, Melvin A. Traylor and George Woodruff, who have

---

* These committees were never appointed and, of course, never functioned.

9

brought me lists of guarantees each aggregating over $1,000,000, and the other friends who have cooperated, both by solicitation and by direct guaranty, I want to give my thanks. Though they would wish that I should, I cannot refrain from publicly thanking that friend of humanity and civic leader, Julius Rosenwald, and as well Samuel Insull, William Wrigley, Albert D. Lasker, Charles F. Glore, Don McLennan, James Simpson, Silas Strawn, Col. R. R. McCormick, Walter Strong, Clement Studebaker, Eugene Thayer, Walter Wilson, Fred Rawson, John C. Shaffer, Vincent Bendix, Paul H. Davis, George Pick and Knowlton L. Ames, whose names occur to me with many others.

In conclusion, let me say this about this celebration: It will be properly managed as a business enterprise. Its garment will be cut to accord with the cloth of its financial resources. The management will be the best the country can afford. I take pleasure in vouching for the man selected by the Board of Trustees as Manager of the Fair, Major L. R. Lohr. With him will be associated Colonel F. C. Boggs, fifty-three years of age, just voluntarily retired after thirty years' service in the United States Army—the man who for eight years was the Purchasing Agent of the Panama Canal during its construction and who, in addition, selected all the engineer, civilian and other personnel used by General Goethals in that great work. As Chief of Supply Procurement for the American Expeditionary Forces, I had him for a time upon my staff where he was the supply officer of the engineers' service, whose purchases in France ran to nearly $300,000,000. Of him and of Lohr I know whereof I speak.

And finally to the guarantors I would say: We have joined in a great enterprise for our imperial city. We are proving that it does not lie down, and registering our faith in its glorious future. We believe in the destiny of Chicago. We have faith in our own.

To wind up the account of this strenuous episode—so easily recounted and yet so desperate in its demands—I append a copy of the resolution of the Board of Trustees which they passed the morning that I left Chicago, and wired to me on the train for Washington.

WHEREAS, General Charles G. Dawes, as Chairman of the General Finance Committee, has lately directed a campaign for the guaranty of Chicago Centennial Gold Notes, in the sum of $10,000,000; and

WHEREAS, the campaign has resulted in the enrollment of guaranties for the whole sum desired in less than ten days;

BE IT RESOLVED that the Trustees of the Chicago World's Fair Centennial Celebration of 1933, hereafter to be known as "A Century of Progress" exposition, express to Charles G. Dawes, their grateful appreciation of this signal service toward a fitting observance of the first Centennial of our city; and further, their confidence that the brilliant success of this effort was due in large part to the distinctive elements of personality and leadership which he injected into the campaign; and

ARRIVAL AT SOUTHAMPTON, JUNE 14, 1929

First four in front row, right to left: Mayor of Southampton, Mrs. Dawes, General Dawes, Captain of *Olympic*.

Journal as Ambassador to Great Britain

BE IT RESOLVED FURTHER that this acknowledgment shall be spread upon the minutes of this meeting and a copy be telegraphed to General Dawes on the eve of his departure to begin his services as the Ambassador of his country to the Court of St. James's.

S.S. Olympic,
Wednesday, June 12, 1929.

I reached Washington again Thursday morning, June 6th, having been requested to stop on my way to New York for a conference with President Hoover and Secretary Stimson. This was had between the three of us at luncheon at the White House—a session lasting about an hour and a half. It was devoted almost entirely to a discussion of the problem of securing naval disarmament and how to go about it along the lines Hoover had laid down to our own navy, covering the matter of a naval yardstick to be used to determine naval equality.

As a result, I left in the late afternoon for New York with these suggestions to be made to the British Government by authority of the President.

1st. That discussion of controverted questions involving a yet unsettled public opinion in both the United States and Great Britain, such as freedom of the seas, should not be allowed to retard immediate steps toward naval disarmament.

To this particular matter I had given some preliminary thought, and read to the President a prepared memorandum which I will insert below. Let me say here, however, that before I read it to the President, he had already expressed practically the same views in opening the subject, and this memorandum represented, therefore, an agreement with him—not his agreement with me.

2nd. That we had best abandon the present method of attacking the problem by a mixed commission of naval experts and statesmen and, what is more, endeavor to settle upon the naval yardstick without convening an International Naval Board in some such way as I will outline in my Pilgrims' speech.

On June 7, 1929, I gave the President the following memorandum:

The question of first importance, at the present time, is that the friends of

11

world peace move unitedly toward that objective. To avoid confusion and delay, endangering their common objective, they should now unitedly consider not only what steps should be taken toward it but the order in which these steps are to be taken, remembering that each step necessarily will involve certain differences of opinion.

It would seem important at the present time that the question of naval reduction, involving the principle of naval equality between Great Britain and the United States, should be settled first. Congress has committed the United States to a billion-dollar naval program, giving, however, to the President in his discretion the right to delay it, in order, through an agreement for international naval disarmament, to avoid it. This particular question, so far as the national policy of Great Britain and the United States is concerned, is settled, and to get it out of the way involves only agreement as to naval technical principles. If at this time negotiations involving the question of the establishment of freedom of the seas be taken up, it may endanger the naval reduction step or at least delay it. The settlement of naval reduction involves no commitment necessarily upon the controverted question of freedom of the seas, but the concurrent discussion of this latter controverted question with one out of the realm of debate upon policy and in that of technical naval principle alone, should be avoided, if possible, by both the friends of freedom of the seas and of naval reduction. Agreement upon naval reduction will hereafter, at least, not embarrass the friends of freedom of the seas, but failure or postponement of naval reduction would certainly make more remote any agreement as to freedom of the seas. Whatever differences of opinion there may be upon the desirability of agreement upon the policy of freedom of the seas, it is safe to say that it is not endangered by a cessation of an enormously expensive naval competition in progress during its discussion. It would seem that all controverted questions such as freedom of the seas—and this particular question involves a yet unsettled domestic public opinion in the United States—should not be allowed to retard the great forward step toward World's peace which it now seems possible to take in an agreement for naval reduction. Should the discussion of freedom of the seas and of naval reduction proceed concurrently, public opinion may become confused by the question of which should take precedence over the other, thus endangering both. All questions involving an unsettled public opinion in both Great Britain and the United States will be resolved more easily if the step of naval reduction is taken now.

I insert here copies of certain radiograms sent and received on the ship.

At sea,
S.S. Olympic.

ATHERTON,
American Embassy, London.

What date, if any, fixed for Pilgrims' dinner? Had planned make my first address that occasion. Essential for me to have interview with MacDonald before making address which is upon naval disarmament. This preliminary conference involves presentation to MacDonald of suggestions from our gov-

HIS MAJESTY KING GEORGE V

17TH ENGINEERS (RAILWAY)
Passing in review before the King and Queen.

ernment. Note by radio news this morning that MacDonald is leaving for vacation at Lossiemouth. Have been informed indirectly that Pilgrims' dinner date was June eighteenth. If this is so, would you ask MacDonald if he would kindly receive me at Lossiemouth in time for me to return to London by that date. If this is satisfactory to him, please arrange other official dates if possible so as to be consistent with this arrangement. Answer by radio, Olympic.

CHARLES G. DAWES.

GENERAL DAWES,
S.S. Olympic, Portishead.

Conference with MacDonald arranged for Sunday in Scotland. Pilgrims' dinner June eighteenth. Letter forwarded you yesterday in care of American Consul, Cherbourg.

ATHERTON.

American Embassy,
London, June 23, 1929.

The first American troops ever to march through London were four Engineer regiments of the American Expeditionary Forces, on their way to France, which, in August, 1917, that terrible year of the war when the fate of Britain hung in the balance, passed in review before the King and Queen who stood on the sidewalk in front of Buckingham Palace.

To those five thousand American soldiers and to me, as one of them, passing through thronged streets from which, for hours, roared a British welcome from millions of people, the most impressive moment of that memorable and emotional time was when we passed Their Majesties who, to us, as to the British people, represented the dignity and power and greatness of the British Commonwealth of Nations. It was then I first saw the King to whom, at Windsor Castle, on last Saturday, I presented the letter from the President of the United States accrediting me as the American Ambassador.

For a half-hour I had the privilege of conversation alone with His Majesty. While showing the effects of his recent illness, he spoke with energy, clearness and great common sense. He inspires respect, not only by the expression of his views on important world questions and the range and thoroughness of his information, but by that naturalness and charm which so befits high position. The King, by custom, is not quoted, for it is recognized that the weight which is attached to his words should not be endangered by possible misquotation. I regret, therefore, I cannot include in these notes his interesting and inspiring comments to me.

My visit only emphasized my former impressions of his fitness for the exalted place he occupies. Both the King and Queen of Britain are justly honored with that highest of decorations—universal public respect and regard.

At the end of the interview, he took me to the room in which the Queen had received Mrs. Dawes, and the four of us chatted for a time. The King and Queen then retired, and the staff of the King showed us through the lower rooms of the castle.

That evening (Saturday) I left for Forres, Scotland, to meet Prime Minister J. Ramsay MacDonald, accompanied by Ray Atherton, the counsellor of the Embassy, and my nephew and secretary Henry Dawes, and a large number of correspondents and photographers. I had been asked by the President to show MacDonald my Pilgrims' dinner speech. On the ship coming over, I learned from the Radio News that MacDonald was leaving London for a rest and would not return until after June 18th, the date I was to speak.

This was the reason for my hurried movements.

London,
June 24, 1929.

My interview with MacDonald at Forres, the residence of Sir Alexander Grant, lasted some two hours. My purpose, of course, was not only to submit for comment the text of my speech at the Pilgrims' dinner next Tuesday, but to secure his acquiescence in the program of our government which it contained, and to secure his agreement to relegate the present discussion of the question of the freedom of the seas and all other controversial questions pending the settlement of naval reduction as the probable first step to be taken.

Knowing also that the President feared the effect upon the

J. RAMSAY MACDONALD

Keystone Views, London

TREE PLANTING AT LOGIE HOUSE

Prime Minister MacDonald and gardener in front; in rear, from left
to right, General Dawes, Ishbel MacDonald, Lady Grant, and Sir
Alexander Grant.

naval reduction efforts of the extraneous discussion about his possible trip to the United States, I hoped to convince him that it would be unwise to go prior to the practical settlement of the naval matter.

Our interview was most frank and friendly, and at its conclusion the Prime Minister had thoroughly approved of all the suggestions made, and expressed his satisfaction. He did not discuss with me what he would say in his speech, to be made elsewhere the same night I delivered the address before the Pilgrims of Great Britain, except to state that it would be entirely consistent with the American propositions as outlined in my address.

He said all steps which he would take in the matter he expected primarily to discuss with us and he hoped that we would show like confidence in him, which I assured him would be the case—the President having already expressed the desire to keep him informed as to all contemplated steps, including information as to how he (the President) was handling his own navy situation.

I was much impressed with MacDonald. His constructive purpose in this navy matter is unquestioned. His ability to deal with it and the clearness of his mind upon the subject were fully demonstrated. He was agreeable, confidential and frank throughout all our interview, and I left him with a high respect for him. He intimated that he believed his Admiralty would be more cooperative than formerly. He wrote out a statement for the Press representatives (who were waiting in large numbers outside the conference room) which I approved. This I attach.

Logie House,
Dunphail, Morayshire,
June 16, 1929.

Statement to the Press

We have had a conversation regarding the present position of the question of naval disarmament as between the United States and Great Britain. It has been informal and general and most satisfactory. His Excellency proposes to refer to the subject at his Pilgrims' dinner on Tuesday night, and I shall do the same almost at the time at Lossiemouth, and that is intended to be the beginning of the negotiations. We both wish to make it clear that the other naval powers are expected to cooperate in these negotiations upon the successful outcome of which the peace of the whole world must depend.

Journal as Ambassador to Great Britain

In our entirely unrestrained and frank interchange of views, MacDonald spoke of his possible visit to America. As he asked for natural reactions, I gave them, saying to him that I could qualify by contact as a former presiding officer of the United States Senate, as a prognosticator of senatorial criticism—that a portion of the Senate, always exceedingly jealous of executive initiative in international affairs, would interject into the situation a demoralizing and demagogical discussion if the trip were taken during the continuance of negotiations for naval disarmament.

Of any treaty framed after, and not necessarily because of such a conference with the President, they probably would say that the Premier had left the United States with the nation sewed up in his pocket, and this American view could not be rectified because of the counterclaim of many of his own countrymen that he had simply been seduced into surrendering British sovereignty to the United States. I suggested that any such unusual event as the visit of the Prime Minister of Great Britain to the President of the United States at the present time would be used to create a fog-bank to conceal an understanding of the real merits of the case from the ordinary man, and that this would be done with diabolical ingenuity.

At my conclusion, MacDonald remarked that he hoped to take a trip to America some time, but that it was decided now that it would not be until after further progress upon the disarmament treaty. I then told him that whenever he was ready to come I was sure the President of the United States and our whole people would give him a most sincere and hearty welcome.

All I did relative to the question of the wisdom of relegating the present discussion of the freedom of the seas was to read him my memorandum prepared in Washington June 7 (already inserted in these notes).

To this he agreed.

On the train coming down from Forres, I realized from suggestions made by the able correspondent of the *Chicago Tribune*, John Steele, that my speech had better be qualified somewhat so as to indicate more clearly that it was largely a proposition for a change in the manner of naval negotiations, in the discussion of which all the nations were interested—that it was not simply concerned with the relations of the United States and Great Britain. Accordingly, I re-wrote the first two pages of my address on the train that night, not changing the meaning but making it more clear.

On my arrival in London (June 15), in pursuance of the commonsense policy of having friendly and confidential relations at the beginning, with those whose cooperation is essential at the ending of negotiations, I conferred with the French Ambassador, Aimé de Fleuriau, the Japanese Ambassador, Tsuneo Matsudaira, and the Italian Chargé d'Affaires, Signor Rogeri (the Ambassador being out of the country) and with the Canadian High Commissioner, Mr. Ferguson.

I went over carefully with them what I was to say at the Pilgrims' dinner Tuesday evening, and presented fully the President's suggestions for a new method in negotiations. They were all agreed as to the wisdom of these suggestions, which they were to submit to their respective governments.

On Tuesday night (June 18) I delivered my address at the dinner of the Pilgrims of Great Britain at Hotel Victoria, and it was well received. I sat next to Sir Austen Chamberlain, with whom I had a most interesting conversation. He is the living image of my old friend, Albert Beveridge. Many of my old war and reparations friends were present and by arrangement were seated together.

I insert here my speech.

We are in a period when mankind, emerged from its greatest cataclysm—the World War—is lifting its eyes from the darkness of the past toward the sunlight of international peace and tranquillity. It is the era of effort for world construction—moral and material.

The ratification of the Kellogg Peace Treaty, which is the agreed-upon expression of a World intention, has one of its first effects in a pronounced change in the form of the international discussion of the World's peace. The closing of the discussion upon the form of the expression of the principle and the inception of the discussion of the practical methods by which to make it effective, prove the existence of the general determination to make the Treaty not a mere gesture, but the foundation of an era of "Peace on earth and good will toward men."

The matter of first importance at the present time is that the friends of the World's peace move unitedly toward that objective with a clear understanding among themselves that any effort which is not a united effort is liable to be ineffective and tending toward disintegration. To avoid confusion and delay endangering their common objective, they now should not only unitedly consider what steps should be taken toward it, but the order in which those steps are to be taken.

The importance of an early agreement on naval reduction by the nations is of outstanding importance at the present time, and it would seem to be the next step to be taken toward world peace. As to any other controverted questions between any nations or between Great Britain and the United States, their future peaceful settlement, either way, will not be endangered by the cessation of an enormously expensive naval competition in progress during their discussion.

Congress has already by law committed the United States to an immediate naval program involving over $250,000,000, giving, however, to the President the power to suspend it in the event of an international agreement for the limitation of naval armament.

On May 31 last, the Secretary of State of the United States said: "I have in my possession a memorandum from the Director of the Budget showing the cost of the program recommended by the Navy Department in case the policy of naval reduction which the President advocates is not adopted. That memorandum shows that the authorized and contemplated naval program for the construction of new ships alone amounts to $1,170,800,000. . . . When it is borne in mind that the foregoing figures involve the construction program of only one nation and that, if it proceeds, other nations will be impelled to follow suit, the burden of unproductive expenditure which will be imposed upon the economic world during the next fifteen years can be to a certain extent realized.

My address tonight concerns itself with suggestions as to a change in the method of future negotiations for naval disarmament. Agreement upon a method of negotiations must concern, from the very beginning, all interested naval Powers and should have not a partial, but a whole, sanction. While in the course of the discussion I may refer to the principle of equality of naval power as between Great Britain and the United States, it is only because the outcome of previous conferences shows that this is the agreed policy of both governments. My theme is what method of procedure had best be adopted to translate a policy of naval reduction into a fixed agreement between the nations—a step so important to the peace of the world and the happiness hereafter of mankind.

Edmund Burke, in his Observations on the Present State of the Nation, once made a profound remark about politics which he could have made with equal truth of law, of governmental systems and of dealings with international relations of all kinds, including methods of negotiation for reparations settlements or reduction in naval armament. "Politics," said he, "ought to be adjusted not to human reasonings but to human nature, of which the reason is but a part, and by no means the greatest part."

The long time which elapsed after the ending of the Great War before a proper method of negotiation for reparations settlements was evolved was because the first method was adjusted to human reasoning and not to human nature. That method was to have the recommended settlement prepared by the continuing and concurrent work of economic experts and statesmen combined.

THE PILGRIMS' DINNER, JUNE 18, 1929

Left to right: Sir Austen Chamberlain; Ambassador Dawes; Lord Desborough;
Rt. Hon. Arthur Henderson, Secretary of State for Foreign Affairs.

Journal as Ambassador to Great Britain

Since the reparations settlement involved, in each one of the nations interested, both an economic and political problem, it was reasonable to suppose that it would be best determined by the joint effort of statesmen and economists working together. This futile effort continued so long before its abandonment that all Europe was brought to the brink of economic and political chaos. And then only, in the latter part of 1923, did the Reparation Commission, as an experiment, decide upon the separate formation of the First Committee of Experts. This expedient, viewed at that time as almost hopeless by most economists and entirely so by most politicians—then designated by one great member of the Reparation Commission as the "Prescription of a pill for an earthquake"—proved successful.

The formation of that Committee was not a triumph of intellect—it was the triumph of despair. It was adopted because nothing else had worked. Its success was due to its unconscious but proper adjustment to the law of human nature. What happened thereafter demonstrated that by accident the world had discovered that the proper method of settling an international problem, involving a separate economic and political problem in each country, was to use independent experts whose suggestions involved their interpretation of the correct and fundamental economic principles involved in the situation, their formula then to be handed over to the statesmen who, reinforced by general public confidence in the impartiality of expert opinion, could better bring the respective public sentiments into acceptance of the necessary working compromise between political expediency and economic principles.

In committees formerly composed of co-laboring statesmen and economists, the economists had always stood rigidly for conclusions endangering the statesmen and the acceptance of the Plan, and the statesmen for conclusions which would stultify the economists and endanger the success of the Plan. Under such circumstances, the arrival at a constructive compromise was well nigh impossible. The method was not adjusted to the law of human nature.

Economic and technical problems are one thing—governmental and political problems another. The rigid attitude and determined expressions of international economic and technical principles are perhaps praiseworthy, but we must remember that these expressions are often incident to a doubtful embodiment of them in a personal interpretation of their applicability to international political situations, of which the experts are not always competent diagnosticians.

One who is inclined to believe that economists and technicians, claiming to be guided in their intellectual voyages by the stars and compasses and high light-houses of fixed principles, never compromise, as do the alleged unworthy politicians, is lacking in experience in international economic negotiations. For six years after the War, the unhappy Reparation Commission, besides its other misfortunes, was surrounded by an army of economic experts representing the different nations interested in the problem. These experts delivered innumerable written ultimatums as to the correct economic principles which underlay their divergent recommendations which filled vast untouched libraries and now moulder in their unruffled dust. The disagreements of these experts with each other, each swearing devotion to infallible principle, was as complete and overwhelming as those which characterized the deliberations of the supposedly less worthy, entirely confused, but fully as determined, politicians and statesmen.

I remember during the last two weeks of deliberation on the part of the First Committee of Experts appointed by the Reparation Commission that, as the inside expert Committee was laboring with the formulation of its conclusions, almost all of them more or less the result of a compromise, they faced a snowstorm of protesting papers filled with the voluminous but disagreeing economic advice of outside experts removed from the field of negotiation.

What I have said has a most direct bearing upon the question of the method of conducting the great negotiation for naval disarmament soon justly to occupy the attention of the world. The question is how best to adjust the methods of negotiation to accord with the laws of human nature so that a successful outcome, so vital to the welfare of the world, may not be unnecessarily endangered.

International naval reduction is a task, the successful accomplishment of which requires the cooperative employment of two distinctly unrelated talents—that of naval technical experts and of statesmen.

Important as is a preliminary expert examination of economists to report to the statesmen on an international problem involving both an economic and political phase, it is even more important where naval technicians and statesmen confront a problem involving both a technical and political phase. But here we must keep in mind the law of human nature. In the case of a preliminary use of economic experts, their prime objective is a formula which will recognize the dominance of economic law, and the success of the statesmen in reaching the second objective of accommodating the expert formula to the political conditions in the respective countries, is something as much desired by the economic experts as by the statesmen themselves. That later achievement only will crown with success the preliminary expert effort. This attitude has recently been twice demonstrated. So anxious was the first economic committee of experts, Reparation Commission in 1924, that their report should be the basis of a successful settlement that they were engaged continually during their work in adjusting the form of their statement to expected political repercussion.

It was their constant endeavor to frame their conclusions in such language as would make them easily understood and be as inoffensive from a political standpoint as was possible. This effort to adjust economic necessity to political expediency led them to many collateral individual conferences for advice from European statesmen during their work. As a result, when the report of the First Committee of Experts was delivered to the statesmen of the London Conference, the latter found it unnecessary to change the Plan but only to supplement it by collateral international agreements relating to it, making it politically acceptable to all the nations concerned. And thus it was with the world-important report of the Second Committee of Experts just completed. It was their intense desire to have a constructive outcome of their work as much as because the work itself was a diplomatic as well as an expert employment, that led them to consult constantly with the leading European statesmen during their epoch-making labors. This desire on the part of these economic committees accorded with the law of human nature. But in the case of naval technical experts, working for a formula for naval equality, the law of human nature runs contrary to such an attitude. It would be vastly more difficult, other things being equal, for a mixed commission of navy technicians and statesmen to agree on a plan for naval disarmament than for a fixed commission of economists and statesmen to agree upon a reparations settlement—practically impossible as history has shown the latter to be.

A naval expert is qualified to define accurately the principles which should determine abstract naval equality, but the law of human nature decrees that his opinion is relatively not as safe in a program which he formulates as a practical interpretation of these principles applied to a partial destruction of his own navy. The proper pride of a naval officer's life is his navy. His whole professional career impels him to think of a navy only in terms of victory. He not only instinctively feels, but he is rightly taught to feel, that he must strive not for equal navies, but for a superior navy. It is difficult for him to forget that with a superior navy, victory is probable— with an equal navy doubtful, with an inferior navy almost hopeless. Other things being equal, I fear no naval officer ever inherently favors equality.

The naval officer has his duty to perform to his State and it is primarily to secure it against attack. He therefore trusts to his ships and his armament. It is the duty of the statesman to remove from his State the danger of attack. Upon the latter primarily lies the duty of peacemaking, and in these negotiations he must hold the initiative. He is the one to build up the new order and to start the new policy, guided as he goes by the advice of those competent and patriotic naval experts who serve him. What differences there are in their respective duties can be coordinated into a policy of statesmanship, and that and that alone is what I have in mind in what I now say.

I have no knowledge of the qualifications and records of any naval officers heretofore engaged in these negotiations, or acquaintance with them. I am concerned only that the methods under which this work is to be done; whoever may do it, shall be adjusted to the laws of human nature.

At the beginning of the work, the contribution of the naval experts to the problem should be a definition of abstract equality. It is certainly possible for naval experts to arrive at a definition for evaluation of fighting strength of ships. Thus, for instance, one might find a yardstick with which to determine the military value of individual ships. These ships might differ in displacement, size of guns, age, speed and other characteristics, and yet such an agreed properly weighted value might be given to each of these differing characteristics as to make it possible to compare, for example, the cruiser fleets or combined fleets of two navies, and establish a parity between them. If naval experts rise to the proper sense of their responsibility, the use by statesmen of their yardstick will not be one which will invite peril from those extreme pacifists and extreme militarists who form the "lunatic fringe."

But, again, in connection with the method of preparing the naval yardstick, let us consider the law of human nature. Should a commission composed of the representatives of each navy concerned meet to reach agreement upon this yardstick, they would be asked to agree upon something, the use of which will reduce in number the idols of their hearts—the ships of their navies. I am casting no reflection here upon the Naval Officers when speaking of the law of human nature which subconsciously influences the actions of all mankind, learned or ignorant, good or bad, rich or poor, skilled or unskilled, great or humble, old or young, of every race and nationality of the world.

I have already spoken of the fallibility and lack of agreement of expert and economic opinion as exemplified by the experience of the Reparations negotiations. I will say, frankly, that from a commission of naval experts of the respective nations meeting together and called to evolve a final definition of the naval yardstick, I personally should expect a failure to agree.

It would seem that to adjust to human nature the method of arriving at naval reduction, each Government might separately obtain from their respective naval experts their definition of the yardstick, and then the inevitable compromise between these differing definitions, which will be expressed in the final fixation of the technical yardstick, should be made by a committee of statesmen of the nations, reinforced from the beginning by these separate expressions of abstract technical naval opinions and able again to seek further naval advice, if necessary, before the final fixation.

These statesmen should further be the ones to draw up for the world the terms of the final agreement upon naval reduction, which should be couched in those simple terms understandable to the ordinary man on the street, which, while the pet aversion of the casuist, are the highest expression of true statesmanship. That final agreement, covering the quantitative dispositions, will go to the nations for approval or rejection.

If this should be the outcome, let those entrusted with the last draft of the conclusions of the last conference be men born with the faculty of clear and concise statement, for that document will appeal to the composite will of the peoples of the nations and, in order to make the proper appeal, it must be read generally and understood.

There, again, we remember the operation of the law of human nature, and will hope that in these men the temptation to show erudition be subordinated to writing that which, while properly covering the case, may be understood by the audience. A clear statement of the case, understandable by all, should mean success.

And here let me anticipate the possible comments of those whom we have always with us on both sides of the ocean—the social purveyors of the trivial in international discussions who talk so continually about good relations and do so little to forward them.

In all I have said tonight, I intend nothing in derogation of the absolute necessity for the consideration and presentation of the naval side of this question by its ablest experts the world over and, on the other hand, nothing in derogation of the absolute necessity of bringing to the political side of it the highest qualities of statesmanship which the world can provide. But to properly solve the problem we must adopt a method which brings the full weight of both of these classes of men to bear upon it without their unnecessary collisions during the first formulating period when they are primarily concerned with two separate objectives.

Again, and also anticipating certain comment, let me say that while it is the fashion of these sensational days to attribute to any statement of irritating fact by a public man some malevolent purpose towards individuals, there is nothing of this in my mind.

The Committee from the Governments which met at Geneva to agree upon naval disarmament was a mixed commission of statesmen and naval technicians, and, in my judgment, that was the reason for its failure. The method was adjusted to human reasoning but not to human nature.

We should not look upon the failure at Geneva in 1927 as the failure of individuals, but of the method under which they were asked to function. This may be said, however, that under the laws of human nature, probably ninety per cent of Englishmen think the American delegation was responsible for the mistake, and ninety per cent of Americans think that the British members of the .Commission were responsible for the mistake. The great, overwhelming and soul-satisfying fact about it is that the British and American people are a unit in agreeing that whoever was responsible for it, a mistake was made. And of what is this significant? It means that in the inarticulate consciences and hearts of the two great English-speaking peoples there is upheld, sacred and inviolate, the principle of the equality between them of naval strength. Their attitude upon this question—unmistakable—assumed as out of the realm of debate even by the nationalistic demagogues of both countries—while decorated by reason, is based under the providence of God upon fundamental human instincts and a co-mingling of the blood.

Under these circumstances, let us be hopeful for the cause of world peace and the progress of civilization, for in the joint hands of these same English-speaking peoples rests not only their secure guaranty, but as well the ark of the covenant of human freedom.

On Thursday, June 20th, I came to realize more and more the possibly injurious results which would have come from a visit of MacDonald to Washington at this time. The Japanese Ambassador called with inquiries about the alleged proposed visit, and when I told him that it would not be made until after the negotiations for naval disarmament were much further along, he received the news with evident relief.

It was evident that the effect on his mind of the trip proposition was that the United States and Great Britain were preparing to proceed with these negotiations themselves and simply call in the other Governments for their ratification.

As the President had spoken to me about Gibson's coming over from Brussels for a conference, I cabled our Government that I would like to have them announce that fact from Washington. I did this because I thought it was due to Gibson to have his connection with the matter properly announced to the public, and because it would indicate on the part of our Government a realization that in view of the conditional legislative commitment of Congress to a large naval program, the negotiations should proceed with as little interruption as possible.

Of course, while speed is desirable, we must avoid any haste that will militate in any way against the most painstaking and careful technical preparation. However, the whole psychology of the situation is now at its most favorable state, and the sooner we can arrive at a proper conclusion, the more certain it is to be accepted.

On the next day (June 21st) the French Ambassador also spoke to me about the proposed MacDonald visit, of the wisdom of which he seemed in doubt, and he was gratified at my explanation of it.

On Saturday, June 22nd, I wired the State Department that it was in my mind that MacDonald, Gibson and myself should invite Matsudaira to join in these preliminary conferences.

London,
June 29, 1929.

Gibson arrived Monday evening, June 24th, and stayed at the Embassy. In reply to the inquiry of the Department of State as to what steps we thought would be most effective to carry on the work, we sent our suggestions, which in general were that the next logical step would seem to be to convene a meeting of technical, non-government experts to take up the problem. We said it seemed better from our point of view to leave this next step to some other Power. It would be understood, we suggested, that the first objective is a full and formal exchange of views which the representatives of the five Naval Powers had agreed upon last month at Geneva, as the necessary preliminary to further possible endeavor.

Gibson and I then saw MacDonald, at 10 Downing Street (the official residence of the British Prime Minister), and went over in general the suggestions we had made to our own Government. This again I explained to the Japanese Ambassador. In our long discussion of the matter, MacDonald expressed tentatively the idea of the invitation by England to all the Naval Powers for a

HUGH S. GIBSON

preliminary consultation as to the methods to be adopted in negotiations.

Gibson left the next day (Thursday, June 27th). Shortly thereafter I received a short telegram from the State Department, suggesting I caution the Prime Minister about making a public statement until the views of the American Government on the suggestion of an immediate informal conference, which MacDonald had in mind, be received. This I communicated to him through his Secretary. He wrote in reply as follows: "My Secretary told me yesterday of the cable which you had received and which I interpret to mean that for the time being the matter is held up until I hear from you further."

However, on the morning of June 28th, I received suggestions from the President and Secretary of State to be considered with MacDonald.

American Embassy,
London,
June 29, 1929.

By dictation at the office, I am trying to keep a record of my more important official work, but it lacks any description of the interesting environment, both of personalities, and the material in which it is transacted. In the evenings I feel little disposed to continue the day's activities, and can give but an outline of them from recollection.

From the time of our arrival here, we have been overwhelmed with kindness and attentions. The nature of the diplomatic work concerned with Naval Disarmament, or rather Naval Reduction, as President Hoover desires it, is exacting and requires close attention, and yet I am constantly interrupted by diplomatic calls of courtesy, and my own official requirements in reciprocation. At the beginning of an ambassadorial assignment there is a lot of official routine to go through, which is all right enough, but it is unimportant as compared with the work allotted me under specific instructions from Washington.

But I am wandering back to "work" as a subject—which was not my intention.

Journal as Ambassador to Great Britain

As I am not accepting anything but official invitations, when I receive an invitation to lunch by someone important for me to consult in my work, I take them to lunch with me at the Embassy. Among those I have thus entertained are Geoffrey Dawson and Sir Harry Perry Robinson, both of the London *Times;* Lord Astor and J. L. Garvin, of the London *Observer;* Myron Taylor, of the United States Steel Corporation; F. W. M. Cutcheon of the Reparation Commission. At Atherton's house I met Sir Ronald Lindsay, permanent Under-Secretary of the Foreign Office, Robert Gilbert Vansittart, the Prime Minister's Secretary, and Sir Warren Fisher, of the Treasury.

Of my interesting callers at the Embassy I will not try to make a list. One of my most frequent callers on business has been my friend, Matsudaira, the Japanese Ambassador, and I have called at his Embassy at least as many times. We were old Washington friends and each tries to save the other the trip necessary to get together.

I have called on all the Ambassadors—and vice versa.

An interesting happening was the dinner of the British Empire Service League, Tuesday, June 25th, where the Prince of Wales presided, and where, as nominated by Colonel Paul V. McNutt, National Commander of The American Legion, I conveyed its cordial and affectionate greetings to their British comrades of the Great War. The dinner was at the Claridge Hotel.

As I was seated by the Prince of Wales, we renewed our pleasant acquaintance made at the dedication of the Peace Bridge between the United States and Canada, when I was Vice President. All that I wrote then of his charm of manner and friendliness would apply here.

Yesterday I called on him at his rooms at St. James's Palace, and on the Duke of Connaught, at Claridge House, who had sent General Hanbury-Williams to the Embassy to invite me to do so. These two calls were most enjoyable, and the two of them occupied over an hour. Both the Prince and the Duke were much interested in the naval situation.

The Prince said that heretofore when he had gone to the United States it was chiefly to see polo, but that next time he

PROCESSION AT OXFORD UNIVERSITY

At the left of General Dawes is the Spanish Ambassador, Merry del Val,
then dean of the diplomatic corps at London.

Journal as Ambassador to Great Britain

wanted to go into the more real world of industry, visiting the industrial and agricultural sections and their people.

On Wednesday of this week Caro and I motored with my nephew and secretary, Henry Dawes, to Oxford, going to the home of Dr. G. S. Gordon, President of Magdalen College. There I was given a robe and taken to a group of notables who were to march to the hall where the conferring of degrees took place.

ADDRESS OF THE ORATOR IN PRESENTATION
TO THE CHANCELLOR

Bound as it is to Americans by the tie of scholarship, this University could have no more welcome visitor than the Ambassador of the free Republic across the Atlantic. Here is one who in war rendered strenuous aid to the common cause of the Allies by his administration of the problem of supplies, and who after returning home on the restoration of peace actually crossed the Atlantic again to strengthen by his "plan" those who were trying to repair the damages of war. But why do I, the public orator of the University, mention damages and losses, especially on this festal Founders' Day when no one cares how much any one has or how much he owes and Grammarians themselves pay no attention to the Dawes rule? In high esteem we hold this well-beloved founder and sponsor of the prosperity of nations and it is our hope that the way he has pointed out will redound to the peace of the world and the safety of our country.

I present to you his Excellency, Charles Gates Dawes, officer of high rank in the American army, Companion of the Most Honorable Order of the Bath, Ambassador of the United States of America in London at the Court of St. James's, to be admitted to the honorary degree of Doctor of Civil Law.

Among the interesting talks I had during the day were those with Viscount Grey of Fallodon and Viscount Chelmsford, whose wife I took to the lunch given at All Souls College after the exercises. We returned to London by five o'clock and Ambassador Gibson, who was visiting me at the Embassy, called with me at 6:00 P.M. on Ramsay MacDonald at 10 Downing Street for a most important interview.

London,
Sunday, June 30, 1929.

Yesterday I received a letter from Parker Gilbert, the Agent General for Reparation Payments at Berlin, saying he had written Secretary Mellon urging that I be designated as the represen-

27

tative of the United States at the conference of Governments which must soon be called to consider the Young Committee's proposals for the final settlement of the reparation problem. If our Government is unwilling to appoint a direct participating representative, he urges that I be named as an "official observer." He seems to think this is important, and says that he may come over to see me before the conference is convened.

He sends me a copy of his letter to Mellon, and if the United States desires to be represented it will have its due influence. But while, of course, I will do whatever is officially assigned me, this particular task, under all the circumstances, is both embarrassing and difficult. This I talked over with Sir Robert Kindersley somewhat. It would seem quite probable that our Government may decide to have in attendance neither a direct representative nor an "official observer."

I have now received the press returns from different parts of the world upon my Pilgrims' speech. All British newspapers I have seen accept it—as do the great preponderance of American papers. The Government of Japan is reported as approving of it, while the French and Italian press is indifferent or critical. But I think it is fair to say that there is quite general approval of the soundness of the argument for an improved way of handling the relations of the naval experts to the problem. This latter may be reasonably expected if things are carried on in the thorough and careful way which President Hoover recommends in his last message to me, the terms of which I have submitted to the Prime Minister, and also discussed with Matsudaira, the Japanese Ambassador.

Our Embassy messenger, just returned from Brussels, brings me confidential official messages from Gibson which are just handed to me, and I must therefore close these notes and read them.

LATER. I have just finished reading Gibson's long letter of ten typewritten pages giving me his general idea as to how the naval problem should be approached. In a note attached to the letter, he calls it "wandering." So far from being that, it is one of the clearest and ablest statements of a case which could be made.

Journal as Ambassador to Great Britain

With the help of the "half-hourly appointment book" which Henry keeps for me, I will try a rough sketch of the happenings of the last six days. As I am awaiting word from the Prime Minister, who is still considering the American suggestions as to immediate procedure in the naval reduction matter, the week, while a very active one, was devoted to business of lesser importance.

On Monday evening Mrs. Whitelaw Reid, whose husband was one of my predecessors in this place, and Lady Bryce—two very able and interesting ladies—dined with us at the Embassy. Lady Bryce told me many incidents of her great husband's career.

On Tuesday morning, with Henry, I attended the levee of the Prince of Wales at St. James's Palace—a brilliant affair and formal. In the evening went to a large dinner given in honor of my dear friend, Sir Josiah Stamp, just back from the Mediterranean, by the Society of Incorporated Accountants. His speech was very able and also kindly in its references to me. I responded extempore, and paid the tribute of a sincere heart to Stamp and Young.

In recalling my failure at Paris to get the London papers to print my commendation, as Chairman, of the work of Stamp and Kindersley, the English representatives on the First Committee of Reparation Experts, I repeated what occurred.

A leader among the British correspondents, as I handed him my written tribute, said: "We Englishmen do not praise each other in the press." "I understand," I replied. "Naturally." "But, at last, I have found two Englishmen who deserve it."

On Tuesday Geoffery Dawson, editor of the *Times,* brought Lord Bridgeman, First Lord of the Admiralty in the Baldwin cabinet, to lunch with me at the Embassy to discuss naval matters. Bridgeman, with Viscount Cecil, took part in the recent unsuccessful naval conference at Geneva.

On Wednesday I lunched as the guest of Major John Jacob Astor with the staff of the London *Times* at its office, Printing

House Square. The other guest was the Premier of New South Wales.

Thursday was a most busy day—our national birthday—and always celebrated at the Embassy. At noon I went to the house of Lord Astor where I lunched with him and Lady Astor, David Lloyd George and Philip Kerr. Lloyd George was at his best. Lady Astor I found unique and with the easy and direct address generally characteristic of the intellectual public woman. Lady Astor cited Lloyd George to me as an example of the "never-to-be-forgiven" by the Peers.

In speaking of the right of primogeniture it seems he had once said that "there was no law of nature which decreed that the first pup of the litter should be the best." Lloyd George agreed with her that he was still remembered for it, but seemed resigned to the idea.

Lady Astor reminds me of Alice Roosevelt Longworth and Ruth Hanna McCormick in her audacity and brilliancy.

From 4:00 to 6:00 P.M. we held the Fourth of July reception for the Americans resident in London at the Embassy. Caro and I shook hands with 2600 people who passed us as they entered the dining room from the front hall, and then passed to other parts of the house and to the garden where refreshments were served. For music we had the Irish Guard Band of 46 pieces, which was the band which played the old 17th Engineers A.E.F. through London in 1917.

In the evening I presided and responded to a toast at the annual American Society dinner. Over 400 were present. The other speakers were Dr. John Grier Hibben, of Princeton University, Lord Reading, and William Robert Gourlay.

On Friday in the afternoon, for a time, I was at the British Museum to see the temporary exhibition of the articles excavated by Dr. C. Leonard Woolley during 1928 and 1929 at Ur, acting for the British Museum and the University of Pennsylvania. This visit was one of enthralling interest.

Journal as Ambassador to Great Britain

Embassy, London,
July 7, 1929.

This morning Caro and I attended the thanksgiving service for the recovery of the King at Westminster Abbey—a glorious service. It was England at her best. The prayers, the hymns, the chanting, the Abbey itself—all were symbolic of the Christian faith of a great people; but along with them there came at intervals the impressive rolling of the drums and the sounding of clarions, bespeaking, at least, a most militant Christianity.

The King and Queen, the Prince of Wales, and others of the Royal Family, preceded by the dignitaries of the Church of England, entered at eleven o'clock and the exercises were through in less than an hour. The Ambassadors, as usual, were seated together.

The British discuss each other—their merits and demerits—in a surprisingly frank way and other matters as well. Some of the Ambassadors, however, are more reserved. I told my friend de Fleuriau, the French Ambassador, the other day that to him I was as transparent as a piece of glass—that he could see through me at any time—but to me he was like the rose window in Notre Dame—magnificent, unquestionably altogether excellent, but quite opaque.

Embassy, London,
July 9, 1929.

This evening we were the guests at dinner of the Prince of Wales at St. James's Palace. The Prince escorted Caro in to dinner. I followed with the wife of the Swedish Minister. Was interested in the Maharajah of Alwar, who was present and who speaks English perfectly. He told me of great times tiger hunting in his country from the back of an elephant.

We had a delightful time, as always, with the Prince of Wales. He says the King is naturally "fed up" with operations, but has to go through another slight one soon. Philip Snowden, the Chancel-

31

lor of the Exchequer, was present. Had a short talk with him and shall call on him soon. He is able and interesting.

Am impressed, more and more as I know him, with Arthur Henderson's method of dealing with matters of moment in his responsible position as Secretary of State for Foreign Affairs.

The antiquities of the Hyksos and the Philistine ages, discovered by Sir Flinders Petrie in Palestine, are on exhibition at University College and I received from him today an invitation to visit them. This I shall certainly do.

Embassy, London,
July 13, 1929.

I will try to dictate a reasonably consecutive account of the progress of the very important, though informal, conferences I am having with the Prime Minister.

In the last few days I have had three interviews with him—two of them at his office in the Parliament Building, and one this afternoon when we rode together to the great aviation show at Hendon. We have become friends, each believing in the honest purpose of the other—an indispensable basis for sure progress.

On July 10th in the House of Commons Mr. Day asked the Prime Minister "whether he is in a position to state when his forth-coming visit to America will take place, and whether any representatives of the Dominions will be present at any conference that takes place." MacDonald answered: "I am not yet in a position to make any statement." He will now answer in effect that the matter of his visit was a subject of diplomatic conversations with a view to determining how the trip might be arranged to best advance our common interest in naval disarmament. This should help to quiet the incessant discussion of the trip in both countries.

But the most important event of the week was the decision of the Prime Minister to stop work on the laying down of the two cruisers in his 1928–1929 naval program, which he outlined in a memorandum which he wrote out and handed to me at one of these conferences. In this he stated that it would help him in

Parliament if our Government could respond in kind, and this evening I have a message from Stimson that the Prime Minister's statement will be reciprocated by an announcement by us that "our preparations for laying the keels of the three cruisers, undertaken by our own yards have been slowed down." This statement will be given out in America in response to MacDonald's statement in Parliament here. This is the partial beginning of the new naval disarmament.

Besides the above matters, most important progress has been made in our discussions of the method of general procedure in naval disarmament negotiations between the United States and England and the other naval powers. I keep Matsudaira currently informed, as he does me.

American Embassy, London,
July 14, 1929.

In the afternoon our family drove to Chequers—the country house of the Prime Minister, where we had an interesting visit with both Ramsay MacDonald and his family.

To MacDonald's decision to delay the laying of the keels of two new large British cruisers, the President will announce that the United States will slow up construction on three large United States cruisers. This is the first tangible result of the naval conversations of the last month.

MacDonald was much pleased and said he wanted time to prepare a letter suitably expressing his appreciation. We all took tea with the family. MacDonald, while showing me through the house, took from a mantel the sword of Oliver Cromwell, which he had used at the battle of Marston Moor, and handed it to me for examination. Spent a time with the fine old books in the library. Half of the time MacDonald and I spend together we talk of other things than international relations. He is sending us the book he wrote about his wife after her death; he talks much to me about her and his earlier life.

His knowledge of history and of literature is exact and comprehensive. It is a delight to be with him. He talks of the problems which he has on hand—and few men have had more difficult ones—and always in his views, so far, he has never descended from the high level of a sincere statesmanship. I have faith that he will stand all tests with continued public respect, irrespective of what happens to him politically. Time will tell—but this is the way I feel about him.

Met Lord Dawson of Penn, the King's physician, who was at Chequers to tell MacDonald of the nature of the slight operation on the King tomorrow. He reassured MacDonald as to its slight nature.

July 20, 1929.

Of what I said in my speech before the Travel Association of Great Britain and Ireland this week, no criticism seems to have been made. But my emphatic method of extempore speech was disparaged by one or two English newspaper critics who are accustomed to more repose in public expression. Partly in self-defense, therefore, I insert this note received next day from the Lord Bishop of London.

Fulham Palace, S.W.6,
July 16, 1929.

DEAR GENERAL:

I felt sure that I would like you but after your speech today I feel that you are "a man and a brother." Now could you and Mrs. Dawes step down quite informally and lunch here on Tuesday, the 23rd, at 1:30 and meet my five brother bishops who help me with my little 4,500,000. They are all jolly fellows and you would like them, and you and your wife would enjoy seeing this old place where the Bishops have lived for 1300 years. Don't let them take you by mistake to the Fulham Palace of Vanities to which many of my guests are taken.

Of course, if the date doesn't suit, I can easily fix another, but I want you to meet the other Bishops if possible. There are no speeches and you can leave at 2:30 if you must.

Yours very sincerely,
A. F. INGRAM.

The Rt. Rev. The Lord Bishop of London.
Arthur Foley Winnington-Ingram, P.C., K.C.V.O., D.D.

On last Thursday morning, Caro and I called by official suggestion upon the Princess Beatrice, the aunt of the King, and a

STANLEY BALDWIN

daughter of Queen Victoria, an elderly lady of most amiable and pleasant address. Her home is at Kensington Palace, and upon the wall of the room in which she received us, I noticed the well-known painting of her mother as a young girl.

On Friday morning we made a similar official call upon the Duke and Duchess of York—both most pleasing young people.

At noon Friday, at Atherton's house, I took lunch with Stanley Baldwin and Sir Ronald Lindsay, the permanent Under-Secretary of State for Foreign Affairs. Here, the conversation was almost entirely upon literature and archaeology. Baldwin's competency in the classics is well known, and I could not resist encouraging such a conversation.

This (Saturday) morning I took Silas Strawn, of Chicago, to call on Arthur Henderson to talk over the serious situation threatening war between Russia and China. Strawn was recently the Chairman of the International Commission in China dealing with the question of "exterritoriality" and had interesting news.

Henderson read us his dispatch to our State Department endorsing the suggestion of the United States for mediation, as well as his dispatch to France. He also read me a dispatch from the United States answering the suggestion which the British and French Governments had made to our Government that I be named as the "official observer" at the Conference on the Young Plan which it is now decided will be held at Brussels.

Our State Department replied that they felt I had enough on my hands already.

> American Embassy,
> London,
> July 22, 1929.

The Prime Minister having asked me to call on him at his Parliament Office at 4:00 P.M., I took with me a cable message from our State Department which I had just received, answering his last message to our Government. The cable was not completed. More of it will be received and decoded by tomorrow. It was complete enough, however, to give the United States' attitude considerably more in detail than had been given before, including some comments on the British cruiser situation as compared with ours.

10 Downing Street,
23 July, 1929.

MY DEAR GENERAL:

I have been thinking over the despatch you showed me yesterday, and though I have not yet had it (I am writing this early in the morning when only the birds are up, and they even are sleepy) to study. It is clear that it raises a problem which we have assumed was smaller than it appears to be. We have been waiting for the "yardstick," but this despatch of yesterday says that this gap between us is too wide for a yardstick to span. So we must examine it and we must get advice and guidance.

I propose, if it meets your convenience, to stay in town till we settle something. This week finds me full of concern till the House rises. Would it be possible for us to meet on Monday morning to go into this whole matter of this tonnage of cruisers and go at it till we agree on how we stand. If Mr. Gibson could be with us, I would bring Mr. Alexander, the First Lord (Civil), and a day or two ought to see the end of our preliminary conversations. Then I shall go on a holiday.

I am, my dear Ambassador,

Yours very sincerely,
J. RAMSAY MACDONALD.

MacDonald sent for J. H. Thomas (Secretary of State for the Colonies and Vice-Chairman of the Parliamentary Labour Party), to meet me, and I met for the first time the unique character upon whose shoulders there rests at this moment such a burden of responsibility.

American Embassy,
London,
July 24, 1929.

11:00 P.M.

This has been a busy day and a most important one in the progress of the cause of naval disarmament. If the United States and Great Britain can agree upon what constitutes between their navies a parity of fighting strength, the result should be a general naval reduction among the three great naval powers—Great Britain, Japan and the United States—and probably also France and Italy.

Journal as Ambassador to Great Britain

If we cannot reach such an understanding, the cause of naval disarmament is lost for the present.

Yesterday the cable from the United States disturbed the Prime Minister, who recognized the considerable apparent discrepancy between the statements of British naval strength made by his advisors in the Admiralty and the estimates of it made by our naval experts and given in our cables.

When I called on him this morning at 10 Downing Street he was more encouraged as the Admiralty had given him reassuring explanations which he was reducing to a written statement to me which I will receive tomorrow, and which we will consider at the meeting next Monday of MacDonald, Alexander (the First Lord of the Admiralty), Gibson and myself.

I visited MacDonald at 10 Downing Street twice this morning.

Our Government, basing its opinion on the figures of the British Admiralty which I had cabled, held that if we are to reach parity in cruisers the present British building program must be stopped until the year 1936.

MacDonald thinks the figures he will give me tomorrow will lead to a modification of this view. His visit will be made probably in October and he expressed himself in relation to it in his speech of this afternoon, along the lines outlined together the other day.

At 3:30 P.M. I went to the House of Commons to hear MacDonald make his statement, which he did in an effective and impressive way. In answering the questions it evoked, he showed himself master of the situation. As I left the gallery of the House after the completion of his statement, I found his secretary waiting to take me to the terrace to meet him, where MacDonald, Lady Cynthia Mosley and myself took tea. The Prime Minister was happy at the fine reception of his statement, and we had a pleasant visit—the third during the day.

Lloyd George stopped with us for a time and arranged for Stanley Baldwin and himself to meet the Prime Minister at 6:30 this evening.

Tomorrow, or soon thereafter, President Hoover will issue a statement approving the Prime Minister's statement, expressing gratification at the new departure taken. He will say that future

American naval plans will await consultation and specifically that we will slow down preparation for laying the keels of the three new units of the American cruiser program which our Navy Yards are to build.

I wired Gibson to meet me here by Sunday evening, ready for our important Monday conference.

American Embassy,
London,
July 25, 1929.

The papers this morning contained both the Prime Minister's statement in Parliament and the response by President Hoover on naval disarmament.

At Their Majesties' garden party this afternoon, the Prime Minister expressed his appreciation of our President's fine statement, and the promptness with which it was made.

This morning I received a long letter from the Prime Minister —a further discussion of the figures of the Admiralty and United States—which, together with some comments, I cabled to the State Department at Washington.

I append the statement of the Prime Minister on naval policy as reported in the London *Times* for July 25, 1929.

Replying to Lieut.-Com. Kenworthy, Mr. MacDonald said: "I am now in a position to make a statement of the immediate intentions of the Government regarding the Naval Building programme. The Government's general position is that the defense of a country must be devised with two main considerations in view; first, the chances of the defense having to be used; then, the efficiency and economy shown in their magnitude and character. The Government has kept in view the changes in policy and in the problem of national security affected by the Peace Pact, if that Pact is to be made an effective influence in international relations. To make it so is the controlling purpose of the Government, and a systematic policy is being developed, which will take a little time to complete, to carry out that intention.

"As is well known, in the midst of the multifarious concerns which the formation of a new Government entails and the specially pressing and complicated nature of our tasks, conversations have been actively carried on between the United States and ourselves for the purpose of opening a way for an agreement on naval matters which hitherto have defied a settlement.

38

Journal as Ambassador to Great Britain

By a happy coincidence our assumption of office corresponded in time with the arrival in this country of the new American Ambassador, Mr. Dawes, who has come here charged by the President of the United States of America with a mission for preparing the ground for an International Agreement on the reduction and limitation of naval armaments. Already the whole field of these differences with the United States has been surveyed, and the two Governments have made a fresh start on their solution. We have agreed upon the principle of parity, we have agreed that without in any way departing from the conditions of parity, a measure of elasticity can be allowed so as to meet the peace requirements of the two nations. We have determined that we shall not allow technical points to over-ride the great public issues involved in our being able to come to a settlement. And, so soon as the rising of the House releases me from its day to day work, I propose to make this matter my chief concern until an issue is reached. A visit to the President of the United States is now the subject of conversation so that it may take place, when it will be most helpful to promote the cordial relations of our two countries and in particular advance the ends of disarmament and peace which we hold in common. It has to be fitted in with certain international conferences, but October at present looks a likely month.

"A committee to co-ordinate the three services for the purpose of Cabinet consideration has been set up, but, as that co-ordination is not comprehensive enough to meet the requirements of State policy, the Foreign Office is also represented upon it. This will enable us to systematize our work. In the opinion of this committee, the general outlook is such as to justify a review of our programme. Our predecessors did this from time to time as the outlook brightened. Therefore, after a thorough examination of our naval position, and not only as a proof of our own sincerity, but as a duty imposed upon us to guard the expenditure of national money, we have decided as follows:

"To suspend all work on the cruisers Surrey and Northumberland.

"To cancel the Submarine Depot Ship Maidstone.

"To cancel two contract submarines.

"To slow down dockyard work on other naval construction.

"As regards the 1929–30 programme, in any event no commitments would have to be entered into before the autumn, and no steps will be taken to proceed with it until the matter has received further consideration.

"The Government, of course, recognizes that a reduction in the naval building programme must have a direct effect on employment, in the dockyards, but I am glad to say that, as a result of special arrangements suggested by the Admiralty, it is hoped to be able to secure the absorption of a large amount of labor which would otherwise be discharged from the Royal Dockyards. The representatives of dockyard labor will at once be consulted.

"We are indebted to the Board of Admiralty for the help which they have rendered, and I desire to state that, having expressed their technical view on the minimum armaments they consider to be necessary, they have furnished us with loyal help in achieving our object with the least possible dislocation and hardship.

"I ought to add that it is recognized by all the Powers concerned that a preliminary agreement on Anglo-American differences is essential to a general agreement on naval building, and the Governments of the Powers represented at Washington, 1921–22, have been informed of the conversations. So soon as the way is cleared, they will be invited to a preliminary conference, so that we may all together try to come to an agreement of a comprehensive kind. The final agreement would be ratified at a place which I hope will by common consent be chosen by the United States as a recognition of the splendid part played by the President in these transactions, and then reported to the Preparatory Commission of the League as a contribution to its work.

"If these intentions are fulfilled, the request of the chairman of the Preparatory Commission on Disarmament made at Geneva on March 15, 1928, that the Powers should make an attempt to agree among themselves will be accomplished, and we shall be in a position to pursue with that Commission the difficult and essential problems of how to reduce other forms of armament in accordance with the pledge given by the Allies at Versailles when imposing disarmament on Germany and its associate nations, and in pursuance of the Pact of Peace. To that His Majesty's Government will direct its thoughts and its energies, in cooperation with other nations, as soon as this more immediate work on naval agreement has been finished. A general disarmament conference will then be possible. I am anxious that the House should not minimize the difficulties in our way, nor the time that will be required for the negotiations, but they may be assured that it will be our care to make our own policy clear and our desire to put our energies into a settlement without unnecessary delay." [Cheers]

The statement on naval reduction by President Hoover as published in the newspapers this morning reads:

I have read with real satisfaction the statement which the Prime Minister has made in the House of Commons. The American people are greatly complimented by his proposed visit, and he will find a universal welcome. Mr. MacDonald's statement marks a new departure in the discussion of naval disarmament. The Prime Minister introduces the principle of parity which we have now adopted, and its consummation means that Great Britain and the United States henceforth are not to compete in armament as potential opponents, but to cooperate as friends in the reduction of it.

The Prime Minister has stated clearly and unmistakably the principles on which he is acting. I cannot but be responsive to the generous terms in which he has spoken of the attitude and purpose of the United States. We join in his efforts in the same spirit. Mr. MacDonald has indicated good will and the positive intention of the British Government by the suspension of the construction of certain portions of this year's British naval programme. It is the desire of the United States to show an equal good will in our approach to the problem. We have three cruisers in this year's construction programme which have been undertaken in the Government Navy Yards, detailed drawings for which are now in course of preparation. The actual keels would, in the ordinary course, be laid down some time this fall. Generally speaking, the British cruiser strength considerably exceeds the American strength at the present time, and the actual construction of these three cruisers would not be likely in themselves to produce inequality in the final result. We do not wish, however, to have any misunderstanding of our actions, and, therefore, we shall not lay down these keels until there has been an opportunity for full consideration of their effect upon the final agreement for parity which we expect to reach, although our hopes for relief from construction lie more largely in the latter years of the programme under the law of 1928.

London,
Friday, July 26, 1929.

There being a lull in naval disarmament negotiations until Monday afternoon at 2:30, took it easy today, writing a few letters and going to University College, Tower Street, where I saw Sir Flinders Petrie's exhibit of the antiquities found at Beth-Pelet, Palestine, of the Philistine and Hyksos ages. Sir Flinders explained them to me and I spent a wonderful time.

London,
July 29, 1929.

This afternoon at 2:30 P.M. Gibson, Atherton and I met MacDonald and Alexander at 10 Downing Street. We remained in conference for two hours. When we left, the only remaining question involving naval parity between our two nations which was unsettled related to the cruiser class and that was much simplified.

This considerable progress was made possible by the masterful statement of the present position of negotiations and suggestions in connection therewith contained in a cable to me from the United States, which I recognize as chiefly the work of President Hoover and the contents of which I read at the opening of the conference.

We agree to equate by 1936.

This afternoon we received a first tentative proposition on cruiser equation from the British, which the Prime Minister, after a general discussion, wrote out in our presence. This is in effect that by 1936 the British should have 15 of the large 10,000 ton, eight-inch gun cruisers, and the United States 18. Of the small six-inch gun cruisers, the British should have 45 and the United States her ten Omaha cruisers of 6600 tons each, and ten new six-inch gun cruisers.

The proposition is tentative. Tonight the Admiralty is probably studying it as MacDonald has given it to them and after their reaction has been received it may be modified. Again we have cabled it to our State Department for their comment.

But our methods of arriving at it well illustrates the entire confidence we are placing in each other's fairness and honesty, and what our idea is of the way the English-speaking peoples should negotiate with each other.

Alexander seemed to have a good grasp of his navy situation and Gibson, as usual, was of invaluable aid to us all. It is an honor and privilege to have a connection with negotiations between two such able and purposeful men as Hoover and Mac-Donald.

Tonight Caro and I attended a dinner given by the Prime Minister and his daughter at 10 Downing Street. Of the Cabinet, Henderson and Snowden were present. Among the others, were the Lord Chancellor, Reginald McKenna, the Spanish Ambassador, and Malcolm MacDonald, son of the Prime Minister and a member of Parliament.

London,
July 30, 1929.

This afternoon I received a satisfactory letter from the Prime Minister which I transmitted by cable to the State Department. In it MacDonald stated his satisfaction with our conversations of yesterday as he thought them over more, and said that he expected to be able to reduce the number of six-inch gun cruisers necessary to the British peacetime requirements, which yesterday he estimated as 45. The prospects for naval reduction are steadily improving.

My friend Thomas W. Lamont, who was a member of the Young Committee, is here. He was made somewhat anxious about

A. V. ALEXANDER

10 DOWNING STREET, LONDON

the present attitude of England toward the ratification of the Young Plan at the coming Hague conference by the recent comments of Snowden and Lloyd George in Parliament. Accordingly, he saw Snowden yesterday. When I saw Snowden at the Prime Minister's dinner last night, he told me Lamont had given him a new light on the Young Plan and had explained "the other side."

This morning I took Mr. Lamont over to the Foreign Office to see Henderson, who will be one of the British representatives at the Hague conference. Henderson is heartily in favor of ratification and was pleased with Tom's explanation of the reasons for the slight rearrangement of the Dawes Plan allotment percentages.

This noon Caro and I took lunch at Fulham Palace with the Lord Bishop of London, who had some of his fellow bishops and other friends there. It was a delightful gathering. The most of those present were elderly. I do not know when I have enjoyed myself more. The Lord Bishop took us through the historic old place after lunch. He is the soul of dignity, affability and goodfellowship.

London,
Wednesday, July 31, 1929.

11:15 P.M.

This has been a full and important day. Will try to take it in order.

My morning was taken up by two calls—one from the Japanese Ambassador and one from the French Ambassador. Matsudaira had a letter from MacDonald which he showed me, telling him to keep informed of the naval conversations between Great Britain and the United States through me and to regard any statement of fact made by me as from him. I had just received a telegram from the State Department saying that my cables conveying the last two statements from the Prime Minister were disappointing and that they would comment in detail today.

Posted Matsudaira on the situation fully.

The French Ambassador called about the Young Plan conference. Thomas Lamont should be at the conference, and I informed de Fleuriau to this effect. He suggested that his Government and the British representatives on the conference suggest at an early meeting of it that the British and American members of the Young Committee be on hand at The Hague, prepared to give their help in elucidating matters if needed. I had found that Matsudaira regarded Tom's presence most important.

Skipping to a later time in the day, I took Tom with me to the Prime Minister and the latter, upon my explanation of the dangers of disagreement on the conference without the presence of some of those who had been through the mill of the Expert Committee at Paris, like Lamont and Stamp and Addis, will take the matter up with Snowden who is inclined to kick over the traces and endanger ratification. I pointed out to the Prime Minister from my viewpoint the chaos which would result from the failure to ratify the Young Plan at the Hague conference. He stated that he favored ratification, but the British would seek some modifications. He intimated, however, that they would not block ratification—but one senses that he feels that Snowden's attitude creates serious difficulties.

In order not to mix subjects, I now skip to a later time this evening, when I saw Stamp at his home, where my family dined with his, and found Stamp disgruntled because of Snowden's and Lloyd George's attack on the Plan in the House of Commons. He is going to Switzerland. He agreed, however, he would come to The Hague on call. The French, I think, realize how serious may be the difference which will develop unless the best brains of the old Young Committee can be called upon when needed.

The interests of the United States are involved in the ratification of the Young Plan, as it will be a recipient of payments under the Plan on account of the expenses of the Army of Occupation. Frankly, I am worried at the apparent lack of appreciation in some quarters of what disagreement upon ratification involves.

At 3:00 P.M., Winston Churchill called. I had never met him before. We talked over his coming trip to America, and he outlined what was in his mind to say. He said frankly that he did not favor naval limitation agreement. There was an interesting but general talk.

WINSTON CHURCHILL

RAY ATHERTON

Journal as Ambassador to Great Britain

Later in the afternoon I called on MacDonald at 10 Downing Street and told him of the telegram from the State Department stating its disappointment with the results of my last conversation and saying that it would send comments today. We had a long talk over the situation, MacDonald calling in Alexander, the First Lord of the Admiralty.

The Prime Minister has made his arrangements to fly to Lossiemouth, starting at 9:30 A.M. tomorrow. He wants to do this if possible. He offered to get up any time tonight we could bring to him the answering cable from Washington which we await.

London,
August 1, 1929.

This morning at 6:45, Atherton called for me at the Embassy with the Washington answer to our cables and we met the Prime Minister at 10 Downing Street at 7:00 A.M.

I presented these answers, in which it was maintained and demonstrated that the tentative program proposed by MacDonald apparently presented unsurmountable obstacles to agreement as amounting to a total abdication of the principle of decrease in naval armament and abandonment of the principle of parity and equality between the two navies of which the crux lies in the cruiser class. The First Lord of the Admiralty Alexander was there.

Hoover's telegram seemed unanswerable, for, without mistake, it was from his own hand chiefly. I shot it into MacDonald with full force for the necessity of the moment is a precipitation of the real issues between us, in order to determine whether we can proceed further or not.

He took it pleasantly and like a thoroughbred. He immediately sat down to write a reply and I left.

About noon his secretary said he wanted to see me again and I went to 10 Downing Street where he read me the first draft of a letter of about 2000 words. In the meantime I had drafted a cable to the State Department which I felt was due MacDonald and as well to Hoover as shedding some light on MacDonald's dilemma.

45

To secure real cruiser reduction, MacDonald has to scrap existing cruisers while Hoover has only to scrap cruiser programs in part and then build some cruisers.

I informed President Hoover that it was only due the Prime Minister to say that in our conference last Monday, resulting in the tentative figures suggested by the Prime Minister, the attitude of Gibson and myself, while pressing the necessity for more reduction was such as to justify him in the belief that we considered these propositions were a contribution to progress.

It would seem that MacDonald must stand for such a reduction as will give some basis, whether well founded or not, for an opposition attack supported by the Admiralty that he is endangering the safety of the Empire, or he must take the position which will have some public appeal, that a parity which includes some limitation of building programs and a cessation of competition, but without substantial present reduction except in programs, is the one he must now urge as the most consistent with British safety. Inevitably this situation will test his statesmanship. Delay with him, if he should suggest delay, is not a refuge for any great length of time. MacDonald has acted up to the present as a statesman being ground between the upper and nether millstones of the American proposition and the proposition of his Admiralty. He is sincere and entirely frank with us, concealing neither the facts as he views them, nor his reactions to them.

It was late in the afternoon when his long letter was delivered to me. In general it is a statement of his desire for reduction and to meet the President's views, and of the necessities of the British situation, which make it difficult to do so. He states that if he had only to consider the relations of Great Britain and of the United States, he could meet the President's desires for reduction and more, but outlines the British situation as affected by its relations to other countries.

It is written in the most friendly and conciliatory terms, and its effect, while it will be clarifying to Washington, at any rate is to check progress pending more discussion.

The above constitutes one of those hard spots in the naval matter of which important international work is generally full.

Journal as Ambassador to Great Britain

London,
August 2, 1929.

In the morning I took the train for Birkenhead with my son Dana and my nephews Henry and Carlos. We travelled with Marshal Lyautey of France, the French Ambassador (M. de Fleuriau), the Brazilian Ambassador and the Minister from Poland. I had an interesting visit with the Marshal—an example of the best French military and civil leadership.

On our arrival we were met by automobiles and taken to the camp where the great jamboree of the Boy Scouts was being held —50,000 scouts being in attendance. Before the arrival of the Prince of Wales and Sir Robert Baden-Powell to review the scouts, I was taken to the American scouts, 1300 strong in formation ready to enter the parade. The Evanston scouts—ten in number—were brought to me and afterward, with Mr. West and Dan Beard, I walked around on inspection.

After receiving the American scouts' salute, we went to the Royal Box and reviewed the parade. During the parade I sat between Marshal Lyautey and the Earl of Meath, an Irish nobleman 89 years of age who, for a quarter of a century, has been the head of the Irish scouts. He told me four of his sons had been in the war; one had been killed and the other three severely wounded. His fine philosophy of life which he described to me explained his vigor and cheerfulness at such an advanced age. To best grow old in happiness, one should keep in touch with youth in a common high purpose.

The Prince and Baden-Powell made fine addresses. Altogether it was an inspiring day, which I much enjoyed. Inspected the camp of the American scouts after the parade. We returned on the afternoon train to London arriving at 9:30 P.M.

Journal as Ambassador to Great Britain

London,
August 3, 1929.

Received another cable from the President and Stimson to transmit to MacDonald who is at Lossiemouth. Sent a paraphrase of it to Scotland to MacDonald by Henry as I did not wish to risk either loss or delay by mail. Henry will deliver it by tomorrow afternoon. Read it over the telephone to Gibson at Brussels. Sent two cables to the State Department.

Like everything received from Hoover and Stimson, this cable means sensible progress and places the negotiations on more of a "brass tack" basis.

Matsudaira is coming back to town to get posted on our next conference Tuesday night, to attend which MacDonald will fly down from Lossiemouth. I regret to see him take such risks in this stormy weather.

Gilbert, Agent General for Reparations, is interested in the report of our Dominican Commission. He took it with him saying he would bring it to the attention of the German treasury officials, inasmuch as the situation there needs a better system for the executive control of governmental expenditures.

Having been in the Treasury Department with me at Washington, when he was Under-Secretary and I was Director of the Bureau of the Budget, he thoroughly understands the advanced step we took when we incorporated into the Dominican Budget law the system of control which, in our country, was set up and now exists only by executive order.

London,
Monday, August 5, 1929.

Caro, Dana, Virginia and I went by train to Salisbury in the afternoon to visit Major General and Mrs. Alexander Anderson McHardy. The General, then a Colonel, became a member of the Military Board of Allied Supply for Great Britain, succeeding Lieutenant General Sir Travers Clarke. For years he was engaged

Wide World Photos, London

LOGIE HOUSE, DUNPHAIL

in the work of the Board which resulted from the orders to the General Staffs of the Allied Armies which, when American Member of the Board I had caused to be issued, to prepare an official statement of the status of Foch's command in the Franco-Belgian theater of operations as of October 31, 1918, just preceding the armistice, and the statement of the supply services of the Allied Armies from the beginning of the war. Thus he was an important factor in producing the report of the Board which has been published by the Allied Governments.

His home is in the close of Salisbury Cathedral—a house three hundred or so years old. The Bishop and the Dean of the Cathedral were at dinner and Mr. and Mrs. Stewart, relatives of Mrs. McHardy.

After dinner we went to Tidworth "Tattoo" given by several thousand troops and a massed band of about 500. It was an inspiring spectacle. We sat by the General in the Royal Box, the American flag and the British flag draping it. The affair was so enthralling that 20,000 people sat for several hours in a pouring rain to see it.

London,
Tuesday, August 6, 1929.

Arrived at 11:30 A.M. from Salisbury. Gibson was at the Chancery, having arrived from Brussels the night before. A long cable was awaiting us from Washington.

After lunch, Atherton, Gibson and I went to see the Prime Minister at 2:30 at 10 Downing Street. He had come by train from Lossiemouth as the weather was too bad for flying.

This conference, at which the First Lord of the Admiralty was present, lasted two hours. The Prime Minister had been working hard to find some way to meet Hoover's demand for reduction. He read us his rough notes for discussion. He is taking the initiative instead of allowing his Admiralty to do so, and as a result we are again making progress. We talked most freely. Mutual confidence and complete exchange of information is the only possible foundation for success in this difficult adjustment.

MacDonald would like to have me go to Elgin on the 23rd,

when he receives the freedom of that Scottish city, and I have told him I would do so.

After the conference, Gibson and I wrote a long cable to Washington. Tomorrow I will receive MacDonald's letter and cable it to Washington. Gibson left this evening for Brussels. He is much over-worked, the State Department having detailed away the effective staff at his Embassy. I am sorry for him but he is simply invaluable. It is hard for him to take these trips.

London,
Sunday, August 11, 1929.

6:00 P.M.

Things have been happening at The Hague, where the division of reparation proceeds under the Young Plan is being discussed by the interested Governments. The United States is concerned because the costs of its army of occupation are to be met out of the Young Plan payments.

J. P. Morgan just called me on the telephone from his country place and told me of the situation resulting from Snowden's ultimatum at The Hague regarding England's share of reparations. It looks as though the Chancellor of the Exchequer had taken the bit in his teeth. Montagu Norman and Tom Lamont, so Morgan said, had lunched with MacDonald at Edinburgh yesterday and outlined to him the seriousness of things. Morgan says that he will meet me at the Embassy at 10:30 A.M. tomorrow.

In the meantime, this morning I received a telegram from Tom Lamont from North Berwick, saying that he had not gone to The Hague as the matter "had become political and must be settled first by Prime Minister here," and asking if I had any suggestion to make.

When I arrived from Ireland at the Chancery last evening, I found that Alberto Pirelli of Italy had called me by telephone from The Hague during the day. Morgan wants Parker Gilbert to meet me tonight.

Told Morgan over the telephone my first reflections. Snowden has aroused Britain over the proposed division of reparation proceeds between the interested Governments, and probably by the same token France. Public sentiment has now to be dealt with—not Prime Ministers or individuals—for public opinion is in the saddle, and, in my judgment, will continue to ride for some time. For a time events will take charge of things and while there may be delay, they must come out right in the end.

During the period of the Young Committee a similar impasse occurred. If it had not occurred, the Plan could not have been agreed upon. It was the impasse alone which compelled the public opinion to consider alternatives, and then only did it manifest itself strongly enough to influence the Committee. The immediate prospect of a financial debâcle in both Germany and England appeared and the Committee, being composed of laymen, and not of politicians who are always apprehensive of a political repercussion which would injure them personally, did the obvious common-sense thing and agreed. It cannot be too strongly stated that public sentiment dominated in these crises.

But now the public pressure falls upon a political and not an "expert committee"—and this committee is dealing with parliaments in its mind.

I am afraid there is nothing to do for the moment but to keep the committee together until events operate—and if I am not mistaken, a prevailing general impression that the Plan will not be ratified will bring the people of all the countries involved face to face with realities in the only way which can bring about the final settlement. But while the way will be rough and many may suffer meantime, the Plan (perhaps slightly modified) will stand.

Caro, Dana, Virginia, Miss Decker, Mr. and Mrs. George Earle, and my nephews, Carlos and Henry Dawes, left with me for Dublin Wednesday evening. The High Commissioner for the Irish Free State in London, Professor Timothy A. Smiddy, accompanied us.

Arrived at Dublin about 7:00 A.M. President William T. Cosgrave met us at the boat. Smiddy took us to the museums and other points of interest until noon. Then we were given a luncheon by the Governor General. Afterward we went to the horse show. Awarded some prizes. In the evening President Cosgrave gave us a dinner. The next day Smiddy took us in government cars on a wonderful trip to Glendaloug and to Bray coming back. We were accompanied on this trip by our Chicago friends, James O'Donnell Bennett and his wife. In the evening attended a reception by the Governor General.

Left Dublin yesterday morning early. Again President Cosgrave came to the boat to see us off, notwithstanding it involved a trip of six miles each way from Dublin. I only wish I could write more now of the wonderful and generous reception we had and of my admiration for the Irish Free State and its executives. Cosgrave is not only a charming and brilliant man but a great man.

Ex-Senator and Mrs. Joseph S. Frelinghuysen and their son and daughter returned with us.

London,
Monday, August 12, 1929.

In the morning J. P. Morgan and Parker Gilbert called at the Embassy. Our talk was of the situation at The Hague. Morgan fears a financial upset of a serious nature will occur if a deadlock even for a time creates a feeling that the Young Plan may fail.

At 3:00 P.M. I called on the French Ambassador, at his request, as he was unwell. He wanted my ideas as to the Hague situation. He felt that the French feeling, while aroused against Snowden, was not hostile toward England, and regretted the absence of Poincaré at The Hague who, he thought, would have had the exact knowledge to make an immediate reply to Snowden when the latter finished his remarks, which would have clarified the situation and made it generally and properly understood.

At 4:00 P.M. the Japanese Ambassador called on me at the Chancery to inquire of the present state of the naval negotiations between us and the English. He notified me that in the negotiations hereafter, when they were extended to the other powers, Japan would ask that the present ratio in capital ships of 5-5-3 between England, the United States and Japan be made 10-10-7, the same to extend to all categories. He also stated that Japan would favor reduction in all categories. This I duly transmitted by

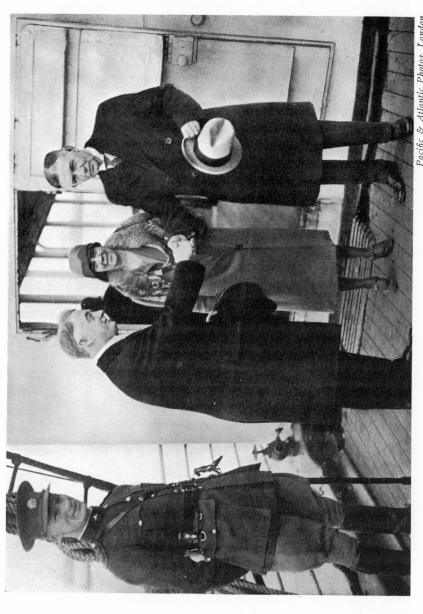

ARRIVAL AT DUBLIN, AUGUST 8, 1929

Left to right: Military aide, President William T. Cosgrave, Mrs. Dawes, General Dawes.

PHILIP SNOWDEN

cable to the State Department. Gibson is in bed at Brussels and is threatened with an operation—the result, according to his doctor, of over-work.

London,
Tuesday, August 13, 1929.

Tom Lamont called at the Embassy, having come from Scotland. He went over his talk with MacDonald. Yesterday afternoon MacDonald had informed me, through his secretary, by telephone that he would be glad if Tom would go to The Hague as Pirelli of Italy desired. But this afternoon his secretary telephoned the Chancery from Scotland that MacDonald had heard from The Hague that things were going better and that it would be best for Tom not to go. This we communicated to Tom, who said he had already decided not to go.

Considering the outburst of natural sentiment altering materially the "status quo" of the negotiations which he has invoked, Snowden will probably win his point. It would seem that after all public sentiment has not been aroused in France in a dangerous way, and that the rest of the delegates are now trying to find a way to meet, or at least to compromise on, the British demands.

Snowden has played his part well. The question is, can the other countries meet his demands without creating a hostile public sentiment among their own people which would prevent ratification? The Young Plan must be ratified. In time it is certain to be. Even if this conference breaks up, it will be ratified. It will be modified in details but not in general.

Snowden, as it transpires, has rendered a real service, not only to England but to the other Allies. By his ultimatum which precipitated the vital issues involved, the reactions of the public opinions of the Allies will be determined at once. It will soon be known, therefore, whether the settlement will come now or whether, impossible now because of the callousness of domestic sentiment, it must await these calamitous public events caused by uncertainty, which will favorably change public opinions toward acceptance.

Journal as Ambassador to Great Britain

In the morning Tom Lamont called me up by telephone to say that Pierre Quesnay, who represented France, had called him up from The Hague in behalf of himself, Émile Francqui of Belgium and Pirelli, to come and assist them in settling matters in the present Hague situation, between France, Belgium and Italy. Tom replied that they must go to Snowden and ascertain if he had any objection.

Accordingly, in order to keep the Prime Minister in touch with the situation, we telephoned this to his secretary at Lossiemouth. He answered that while he had desired Tom to be at The Hague, he had determined to let the British delegates there control the present English program, and would be satisfied with their decision in the matter. He desired me to keep him informed of anything I deemed of importance.

When Tom was telephoned this by Belin, at my instruction, he replied that he had decided not to go.

Uncle Will Mills and General Pershing will arrive at the house this evening for a visit and Tom will be here for dinner.

LATER: Tom Lamont said that when Snowden was approached by Quesnay he said that he would prefer to call in the experts later, if necessary, and let the present situation be handled by the statesmen.

By the way, Snowden is doing a good job in handling.

Had a fine time in the evening with General Pershing.

Parker Gilbert came in this morning to say "good-bye" as he is leaving for Berlin today. He called while General Pershing, Uncle Will Mills, Major Price and I were having breakfast, and sat down with us. He thinks things are going well at The Hague and that the other Allies will concede something to Great Britain along each of the three demands of Snowden. This is his last information from The Hague.

London,
Friday, August 16, 1929.

During the day I received from the State Department the reply to the Prime Minister's last proposition.

In the afternoon I telephoned the Prime Minister at Lossiemouth that the answer had arrived and he asked me to come to Lossiemouth on Monday. Will leave for there Sunday evening.

The answer practically accepts the Prime Minister's proposition but raises some points which must be accorded much attention. We are about up to the point where the "yardstick" must be decided upon between the navy men.

The message suggests the possibility that the United States must build the whole of the 15 eight-inch gun cruiser program, bringing our total of 10,000 ton cruisers to 23, if we are to reach parity by 1936 with the 15 eight-inch gun, 10,000 ton cruisers and thirty-five of the smaller cruisers which MacDonald proposes for the British at that date.

The fact is that we are about agreed "in principle" but if the principle works out in detail, something which does not express a clearly understood parity by the public opinion of both countries, we will be in trouble. At best we have got to "lump things" in our decisions, yardstick or no yardstick.

Sent the message by the King's messenger by train to Mac-Donald this evening.

London,
Saturday, August 17, 1929.

At lunch at Embassy were Justice Pierce Butler, of the United States Supreme Court and his son, and Sir Warren Fisher, Permanent Secretary to the Treasury and his son, who is now in the English Navy. Received from Fisher my first real explanation of the machinery for the control of the English Government expenditures and we compared it with that which I set up by executive order when I was the first Director of the Bureau of the Budget in Washington. He is studying my book on the budget and we will continue our comparisons and recounting of experiences at another session.

Fisher thinks that there will be agreement without adjournment at The Hague. I hope so, but it depends upon what kind of public reactions the statesmen are sensing in their respective countries.

Agreement will finally come, but whether before or after a first break—that is the question. Upon the answer depends whether or not Europe is to have common sense jolted into it by a time of financial trouble. I hope it will not prove necessary, but one does not know.

Am leaving tomorrow afternoon for an interview on Monday at Lossiemouth with the Prime Minister.

London,
Saturday, August 24, 1929.

Uncle Will Mills, Dana and I arrived at Lossiemouth on Monday morning, the 18th. The Prime Minister was at the depot to meet us and took us to his house. (Hillocks). He and I had a two-hour talk over the naval disarmament. He is gathering information from the Admiralty in preparing his reply to the last message from our State Department, and told me he would have his answer ready by Friday when I was to rejoin him at Elgin.

John F. Harris, an old friend, met us and he and the others of our party were entertained by the Prime Minister and his daughter, Miss Ishbel MacDonald, at the Marine Hotel.

After another short talk with him, Uncle Will, Dana and I took a motor with John Harris for Lude House, Blair Atholl, which he has rented for the grouse shooting.

There are some 9000 acres in this place. The mountains of Ben-Y-Ghlow surround it. The moors are covered with purple heather and the panorama is a wonderful one.

On Wednesday, Uncle Will left for London and America, much to our regret but after a visit enjoyable to him and to us.

SHOOTING BUTT ON GROUSE MOOR AT BLAIR ATHOLL, AUGUST 20, 1929

Left to right: Mr. Mackey, in charge of moor; Hugh Gow, loader; General Dawes.

Journal as Ambassador to Great Britain

On Thursday afternoon, Dana and I motored to Forres, where we stayed all night at a fine hotel, called a "hydropathic hotel," which the Prime Minister had recommended.

On Friday morning we went to Hillocks. There the Prime Minister and I had a short talk before going to the ceremonies at Elgin. At the hotel at Forres I found a long letter from him professing much discouragement about the naval outcome.

Realizing that I must speak at the ceremonies attending the giving of the "Freedom of the City of Elgin" to the Prime Minister, I had evolved at Glen Atholl, at the expense of an evening, some remarks upon the value of effecting a settlement by the progressive simplification of the problem now going on which is circumscribing the power of the naval specialists to block action. This I read to him and he approved it as useful.

Parenthetically I would say that when one realizes that what he says on the naval question will be printed on both sides of the ocean, he cannot safely dash things off. My encouragement to the Prime Minister was probably not necessary, for upon reflection I am inclined to consider his pessimism, now that expressions of a similar hopelessness from America were answered by him with a ten ship reduction in the estimate of British needs, is calculated to spur the intelligent minds of President Hoover and his associates in Washington to endeavors to relieve it by a concession of some kind. A verbal expression of despair from him would have been more convincing to me than his written one, the substance of which he realized, of course, that I would transmit to Washington.

At this time I had not seen his formal letter in reply to the last Washington cable, which he said would be handed to me by the Foreign Office when I reached London the next morning.

Here is his letter to me:

Lossiemouth,
August 22, 1929.

MY DEAR GENERAL:

I have now finished my study of the last note you transmitted to me from Washington and have refreshed my memory by papers sent up to me here. The result is that I am more depressed than I have been since we began our conversations. You will remember that we started on the yardstick which was the proposal which brought back hope for Geneva. You were to give me a formula and we both agreed that it should be examined by subordinate experts. That has all gone. In your speech at the Pilgrims, you said so truly that the statesmen should handle this matter and that as there was the desire for an agreement, and as a naval conflict between the countries was unthinkable, the technicians should not thwart the statesmen. That has gone, and we are back into exactly the same atmosphere and facing exactly the same presentation of the problem as we were at Geneva. We are drifting away from the only road which offers a solution of a problem which does not consist of reality at all, but of words and appearances. Experts and lawyers make nearly all the reefs in the seas of life upon which men and states founder. I am working at my formal reply which I am sorry cannot be ready today, as I led you to expect. It will be ready tomorrow however. I thought I should tell you this so as to keep my promise to you.

With all best wishes for a good time in the Highlands.

Yours very sincerely,
J. RAMSAY MACDONALD.

His Excellency General Charles Dawes.

After a short time we left Lossiemouth for Elgin. The Prime Minister and Miss Ishbel occupied the first car, and Lord Dunedin and myself the second. We were met formally by the Lord Provost of Elgin, and other dignitaries, including Lord Forres, Sir Alexander Grant, the City Council and others.

The meeting was impressive. The speech of the Lord Provost was able and at times most touching in its references to the Prime Minister. The latter made a most dignified, cultured and eloquent reply. His command of language, his power of description, and his magnetism are most unusual. He was master of himself and of the occasion.

I append my speech, made at Elgin in Scotland, on August 23, 1929.

It is to me a deeply appreciated privilege to participate in this ceremony by which this historic city honors the Prime Minister whose distinguished career had its humble beginning in its neighborhood—a participation all the more valued because it enables me to express the appreciation and gratitude which all of us present here feel toward you, my Lord Provost, who have presided over these dignified proceedings, and directed the preliminary efforts which have given to them such interest and success.

My official duty at the present time, to keep in touch with a most active Prime Minister, has not only given me an undeserved reputation for energy but the invaluable opportunity to see this great country of Scotland as it is —a country whose history is familiar to every American schoolboy and whose traditions are a heritage to the world. Your cities, your mountains, lakes and valleys are enhanced in their beauty and interest to every stranger visiting them because they are decorated with historical memory—not only of ancient times but of the present period.

The other day I stood before a little monument in a Scottish village and on its face was a pathetically long list, for so small a place, of those from there who had died in the Great War; and I uncovered then, as has the world for centuries, to the glorious memory of the unsurpassed bravery and self-sacrifice of the Scottish soldier.

My personal acquaintance with him upon whom you have conferred the honor of the "Freedom of the City" of Elgin, has covered but a short time in one sense—but a long time if measured by those important contacts which have enabled me to judge his high character, to measure his motives and to realize that feeling of true friendship which, while invited by lovable qualities, endures because based upon sincere respect.

The great position of Prime Minister brings to its possessor heavy burdens. To succeed he must have all the qualities of a skilled executive, and, in addition, one other attribute often unrequired in other executive positions, that of the ability to meet in open debate upon controversial questions, and, without time for extended preparation, the ablest statesmen and parliamentarians of the Kingdom.

It is indeed a gruelling process under the law of "the survival of the fittest" to which Britain submits those to whom she would entrust the administration of her power. To the Prime Minister, the sense of his responsibilities must be ever present. He is not allowed to forget them, even if he would or could. At all times and everywhere he is sought out—even upon his vacation here in Scotland—sometimes by Ambassadors, who are by no means the least of his disturbers. And this leads me to say a word about the discussions which, in carrying out the directions of President Hoover, I have recently had with him.

When last Tuesday, after my visit to him, the Prime Minister issued his statement of the nature of those naval problems which Britain and America are discussing as a preliminary to taking them up with the other naval powers, and said in it a distinct advance had been made, I noticed shortly thereafter a press comment to the effect that this indicated he had no progress to report.

I think we should remember that naval negotiations may have favorably advanced, though they may not have reached necessarily the proper stage for useful discussion in detail by the press. The arbiters of the ultimate fate of this naval effort will be the respective public sentiments of the naval powers, and time must be taken to reduce to their simplest terms, before their public discussion, the problems it involves, so that the average man can then understand the better what it is all about.

If the problem is not mastered so that its final solution is clear and satisfactory to the average man, even though Governments may come to preliminary agreement, Parliaments and Congresses may not ratify it in the end.

Whatever is agreed upon now as an easily understood matter of common sense and fairness, and which constitutes part of a progressive simplification of the terms of the problem, is a most important step in advance.

The smaller the compass into which the necessary technical naval differences can be reduced, the clearer will be the public perception of the relative insignificance of the quantities involved when compared with the total naval strength of the powers, and the more general will be the demand that these smaller technical differences be fairly adjusted in order that the cause of the world's peace may not be jeopardized unjustifiably thereby. We must realize that the one unforgivable thing now would be an inadequate preparation for the proposed Naval Conference.

After a lunch, where the Lord Provost, the Prime Minister and his able son (Malcolm), now a member of Parliament, spoke, Dana and I left for London on an afternoon train.

This afternoon I received from the Foreign Office and transmitted to Washington a formal reply to Washington. This again fixes the minimum of British cruisers requirements at 15 large and 35 small ships. The disturbing part of the letter, and it does not surprise me, for I have long foreseen it, is that the Foreign Office states that it will be impossible to satisfy British opinion that America has not achieved superiority if it builds up to 23 cruisers, as Washington has indicated was necessary for an equivalent strength. The Japanese Ambassador called during the day and was posted on the situation.

London,
August 26, 1929.

This afternoon Craigie, one of the under-secretaries of the Foreign Office, asked one of our secretaries, Belin, for a conference. It was for the purpose of transmitting informally word from the Prime Minister that he was "determined upon agreement on naval disarmament with the United States"—that he was anxious to have an early answer to his formal message now at Washington so as to be able to report progress when he goes to Geneva Thursday to forestall a possible proposition there for the disarmament committee to take the matter up, and that he was addressing another letter to me. This "news" I "informally" transmitted to Washington as the Prime Minister evidently wants them there to know this attitude of mind on his part before they answer the former message they are now considering.

This morning over the radio I learned that Lord Cecil and

Journal as Ambassador to Great Britain

Albert V. Alexander had called upon him today, and I attribute this word from him as the result of Lord Cecil's representations. As to this I may, of course, be mistaken.

If this is the attitude of Great Britain, I now predict the beginning of an effort to fit a yardstick to the settlement instead of a settlement to a yardstick.

After the process of reducing naval technical differences to the simple terms they are now assuming, their danger is lessening. The public will soon be able to judge of their relative importance as compared to the cause of world's peace, while they may not understand the naval arguments they involve.

One may not understand the professional arguments of two doctors as to a proper course of medical procedure, but one can judge of their relative importance to the life of a patient when the argument involves an agreed serious case of smallpox or an agreed light case of measles.

The news from The Hague is no better. Dr. Hjalmar Schacht, President of the Reichsbank, telephoned he would call on me tomorrow. Invited him to lunch.

London,
August 27, 1929.

My 64th birthday, which I celebrated by a good day's work, in which, among other things, I caught up with my mail.

Upon direction of our Government I called in the morning upon the Foreign Office and officially requested the British Government to make every effort to protect the lives and property of Americans in Palestine, where the chronic trouble between the Arabs and the Jews has developed into a serious conflict, in which a cowardly and cruel attack was made by Arabs upon inoffensive orthodox Jews and many were killed and wounded, including, it is estimated, some twelve or more American citizens. The immediate cause of the trouble was an effort by Arabs to interfere with the centuries-old habit of the Jews to congregate at the "wailing wall" to mourn their departed sovereignty.

Sir Ronald Lindsay, the Permanent Under-Secretary of the Foreign Office promised to comply with this request, saying that every effort is being made, and will be made, to protect American lives and property. He said the English cruisers *Benham, Sussex* and *Courageous* were probably in Palestine waters by this time, that the Trans-Jordan forces were being used to prevent Arabs from infiltrating across the river and making things worse, that a battalion had been sent from Egypt, and one battalion and a half from Malta, a British battalion abroad consisting of about 700 men.

At noon Dr. Schacht, Roland Boyden, Congressman Anthony J. Griffith of New York, Henry Copley Greene of Boston and Walter Wilson lunched with us at the Embassy.

Had a long talk with Dr. Schacht who is, as I have already said, the President of the Reichsbank. He does not expect a temporary break on the Young Plan, if it occurs at The Hague, to result in the heavy drain upon the gold reserves of the Reichsbank which followed the near-break of the Young Committee at Paris, saying that a break of the politicians for a time is to be expected by the public and would not be regarded so seriously as a break of economists. He does not expect a break of any duration if at all. He is here for two days to consult with Montagu Norman, Governor of the Bank of England, upon ways and means of dealing with financial emergencies which may arise. He spoke of the fine work of Young and Stamp at Paris. He said he was disappointed that I was not at The Hague now in some capacity. We talked over reparations for a long time.

Answered a letter from Sumner Welles, asking me to recommend to President Vasquez, of the Dominican Republic, an expert to advise upon the revision of the tax laws of that country. Suggested Stamp or Pirelli, but as they are almost certainly unavailable, named ex-Senator James W. Wadsworth.

London,
Wednesday, August 28, 1929.

The news from The Hague this morning is that agreement has been reached among the Allies, including Great Britain, and now awaits only the agreement of Germany. It would seem that at

Journal as Ambassador to Great Britain

last the long and weary work on the reparations problem is to end.

I wired my friend Young congratulating him even though it may be a little premature. For ten years the Allies and Germany have wrestled with this complex and difficult adjustment. It seemed at times a problem almost insoluble.

Having noted press dispatches to the effect that the Arabs in Trans-Jordania were organizing to move into Palestine, I called on Lindsay again at the Foreign Office this morning. He explained the method of air patrol in this section which he said was effectively organized and in position to break any organized movements in this open country in a way impossible in city districts. I cabled this to Washington with the suggestion that consideration might be given to the moving of some available American cruiser to a point nearer Palestine to be on hand in case of unexpected but possible emergency that might endanger American lives and property.

The Prime Minister sent me a most cordial birthday letter, as follows:

10 Downing Street, Whitehall,
August 28, 1929.

My dear General:

For once the staff of the American Embassy has failed in a most culpable way, and I shall put in a firm protest to the President. There you were passing a milestone yesterday and none of your folks told me so that I might be there waving a "Stars and Stripes," a "Union Jack" or "Chicago Blazer" and playing the instrument into which you are blowing your soul in *Punch* this week. This morning you are past the mark, but I am shouting "good luck" behind you. May your days be long in the land, and be full of happiness, and may you have every satisfaction out of the coming years.

With kindest regards to Mrs. Dawes and yourself.

Yours very sincerely,
J. Ramsay MacDonald.

The cartoon in *Punch* to which MacDonald refers is one in which he is smoking one of my pipes and I am playing one of his Scottish bagpipes, with the suggestion that this arrangement "ought" to disarm everybody.

63

Journal as Ambassador to Great Britain

We seem about arrived at a successful conclusion of the first stage of the naval negotiations—that general agreement and understanding between the United States and Great Britain as to what constitutes parity which will enable a conference of all the naval powers to be called, with a prospect of reaching a general and final settlement assuring naval disarmament.

From 10:00 to 12:00 P.M. last night I was at the house of the Prime Minister at 10 Downing Street taking with me the paraphrase of three cables of some 4000 words altogether, conveying a precise statement of understanding at which, if the Prime Minister agrees, we have arrived as our first destination in the negotiations. We had a discussion of the cables and the Prime Minister agreed to the statement subject to a further consultation with his Admiralty, in order to check figures. He promised me a letter making a preliminary agreement by tonight for which I am now waiting; but his secretary telephoned the Embassy that they were running into snags in the Admiralty conference which might delay it for a short time.

The Prime Minister leaves for Geneva tomorrow and will reply formally to the United States on his return from there in a few days.

The above was my second conference yesterday with the Prime Minister, at 10 Downing Street, for I brought him a paraphrase of the first part of the cables so far as decoded by noon, as it indicated the nature of the whole of the document.

I sent today to Washington a long comment on the messages, as I think that the form of the statement of agreement which may finally go to the public should be altered materially before decided upon so as not to magnify in the public mind, out of their proper proportions, the technical differences yet to be adjusted.

The successful settlement at The Hague which establishes in operation the Young Plan has made MacDonald happy and our conference was a pleasant one. I outlined the changes which I proposed to recommend to our Government, deleting those sec-

OWEN D. YOUNG

tions in the form of the present memorandum of agreement which refer to the yardstick, and although he could not, with propriety, make an official representation, he said that he agreed with me entirely, and that he would really prefer to drop the yardstick idea altogether.

Yesterday I again called on the Foreign Office at the request of our State Department to ask a military guard at our Consulate General in Jerusalem.

In answer to a telegram which I sent congratulating Young, he said he had been urging the President to send me to The Hague to help in the settlement.

I have agreed to stay up until 11:30 P.M. for the Prime Minister's letter. I think it will come for he wants to announce at Geneva this preliminary agreement on naval reduction between our two countries.

London,
Sunday, September 1, 1929.

On Friday night late I received at the Embassy two letters on the naval negotiations from the Prime Minister. In them he raises his estimate of the minimum tonnage necessary in cruisers for British needs to 339,000 tons, an increase of 9000. He agreed to the most of the American statement, defining agreements reached at the present stage, but stressed the prospects of difficulties over the effect of the necessary increase in American large cruisers upon the acceptance by British public opinion of what he feared would be a resulting equality between Great Britain and Japan in the large cruiser class.

Received instructions from our State Department to thank the British Government for compliance with our request to place the military guard at our Consulate General in Jerusalem.

Journal as Ambassador to Great Britain

London,
Tuesday, September 3, 1929.

Called at the Foreign Office in the afternoon with a cautioning cable relative to publicity on the proposed naval agreement. Up to date the leakage has been altogether from the Washington side. The press dispatches in the British papers from Washington have been giving reports so correct in some details of what is transpiring that the Foreign Office has complained, and I have informed Washington.

The enterprise and intelligence of our Washington correspondents is such that when important governmental matters necessarily involve discussion with several governmental services with each of which they have a contact, it is almost impossible to prevent premature publicity.

Once in a while a liberal or conservative of prominence indulges in criticism to me of the inconsistency of MacDonald or Henderson or Snowden when they stand for sensible and sound public measures, as if resort to conservatism, when impressed with public responsibilities, should be regarded as reprehensible in one who is alleged to have expressed contrary views in a political contest. To me, accustomed in America to see politicians nominated by a conservative party and elected to office by reason of their conservative professions or silence in the campaign, turn radical when in office, such inconsistency indicates a higher regard for the public interest.

One loses impartial judgment just in proportion as he absorbs prejudice. MacDonald and his colleagues have my confidence, my admiration and my trust. I shall not allow it to be undermined by a discussion of their past campaign speeches. I am accredited to governmental officials, bearing responsibilities—not to candidates—nor to gossiping "diners out," the last ones to whom, in important diplomatic negotiations, an Ambassador can look for helpful information.

Journal as Ambassador to Great Britain

I saw the Prime Minister at 10 Downing Street at noon upon his arrival by airplane from Geneva, via Paris.

We are at another hard spot in our negotiations, and the message I gave him from the State Department is preliminary to a more comprehensive one to be received next week. The Prime Minister had seen Briand, to whom he frankly explained the present situation in our efforts to agree, and also Beneš. He is hopeful as to cooperation from them.

Australia and Canada are questioning British central control of its naval policy by Great Britain and the former country intimates that if the proposed agreement is not satisfactory, it may build cruisers on its own account.

At Geneva, Matsudaira and MacDonald talked over Japan's attitude, which the former stated as a determination upon a request for its proper ratio to the number of United States large cruisers.

MacDonald said his Admiralty would agree to 12 eight-inch gun cruisers to Japan as against 15 eight-inch gun cruisers for Great Britain.

At Geneva he found that our conversations were uppermost in the minds of everyone, and felt that our failure to agree would be as disastrous in its effects upon the cause of world peace as our success would be beneficial.

He told of the machinations of the mischief-makers, but thought his going straight to Briand and giving him our exact status was the proper method of dealing with them.

London,
Tuesday, September 10, 1929.

This morning I received a most important letter from the Prime Minister on the naval problem. It was in answer to an interim letter from our State Department which was not intended to elicit a reply, but to explain the reasons for a probable delay in its formal reply to MacDonald's former message.

MacDonald in this letter received today makes suggestions to the United States, which I think anticipated what is already in the President's mind. I believe now that we will reach a preliminary settlement between the United States and Great Britain very soon. These suggestions are relative to placing six-inch guns instead of eight-inch guns on a few of the United States 10,000 ton cruisers (five), and fixing her number of large 10,000 ton cruisers at 23 instead of 18 as before proposed by Great Britain. This may simplify matters as they stand at present.

I may be mistaken, but I think that both Great Britain and the United States were led to think along these lines as leading to a solution of their present differences as a result of information which I received from Matsudaira, and reported to both governments—that Japan was planning to meet Great Britain's desires by the device of placing eight-inch guns on a few of her six-inch gun (small) cruisers.

London,
Friday, September 13, 1929.

Yesterday morning I conferred with Matsudaira, and later with the French Ambassador.

During yesterday the awaited answer to MacDonald's last proposition arrived and after it was decoded I saw MacDonald at 10 Downing Street at 6:15 P.M. It was in three sections, and one of them contained the first draft of the memorandum of agreement, which it is now agreed by both parties constitutes a sufficient basis for the success of a general naval conference to justify its assembly. The two sections to which I objected were deleted.

As between our two countries, differences of naval technical opinion have now been so reduced that quantitatively they concern less than 25,000 tons out of an aggregate tonnage of both nations of about 2,400,000 tons. A failure in conference to settle as between us this small remaining difference is unthinkable, even if it is not settled before the conference when MacDonald visits America next month.

Journal as Ambassador to Great Britain

After our discussion of the cables, lasting less than an hour, MacDonald announced to the press last night that he would leave for the United States on September 28th.

This evening, MacDonald having been in conference with the Admiralty during the day, I received from him here at the Embassy his formal reply to yesterday's cables. This is being transmitted to the State Department tonight. It is voluminous but satisfactory, and already is reaching toward a preliminary settlement before conference of the small tonnage question still at issue between our Naval Board and the British Admiralty.

I confess to satisfaction with the way in which we have used the naval technicians, for never in my judgment could there have been a naval conference in which consultation with them has been more continuous and thorough on both sides. And yet, while these officers fought their fights right along, they composed, with the aid of statesmen, their technical differences almost entirely. They were unable to block the continuing and progressive simplification of the quantitative terms of their unsettled differences until now these differences have become so small that they no longer are formidable.

At no time did they get the middle of the stage where their continuous bonfires would have presented to the audience the appearance of a general conflagration. By consulting them separately and not allowing the two sets of naval experts to confer— the course advised in my Pilgrims' speech—we deprived each of them of any opportunity to escape full responsibility to their respective chiefs by blaming the other for a failure to agree.

In the MacDonald letter, received this evening, he ends with this personal allusion, which I am vain enough to include here, but sensible enough to feel that it is due largely to his friendship and loyalty:

"When I have a little more leisure I really must put on paper an expression of some of the obligations we all owe to you for what you have done since you set foot on our shores. I feel that if this were to end one's service for the world, it would have been worth while."

69

Journal as Ambassador to Great Britain

London,
Sunday, September 15, 1929.

The papers this morning are full of comment on our naval agreement. Washington has wisely made public that the only point upon which the naval experts of both countries are apart is whether three of the American cruisers are to be 10,000 tons each with eight-inch guns, or there is to be substituted for these three cruisers, four smaller cruisers, say of 7500 tons, with six-inch guns. Thus has a mountain shrunk to a mouse.

I was pleased with the comment in this morning's editorial in the (London) Sunday *Times:* "Success has been due to the improved methods by which the discussions have been carried on. The experts and the yardstick have been kept in their proper places, and the will to agree has never been allowed to weaken under the assaults of technicians."

As to my own contribution to the matter of improved methods of negotiation, apart from my Pilgrims' speech, I regard the deletion of the old eighth and ninth paragraphs of the first form of the agreement as, perhaps, the next important from the standpoint of keeping the real difference down to its simplest and most understandable form in the public mind.

Have received the Prime Minister's cooperation in fixing a site for the American Government's memorial to the lost sailor heroes of the war as General Pershing desires to be done as soon as possible. This means, I hope, a quick and satisfactory decision upon a too-long delayed matter.

LATER. 10:00 P.M.

After writing in these notes this morning, Secretary Cox brought me two dispatches from the State Department. They suggested a postponement of the publication of the agreement until after MacDonald's visit, and the deferment of further discussion of the settlement of the small remaining difference until the visit. It was also suggested that MacDonald bring a naval representative on his visit. Having heard that MacDonald had called a meeting of the press representatives for a conference tomorrow

70

morning, I got in touch with 10 Downing Street, located the Prime Minister, and arranged a meeting for us at 5:45 P.M. I felt it essential that he should have this information before making a public announcement.

This meeting at No. 10 resulted in a most confidential talk as to the respective difficulties each Government is having with its naval experts. For myself, I stated that I should advise our Government against the opening of any discussion as to further details of settlement between the President and MacDonald on the visit and especially against the suggestion that the latter bring a naval expert with him. My views are decided.

If it became public that the President and MacDonald would discuss with naval technical advice the small remaining technical difference, it would be magnified in the public mind out of its true significance. The public no longer regards the difference as serious. It regards the United States and Great Britain as in substantial agreement. There is danger of creating the impression that this difference is so important as to have required the visit of the Prime Minister to settle it. If the public should get that impression, what would be the effect of any inability of the President and the Prime Minister to settle this difference in conference? What would be the reaction upon the respective naval contingents as to the importance of their relation to a final settlement or the lack of it? What would be the reaction upon the Senate and Parliament—those breeding grounds for ingenious and imaginative deviltry and international demagogy? What would be the reaction of Japan?

The approaching visit of the Prime Minister, now that the substance of agreement is assured, should be regarded as evidence of the friendly and united constructive purpose of the two nations to promote world peace, and not as a coming joint technical debate, on agreement or disagreement, which would constitute both an invitation and an excuse for misrepresentation in both countries, to say nothing of Japan.

MacDonald and I talked over the form of his proposed statement tomorrow. In view of the press interviews given officially in America, the London newspapers are pressing for one from him.

Journal as Ambassador to Great Britain

When Matsudaira came this evening, I told him of the present status of things and discussed the Japanese requirements. What he told me as to the attitude of his Government in regard to the American propositions for 21 large eight-inch gun cruisers, in my judgment, makes it important that both Great Britain and the United States should reach agreement with Japan on the large cruiser matter at the same time we reach it with each other— whether now or later at the conference itself.

This has a bearing on the advisability of the direct discussion between the President and MacDonald, especially with naval technical assistance, as Matsudaira fears it would create an impression on his Government that we desired to present Japan with a *fait accompli,* with the alternative of acceptance or rejection without a preliminary understanding and recognition of her political and technical needs.

We must keep Japan satisfied and informed in every way as a matter of justice, fairness and common sense, and I know this is what both Hoover and MacDonald desire. So far I have done this at my end of the negotiations, to the satisfaction of Japan, according to Matsudaira; but I am going to suggest to MacDonald tomorrow that he call in Matsudaira to hear his views. Matsudaira's views are as important to us as they are to him, for the three great naval powers must stand or fall together in the negotiations.

London,
Monday, September 16, 1929.

10:00 P.M.

Busy all day, and wound up this evening at 10 Downing Street for another conference with MacDonald after a long conference with the Japanese Ambassador at the Chancery this morning.

MacDonald had a meeting with the press this afternoon to convey information as to the details of the present state of our negotiations with the understanding he was not to be directly quoted. The *Times* telephoned asking me to see Charles R. S. Harris, who would write tomorrow's editorial, based on the Prime

TSUNEO MATSUDAIRA

Minister's statement. Mr. Harris called at the Embassy this evening and I suggested that in his editorial he emphasize the triviality of the remaining differences of opinion by reference to the gross tonnage involved in and covered by what we had agreed upon.

I again expressed my views to MacDonald this evening relative to the inadvisability of a discussion in America of the remaining naval differences and he agreed to the wisdom of them. Unfortunately, in the interview with the press, he had stated that one purpose of his visit was to settle the remaining technical differences with Hoover. This statement, however, Harris deleted from the *Times* news report.

I regret that the figures in detail, representing our differences, have been made public by the British Government at this time.

London,
Wednesday, September 18, 1929.

Two long sets of cables have been exchanged. The British step of making public the exact figures of the two differing naval proposals of the Government as they stand at present has disconcerted our people.

Secretary Stimson called me by telephone this afternoon and supplemented somewhat the cables he has sent, including a most able letter from the President on the whole situation, to be delivered to the Prime Minister. Stimson is much annoyed by the publication by Great Britain officially of the details of an unsettled negotiation.

The form of the statement also which the Foreign Office prepared, sent to me by MacDonald and forwarded by me to Washington, to go from the British Government through its ambassadors to Japan, France and Italy, is objected to by our Government. It outlines the present differences between the United States and Great Britain which our people at Washington think is inadvisable.

The bulk of the communications between the two Governments, which have passed through my office during the two days, has been such that one is kept constantly engrossed in the study of them. While it is not going to interfere with MacDonald's trip, another one of the "hard spots" in these negotiations has been reached, which, when passed, will seem small like the others, but now it is most troublesome.

The American Ambassador, as an intermediary, becomes during such a time a sort of "punching bag" for both sides, for he transmits the unpleasant news to both. However, calmness on my part is essential, as is also diligence, whenever I receive an impression which has an important bearing on the situation, to transmit it in full force in either direction.

How fortunate it is that at the inception of a large undertaking over-confidence generally induces in men an under-estimate of its difficulties and an over-estimate of their capacity to deal with it. Otherwise many successful undertakings would not have been commenced. But where many men are engaged in a great effort, since the deficiency of a man in one direction is generally offset by his usefulness in another, somehow, between all of them a way out is found.

My admiration of the indefatigable energy, high ability and statesmanship of Herbert Hoover constantly increases.

Last night the Prime Minister and I had a "surcease of sorrow" together. We went to an early dinner at Lady Astor's house from which she took us to the first night London opening of Bernard Shaw's "Apple Cart" at the Drury Lane Theater. Mrs. Dawes and some of Lady Astor's immediate family were in the party. We were duly introduced before the play to Mr. Shaw, to whom the Prime Minister remarked that he hoped his play, which incidentally satirizes both the Prime Minister and the American Ambassador, would not make more trouble between us than we had now.

The Prime Minister and I sat together almost in the front row of seats and I noticed that people would look at us now and then when our counterparts on the stage got a swipe. A question asked at the Cabinet meeting on the stage as to why the Prime Minister had been appointed was answered: "Because he was not fit for anything else."

I do not report this as being any more pointed than what he

heard every few minutes or so, but only because I remember it. Comparatively, the "Ambassador" got off easily.

I will meet MacDonald at 3:00 P.M. tomorrow at 10 Downing Street with a large piece of raw meat to digest in the shape of the President's letter with its new proposals.

London,
September 19, 1929.

At 3:00 P.M. I called on the Prime Minister at 10 Downing Street and delivered the President's letter. This was in the form of a letter from him to our Secretary of State. While I purposely refrained from detailed discussion of the accumulation of important cables, MacDonald opened a general talk on the whole situation.

The influence and prestige of the admiralty here and everywhere is very evident. As naval officers here and with us under the operation of the laws of human nature, are naturally adverse to both naval equality and reduction, our minds are constantly on the problem of how to bring to this difficult question the full advantage of their technical knowledge and experience without placing them at the conference in a position of power to do injury from any ulterior motives.

I append the text of the letter cabled from President Hoover which I delivered to the Prime Minister.

September 17, 1929.

The Honorable
The Secretary of State,
Washington, D. C.

My DEAR MR. SECRETARY:

I have been giving a great deal of thought over the week end to the Prime Minister's latest dispatches.

I am, of course, glad to discuss with him on his visit the gap between our two cruiser proposals, but I suggest later on a method of closing it before Mr. MacDonald's visit. I dislike the idea that Mr. MacDonald's visit might become one of negotiation or split on such a question as this for our whole great program might in public mind degenerate into a huckster's quibble; nor does it seem to me that we should fail to call the conference because of such a gap. The purpose of the conference is to find methods for surmounting difficulties that we cannot solve otherwise.

Journal as Ambassador to Great Britain

The position as I see it, on the two proposals as to cruisers, is that the British with 339,000 tons would have a superiority of some 24,000 tons over the American 315,000 tons, a superiority to the British equal to, say, 4 medium sized modern cruisers, as against the American Navy having the advantage of two inches in gun calibre on 60,000 tons, or 30% of its fleet. It is true that part of the British cruisers will be less modern than ours, yet our Omaha class is in turn less modern than other important British classes. I am, therefore, convinced that we have gone as far as we can go on this line. We have on our side a great burden indeed to prove to our people that we have parity in the two programs when the American Navy will be 24,000 tons and 13 ships less than the British Navy even if it be compensated by larger gun calibre and an average more modern fleet—that is by the yardstick.

I am willing to try to carry this burden through but I do not believe if Mr. MacDonald understood the difficulties of our situation he would insist upon enlarging this margin by 15,000 tons and decreasing the compensation in gun calibre. Our situation is necessarily different from his because, having arrived in a position in which his own political colleagues have agreed to support him, he can carry through Parliament.

We, on the other hand, have to persuade an independent branch of the Government to vote with us by a two-thirds majority. I am, however, very anxious to find a way around this difficulty by mutual concession especially as the twenty-one large cruisers on our part may affect the program for the other powers.

It seems to me that the emphasis which the Prime Minister properly lays upon the importance of a second conference in 1935 to again reduce the world's naval arms, suggests a new line of thought and presents a basis to reorient our whole discussions and proposals.

Under the cruiser programs which we have been discussing the British will between now and the conference of 1935 lay down 91,000 tons in new 6-inch cruisers. We must lay down 145,000 tons further. This in addition to the ships which we now have in construction. In other words, we shall between us have imposed upon ourselves, say, 236,000 tons of new warships at an expense of, say, $1,500 a ton, a total expenditure of over $350,000,000, some part of which at least would be much better invested in works contributing to real human welfare. And then after we have done all this, the whole purpose of the proposed 1935 conference and the aspirations we have with regard to it, would be that after we have built up all this tonnage and expended all this money, we shall then try to find a method by which we shall scrap it, or some large part of it. And in any event we shall then determine that some of it was not necessary.

It seems to me that there is the most profound outlook for peace today that we have had at any time in the last half century, more especially if we succeed in our conference of January next, yet in effect we are plunging along building more ships at fabulous expense only with the hope and aspiration that at the end of a period so short as 6 years we shall be able to sink a considerable part of them.

In the same line of thought it occurs to me that the dangers of war during the next six or ten years for either of our countries in any direction are inconceivably less than they have been at any period since the Great War. But I find on examination that the British Empire has apparently, during the past few years, been able to preserve peace and provide for its naval defense with a very much smaller cruiser fleet than that now contemplated.

The figures given to me indicate that the British cruiser strength actually in commission in 1922 was 285,000 tons; that it decreased to 244,000 in 1925 and that after allowing for recent disposal of three old ships it comprises only 300,000 tons actually in commission today. Yet we are proposing at this moment that the British fleet should be increased to 339,000 tons. Again in the American fleet I find that we had in commission a total cruiser tonnage of 161,000 in 1922, 153,000 in 1925, and that we have today a tonnage of 100,000 tons afloat—and we are likewise proposing to increase this to 315,000 tons by 1936. In the same breath we are promising the world that at that date we shall use our best endeavors to sink a considerable portion of these fleets. All this is illogical and is the simple negation of our own aspirations and I believe also of public opinion on both sides of the Atlantic.

This discussion between our governments has been in progress now for about three months. There has been time for public opinion to react on all sides, and there is the most extraordinary unanimity and prayer throughout both countries and the whole world that we shall succeed in actually reducing naval strength, not that we shall increase it.

The major discordant note we have is the criticism in the United States over the published statements of proposed cruiser programs—that it is not a program of reduction but a program of expansion. We are faced with the practical fact, however, that to abolish competition and to get any program accepted, we must reach what will not only be parity but what will carry to our people a conviction of parity.

In view of all this situation I am anxious that before Mr. MacDonald arrives he shall have opportunity to find whether or not it will be possible for him to reduce the proposed tonnage of the British fleet from 339,000 tons to at least 300,000 tons. I would be glad to join with him in so bold a move. On such a gross tonnage we could in turn reduce our program by 39,000 tons, thus solving the question of reduction of our 8-inch cruisers from 21 to 18, and allowing us to make a further cut of one proposed new 6-inch 7000 ton cruiser.

I know that upon turning to his charts, Mr. MacDonald will find that with his proposed replacement program of 14 new ships, this could not be accomplished. If, on the other hand, after scrapping the Hawkins class, he limited his replacements so as to provide the laying down of one cruiser per annum, or a total of six replacements, he would keep constant employment in his yards and he could perhaps worry along with his policing of the British Empire by extending the life of some of his older ships for a few years and we would thus each of us arrive at 1936 with at least 39,000 tons less of new ships to deal with. Such a program could apparently be worked out to about fifty ships. I may mention that we have four cruisers now in service that are over 25 years old and one 30 years old that do most effective police duty in various parts of the world. Even a reduction of 39,000 tons in our cruiser programs seems small in the face of all our public backing in this situation, and I should like to see it down another 50,000, but I do not wish to seem impractical.

I would call your attention to the fact that if our present agreement is proposed to be binding only to 1936, if at that time the reduction of the British fleet to 300,000 tons proved too severe, it could be corrected then.

There are some other phases of the problem which seem to me also of the utmost importance and could quite well be taken up on Mr. MacDonald's arrival here with view to making an announcement after his visit of an accord much more powerful from a world point of view. At various times in these discussions we have referred to the maximum destroyer strength of somewhere about 150,000 tons for each country. If we could agree on this figure, it would in itself mark a great tonnage reduction on both sides, although we would each require some construction for replacement. Likewise on submarines, if we could agree on some maximum tonnage for each country, at say 75,000 or even 50,000 tons, it would be helpful to have such a figure declared to the world as a part of our accord.

Another still more important phase of the whole discussion that I think we should bring in, and which I would appreciate Mr. MacDonald's having in mind, is whether or not as a part of this preliminary accord we could not settle the proportion of replacements of battleships we should propose to the January conference that are to be undertaken prior to 1936.

By reference to the Washington Arms Treaty I find that we each of us are presumed to lay down cruisers C and D in 1931, E and F in 1932, G in 1933, H and I in 1934, and K and L in 1935. As these ships are 35,000 tons each, this amounts to each country laying down ten ships, or 350,000 tons which will represent a commitment to an expenditure to our two countries of over $1,000,000,000.

I recognize the Prime Minister's feeling that he must keep some continuous construction going in his navy yards, but it would seem to me this could be accomplished if we laid down a maximum of one ship each 18 months which would reduce the number laid down from ten to four on each side. The net effect of all this would simply be that we should maintain in service our present ships for a longer time than we contemplate in the Treaty, which would give opportunity in our second conference of 1935 to reconsider whether or not we should scrap these older ships and thus reduce the capital ships in the world. It would seem to me a most effective and comforting statement if we could arrive at some such proposal as this during Mr. MacDonald's visit and could announce it as part of the conclusions at which we have arrived.

Obviously proportionately the same reduction would need be accepted by the other signatories to the Washington agreement and they should be glad to have such an opportunity.

I shall look forward to the Prime Minister's visit as an opportunity for most distinguished accomplishment.

Yours faithfully,
HERBERT HOOVER.

Journal as Ambassador to Great Britain

London
Tuesday, September 24, 1929.

The following letter was received from the Prime Minister this morning. He has been at Chequers during the week-end and my last interview with him was on September 19th.

23rd September, 1929.

MY DEAR GENERAL DAWES:

What I take as a personal letter from your President to myself has given me the greatest pleasure. Its candor is a proof of that trust which we must have in each other if we are to overcome the difficulties which face us. Moreover, its line of thought and its subject matter have been giving me concern and he may have some comfort in knowing that before his note came I had addressed inquiries to my advisers on some of the points he discusses. Further, it is just that line of country which I hope to go over with the President when I see him. I want no bargaining and that sort of thing, but primarily a political talk on the world situation so that our hands may be strengthened by an understanding of each other's problems and purposes.

But it will be helpful to both of us if I make a few comments with a view to carrying the President's letter a further stage.

The mind of our European neighbors who will be invited to the Five Power Conference is not tranquil but is suspicious that we are to come to some bargain with the United States against them. We have to walk warily lest we upset them, and they may decline to attend a Conference. Upon that I am now making private and unofficial inquiries but their press is illuminating. The President is free of that troublesome part of my problems. It has been increased by the leakages which have come from Washington and which forced my hand and compelled me to prevent a stampede of the British press by seeing journalists much against my will. When I found the contents of my notes appearing here within two days of their receipt in Washington, it was like a net about my feet. I know my statement might give trouble but on thinking it over concluded that it would be a puff of bad weather that would soon pass over us.

This parity business is of Satan himself. I am sure it has struck the President as it has me as being an attempt to clothe unreality in the garb of mathematical reality. Opinion in the United States demands it and the Senate will accept nothing which does not look like it. On my side I am not interested in it at all. I give it to you with both hands heaped and running down. When I am forced to scrutinize your program which you say embodies it, I turn from you altogether and have to think of things which, but for my importunities, you would not think much about vis: the fleets of other nations. Therefore, although in our talks with each other, we assume that the discussion takes place between us two, that is really not the case. There are shadowy entities behind us. A spirit photograph would show you unaccompanied, but round me would be the ghosts of the other nations. In

79

its ultimates, the parity we are trying to devise is one between you and the rest of the world in relation to the British position in it. If the appearance of parity is to be obtained, neither of us can get away from the fact that the standard must be fixed by British needs. The tides of events swelling upwards and downwards, backwards and forwards, change our defense problems every year and with that the figures change.

Now what am I trying to do? First and foremost, I am trying to stop the daily swell so that we may fix levels which cannot be exceeded and then create a confidence which will permit those levels to be steadily lowered. I want to substitute the security of peace for that of military preparation. But if in the lowering we act impatiently there will be a break back. That psychological fact fixed my present limits. Stabilization downward is the only road by which Europe will move to disarmament.

In consequence of this, the nearer our two countries come to an agreement the larger in my mind becomes the Five Power Conference and its results. Let me illustrate by referring to what the President says about three categories.

(a) The First Class Battleships. Our Admiralty, I believe, would be willing to agree to reduce the replacement ships from 35,000 tons to say, 25,000, to reduce the calibre of their guns, to increase their age, and to propose that at the conference. But I am warned that the offer will be rejected. Therefore it will not be the fault of Great Britain if that reduction is not made.

(b) and (c) Destroyers and Submarines. I believe I should have no difficulty in closing at once with figures in the region of the President's proposals. But the tonnage in destroyers depends largely on the tonnage put by other powers into submarines. I am warned that certain other Powers will not agree to a limitation in submarines. I might be willing to support something like the President's figures, but what can I do if the Five Power Conference were to reject them?

Under the geographical and political conditions of the British Empire, the cruiser category is that upon which public opinion can be most easily stampeded, and is also the chief concern of the Admiralty. When we came into office, we found a program of considerable expansion being built on the ground that in view of the building of other Powers we were too weak. Three 8″ cruisers were to be added at once, making 18. We stopped it and that must be counted as a reduction. We have stopped other expansions. The whole of my resistance to your proposal of 21 is that its effects upon other Powers will compel me to expand whether I like it or not. The Admiralty view is that it is not parity; the political view is that it inevitably means expansion. The narrow margin which divides us does not really lie between you and us but between both of us and the rest of the world. If by hook or by crook the United States could say regarding something like 30,000 tons, "we shall not use them," or, "we shall use them in such a way as not to have world repercussions," our agreement would be pretty complete.

Involved in this is a valuation of the relative efficiency of the 8″ and 6″ cruiser. I find so far as I can lay my hands on discussions on the subject that in actual battle the relation is almost infinity; in the general operations of war the relation is at least 4 to 1. I have had the relation implied in the

Journal as Ambassador to Great Britain

President's figures worked out for my guidance and I find that they vary, but that his latest proposal is 10 to 3 in individual ships irrespective of guns and gross tonnage. Here there might be found a way of coming still nearer and critics could be silenced by naval opinion itself on the relative value of the two classes of ships.

The major difficulty is indeed with the 8" cruiser. If the three biggest naval powers would agree first of all to a ratio of 6, 5, 4 (18, 15, 12) that, as I am advised, would be a world equilibrium unless some of the other Powers disturbed it. But Japan wishes instead of two thirds of the largest cruiser fleet, 70 per cent, though, on an American force of 18, it might be induced to build no more than 12. It would certainly want more than 12 or 21, and then we should have to move up our figure of 15 by four or five and the whole plan would fall to the ground.

This is so important that I must emphasize it. If I had the shadow of dread that the United States and ourselves would ever be at war, it would be impossible for me to agree to parity being expressed by any number of 8" cruisers beyond our own, e.g. 15. I should be willing to refer the issue to any body of able and impartial authorities on sea warfare to decide between us and I should be assured of their verdict. But that is not in my mind at all. Everybody here is anxious to accommodate themselves to an agreement with you on the assumption that there will be no war and no interference in which our fleets are involved. But I am not justified in making the same assumption as regards the rest of the world, and Mr. Kellogg himself used language which justifies that. He refers to the possibilities of wars of defense. I may regret it, but he did it, and if I am to get Parliament to agree to our programs I cannot at the moment overlook that fact.

As I am most anxious that the President should be fully aware of the facts as I have to look at them, let me refer to guns—a very important consideration so soon as our people examine the agreement in cold blood. On its 8" ships (assuming 21) the United States will carry a superiority of 75 guns and on our 6" ships our superiority would be 47 only, a very hard bit of mathematics for me to prove to be parity. Even on our proposals my task will not be easy for they give the United States a superiority of 48, 8" guns to ours of 23 in 6" guns, but the numbers are substantially diminished.

I have spent every spare moment at Chequers this week-end trying to see daylight through this entanglement and the only conclusion I can come to is that if the United States insists upon more than 18, 8" cruisers British expansion is inevitable, especially in view of the hostile reception which the 21 figure has received in both the French and Japanese press.

Another point which the President has overlooked when he writes that on present proposals we shall have actually increased warship tonnage by 236,-000 is that of that total 145,000 is new construction by the United States, whereas our addition of 91,000 is offset by 115,000 scrapped. This unsatisfactory result arises from the fact that your ships actually built must be increased if you now put the parity agreement on the seas and do not accept it as something you can build up to if you think it is necessary. Again and again, I have been driven back upon this fundamental difficulty. It is the insuperable problem and we must get round it somehow. I shall continue to work away at it but the peace of Chequers has yielded barren results. I am however, looking forward with hope to continuing my ponderings with the President himself in the intervals of the all too generous hospitality which, according to the press, he is preparing for me.

Believe me to be

Yours very sincerely,

J. Ramsay MacDonald.

London,
Thursday, September 26, 1929.

The Prime Minister leaves for America tomorrow evening, and I had a conference with him this morning at 10 Downing Street. We did not discuss at length the naval problem as the Prime Minister's last letter was intended by him to fix the present "status quo" before commencing his American conversations.

He is arranging that General Pershing, for the Battle Fields Monument Association, may have one of the locations for the United States Naval Memorial monument in London.

He said he had read his last letter to the President to Sir Charles Madden, Admiral of the Fleet. So it is evident he is keeping in close touch with his technical advisers. To the inquiry from the United States as to whether Miss Ishbel (his daughter) would accompany him as his daughter or as his hostess, he replied to them: "Miss Ishbel does not care where she sits."

He intimated a possible 3000-ton concession he might make on the British proposition on account of finding that two of the ships he had rated before as of the 10,000-ton class were of only 8500 tons each. He did not again refer to the possibility of reducing the number of proposed 10,000 cruisers for the British from 15 to 14.

I saw Vansittart and Robert Leslie Craigie who are to accompany him. Vansittart, in response to a statement of my hope that Great Britain could issue the invitations to the Conference to the other powers before the Prime Minister arrived in the United States, in order that the public impression might not be created that we were in a tangle as to its terms upon which we are practically agreed, cabled Australia, Canada and the Irish Free State, who must approve, asking them to pass on the form of the invitation submitted to them, and reply as soon as possible.

THE PRIME MINISTER AND MISS ISHBEL MACDONALD
LEAVING FOR AMERICA FROM WATERLOO STATION

Journal as Ambassador to Great Britain

My last notes were on Thursday. On Friday noon the Prime Minister sent for me to say that he had concluded arrangements for a site (in London) for the United States Naval Monument which had been requested by General Pershing.

At 10 Downing Street I also had a short talk with Stanley Baldwin, who was just leaving after a call. MacDonald, of course, talked about his trip and his confidence in its good results. He is happy at the prospects. We talked over naval matters somewhat.

I then went to the Foreign Office and from Lancelot Oliphant and Craigie received the last draft of the invitation to the powers for the Naval Conference.

In the afternoon I cabled it to America for comment. All the Dominions have agreed to the form.

Today (Sunday) I received a cable from the State Department agreeing to the form save in two or three comparatively unimportant particulars. I think the Foreign Office tomorrow (Monday) will accept these minor suggested changes and issue the invitations without resubmitting the form again to the Dominions, as they would not be affected by them. Possibly they will resubmit them, but in any event I think the Foreign Office will be able to issue the invitations before MacDonald's arrival at New York, which is desired by both our Governments, demonstrating that its form is settled upon before the Hoover-MacDonald conversations commence.

On Friday evening, together with Mr. and Mrs. John Finley (most delightful guests of ours) and with Atherton, I went to Waterloo Station to see MacDonald and his party off. A large and enthusiastic crowd was present. The Prime Minister and I had to shake hands and exchange felicitations before the camera men who had gathered in large numbers for the occasion. And then took place MacDonald's departure on his eventful visit to our country—the first ever made by a British Prime Minister. Certainly, no trip could be undertaken in a better cause—that of the world's peace.

Journal as Ambassador to Great Britain

I have obtained leave from the State Department to go to the United States during a part of MacDonald's absence from England, if my duties as Chairman of the Finance Committee of the Chicago Exposition should demand my presence. The $10,000,-000 bonds of the Exposition, to secure which Chicago citizens have signed $12,000,000 in guarantees, must be issued soon and sold.

London,
Friday, October 4, 1929.

Diplomatic work has slowed down inasmuch as MacDonald, by his journey, has transferred the field of activity to the United States. I have kept in touch, however, with the Japanese and French Ambassadors and with the Foreign Office. It has now been decided not to issue the invitation to the naval powers to the Conference, the form of which has now been agreed upon, until October 9th, after MacDonald has reached Washington. The Prime Minister arrived at New York today and the evening papers contain an account of his great reception there. I requested, and was granted, leave of absence by the State Department to go to Chicago during MacDonald's absence, to attend to the Exposition finance matters.

I announced my proposed trip before MacDonald reached America, having talked it over with him before he left. By arriving in the United States after he leaves, going straight to Chicago from New York, and visiting Washington only upon the return trip, I hope to prevent any wrong inference that my visit is concerned with official business.

Caro is going with me. We will sail on the *Ile de France*, October 9th, reaching New York October 15th, and will return on the *Berengaria* sailing from New York on October 30th.

On Tuesday, October 1st, Mrs. Dawes, Henry, Miss Decker, Mr. John O'Leary of Chicago, and I went to Sudbury by automobile, where I received the freedom of the Borough in elaborate ceremonies covering the entire day. The crowd, including the school children, which I addressed at the town market square, in

84

front of the Gainsborough statue, must have numbered at least 5000—a great assembly for so small a community. The account published in the London *Times* for October 2, 1929 reads:

GENERAL DAWES, HONORARY FREEMAN OF SUDBURY
A Link with the Early Puritans

The American Ambassador, General Charles G. Dawes, is descended from one William Dawes, who left Sudbury for New England as a boy of 15 in 1635. Today General Dawes came to Sudbury to be made an honorary freeman of the town, and Mrs. Dawes came with him.

A small town like this can achieve an artistic unity when it sets out to celebrate an occasion, and every element in the community, from the Mayor and Corporation down to the school children, had a share in the festivities. If the Council Chamber was too minute to allow more than a fraction of the townspeople to see the actual admission of General Dawes to the roll of honorary freeman, there were outdoor ceremonies with life and color enough about them. Flags and streamers decked every street, and almost every building. The band of the 1st Battalion of the Suffolks was there to play, local and visiting dignitaries from the Town Hall to the Drill Hall for luncheon, and the fire brigade, ten strong, together with the town crier and his bell, to march in front of the procession. Many of the visiting Mayors, themselves in robes of office, were attended by mace bearers in wonderful old liveries. The children from the schools greeted General Dawes on the spacious Market Hill in the afternoon. A place had been chalked out on the ground for every school, a band stand had been set up, and another temporary platform stood before the statue of Thomas Gainsborough, who was born here 200 years ago. Mr. Pickwick might also have been imagined looking benevolently on, for Sudbury claims to be the town in which he tried his hand at electioneering, and the old hustings stood on, or very near, the spot from which General Dawes addressed the children today.

Spirit of Pilgrim Fathers

The freedom was conferred on General Dawes at a special meeting of the town council. The Mayor (Councillor E. P. FitzGerald) who presided, moved the resolution. He paid tribute to the spirit which upheld the Pilgrim Fathers in their hazardous adventure. "They and their Descendants," he said, "are bone of our bone, flesh of our flesh, forming a mighty nation whose common heritage with ourselves is the same mother tongue, the same translation of Holy Writ, the same literature, and a similar jurisprudence; and each is inspired by the same lofty ideals." The Mayor's motion was seconded by Alderman J. W. H. Alston, who said that the Prime Minister also would have been present to share this honour with the American Ambassador, had not the original date of his departure for the United States been anticipated.

The resolution having been passed unanimously, the Recorder (Sir Harry Courthope-Monroe, K. C.) administered to General Dawes the Freeman's oath, in which he affirmed his readiness to "uphold, support, maintain, and defend all the good and useful rights, privileges, customs, decrees, by-laws, orders and hereditaments of and belonging to this town."

After signing the roll the new freeman briefly acknowledged the honour, reserving his main address till after luncheon. He was given a scroll recording his election "in commemoration of his ancestral connection with the borough," and "in recognition of the eminent services to the cause of peace and disarmament to which he has whole-heartedly devoted his life." To Mrs. Dawes the Mayoress presented a cushion of brocaded silk and a model of an early Stuart room, containing furniture of the period.

The toasts of "The King" and "The President of the United States of America" were honoured at the luncheon, and the health of the American Ambassador was proposed by the Lord Lieutenant of Suffolk (Colonel Sir T. Courtenay Warner), and supported by the Rev. Sir William Hyde Parker. The Mayor and General Dawes then drank together from the borough's silver loving cup, which dates from 1666. "Your Excellency, my love to you," said the Mayor as he drank, and General Dawes replied, "Your Worship, my love to you." The wives pledged each other similarly.

Puritans of Old Sudbury

The American Ambassador, acknowledging the toast, explained that there was a William Dawes who went out with the early Puritans to New England in 1628 or 1629. It would seem that he did not remain there for any length of time, and that it was his son William, who sailed on the *Planter* in 1635, who was regarded as the founder of the American family.

"In these easier days everywhere" [General Dawes continued] "with their inexpensive and alluring temptations to carelessness and indolence and their many distractions and frivolities, when we think of the character of the Puritans of old Sudbury and their steadfastness in standing for their high principles there seems to be ringing down to us through the centuries the sound of a clear bell in the midst of a fog. But the fundamental character of the British people has not changed. And, in addition to character, which is the most important, they are possessed of capital, leadership, technical skill, and every quality which they have manifested in their wonderful career of the centuries.

"Before coming to this country I had read some statements from British sources as to its industrial prospects which seemed discouraging. Since my arrival I have discovered that this resulted alone from the customary British courage in frankly and openly discussing the disadvantages as well as the advantages of a situation, despite the fact that the disadvantages are the enduring heritage of a proud and fortunate people. The reasons why British industry, now so active in taking steps for its necessary readjustment to post war conditions, was late in commencing, constitute in themselves a firm basis for confidence in the return to the old time industrial prosperity. Take, for instance, the basic steel industry. The revolutionary changes in the mechanical methods of production of coke, iron and steel now in process in England are necessary to bring about what used to be considered paradoxical—a decrease in the cost of production with an increase in wages—a

NOMINATION IN COUNCIL CHAMBER FOR FREEDOM
OF THE BOROUGH OF SUDBURY, SUFFOLK

FROM HERE EMIGRATED WILLIAM DAWES IN 1635

Journal as Ambassador to Great Britain

truth which was so well expressed by Mr. Ben Tillett the other day at Belfast, before the annual Trades Union Congress. I will state what in my opinion constitutes three of the reasons which have delayed prosperity in the British steel and iron industry, in each one of which is embodied a promise of its certain return—

"(1) The natural advantages of Britain themselves, unsurpassed in the world, in an unlimited supply of easily accessible iron ore, limestone, and coal, within short distances of each other and near by fresh and tide water which have had the effect of delaying the pressure of necessity for a change in British production methods years after it had been felt in full effect by outside competitors forcing them to necessary changes in their mechanical methods of production if they were to survive.

"(2) The fact Great Britain was the pioneer in the development of the steel industry and naturally for a longer time retained the older form of equipment because in the midst of these natural advantages, it could function profitably longer than in other countries.

"(3) The commendable British pride in family and corporate tradition fortified by custom and habit, where for generations business has been conducted under certain family names and trade marks.

Future of Britain

"With a tremendous domestic consumption of steel and iron, amounting in 1928 to 7,200,000 tons, of which 40 per cent was supplied from abroad, chiefly from the continent, but which should soon be supplied in much greater part from home with a great export trade to the Colonies and foreign countries, amounting to 4,260,000 tons last year and capable of expansion through the adoption of more efficient methods of production, with its leaders of business aroused to the situation and its labour envisaging and intelligently advocating the proper and necessary changes in productive methods, which its leaders are initiating, with all these natural resources in easily transported raw materials ready to be transformed near the sea for consumption at home and export abroad, it seems to me that the future prosperity of this fundamental British industry is assured. And what is going on in the steel and iron industry is going on in other industries and business, and for much the same reason. Since the Great War, no nation has dealt more successfully with the serious problems which it left than Great Britain, and no nation in Europe, in my judgment, faces a more encouraging industrial future."

The toast of "The Visitors" was given by the Deputy Mayor (Councillor W. P. Cook) and acknowledged by the Mayor of Ipswich (Councillor J. F. C. Hossack) and Mr. Wickham Steed. In a tribute to the American Ambassador, Mr. Wickham Steed recalled his great reputation in France during the war for getting things done and the work he had since accomplished for the welfare of the world in his scheme of lifting Europe out of the awful morass of reparations, debts, and all those extraordinary legacies of the war. As Ambassador at the Court of St. James's they now saw him steadily working with Mr. MacDonald as he would have worked with Mr. Baldwin or any accredited representative of the British people, to bring

87

about complete concordance of view upon naval matters, and matters going beyond them.

In his few words to the children on Market Hill, General Dawes told them that he had been thinking a good deal that day about those forgotten pioneers who, in the America of those early times, had formed an unbroken chain from the North to Florida, and in the movement of civilization toward the west first conquered, subdued and planted the wilderness. "They had common ancestors with all here," he said. "There is one great lesson that old people as well as young people can learn from their lives: that they were not afraid to stand against the crowd. It is the weak who follow the crowd and in these days when temptations are so many and it is so easy to be a bad boy or a bad girl, we can be sure that a thought now and then of those young people who went across the ocean will do us a great deal of good." He was very proud that his young ancestor was a Puritan stonemason who tried to construct things instead of tearing them down. "It is a long time since any of my people lived here," he added, "but if they had selected the place consciously they couldn't have done better in all England."

My brother Beman and his wife are visiting us, having arrived Wednesday. We are greatly enjoying their visit which our departure makes all too short.

Our friends, Mr. and Mrs. R. H. Little of Chicago, dined with us this evening. Mrs. Little has just published a life of George Washington which gives a fine picture of the real man.

London,
October 6, 1929.

Busy preparing for my trip home. Last night I attended the first seasonal dinner of the Press Club composed only of active journalists, Lord Riddell presiding. As the guest of honor I had to respond to a toast, which I did extempore, having had no time for preparation. It was more or less informal and a most enjoyable affair, conducted much as the Gridiron Club dinners. My friend Richard Henry Little, of the *Chicago Tribune,* made an impromptu and most happy speech. I spoke about twenty-five minutes.

The Prime Minister had sent the following letter to Lord Riddell: "When you read this letter I shall be in the country which your guest and my friend, General Dawes, so ably repre-

BEMAN G. DAWES

sents in London. He, of all people, needs no explanation of my absence, for he has been continuously engaged for some time in helping to arrange that I should be absent. I do regret, however, that I am not able to attend the Press Club on the occasion of his first visit, and I send you my best wishes for the enjoyable evening which I am sure you will have."

Upon the death of the great German statesman, Gustav Stresemann, I made a written expression of my sympathy which the German Embassy sent to the Government and to Frau Stresemann. I insert an editorial from this morning's London *Observer*, which is the best tribute to Stresemann that I have seen and was probably written by the able editor of that paper, J. L. Garvin.

THE GOOD LIVES AFTER HIM

The death of Dr. Stresemann is a European calamity. He had become so central, so indispensable a figure, that it is hard to realize his constructive achievement as falling within six years. He re-made Europe. That and nothing less is the verdict which history will pass on him. Bismarck—the comparison, no less than the contrast, is inevitable—took longer to re-make Germany.

He re-made Europe. He taught his countrymen the truth, so hard to realize after fifty years of Hohenzollern chauvinism, that a German could be at once a good patriot and a good European. He accepted the Chancellorship to restore order in an almost anarchic country. He transferred himself to the Foreign Office because he realized—and this in a state still almost cut off from the outside world—that Germany could regain her strength only in her proper setting.

Its construction forthwith became the aim for which he deliberately shortened and at last sacrificed his life. But he saw his policy triumph. He found a Europe at war in everything but name. He left a Europe trebly vowed to peace by the steps which had given Germany her rightful place among her equals. He did not live to see Germany free. But he saw evacuation begun, and knew the date when it would be completed; and we British are proud to think that, when time was visibly pressing, the clear expression of British opinion and the resolve of the British Foreign Secretary facilitated the fulfillment of his aims.

His work survives, and not only his work, but his example. No statesman in history has shaped and carried on a policy amid more formidable difficulties and he must sometimes have wondered whether his conduct was consistently worthy of his ideals. If his spirit has lingered to hear how this world answers that question, it must now rest content. Such was his quality and so potent his influence that not one hint of the war hatreds which he exorcised has sullied the tributes to his memory.

Journal as Ambassador to Great Britain

London,
Monday, October 7, 1929.

The invitation of the British Government to a Naval Conference, to be held in London at the beginning of the third week of January 1930, the form of which has so long occupied the attention of our two Governments, addressed to me as the American Ambassador and signed by Arthur Henderson, head of the Foreign Office, arrived at the Chancery this afternoon. Since our Government already had received from me by cable its contents before its issuance, all of which have been jointly considered and evolved, I did not re-cable it, simply notifying the State Department of its receipt in the form agreed upon. An invitation, in similar form, has gone to the Japanese, French and Italian Ambassadors to Great Britain.

The text will be made public tomorrow. The following is a copy:

Foreign Office, S.W.1,
7th October, 1929.

DEAR EXCELLENCY: (The Japanese Ambassador)
I have the honor to inform Your Excellency that the informal conversations on the subject of Naval Disarmament which have been proceeding in London during the last three months between the Prime Minister and the Ambassador of the United States have now reached a stage at which it is possible to say that there is no point outstanding of such serious importance as to prevent an agreement.

From time to time the Prime Minister has notified Your Excellency of the progress made in these discussions and I now have the honor to state that provisional and informal agreement has been reached on the following principles:

1. The conversations have been one of the results of the Treaty for the Renunciation of War signed at Paris in 1928 which brought about a realignment of our national attitudes on the subject of security, in consequence of the provision that war should not be used as an instrument of national policy in the relations of nations to one another. Therefore, the Peace Pact has been regarded as the starting point of agreement.

2. It has been agreed to adopt the principle of parity in each of the several categories and that such parity shall be reached by December 31st, 1936. Consultation between His Majesty's Government in the United Kingdom and His Majesty's Government in the Dominions has taken place and it is contemplated that the program of parity on the British side should be related to the naval forces of all parts of the Empire.

3. The question of battle ship strength was also touched upon during the

90

conversations and it has been agreed in these conversations that subject to the assent of other signatory powers it would be desirable to reconsider the Battleship replacement programmes provided for in the Washington Treaty of 1922, with the view to diminishing the amount of replacement construction implied under that Treaty.

4. Since the Government of the United States and His Majesty's Government in the United Kingdom adhere to the attitude that they have publicly adopted in regard to the desirability of securing the total abolition of the submarine, this matter hardly gave rise to discussion during the recent conversations. They recognize, however, that no final settlement on this subject can be reached except in conference with the other naval powers.

In view of the scope of these discussions, both governments consider it most desirable that a conference should be summoned to consider the categories not covered by the Washington Treaty and to arrange for and deal with the questions covered by the second paragraph of Article 21 of that Treaty. It is our earnest hope that the Japanese Government will agree to the desirability of such a conference. His Majesty's Government in the United Kingdom and the Government of the United States are in accord that such a conference should be held in London at the beginning of the third week in January 1930, and it is hoped that the Japanese Government will be willing to appoint representatives to attend it.

A similar invitation is being addressed to the Governments of France, Italy and the United States, and His Majesty's Governments in the Dominions are being asked to appoint representatives to take part in the conference. I should be grateful if Your Excellency would cause the above invitation to be addressed to the Japanese Government.

In the same way as the two Governments have kept Your Excellency informed *au courant* of the recent discussions, so now His Majesty's Government will be willing, in the interval before the proposed conference, to continue informal conversations with Your Excellency on any points which may require elucidation. The importance of reviewing the whole naval situation at an early date is so vital in the interests of general disarmament that I trust that Your Excellency's Government will see their way to accept this invitation and that the date proposed will be agreeable to them. His Majesty's Government in the United Kingdom propose to communicate to you in due course their views as to the subjects which they think should be discussed at the conference, and will be glad to receive a corresponding communication from the Japanese Government.

It is hoped that at this conference the principal naval powers may be successful in reaching agreement. I should like to emphasize that His Majesty's Government have discovered no inclination in any quarter to set up new machinery for dealing with the naval disarmament question; on the contrary it is hoped that by this means a text can be elaborated which will facilitate the task of the League of Nations Preparatory Commission and of the subsequent General Disarmament Conference,

I have the honor to be,

    With the highest consideration,

        Your Excellency's obedient servant,

                (Signed) ARTHUR HENDERSON.

Journal as Ambassador to Great Britain

London,
October 8, 1929.

At Chancery most of the day was spent preparing to leave for
the United States tomorrow. At 12:00 M. attended the memorial
services at Westminster for Dr. Stresemann. I was not seated
with the diplomatic corps but was given a seat in front with
Lloyd George and Sir Austen Chamberlain. The form of service
was all printed in a pamphlet of two pages, which was handed
us, and we could thus follow the hymns and prayers. They were
concluded in half an hour, which is the prescribed time allotted
to such occasions here.

Bade good-bye to Matsudaira and de Fleuriau.

At Sea,
S.S. Ile de France,
October 11, 1929.

Before leaving had a talk with Sir Josiah Stamp about an adviser on new tax legislation for the Dominican Republic, a selection which President Vasquez desires me to make. He recommended Sir Ernest Clark, former permanent secretary of the
Treasury of the North Ireland Government, and who had
schemed out the tax system of Cape Colony, remaining until the
taxes of the first year were collected under it. Accordingly, I
wired Sumner Welles recommending Clark. It seems to all, after
consideration, that it is best to have some one other than an
American recommend the new tax laws as less demagogery will
be incited in Santo Domingo as a result.

At Sea,
S.S. Ile de France,
October 13, 1929.

At Owen Young's cabled suggestion, Caro and I called on Madame Curie, the discoverer of radium, at her stateroom yesterday
evening. We found her a most interesting and charming old lady

92

HENRY M. DAWES

with that simplicity of speech, life and conduct which best befits the truly great.

Yesterday, in response to a request from John W. Davis, President of the New York Chapter of the English-Speaking Union, I sent the following telegram of greeting to be read at the banquet to MacDonald yesterday noon, at which Davis said there were to be nearly 5000 guests:

"It is a privilege to join in your greetings to the Prime Minister. During the last few months I have been but a humble intermediary between two great leaders, resolute and fearless in the sacred cause of peace, not only among our two peoples, but for the world. I can thus properly bear witness to their courage, ability and high purpose. I know the Prime Minister is winning the trust and high regard of the American people, as he has long ago won my own."

Finished reading my brother Henry's article on "Branch and Chain Banking" written for a magazine. It is the best article on the subject I have seen. Cabled him my congratulations.

> White House, Washington, D.C.,
> November 5, 1929.

The pressure of work during my visit has been such that I have actually had no time for these notes.

Nothing had been done about the Exposition bonds (Century of Progress) in my absence. What is everybody's business is nobody's business. So on arriving at Chicago I went straight from the train to work. I had no time to be discouraged. The money for the Exposition must be raised now or never, and my stay was to be only for two weeks.

Harry Hurd worked at the indenture and I went to work selling the bonds before they were issued as there was no time to spare. Hurd drew a subscription paper, necessary for that purpose, and I personally presented it to thirty-one of our guarantors. Yesterday, when I left Chicago, I had sold $6,125,000 payable at par on call. The stock panic commenced before I was through but I had sold most of them before that storm broke, and to the people and corporations whose wealth was not jeopardized by stock fluctuations. The amount sold was $1,125,-000 above the $5,000,000 which, under the resolution of Congress, had to be raised before the President could issue the invitation to other nations to participate.

It is hopeless for me to try to write of the last two strenuous weeks. The Century of Progress is firmly on its feet and my brother Rufus is now firmly in the saddle. To protect him, I had the indenture drawn and ratified so as to place control of the funds in myself and two men selected by me, and not only that, but in case the Exposition Board delays or does not make decisions, this committee through Rufus can go ahead under its own authority and build the Fair.

The breakdown of interest and belief in the Fair in one way was fortunate because it enabled me, when I agreed to raise the money, to make my own conditions. This Fair will, therefore, be built by Rufus on a strictly business basis. I know he will succeed in this great work.

Some night last week, I forget which, Rufus and I gave a dinner at the Palmer House to the South Park Board, the guarantors and the trustees of the Fair. At this dinner Rufus, the President of the South Park Board, E. J. Kelly, who is an indispensable friend of the Fair, and I made statements.

During the hectic two weeks, Rufus, Harry Hurd, Major Lenox Lohr and Rawleigh Warner did magnificent work.

I am deeply grateful to my friends who stood so loyally behind me in my efforts to raise this large sum under such distressing conditions—chief among whom were Julius Rosenwald and Samuel Insull.

President and Mrs. Hoover invited my daughter Carolyn with us to visit at the White House during our stay in Washington. We arrived this morning. Had an extremely interesting conference with the President. Will wait until I get on the ship before taking up the thread of naval affairs again.

This panic, in my judgment, is the beginning of a major depression.

Journal as Ambassador to Great Britain

At Sea, S.S. Homeric,
November 9, 1929.

I have lived in such a whirl the last few days that I hardly know where to commence. My three days in Washington were, of course, devoted chiefly to naval matters. My conferences were with Secretary Stimson and Assistant Secretary Joseph P. Cotton, but chiefly with the President. As his guest at the White House during my stay, opportunity was given for hours of consideration without distraction. My admiration for his grasp of the problem, both in general and in detail, already great, was heightened by this continued contact. He has had a constant struggle to get fair play from the Naval Board, and he would never have got it, in my judgment, had he not mastered the technical elements of the question as thoroughly as the Board. To mislead him was impossible. Every report made was checked over with at least the same, if not greater competency, than that with which it was prepared.

An illuminating instance which Stimson gave me will illustrate this fact: the Naval Board had furnished him with a "yardstick" to determine the relative fighting effectiveness of ten-inch and six-inch cruisers. At one stage of the negotiations, when they were endeavoring to cut down the number of small cruisers for Great Britain in determining parity, they announced the result of the application of their "yardstick." At a much later time and at another juncture when they were endeavoring to increase the number of small cruisers to be allotted the United States, they again made a report on the basis of their "yardstick" measurement. At this later juncture the British had come down to the following figures:

15 eight-inch cruisers, tonnage	146,000
14 new replacement six-inch cruisers, tonnage	91,000
21 old six-inch cruisers, tonnage	101,000
Total tonnage	338,000

The President was then considering for the United States 21 eight-inch cruisers, tonnage 210,000; 10 Omaha cruisers (six-inch cruisers) tonnage 70,000, and enough additional new 7000 six-inch cruisers to bring our cruiser fleet to parity in fighting

95

effectiveness. The Naval Board, in their "yardstick" report gave eight as the proper number of these new 7000 ton six-inch cruisers to be added.

At the conference when this report was handed in, Stimson said the President read it, drew from his pocket the "yardstick" formula, and commenced to figure it out for himself. He presently announced that according to their "yardstick" formula, applied in the same way as in their previous report the number of these additional cruisers should be four and one-half instead of eight. The Naval Board had no answer and withdrew from the conference. Stimson, however, went to the Navy Department and at a meeting with the Naval Board demanded their answer. It was that the "yardstick" after all was only a camouflage and they were but performing their duty of "protecting properly the interests of their country," etc. The Secretary of State said: "Gentlemen, the United States in its international negotiations is not in the habit of camouflaging."

The duty of framing the policy of the United States for the protection of its people and their interests belongs to the President of the United States who is also Commander-in-Chief of the Navy. This duty is not delegated to the Naval Board by the people or by our Constitution or laws.

This impudent assumption by the Naval Board that they possess such power is an evidence of a gross indifference to their military and naval duty. The demand of a board of subordinate officers in the American Expeditionary Forces during the war that General Pershing let them determine his campaign would have been no more ridiculous than this.

The Naval Board not only has no such power but it was organized in its beginnings with no such purpose. It should be abolished or at once reorganized. It is simply an advisory committee. Moreover, the advice of naval officers, taken separately, is more valuable than that of a committee. More officers could be consulted and wider information thereby secured without involving the risk of having a cabal which foments insubordination.

In a great struggle requiring executive leadership, the appointment of an advisory committee is often the last, hopeless and disastrous resort of executive incompetence.

DWIGHT W. MORROW

Journal as Ambassador to Great Britain

In our conferences the President discussed the make-up of our conference representation. He had already decided upon Stimson, Senators Joseph T. Robinson and David A. Reed and myself, and to my delight, he said that he would select Dwight Morrow as one of the additional delegates.

I made a plea for Gibson, whom the President would like to select if Great Britain will agree to six United States members. As Great Britain will be represented by three members from England and three from the Dominions, there will probably be no difficulty in appointing Gibson, who, from every standpoint, has not only earned it, but is unusually qualified.

The other matters we talked over have been largely discussed in these notes heretofore, and I will not go into them again.

He read me his coming speech on Armistice Day, and my last evening was spent with him and Mrs. Hoover in their final revision of it. The comments and suggestions of Mrs. Hoover gave me for the first time the proper sense of her unusual ability and sound judgment. We arrived in Washington last Tuesday. With the exception of lunch with Secretary Stimson at his home, I spent the time at the White House, and the State and War Department building, where I occupied General Pershing's offices.

One afternoon I went to the Senate and met my old friends, including Vice President Curtis.

On Wednesday evening the President gave a dinner at the White House in honor of Ambassador Guggenheim and his wife, who are soon to leave for Cuba, and ourselves. The guests were members of the Foreign Relations Committee of the Senate and Secretary and Mrs. Stimson.

On Thursday my brother Rufus and his wife and Major Lohr arrived. They lunched at the White House and during the day the President issued for Rufus the proclamation inviting the nations to participate in the coming Chicago Century of Progress Exposition, the necessary $5,000,000 to enable him to do it, under the Congressional resolution, having been raised.

Journal as Ambassador to Great Britain

Caro and Carolyn left Thursday morning to visit Dana at Lawrenceville School, and going over Thursday night I met them at New York Friday morning.

The Hoovers make delightful and most considerate hosts, and we all greatly enjoyed our visit with them.

> At Sea, S.S. Homeric,
> November 11, 1929.

Armistice Day. Subconsciously—for all mass movements commence that way—I believe the world has turned toward a long peace, and that this is to be the blessing to many generations which they will owe to the silent and forgotten dead, to whose memory today the world pays the tribute of silence.

Arriving at New York Friday morning, I took breakfast with Caro, Dana and Carolyn, and then met Rufus and Major Lohr at Owen D. Young's office. Young had called in General James G. Harbord (President) and David Sarnoff (Vice President) of the Radio Corporation of America, Andrew W. Robertson, President of the Westinghouse Electric & Manufacturing Company, and Gerard Swope, President of the General Electric Company, of which Young, himself, is Chairman.

Rufus, Lohr and I devoted the morning to a discussion with them of the part to be taken in the Exposition by the electric and radio industries, and went away with their firm promise of complete cooperation. Sailed on the *Homeric* that night.

It occurs to me to say something about the great stock panic and credit contraction through which our country is passing. It is long overdue. For several years I have been expecting it and getting my house in order to meet it. It should have occurred two years ago, and for at least that length of time I have been warning my friends to get out of the stock market.

It was in the panic of 1893, when I was twenty-eight years old, that I learned the greatest financial lesson of my life—which was that a ninety-day note becomes due. Before that time I had regarded them as renewable forever. At the time that panic broke I owed in the neighborhood of $200,000. I passed through it without failure, but my agonies of anxiety and worry and my strenuous endeavors of that period, terrible as their memory is, have proved themselves the safeguard of my business life. They taught me the dangers of debt. I have borrowed since that time but never recklessly, and never without a plan for repayment worked out at the time I contracted the debt. Out of my experience I have given advice to a number of young men during the last two years as to what was ahead of them. I can recall none of them who took my advice. So probably it would have been with me in the years before 1893. I probably would have listened to but not acted upon conservative advice. Experience alone teaches the ambitious young.

To me it seems that the signs of the coming of the present panic were more pronounced than those of any through which the United States has passed. History shows that there is no such thing as an orderly deflation of generally over-expanded credit. Human nature remains the same. The law of human action and reaction is immutable. Federal Reserve Banks, low production costs, low inventories, and all the other things which the optimist has regarded as "making a change in conditions as compared with the past" have not changed human nature.

The longer the spree, the deeper the following depression and the longer the sobering up time.

The stories I was told of the losses, first of paper profits and then of real ones, fed as additional margins to brokers before the final sell-out, seem almost incredible. All classes of people seem to have been speculating. "All New York is a wailing wall," said somebody.

At Sea, S.S. Homeric,
Thursday, November 14, 1929.

While I was in Chicago my friends gave me clippings from the papers containing what the Prime Minister had to say about me in the speeches in America which he delivered while I was on my way over. What he said, I greatly appreciated and I know that it came from his heart. Perhaps, because it did, his statements may seem over-kind but I freely forgive him for this.

Journal as Ambassador to Great Britain

"Speaking of war and war dead," MacDonald said: "The other day I went out to Arlington and I saw those solemn acres where your military dead lie. I saw the care bestowed upon them. Before I was there I had been at some of the graveyards on the continent of Europe and there I saw just as I saw here now how the dead were being kept in reverent honor and the recollection of the romance of sacrifice was their custodian.

"Ah, my friends, we know the stress, we know the pain, we know the losses, we know the privation, and, therefore, we are moved in our hearts by the romance of sacrifice. But a young generation is growing up round about us whose eyes were never moistened by the tears of sorrow on account of war. And the reverence that we show to our dead runs the grave danger of becoming not the romance of sacrifice, but the romance of war itself."

He next spoke of his conference with the President, saying: "We threw aside all the old rectitudes of mid-Victorian and still more ancient clothes; we never beat about the bush. We never employed the methods and the language of circumlocution. We went straight at it. We were informal."

The radio news bulletins on the ship bring the daily tidings of the terrible collapse in speculative credits and stock exchange prices in New York and to a large extent elsewhere. It is without question the beginning of a major depression in general business. It is easy to be philosophical in a panic when one is out of debt. There is wide-spread agony and despair among the venturesome in life; but it is the plodders' day of triumph. After having passed through the panics of 1893, 1907 and 1914—the latter two as a business man—I am in a position, in this panic, to sense the suffering of the one class and the melancholy satisfaction of the other. The latter feeling is natural but not creditable. I notice that some who have escaped disaster in this panic through mere accident, pickled in the vinegar of their own pretended righteousness, are the most severe in their criticisms of the unfortunate.

Journal as Ambassador to Great Britain

At Sea, S.S. Homeric,
Friday, November 15, 1929.

MacDonald's visit to the United States was an unqualified triumph in which his daughter, Miss Ishbel, had her full share. After nearly four months of association and negotiation with him I had implicit confidence in his ability to make the trip a contribution to the good relationship of the two English-speaking peoples. But I had not visualized the greatness of the accomplishment he had left behind him.

Everybody I met at home spoke to me in praise of him and of his daughter—of his addresses—of his tact and complete understanding of his subject and the way to handle it. This was true in official Washington, as well as in Chicago and in New York, among all classes, politicians, statesmen and business men.

What I think made the greatest impression was the fact that his speeches were both long and extempore. The nation-wide radio broadcast of them brought to the public a sense of his sincerity, high purpose and sheer courage and ability.

The sublime self-confidence and skill with which he addressed extempore the Senate of the United States, where a mistaken sentence might at one and the same time have wrecked his administration at home, and the cause of peaceful understanding here, was a revelation of what the long parliamentary training and experience of British Prime Ministers results in. In important announcements of policy our own public men in high positions of responsibility, as an invariable rule, very properly avoid the risk of misquotation or of inexact statements on their own part, and read their speeches.

With MacDonald there is never a risk of misstatement on his part, and the risk of misquotation he accepts.

Journal as Ambassador to Great Britain

London,
Sunday, November 24, 1929.

We did not reach London until the late afternoon of Saturday, November 16th, after a fairly good voyage and just in time for me to attend in the evening the dinner of the Institute of Journalists where, together with Arthur Henderson, J. A. Spender and others who spoke, I made an address. It was the one upon which I had worked so hard on the *Ile de France* en route to America. It was cabled to the United States and will tend, I trust, to keep attention directed to the essentials of the naval problem and the proper methods of dealing with it. I regard the address as a proper supplement to my Pilgrims' speech, and its argument upon method, since the method then recommended has been followed thus far by the Governments. It is as follows:

It is under the aegis of the Kellogg Pact that the coming Naval Conference is called, and in its spirit the great naval powers of the world will meet.

The methods, or if you please, the science of international negotiations in matters involving both a political and a technical problem in each of the respective nations concerned is at present undergoing an evolutionary process which started at the end of the World War.

Like all international evolutions either of method or attitude, this has come about through necessity which, besides being the "mother of invention," is as well an opener of the eyes of the blind.

The current negotiations upon naval disarmament between the United States and Great Britain have thus far well exemplified the greater effectiveness and expedition of the new methods as compared with the old.

These negotiations have been but preliminary and their result is subject to such modifications as may result from the necessities of the other naval powers.

These powers will, from now on, give these results their full examination and consideration, not only in preliminary informal conferences amongst themselves, but as well with the United States and Great Britain.

Thus, hereafter, these informal conferences will be between all of the naval powers as a preliminary to the consideration of the problems by the formal conference commencing the third week of next January.

It may be well, therefore, to discuss at this time the new methods of approach and the basic principles underlying it which thus far have been recognized by Great Britain and the United States.

In the first place, in these negotiations both governments have from the first proceeded upon the assumption that the final arbiter of the outcome of the conference must be not only their own domestic public sentiments but those of the other powers concerned.

Journal as Ambassador to Great Britain

Secondly, they have realized that no temporary public sentiment in the respective powers will crystalize into a matured and compelling public judgment determining national policy unless the public of each power understands exactly the nature of the differences to be adjusted and their relations to domestic as well as international interest and security.

Thirdly, they have realized that as a basis of a general constructive public judgment insuring a successful outcome of the conference, there must be, after a most painstaking and careful consideration by naval technicians of the naval questions involved, a complete understanding of the naval opinion of each country with that of its statesmen.

Fourthly, they have realized that this accord of naval technical opinion between nations, as well as between the technicians and statesmen in each nation, is best reached through a discussion carried on by the principals separately advised by their naval staffs.

Fifthly, they have realized that not until naval technical differences, with meticulous care and after laborious research, are reduced to their simplest terms can there be made, by mutual understanding between the technicians and the statesmen, a proper statement of these differences which the general public will easily understand.

Public opinion will eventually control all and for the proper formation of its final judgment the public should first have a clear statement and understanding of the case.

A successful public debate depends largely upon a proper statement of the subject for discussion.

Naval technicians alone are primarily qualified to formulate the terms of a technical naval difference; and with their findings as a basis, the statesmen should be able to state properly those differences for public consideration. Any other course may be an assistance to the propagandists and other selfishly interested who will endeavor to obscure the real question and the real public interest by the injection of extraneous and irrelevant considerations.

It is important that during the future course of the naval negotiations the method of proper approach be always in mind, and the experience thus far of Great Britain and the United States is worthy of consideration by the other naval powers.

During the last four months in the conversations between Great Britain and the United States, most of the time has been devoted to a technical naval discussion in a preliminary way of the following points:

First: Of the naval requirements of each of the two nations essential to their respective security.

Second: Of whether reduction may be secured consistent with the meeting of these requirements.

Third: Of what will constitute equality in strength between the two navies, particularly in the cruiser category.

The substantial agreement upon what constitutes equality in the cruiser category had involved the settlement of a series of technical questions upon each of which, at first, conflicting opinions were submitted.

In each instance this involved the necessity of further research and reconsideration by both sides before a final agreement of technical naval opinions between the American Naval Board and the British Admiralty was reached. Conflicting opinion remains on only a minor matter involving 30,000 tonnage out of an aggregate tonnage of 2,400,000.

Had this series of technical questions been discussed publicly by a general body composed both of the naval technicians and the statesmen of the two countries instead of being dealt with one at a time and in the order determined by the principals—the President and the Prime Minister—advised separately by their naval staffs, it is probable no agreement would have been reached.

The appearance to the public at least would have been of a general and destructive conflagration involving parity as to the whole structure of the 2,400,000 aggregate navy tonnage dealt with.

As a matter of fact, there was at no time any general conflagration, but instead a series of separate bonfires each one of which, sometimes laboriously, but always loyally, conscientiously and quietly, was extinguished by those who had built it, and this was always done before the next bonfire started.

As I said before, there was always a continuing sense on the part of both principals during these negotiations of the necessity of reaching a conclusion which the general public could clearly understand, and understanding approve.

This was very wise. The average man is not interested in a question unless he understands it; for as Balfour once said: "With the generality of people, they much prefer the continued existence of a problem which they cannot explain, to an explanation of it which they cannot understand."

Again in these preliminary negotiations so in any more general disarmament negotiations the motto "One thing at a time" should be kept in mind.

The discussion of other desirable ultimate objectives such as freedom of the seas and more comprehensive disarmament should never be allowed to obstruct any agreement which is clearly a step in their direction. No average man in his personal or business transactions commits a similar folly. He does not become discouraged in advance because a step in the right direction may not be as long as he personally would desire. If wise, he does not feel discouraged because a staircase must be ascended one step at a time.

The specific objective of this present negotiation is the abolition of the general competitive building of fighting ships and their reduction in number so far as is consistent with the national security and domestic necessities of the respective naval powers.

This objective is itself of vast importance and value to the economic welfare of the world, and, furthermore, its consummation will furnish the only foundation for further procedure and further pacts guarding still better a continuing world peace.

Yesterday the French Ambassador told me that no naval officer will be named on the French delegation to the Conference. MacDonald, last Monday when I called on him, told me the same thing as applied to the British delegation. Our delegation, which has been already appointed, contains no naval officers. The naval officers thus far named will have their relation to the Conference as advisers, not as principals, and it will be due to this fact, as much or more than any other, that its success is possible.

Last Monday morning I called on the Prime Minister and received a call from the Japanese Ambassador before leaving for Paris on the early afternoon train.

It was my desire to learn from the Prime Minister the number of delegates he would appoint to the Conference so as to inform our Government. He stated that from Britain there would be four—possibly five—which number would not include the Dominions. Upon receipt of my cable to this effect, the President on Wednesday completed our delegation by the appointment, in addition to Secretary Stimson and Senators Joseph T. Robinson and David A. Reed, the following: Secretary of the Navy Charles Francis Adams, Ambassadors Hugh Gibson and Dwight Morrow and myself, making seven members in all, with Admiral William V. Pratt and Rear-Admiral Hilary P. Jones as advisers.

The Prime Minister and I talked over his American trip with the results of which he is properly well pleased. He went over his recent conversation with the Japanese Ambassador for my information. From what he said, I assume that the Dominions are asserting themselves considerably and may be an important factor in the coming negotiations.

At noon after this call upon MacDonald, I received a visit from Matsudaira, whose government is pressing for a statement from our country and Great Britain on our attitude on the question of changing the naval ratio fixed at the Washington conference between the United States, Great Britain and Japan at 5-5-3 to a ratio of 10-10-7.

Since the determination of national policy is not the province of a diplomatic agent, but of his chief, I did not enter into any discussion of this, but did urge that Japan should defer the discussion until the Conference. This MacDonald told me he had done, and this I knew also is desired at Washington.

At 2:00 P.M. Monday, Caro and I took the train for Paris. Between Monday and Friday, when I was expected to speak at the Pilgrims' dinner in honor of Frank B. Kellogg, seemed the only time available for me to make the visit to my friend General

Journal as Ambassador to Great Britain

Payot—a visit which I have been planning for so long. General and Madame Payot joined us Tuesday afternoon, coming from Clermont-Ferrand, where his headquarters as Commander of the 13th Corps of the French Army is located. My time until we left Thursday noon was chiefly spent with him. It was too far to try to go to Clermont-Ferrand in the short time we had, much to our mutual disappointment.

On Wednesday we had at lunch General and Madame Payot, Sir Robert and Lady Kindersley, Jean Parmentier, Colonel Philippe Bunau-Varilla and Miss Kindersley. At dinner in the evening besides the Payots, Colonel Doumenc joined us. The latter drew up the regulations issued by our Military Board of Allied Supply for camion transports behind the armies in the zone of the advance. Captain de Marenches, that brilliant and faithful man who was with General Pershing from the first as his liaison officer between him and Foch and Petain, was with me for a morning.

General Payot and I called on General Gouraud, now military Governor of Paris, on the American Embassy, and on Morgan and Company where I saw Pesson-Didion of the French Staff at my old headquarters. Dean Jay and other old friends were out of the city.

The morning we left for Paris (Thursday) Parmentier brought René Massigli, of the French Foreign Office, to the hotel to see me. I had endeavored to avoid any official contacts even though my old friend of war times—Tardieu—is now Premier of France.

Paris is outside my diplomatic reservation, but Parmentier insisted so strongly I felt I could not decline with good grace. I am glad I did not do so, for Massigli came from Tardieu and outlined for my information the attitude of France toward the Naval Conference. It is, according to Massigli, intended to be constructive, although France is preparing a preliminary statement to the effect that her acceptance of any Naval Conference agreement must be subject to revision in connection with any more general disarmament agreement which may arise later out of the efforts of the Preparatory Disarmament Commission at Geneva. I said at this point that in view of the expressed desire to be constructive, it would be well for France to informally consult and

106

advise with the other powers as to the form of this statement as was done between the United States and Great Britain relative to the form of the invitation to the Naval Conference which was issued by Great Britain.

He replied that this was a good idea and they would probably decide to do so. He said France was not opposed to binding commitments among the other naval powers at the Conference.

We arrived at London by the "Golden Arrow" at 6:35 P.M. Thursday.

On Friday Mr. Frank B. Kellogg called on me at the Chancery and we had a pleasant visit. On that evening attended the dinner given in his honor by the Pilgrims. Lord Desborough presided. Kellogg, Lord Cecil and I spoke. Kellogg and Cecil made fine prepared addresses. My remarks were extempore, proposing the toast of the Chairman.

The French Ambassador called to report on a recent visit of his to MacDonald, which he made after a visit with Briand. The latter will be a delegate. Tardieu will also come over for a few days. From the desire of the French to keep me posted now on their procedure, it would seem that they appreciated our efforts in the past to inform them fully as to ours.

The appointment of our delegation to the Conference and the fact that the negotiations between Great Britain and the United States are quiescent, changes the "status quo" to some extent; and for a time, until our delegation arrives, I shall be a reporter of the informal negotiations between the other powers which may go on here, rather than a negotiator myself.

London,
Saturday, December 1, 1929.

Matsudaira called at 3:00 P.M. and fully reported as to the Japanese naval proposition which he had submitted to MacDonald in the morning. I told him I would not enter a discussion of it with him—that our naval delegation was now appointed and although I was a member of it I did not propose to change the "status quo" here in London by personal negotiations at this time unless specifically directed by my Government or the Chairman of our delegation—that I would, of course, transmit any information he desired to our Government.

In repeating the terms of the Japanese proposition, I dictated the Washington cable in his presence and so stated in the cable. Since our Government is already in negotiation with Japan through Dubuchi, the Japanese Ambassador at Washington, I am determined not to allow anything I may do here embarrass them there.

London,
Monday, December 2, 1929.

Yesterday (Sunday) received State Department cable instructing me to submit to the Foreign Office a form of statement to be used, issued by the United States to China and Russia calling attention to their duty under the Kellogg pact to seek peaceful means of settling the Manchurian trouble and to suggest that Great Britain issue a similar one simultaneously. This I communicated to Henderson, who said he would do so.

Today received another detailed cable, giving the status of the trouble as reported to the United States and requesting me to make certain representations relative to the proper attitude for the powers to assume toward it under the Kellogg pact. This I did at 1:00 P.M. to Henderson at the Foreign Office, who read me the statement he will make in the House of Commons this afternoon, in which he announces that Great Britain will issue a statement to China and Russia tomorrow, substantially identical with that of the United States. This statement he is preparing.

London,
Wednesday, December 4, 1929.

At 11:00 A.M. Caro and I went to a private showing of the motion pictures of the Prime Minister's visit to the United States and Canada, at his invitation. It was at a motion picture theater. We sat with the Prime Minister and Miss Ishbel. A number of others, mostly from the Government, were present. As the pictures well indicate, Miss Ishbel, who accompanied him on his trip, combines a modesty and even shyness of demeanor with such evidence of entire self-command and naturalness as to inspire both friendliness and respect.

Both the Prime Minister and his daughter in the pictures were wholly themselves, and it resulted well. It suggests that the natural is always the artistic.

Secretary Stimson cabled that he and the President felt so strongly the desirability of eliminating at the Naval Conference the possibility for the various delegations to take public stands early in the Conference from which they could not recede, thus transforming what is intended to be a peaceable conference into a battle ground, that they felt I should discuss with the Prime Minister, as soon as possible, some arrangement of the Conference by which no opportunity would be afforded for any but the most general of speeches. They further suggested that the methods of procedure be determined as far as possible after the arrival of the delegates at London.

At 5:45 P.M. I went, therefore, to the Prime Minister's at 10 Downing Street, and we had a satisfactory conference over the matter. He fully agrees with the idea and said that no method of procedure would be suggested with which we did not agree. In my cable of reply to the State Department, I suggested that on the day before the first meeting the leaders of the delegations could discuss methods and desirably arrange that the first meeting be a plenary session devoted to organization and division into committees for the conference work, eliminating all save a short opening address by the Chairman, previously submitted to the delegation leaders, which was the course followed with our First Committee of Experts in Paris in 1924.

This was but a slight modification of the suggestion made by Stimson in his cable to me, discussing the proposed programs submitted to him by the British Embassy at Washington.

I do hope that by some departure from the conventional the Conference can properly create a public sense of their earnestness and their determination to indulge in constructive work rather than in declamation.

Journal as Ambassador to Great Britain

The American Embassy at Paris has wired the State Department, sending us a copy, that René Massigli is coming to London soon to consult the Prime Minister as to the form of the statement which France proposes to issue defining the reservations under which she enters the Naval Conference. The cable refers to the statement as one of which Massigli spoke to me when in Paris, so that my advice as to preliminary consultation with the United States and Great Britain as to its form is evidently being followed.

Last night I went with Caro, Henry (my secretary) and Mr. and Mrs. Raymond E. Cox (first secretary of Embassy), to the impressive ceremony of Toc H, in which the lamps are lighted in memory of the "elder brothers," the dead of the wars. This took place in Albert Hall, in the presence of an audience of at least 7000. The program which I append will give but an inadequate impression of the wonderful memorial meeting. The emotions of all were deeply aroused. The Prince of Wales spoke in his fine way and all that was said was deeply touching and appropriate.

As I looked at the scene from the platform, I realized that the British people are a bereaved people. To have lost 800,000 of their youth in war has meant something to them which I have not fully understood until now. Their attitude toward religion and toward life and death is clearer to me.

Lord Forster who stood by me had lost his two boys in the war. When the hall was darkened and the soldiers before him held their little lights in silence and all the people were silent in a tribute to their dead, I saw him put his hand to his heart. That was all, but I understood what it meant.

The Prince of Wales had asked that I be present, which explains the reference to me in the order of exercises.

H.R.H. THE PRINCE OF WALES

Journal as Ambassador to Great Britain

From the Birthday Secretary Toc H
1 Queen Anne's Gate
London, S.W.1.

THE TOC H BIRTHDAY FESTIVAL, DECEMBER 6/8th, '29.
Royal Albert Hall,
Saturday.

7:55 P.M. His Royal Highness, the Prince of Wales, attended by Sir Godfrey Thomas, arrives at the South (Artists') entrance, and is received in the Artists' room behind the platform by Lord Forster, Field Marshal Viscount Plumer, the Founder Padre, and Captain F. W. Bain (Chairman of the Birthday Committee), all of whom will have previously received the American Ambassador.

8:00 P.M. The singing of songs having ceased, His Royal Highness takes the chair and speaks.

8:25.P.M. Approx. The thanks of Toc H are voiced briefly by Lord Forster and the audience sings an Australian ditty, "How we Train 'em at Payneham."

His Royal Highness is then conducted to a chair on a small platform in the center of the Arena. The Prince's lamp is placed on a pedestal by "The Gen" (Arthur Pettifer, M.M.). Tapers are lighted from the Lamp and Lord Plumer and Lord Forster begin the lighting of the (old) lamps and rushlights as the bearers assemble in the Arena. The new Lamps of Maintenance to be lighted for the first time are then brought by members from the following branches, accompanied by their banner bearers.

1. Cottingham (Yorkshire)
2. Sevenoaks (Kent)
3. Barking (Essex)
4. Hinckley (Leicestershire)
5. St. James', Winnipeg (Canada)
6. Valparaiso (Chili)
7. Verulam (Natal)
8. Wandsworth (London)
9. Bardon Hill (Leicestershire)
10. Cannock (Staffordshire)
11. Cawnpore (India)
12. Escombe (Natal)
13. Port Elizabeth (Cape Province)
14. Fort Beaufort (Cape Province)
15. Handsworth (Birmingham)
16. Morton (Lincolnshire)
17. Rainham (Kent)
18. Tavistock (Devonshire)
19. Christchurch (New Zealand)
20. Dunedin (New Zealand)
21. Blackpool (Lancashire)
22. Aberdeen (Scotland)
23. Newport (Monmouthshire)
24. Cowes and East Cowes (I.O.W.)
25. Darlington (Durham)
26. Govan (Glasgow)
27. "Maple" (London)
28. Parkstone (Dorset)
29. Philadelphia (U.S.A.)
30. Poplar (London)
31. Portsmouth (Hampshire)
32. Spilsby (Lincolnshire)
33. Rio de Janeiro (Brazil)
34. Stepney (London)
35. Truro (Cornwall)
36. Watford (Hertfordshire)
37. Carlton (Nottinghamshire)
38. Greenwich (London)
39. Boldre (Hampshire)
40. Wales (Silver Lamp)

111

Journal as Ambassador to Great Britain

Lords Plumer and Forster return to the platform and two verses of "Hail, Joyful Light" are sung as the last new lamp is being lighted.

His Royal Highness and the Founder Padre turn about and face all the lights and banners. The Ceremony of Light is conducted by the Founder Padre, and a third verse of "Hail, Joyful Light" is sung.

His Royal Highness is then conducted up the Stalls Gangway to the main corridor, and thence to his box.

The American Ambassador, Lord Plumer and Lord Forster go from the platform to Royal Box No. 27/28.

9:00 P.M. Approx. The Interval follows.

9:15 P.M. The Orchestra plays for a few minutes, before the performance of the "Mime", "At the Sign of the Star", concluding with the singing of "Jerusalem" and Family Prayers taken by the Founder Padre at approximately 10:15 P.M.

R. R. CALKIN,
Birthday Secretary, Toc H.

December 5th, 1929.

London,
December 19, 1929.

Recently I have been presenting certain of my views to the State Department and the Prime Minister on the methods of self-government to be adopted by the Naval Conference, for my wartime experience teaches me that these require as careful an approach as has been given to the definition of naval technical differences which will be turned over to the Conference.

Nothing is more important in major international conferences than that the primary duty of fixing the order of precedence of a series of interdelegation negotiations should devolve upon the individual leaders of the respective delegations in committee. This situation in conferences is ultimately inevitable, but its results are liable to be less satisfactory in proportion to the delay of the conference in evolving it.

An agreement should be made at the very beginning that a committee composed of the heads of each delegation shall fix the order and nature of the differences to be discussed in any plenary sessions.

Journal as Ambassador to Great Britain

The relation of this committee to the rest of the Conference should be in the nature of that now sustained by the President of the United States to the Naval Board and the British Premier to the Admiralty in determining the nature and order of consideration of the technical differences which were submitted to them for their opinion. This arrangement, which is so necessary to the success of the conference, can be secured at the beginning without acrimony. But if neglected it probably will only be had finally after a painful performance and dangerous waste of time.

When I read the draft agenda of suggested procedure of conference which the British Foreign Office prepared and submitted to the other Governments, including our own, I was disturbed. This was handed to me for my information on December 17th. On December 14th, I had suggested to Secretary Stimson that when he arrives he have a preliminary conversation with Mac-Donald, Briand, and, if possible, with the representatives of Japan and of Italy. An agreement between them as to the best method of self-government by the Conference would undoubtedly be accepted as soon as presented to the Conference.

It would be understood that the discussion at this preliminary meeting of the heads of delegations would relate to nothing but methods of facilitating the procedure of the forthcoming Conference.

The British agenda provided for two preliminary committees.

I took the position that these agenda discussions by correspondence should not be allowed to result in the adoption of a plan but should be considered only as an exchange of views to be discussed at a preliminary meeting of the five leaders of the respective delegations, who will decide upon plans of procedure when they get here. To have two preliminary committees as suggested by the British agenda when it provides that its first committee alone would be in position to acquire the information necessary to determine a method of conference procedure, is most unwise.

Why risk a series of unnecessary discussions and possible conflicts between the two committees? The first committee in developing the situation would develop also the reasons for a proper procedure on the part of the Conference. Why should it be compelled to educate the second committee as to the necessity of a certain form of procedure, which, in turn, would educate the Conference?

The second committee would constitute an unnecessary and dangerous infraction of the principles of effective organization. Why, again, should there be two delegates from each country on the committee of procedure? Committees of this kind lose effectiveness and waste time in proportion to their size.

London,
December 24, 1929.

I have received from Roop, whom I left in Santo Domingo to help install our system, and from Seidemann, who is now in Santo Domingo finishing up his installation of a proper governmental accounting system, most complete reports as to the budget and accounting situation and a copy of the "Budget of the Dominican Republic for 1930" which was prepared in accordance with our recommendation.

Budget and accounting matters and the saving of money for governments and peoples never inspired the songs of the poet or the acclaim or even interest of the ordinary man, but when I gave these documents to Sir Ernest Clark it was with confidence that there would result a commendation of our work from an acknowledged expert.

Clark has agreed to go and I will so cable Welles. When Clark has framed new revenue laws for the Dominican Republic, I believe that government will have as good a business and tax system as can be devised. If President Vasquez lives, and is re-elected next May, this system, in my judgment, should have a fair try-out, for I believe Vasquez to be an honest man as is also Mr. Battle, his Director of the Budget, who is a successful business man serving his country at personal sacrifice.

The man whom Dr. G. H. Grosvenor, editor of the *National Geographic Magazine,* sent to Santo Domingo for photographs and an article on that country has just finished his visit there.

By the way, I had the other day from high Spanish authority

LADY ASTOR

the admission that the body of Columbus is in the Cathedral at Santo Domingo and not at Seville. Indeed, the statement was made that an old chart has been found in Spain showing in the Santo Domingo Cathedral the original location of the three bodies of Columbus, of his son Diego Columbus and of Diego's son.

We are busy this evening preparing for Christmas.

London,
Thursday, December 26, 1929.

Today is called "Boxing Day" in London. While we greatly missed the folks at home yesterday, nevertheless, we had a most interesting Christmas.

We had a Christmas tree at the Embassy for which one never grows too old, and our little family and our staff of servants gathered around it at 10:30 A.M., and presents were distributed to all. Many messages were sent and received between us and our dear ones at home across the ocean.

I received one from Will Rogers in Beverly Hills, California, containing a hint of value relating to the coming Naval Conference. It read: "Merry Christmas to my favorite man in public life. Don't sink anything until you see them sink first."

At five P.M., Caro, Virginia, Henry and I went to Cliveden, to visit the Astors. We stayed all night, and returned this evening.

About fifty, mostly of the Astor family and relatives, sat down to dinner. One daughter convalescing in a neighboring village from a riding accident, at whose bedside Lord and Lady Astor alternate, was absent, as was Lord Astor on this account. On our return to London this evening, I find that the Cliveden establishment is overshadowed in our memories by the genius of the three sisters who were there—Lady Astor, Mrs. Brand, and Mrs. Phipps —who furnished the chief entertainment for the gathering.

Journal as Ambassador to Great Britain

London,
December 29, 1929.

Diplomatic work is temporarily at a lull, and I am devoting spare time at intervals to the study of the naval situation.

Yesterday afternoon I went to the Zoo to see the new tiger recently received from Sumatra. This ferocious beast arrived with the record of having killed three men. I was present at the feeding time of the lions and tigers. The rest of the animals were pacing their cages in a frenzy of anticipation, awaiting the keeper who thrust their meat through the bars. But the man eater did not appear for his share. He was hidden behind a wall in the back of his cage, through which there were two doors, and the meat did not tempt him to come out in the open part of his cage.

After waiting a half hour for him to appear, I introduced myself to the keeper, who took me through an entrance between the cages to their rear. In the solid wall at the back of the man eater's cage was a small circular peep hole covered by a lid. Through this I saw the magnificent but untamed and ferocious animal lying behind the wall within the cage, between the two doors leading to its front.

It seems he will not go out in front save after dark or occasionally when it is very quiet. If he then sees anyone he is apt to jump against the bars after him. I asked the keeper what the tiger would probably do if, as is the keeper's custom with the other animals, he entered his cage. His reply was that the tiger might either attack him immediately or break his neck against the bars in a jump to get away. This tiger and the one that I saw at the Dublin Zoo last summer were the only recently captured tigers I have ever seen. They increased my respect for prehistoric and savage man, who somehow survived their unconfined companionship. What a terrible fighter or runner, or both, prehistoric man must have been!

Journal as Ambassador to Great Britain

London,
January 1, 1930.

Last night we had a wonderful experience even for this era of wonders as we sat here at home and heard over the radio the acclaim by European peoples of the passing of the old and the coming of the new year. As one listened in succession according to the respective differences in time to the bells of Cologne and the voices of the Germans, the whistles and sirens of the boats in the harbor at Rotterdam, the music in Italy, the speakers at Prague, the singing at Copenhagen, the shouts from Paris and finally the ten-minute address of a Canon in Westminster Abbey, and the booming tones of "Big Ben" at London striking twelve, followed by a choral singing of "Auld Lang Syne," he could not but have a sense of awe.

Ambassador Gibson called this afternoon, and we talked over naval matters. After he had gone the French Ambassador called to tell of his recent talks with Aristide Briand at Paris, to assure me of the French desire to cooperate in the Conference. The French hope to be able, if possible, to come to an agreement with the other naval powers, consistent with France's obligations to the League of Nations, and if they find that they cannot agree, then they will not obstruct a treaty agreement among the other powers. He said that Briand hopes that a way will be found for France to join in the agreement.

London,
January 3, 1930.

This evening the Japanese delegates to the Naval Conference called on me at the Embassy. They include Reijiro Wakatsuki (the former premier of Japan), Admiral Takeshi Takarabe, and Ambassador Matsudaira. They expressed their appreciation of their cordial reception in the United States and of my action in keeping them informed in detail of the Anglo-American negotiations as they progressed. This latter I told them was in accordance with my instructions from my Government before I left for

Journal as Ambassador to Great Britain

London, and also at the desire of the British Prime Minister, but was a most appreciated privilege to me personally.

Wakatsuki is a quiet spoken man of dignified and agreeable bearing. Takarabe has a most likable personality and speaks excellent English. In the evening I received from MacDonald a note written on New Year's Day from Logie House, Dunphail, Morayshire, the home of Sir Alexander Grant, where we had our first meeting in June, and where we started the Anglo-American naval negotiations—a beautiful place in the highlands of Scotland on the banks of the Findhorn and in the midst of the forest.

I have not seen the Prime Minister much since our negotiations became quiescent, and, by agreement, ready to be transferred to the Conference, but have followed with sympathy his difficult and exacting political situation. Sir Josiah Stamp, whom he lately had called into conference upon economic matters, told me the other evening that he seemed worn and somewhat dispirited. This is not to be wondered at, for the strain of his official position in these dark days for British industry and trade would break any ordinary man. His note, written as usual in his own handwriting, gave a hint of discouragement. It reads:

MY DEAR DAWES:

I am here for my New Year's lunch and think of you. I wish you were here with us for old associations' sake. The river runs and the trees grow, but shall we be allowed to carry out the purpose we laid down in June? Sometimes I wonder, but we shall have a good try. So I think of you and send you my warmest greetings and hopes for the New Year—all your folks sharing.

Yours, always sincerely,
J. RAMSAY MACDONALD.

London,
January 4, 1930.

Called on Robert Craigie at the Foreign Office this morning to notify him in accordance with a cable received this morning that our government regards it impracticable to attempt to reduce the size of capital ships at this Conference. Also talked over with

118

BARON REIJIRO WAKATSUKI

him the proposed speaking program of the various public social functions.

At each function it is proposed that only one delegate speak, if it can be so managed. The four public *functions* arranged for the delegates are just four too many, in my judgment.

I have engaged in too many inter-allied conferences during the war not to understand the folly of the present society program and its possibilities. At the least, we have probably added weeks to the length of the Conference. First impressions are of vital importance in their effect upon the delegates themselves. If they are led to believe that time and expedition are not of value, they will act accordingly.

As Chairman of the First Expert Committee at Paris, my first public statements were planned to create the impression, not only upon the public but upon the Committee, of the necessity of all possible expedition in our work, consistent with thoroughness. I announced also that we would attend no public functions.

London,
January 9, 1930.

Yesterday sent two important cables which should reach our naval delegates before they sail today. One was the statement brought me by the French Ambassador, which he will present to the British Government Monday asking certain questions and further amplifying their former statement of the French attitude. It is on the whole constructive and evidences a purpose to assist in making the Conference a success. The other related to the French position taken at Geneva.

Today, as representing our Government, I signed a commercial treaty of the United States with Iraq, together with the Minister from Iraq and Arthur Henderson, the Secretary of State for Foreign Affairs. This took place at the Foreign Office.

Sent Stimson a cable today as to a meeting with MacDonald immediately upon arrival and outlining what the Foreign Office had to say regarding the attitude of the Japanese delegation upon the naval ratio.

Journal as Ambassador to Great Britain

London,
January 13, 1930.

Saturday, the Spanish Ambassador called, stating that if the Mediterranean situation was to be added as an agenda for the Naval Conference, Spain, having 700 miles of Mediterranean sea coast, would expect to take part in it. I informed him as to the situation—that the United States and England did not desire to discuss a Locarno for the Mediterranean at the Conference, and that there was no probability that the present program of the Conference would be expanded so as to involve it.

Delivered a letter to Sir Ernest Clark yesterday from President Vasquez, of the Dominican Republic, asking him to come to Santo Domingo in June to suggest improvements in their revenue legislation.

Our naval delegation is now on the ocean.

London,
Tuesday, January 14, 1930.

The approaching Conference fills the days with preparations for it. The informal negotiations going on between the powers, similar to those through which the United States and Great Britain have passed, bring the Ambassadors to my office to report upon their progress as I used to report to them upon ours in the past.

Today, with the *George Washington* nearing the English coast, I cabled to Washington for transmission by code to the ship the information given me by Matsudaira of the conversation between the Japanese delegates and the Prime Minister. So far they are about where they started as far as any concessions on either side are concerned; but concessions are hardly to be expected at this immediate juncture.

Another long cable also was necessary covering details of landing, time of arrival at London, nature of various official receptions, and arrangements for an early meeting between Stimson and MacDonald.

Journal as Ambassador to Great Britain

Tonight I have re-read MacDonald's speeches in America, inasmuch as the publishers, with MacDonald's approval, desire me to write a foreword to them in book form. Am going to do it though I feel somehow a sense of inadequacy as I consider these masterful speeches in retrospect, all of them delivered extempore.

Yesterday I had a fine reunion with Lord Pembroke, who was on the Staff of our Military Board of Allied Supply, at Coubert, France, during the last four months of the war. He had come down to see me from Salisbury, and by a happy coincidence while we were exchanging greetings in the office, Major Craig, another British member of the old staff, walked in on us.

Common experiences in time of strain and emergency certainly cement friendships.

Pembroke said that the terrible gale of Sunday blew a lead roof three hundred years old off of one of the towers of Wilton Castle, where he lives.

London,
Sunday, January 19, 1930.

Notes like these, written in the midst of events, are a strange intermingling of consequential and inconsequential things. The difficulties of telling at the time "which are which" is perhaps one of the reasons why contemporaneous notes so often outweigh in value *ex post facto* dissertation.

I wrote my introduction to the volume of MacDonald's American speeches, and sent it over to him for comment. I was rewarded by one of his gracious acknowledgments in his handwriting, which I append.

10 Downing Street,
Whitehall,
16 January, 1930.

My dear Dawes:

Thank you very much for that introduction. Its spirit of kindness and appreciation touches me, and over and above that I am glad that, in the little volume, you and I walk arm in arm. We should have done it in any case, but I am happy that it is done openly for all to see from its very first page.

With kindest regards and renewed thanks, I am,

Yours very sincerely,
J. Ramsay MacDonald.

121

Journal as Ambassador to Great Britain

On Thursday evening I attended two functions; the first a dinner at the Middle Temple, where I was made a "Middle Bencher" at 6:45 P.M., the other a brilliant reception at the Japanese Embassy, given by the Ambassador and Madam Matsudaira for the Japanese delegation to the Naval Conference.

The first occasion especially was a memorable one to me for I walked with history for a time. I will append the interesting program which the Secretary of the organization gave to my nephew, Henry, as the one through which I would be put on my arrival at the historic Middle Temple. It was not carried out as to myself as I was telephoned in the afternoon that on my arrival I would be met at the door by the Treasurer (or Chairman) and other officials, and the details of the ordinary invitation waived.

Justice Horridge, the Treasurer, gave me a most kindly and graceful introduction at the dinner, where I spoke extempore.

THE MIDDLE TEMPLE

6:45 P.M., Thursday, Jan. 16, 1930, Dress Suit

You should wear a dress suit, even though everyone else will be dressed in ordinary clothes, but all will have academic robes, including yourself. You will be placed at a small table in front of the Bencher's table until you are called to the Bench by the Master Treasurer (everyone called to the Bench is addressed as Master, regardless of other titles, rule of precedence being by seniority). You will then take your place at the foot of the Bencher's table as Junior Bencher. At this time, or a little later, the Master Treasurer will propose your health and you should make a short speech in acknowledgment.

For fruit and coffee, and smoking the Benchers file, according to seniority, into another room where you will sit at the foot of the table (the end nearest the door).

The Master Treasurer will toast "The King" and you will repeat, "Master Treasurer, The King"; no one rises during the toasts because when Charles II was called to the bench he was unable to rise so freely and the port flowed and thus was formed this tradition.

Later the Master Treasurer will toast "Domus" and you repeat, "Master Treasurer, Domus". The next toast is to the Absent Members, and again you repeat, "Master Treasurer, the Absent Members."

Soon the Master Treasurer will order the Junior Master to ring the bell. You do this, making a bow to the Master Treasurer before returning to your seat. (The bell is near the fire place.) After this ceremony you may smoke.

The former Temple Hall was burned in 1560, and the present one erected in 1570. The only remnants of the old building are a pair of oaken doors, dating 1430. In the hall is a lamp which was the poop lamp on Sir Francis Drake's ship which circumnavigated the globe. Just in front of the platform

122

ARRIVAL AT PLYMOUTH, JANUARY 17, 1930

Left to right: Senator David A. Reed; Charles Francis Adams, Secretary of the Navy; Henry L. Stimson, Secretary of State; Senator Joseph T. Robinson; Dwight W. Morrow, Ambassador to Mexico.

is a table made from the wood taken from this ship. These mementoes are kept here because Sir Francis, a member of the Middle Temple, dined here the evening of his return to England. The table at which the Benchers sit is from a magnificent oak from Windsor Forest, a gift of Queen Elizabeth. It is 30 or more feet in length, about four feet wide—the top is a single piece of timber about three inches in thickness. Behind the table are hung large pictures, the center one being a beautiful Van Dyke. One word more about this table. The Queen gave the tree but the Templars had to transport it down the Thames and have it cut. The bill for this, which is still preserved, was ten pounds.

Shakespeare is said to have appeared on this platform in the first performance of "The Midsummer Night's Dream."

Formerly the members of the Temple had their sons educated there before sending them up to Oxford or Cambridge. Thus it is that you find soldiers, sailors and statesmen, as well as lawyers, as members.

It might be interesting to note that five of the men who signed the Declaration of Independence were Middle Templars. It has always been considered the Colonial Temple, and hence it is there are so many Indian Students there now.

The roof of the Dining Hall is of a peculiar design and is noteworthy.

The Benchers hope that you will make the Temple your club, lunching or dining there often. You are permitted to take guests to lunch and twice a term to dinner.

At midnight Thursday I left with Atherton for Plymouth to meet the American delegation. We arrived there at 7:30 A.M., and first met Gibson (who had preceded us from London), Admiral Sir Hubert Brand and the staff of the British Admiralty, and other local officials.

Then we proceeded to the dock where the tender with the delegation was just landing. Secretary Stimson made his reply on the dock to the Mayor of Plymouth who, in a scarlet robe and gold chains, surrounded by four men carrying the maces of the city, had delivered a welcome; and all the American party then boarded a special train of a dozen cars entirely filled with their personnel, and departed for London which we reached about 2:00 P.M. A greeting at the station there from the representatives of the Government followed.

On the train I spent much time with my friends, Dwight Morrow and Senator Joseph T. Robinson, also with Secretary Stimson, Senator Reed, Secretary Adams and Ambassador Gibson.

At 4:00 P.M. Dwight Morrow called at the Chancery, and we had a delightful visit. In the evening, Senator and Mrs. Robinson took dinner with us and the Senator and I had a "long go" at naval matters.

Yesterday (Saturday) I had a lunch at the Embassy, with Dwight Morrow, Will Rogers, Willmott Lewis, of the London *Times,* and John Steele and Arthur Sears Henning, of the *Chicago Tribune.*

In the morning our entire delegation called on the Prime Minister at 10 Downing Street to pay our respects, remaining there about an hour.

In the evening all the delegation and their wives, excepting Secretary and Mrs. Stimson, who went out to Stanhope, dined with us at the Embassy, as did Admiral Pratt and Admiral Jones and their wives.

Most happily Will Rogers also was a guest and he made the dinner memorable to us all.

London,
Tuesday, January 21, 1930.

On Monday morning (yesterday) all the delegates were received by King George V at Buckingham Palace; and in the evening attended a dinner at the Savoy Hotel, given by the British Government, at which the guests numbered over 500. A reception at Lancaster House followed the dinner, at which the Prime Minister and his daughter Miss Ishbel officiated.

This morning, in the Royal Gallery, at the House of Lords, was held the first plenary session of the London Naval Conference, addressed by the King and the heads of the delegations. Although ordinarily a trip from the Embassy at 14 Princes Gate to the Parliament Building by motor only takes ten minutes, the fog was so blinding that it took nearly an hour, and as Caro and I arrived at ten minutes after eleven, the opening hour, I missed the King's opening speech which consumed about that time.

The speeches at the Conference were good; but as all the delegates in their addresses referred in some way to their respective nationalistic standpoints, the King's fine speech was the only one addressed in world terms to the world's people. The occasion, I thought, would have inspired some delegate to include a condensed and simple argument for disarmament, to which some of the time devoted to the coining of graceful and general phrases might well have been devoted.

I thought the addresses of MacDonald, Stimson and Tardieu most admirable, but all were good.

The days since the arrival of our delegation here have been consumed largely in informal conferences between the heads of the delegations. I think we are most fortunate in having Stimson as the head of our own delegation. He will, in my judgment, make no mistakes. I have spent a great deal of time with Dwight Morrow since he arrived, and I find that he also has the greatest confidence in Stimson, based upon twenty-five years of friendship. Stimson keeps everyone well informed of what he is doing, and knows how to keep his team "playing ball."

Last night I had a delightful time with my old friend of war days, André Tardieu. "You and I," said he, "are the only ones here at the liquidation of the war of all who were with us in 1917, 1918, and 1919. . . . If you and I had only the power to decide things now as we decided things then, we would not have to stay here long. . . . In the conference of the heads of the delegations, I discern some tendency to delay decision."

Stimson said that Tardieu told him this morning that he would announce France's position at the plenary session on Thursday morning. Stimson is therefore preparing a statement of the American position, on which Dwight Morrow is also working. This will probably be discussed at the 10:00 A.M. meeting of our delegation tomorrow.

Probably Tardieu, as was his habit in war time, is precipitating discussion of essentials early in our proceedings. This is all right and will save time if informal conferences before Thursday morning will either result in ironing out possible ultimatums or having them omitted for the time being.

The prospects for agreement all around, judging from my talks with our own people, as well as with other delegates, seem outwardly as somehow too good to be true. I fear that in showing their desire to agree, which is sincere, all are assuming that the necessary concessions to respective domestic sentiments and demands are going to be made "by the other fellow." At least I see no "yielding tendency" on our part so far as our previously announced intentions are concerned.

Dwight Morrow and I are spending much time with some of the delegates who can do much to make or mar the success of the Conference. The part of wisdom at a "unanimous consent" party is to look after wallflowers who, feeling neglected, may prove to be poison ivy in disguise.

During the conference at the House of Lords this morning, I drew up a cable to my friend Owen Young, congratulating him upon the final agreement on the Young Plan at The Hague yesterday, which my associates on the American delegation signed with me.

London,
Friday, January 24, 1930.

I am rather glad that three days have passed without attention to these notes, a neglect induced by a whirl of interesting occasions and gorgeous affairs, combined with incessant work on the part of our delegation.

This will enable me to write tonight with a better perspective upon certain important questions of procedure in our negotiations upon which the success of the Conference may largely depend.

We started out with a series of preliminary negotiations between the heads of the delegations. The efforts we (the United States) have been making for weeks before the opening of the Conference against the preparation by the Foreign Office of the agenda upon procedure in advance of the arrival of the delegates, have been successful and the discussion of procedure is now going on between the heads of the delegations in separate consultations from time to time with their respective members. The "town meeting" methods have not been followed. This has resulted in the assumption of informal primary negotiating by the heads of the delegations, a procedure which is acquiesced in without question by all delegates as a matter of plain common sense.

Journal as Ambassador to Great Britain

The importance of this cannot be over-stated. The reasons for it I have stated so fully to the State Department and in these notes long before the arrival of the delegates, that I will not go over them here. To bring such a state of things about weeks ago, I even suggested sole delegates from each country, assisted not by other delegates, but by advisers. This was impracticable, but the method now adopted preserved its general advantages.

Today, during all of which our delegation has been in conference, the discussion ran for quite a time on the question submitted to us by Secretary Stimson as to what attitude he would take in the next meeting of the heads of delegations Monday, which will decide what should be the first question to be discussed at a plenary session with press representatives present. A list of some fifteen or twenty subjects which might be discussed has been prepared by the General Secretary of the Conference, Sir Maurice Hankey, and was in our hands.

Senator Reed today handed over to the rest of us without any preliminary comment a sheet of paper upon which he had been writing, which I reproduce from memory, something like this:

1st. Reduction in battle ships in number to 15-15-9.
2nd. Holiday until 1936.
3rd. We to be allowed in capital replacements a Rodney and a Nelson.
4th. 8-inch cruisers—18-15-12.
5th. 6-inch cruisers—20-35-17.
6th. Destroyers—152-152-90.
7th. Submarines—90-90-60.

Stimson was not present, but the six of us agreed we could make a first stand on this proposition. Admiral Pratt was called in and he approved. Then Stimson, who had been absent during the discussion to attend another conference, came in and agreed.

Of course this statement of our position, which is now being revised by Admiral Pratt with the other technician, will be modified, but we all realized that either this statement or one like it made by us or some other nation or prepared tentatively by the heads of the delegations, will constitute the agenda of the Conference.

Once a general proposition covering all categories and all navies is put before the Conference, the changes which will be proposed will all emphasize the quantitative smallness of the differences which separate us and add to the weight of public opinion for settlement. The public will thus not be easily misled by irrelevant argument for the text will always be forced upon their attention, even by a divergence from it.

The long preliminary work of the past months in reaching the tentative agreements which have induced the present world attitude of support and hopefulness will not have been wasted.

I summarize here the arguments I personally urged at intervals all through the long session of our delegates.

The purpose of this long series of preliminary negotiations which have been in progress for the past six months has been to simplify the terms of the differences between the nations. Because of this simplification, the general attitude of public opinion in the world is that the differences are minor when considered in connection with the magnitude of naval tonnage involved and the injury to world economy and the cause of peace consequent upon the failure of the Conference. Upon the maintenance of this world psychological attitude depends the chance of ratification of any agreement which we may make. To lose it will be a disaster.

For the heads of the delegations to determine on next Monday morning which one of the twenty questions listed before us should be first discussed at the plenary session, which course assumes a similar discussion as to other questions which must be selected from day to day, immediately arises the general inquiry as to whether or not this does not inevitably lead into a method of procedure which will destroy all the advantages which have been gained during the last six months through the informal preliminary negotiations. It involves a deliberate reversal of policy in that it will invite the attention of the world to a rediscussion of all the details which have in effect been settled. It will constantly invite during the Conference definite commitments made in public by the representatives of the different nations, so phrased as to accord with domestic public sentiment at the time. By this method, we would deliberately throw away much that we have gained in good understanding during the last six months.

The trouble is that the naval settlement presents an indivisible question. In the plenary sessions it cannot be discussed publicly, as though composed of separate unrelated elements. Every question as to one category involves another category. Every question which involves one nation involves the other nations. The present situation confronting the heads of the delegations is similar to that which confronts a creditors' committee in business. A creditors' committee laboriously devotes itself to a simplification of the differences between creditors or classes of creditors, and is in a position to state them. What our heads of delegations are at present contemplating is similar to a proposition on the part of a creditors' committee to call a general meeting of the creditors and then, when assembled, instead of presenting to them a tentative and simplified statement of understandings and relationships as

Journal as Ambassador to Great Britain

to essential differences, to invite the meeting to start a new discussion of its own without the report of the creditors' committee to guide them. Such procedure as this will inevitably bring the Conference to an impasse which may change a unified, favorable public attitude of the world into one divided into as many different phases as there are nations involved.

The imperative need of the present situation is a statement from the heads of the delegations early in the proceedings, outlining the limited quantitative differences which, in their present simplified form, stand in the way of agreement. Then, when the discussion starts, they will tend less to divert the attention of the world from the smallness of the difference as compared with the large aggregates involved and the importance of settlement. As to just what such a statement should contain, I have not the technical knowledge to indicate; but such a statement made by all the delegation heads, or even by one country early in the proceedings, would change in a revolutionary and advantageous way the future course of the Conference. This method was followed by Secretary Charles Evans Hughes at the beginning of the Washington Conference, and it was his preliminary statement which simplified and guided the discussions of the entire Conference, inspiring constructive suggestions as to the necessary changes in his propositions to effect agreements and lessening the opportunity as well as the temptation for the making of preliminary nationalistic ultimatums.

The naval situation has been so engrossing that I can hardly recall the evening social and formal events of the last few days.

On one night we attended the Lord Mayor of London's banquet to the delegates at Guildhall. On another we had a large dinner at the Embassy which I gave in honor of the seven members of the Gridiron Club who are here for the Conference. Besides them, there were seventeen other guests, including Admiral Takarabe, Secretary Adams, Dwight Morrow, Senator Reed, Senator Robinson and Will Rogers. The latter alone would make any dinner a brilliant success.

Thursday and Friday the whole delegation lunched with Secretary Stimson whose room at the Hotel Ritz adjoins the delegation offices.

This evening I took Senators Robinson and Reed, Secretary Adams and Dwight Morrow to a dinner at the Middle Temple which we all greatly enjoyed. It was a guest night.

Journal as Ambassador to Great Britain

I confess to weariness at the end of these days, for life is one long debating society at present, and yet progress is being made. This progress comes from informal conferences, and intra-delegation discussions, not at the formal conferences of the delegation heads as yet.

Stimson reported at our delegation meeting this afternoon that at the conference of delegation heads this morning, over two hours was devoted to a dissension between the Italian and French about a minor matter.

All the afternoon, our delegation debated the American proposition first prepared by Senator Reed and since revised in consultation with the technicians. These discussions are educational in a high degree. In the evening, I spent an hour or so with Tardieu and Briand, first with Tardieu and afterward with Briand.

Tardieu chafes under what he believes is necessary procrastination among the leaders, but says that after a short time he will press for decisions. He says that the leaders he is meeting are able and excellent men, but somewhat timid. I replied that, considering his own deliberation, probably that also was their idea of him.

He agreed with my view that in plenary sessions, constructive debate will commence only after the presentation of a tentative but comprehensive and detailed plan of settlement. Upon that as a basis, the various amendments will be suggested and thrashed out, and the final settlement made. He thinks that this first tentative plan ought to be evolved in about ten days. I had a most interesting visit with him and we recalled our war-time negotiations and settlements with comments upon the ineffectiveness of peace-time methods as compared with those of war when parliaments, of necessity, had to "cease from troubling," and in all conferences formalities at once gave way to "brass tacks."

My interview with Briand was my first conversation with him, my acquaintance with him having only commenced last week. It was to me most illuminating in its revelations of his methods and character. He pleased me by his favorable references to my Pilgrims' speech, and emphatically endorsed what I had to say about conference procedure.

As to France and Great Britain, he said they would soon agree and that he felt most hopeful of a successful outcome of the Conference. He discussed his difficulties with admirals just as Tardieu had done. He said the present movements in our conference negotiations, while not apparently progressive, in so far at least as informal consultations were concerned, were actually so.

"They were," he said, "much like the adjustments of our internal bodily organs to age."

He expressed the hope that we would confer often, and when I left this great and charming man my feelings were probably those with which all leave him—a sense of his superior ability and an added, but perhaps unjustified sense, of self-satisfaction. His dealings with men, however, while they may be "adjusted to human nature," are glorified always by unselfish and high constructive purpose.

London,
January 28, 1930.

2:30 P.M. In the morning a long session of six of the delegation was held with naval experts on the question of ratio of effectiveness of 8-inch and 6-inch cruisers, "all things considered" which means a lot. Secretary Stimson, however, attended a meeting of the heads of delegations.

At 1:00 P.M., Senator Robinson and I took lunch with Secretary and Mrs. Stimson to meet the Prime Minister and Robert Craigie of the Foreign Office.

This afternoon at 3:00 P.M., we will continue discussions with our naval experts. The American proposition is nearing its first tentative form. This evening we attended a banquet of the Pilgrims of Great Britain.

We are developing real arguments underlying the Naval Board attitude on big cruisers—thanks very largely to the unusual talents, indefatigable study and clear-mindedness of Dwight Morrow and David Reed.

Journal as Ambassador to Great Britain

Spent all day at conference of the American delegation, much time being given to the questioning of our naval advisers. As usual, the experts radically disagree. It will be impossible to bring them together; and the final Conference agreement, if reached, must be ratified over the opposition of a section of the naval experts of the United States and Great Britain. The points of difference, however, will be whittled down to a minimum, and are already small.

Yesterday Dwight Morrow presented me with a copy of *British Foreign Secretaries, 1807–1916* by Algernon Cecil. This he did because it contained the following quotation from Lord Salisbury: "You listen too much to the soldiers. No lesson seems to be so deeply inculcated by the experience of life as that you should never trust experts. If you believe the doctors, nothing is wholesome; if you believe the theologians, nothing is innocent; if you believe the soldiers, nothing is safe. They all require to have their strong wine diluted by a very large admixture of common sense."

The relevancy of this to our present situation needs no comment. Fortunately, we have on our delegation Senator Reed, whose logical and brilliant mind is equipped with a technical knowledge by his long service on the Committee on Military Affairs of the Senate. Through his skillful questioning of our naval experts, their "strong wine" received a "welcome admixture of common sense."

He discusses no question without shedding light upon it. His memory of relevant naval statistics, naval fact and naval history, is remarkable as is also that of Dwight Morrow. Nothing is more illuminating to all of us than a discussion between these two.

Secretary Stimson does not resent initiative on the part of others, his mind is clear and logical and his judgment sound. He controls the activities of his delegation without trouble, preventing cross wires and keeping each of them advised as to the whole situation which he develops in his delegation conferences.

Gibson's technical naval experience, his originality and natural

CHARLES F. ADAMS

DAVID A. REED

resourcefulness, his wide acquaintance, as well as his great industry, make him an invaluable delegate.

Adams reserves his fire for naval questions and then speaks with force, wisdom and influence. The well-considered and sound judgments of Senator Robinson carry a weight second to none on the Committee of which he is probably the most powerful member because of his commanding position in the Senate.

Secretary of the Navy Adams, of all, probably has the most delicate and difficult situation to handle. He is the natural liaison between our Government and the naval technicians, and has been so throughout the preliminary discussions in America. It is fortunate for our country now, as on former occasions in our history, that an Adams is here to help represent it. He ably upholds the family tradition.

London,
Thursday, January 30, 1930.

We had the third plenary session of the Conference at St. James's Palace this morning, which concerned itself with speeches on a plan of transfer between categories, and ended by providing a Committee for its study. All delegates then attended a lunch given by the Foreign Press Association at the Savoy Hotel. Wakatsuki responded for the delegates.

In the afternoon we had another delegation conference. Things seem going pretty well all around. Tomorrow we will try to get in agreement on the American proposal. The British and French are nearing an understanding. Reed is making progress with the Japanese delegation in informal conferences. Secretary Stimson is in constant touch with the other heads of delegations.

London,
Friday, January 31, 1930.

The American delegation was in session morning and afternoon. The discussion is now upon methods of negotiation. After our hearings with our naval experts, we find them divided and offering us two diametrically opposite opinions as to our fleet's need in 8-inch and 6-inch gun cruisers at the present time.

All the delegation realizes that technical arguments exist for both views, but feel that a reasonable compromise should be made between the two. Five of the delegation feel that Admiral Pratt has the best of the technical arguments in his contention to the effect that the fighting effectiveness of the fleet will best be subserved at this time by 18 of the 8-inch cruisers and with a larger number of 6-inch cruisers, rather than by 21 of the 8-inch with a smaller number of 6-inch cruisers. Two feel that Admiral Jones' contention as to the 21, 8-inch cruisers has the best of the technical argument.

But all of the delegation agree that the practical consequences involved in the difference in these views as to three 8-inch cruisers, more or less, are so insignificant as compared with the total tonnage involved in our conference negotiations as not to justify a split and the failure to agree on the part of the delegation. Accordingly, the discussion, as I said before, is now as to methods of negotiation. Dave Reed's original proposition though in a considerably revised and modified form, has now been practically agreed upon as embodying the American stand. It has been discussed from all angles by both our technicians and our delegation.

TENTATIVE PLAN OF THE AMERICAN DELEGATION
January 28, 1930
(Third Revised)

CRUISERS

For United States

Type

Total Tons		
180,000	18—10,000 ton cruisers, carrying guns of 8-inch calibre.	
70,500	10	existing Omaha's.
76,500		new cruisers, carrying guns not exceeding 6-inch calibre.
327,000		

(A) The United States shall have the option of the following:

150,000	15—10,000 ton cruisers, carrying guns of 8-inch calibre.	
70,500	10	existing Omaha's.
118,500		new cruisers, carrying guns not exceeding 6-inch calibre.
339,000		

For Great Britain

110,000	11—10,000 ton cruisers now completed, carrying 8-inch guns.
20,000	2—10,000 ton cruisers now building, carrying 8-inch guns.
16,800	2— 8,400 ton cruisers now building, carrying 8-inch guns.
91,000	14 new cruisers, mounting 6-inch guns.
101,200	21 existing cruisers, mounting 6-inch guns.

339,000

(A) Great Britain may retain four cruisers of the Hawkins Class, carrying 7.5-inch guns until replacement by 6-inch cruisers.

(B) Great Britain shall have the option of the following:

176,800	18—10,000 ton (or smaller) cruisers, carrying guns of 8-inch calibre.
150,200	cruisers, carrying guns of 6-inch calibre.

327,000

For Japan

28,400	4— 7,100 ton cruisers, carrying 8-inch guns.
40,000	4—10,000 ton cruisers now completed, carrying 8-inch guns
40,000	4—10,000 ton cruisers now building, carrying 8-inch guns.
87,800	17 cruisers, carrying guns not exceeding 6-inch calibre.

196,200

1—6-inch gun cruiser (3,750 tons) scrapped in year 1930, and 3—6-inch gun cruiser (13,200 tons) scrapped in year 1932.

REPLACEMENTS

1. No cruiser may be replaced until it shall have reached a life of twenty years from date of completion, unless it shall have been lost through an accident.
2. No cruiser may be laid down prior to 31 December, 1936, except to replace vessels as provided above (Paragraph 1) other than as agreed to in the following table:

To be drawn up in the Conference.

3. Tonnages are given in Washington standard tons.
4. Old tonnage may be retained over the age limit if not replaced, but the right of replacement is not lost by delay in scrapping after reaching the age limit.

DESTROYERS

Total tonnage of destroyers and destroyer leaders shall be:

For United States	200,000
For Great Britain	200,000
For Japan	120,000

1. Existing destroyers and leaders may be retained and vessels building may be completed up to the above total allowed tonnages.
2. Existing vessels shall not be scrapped except to comply with the allowed tonnages until the vessel has reached an age limit of 16 years.
3. Old tonnages may be retained over the age limit if not replaced, but the right of replacement is not lost by delay in scrapping after reaching the age limit.
4. No new vessels shall be laid down prior to 31 December, 1936, except to replace vessels reaching the age limit or lost through accident.
5. Maximum unit displacements shall be limited as may be agreed upon in Conference. We suggest 1850 tons for Great Britain and 3000 tons for France.

SUBMARINES

Total tonnage of submarines shall be:

For United States	60,000
For Great Britain	60,000
For Japan	40,000

1. Existing submarines may be retained and building vessels may be completed up to the above total allowed tonnages.
2. Existing vessels shall not be scrapped except to comply with the allowed tonnage until the vessel has reached the age limit of 13 years.
3. No new vessels shall be laid down prior to 31 December, 1936, except to replace vessels reaching the age limit or lost through accident.
4. Submarine tonnages are given in Geneva standard tons; surface conditions.
5. Maximum unit displacement shall be limited as may be agreed upon in Conference.
6. Old tonnage may be retained over the age limit if not replaced, but the right of replacement is not lost by delay in scrapping after reaching the age limit.
7. Submarines to be limited to the same rules of international law as surface craft in operation against merchant ships.

BATTLESHIPS

1. The replacement tables of the Washington Treaty are modified as follows to comply with these principles.
    (A) Immediate scrapping of old ships down to a total of 15-15-9
    (B) No new ships shall be laid down prior to December 31, 1936, except as provided below in Paragraph 4.
    (C) Each nation may retain two old battleships for training purposes or for use as targets, provided these vessels shall be rendered incapable of further warlike service as prescribed in the Washington Treaty.
2. Tonnages are in both Washington standard tons and in pre-treaty normal tons. Three thousand standard tons have been added to each of the *Idaho, Mississippi,* and *New Mexico,* to allow for future modernization.

Journal as Ambassador to Great Britain

3. Should any provision be made for replacements of battleships, each nation may retain old tonnage if not replaced, and the right of replacement of that tonnage is not lost by such postponement.
4. In order to realize now the parity of battleship tonnage which was ultimately contemplated by the Washington Treaty by balancing the *Rodney* and *Nelson,* the United States may lay down one 35,000 ton battleship in 1933, complete it in 1936, and on completion scrap the *Wyoming.* This would give the United States, in 1936, the following:

	Standard Tons
On hand 1 January, 1936,	462,400
Scrap *Wyoming*	26,000
	436,400
Add 1 new ship	35,000
Total at end of 1936 under option	471,400

Modernizing existing ships includes increase in gun elevation.

Minimum limitation of 10,000 tons shall be stricken from definition of aircraft carriers so that all such vessels shall be charged against limited tonnage.

For United States

	Standard	Normal
1. Scrap *Florida*	21,900	21,825
Utah	22,000	21,825
Arkansas	26,100	26,000
Total	70,000	69,650
2. Total tons now on hand	532,400	525,850
Scrap in 1930–31	70,000	69,650
Remaining until 31 December, 1936	462,400	456,200

For Great Britain

	Standard	Normal
1. Scrap *Iron Duke*	26,250	25,000
Marlborough	26,250	25,000
Emperor of India	26,250	25,000
Benbow	26,250	25,000
Tiger	28,900	28,500
Total	133,900	128,500
2. Total tons now on hand	606,450	558,950
Scrap in 1930–31	133,900	128,500
Remaining until 31 December, 1936	472,550	430,450

For Japan

1. Scrap *Kongo*	26,330	27,500
2. Total tons now on hand	292,400	301,320
Scrap in 1930–31	26,330	27,500
Remaining until 31 December, 1936	266,070	273,820

Exempt Class

(A) That all naval surface combatant vessels of less than 500 tons standard displacement be exempt.

(B) That all naval surface combatant vessels of 500 to 3,000 tons individual standard displacement should be exempt from limitation provided they have none of the following characteristics:

    (1) Mount a gun greater than 5-inch calibre.

    (2) Mount more than two guns above 3-inch calibre.

    (3) Are designed or fitted to launch torpedoes.

    (4) Are designed for a speed greater than 16.5 knots.

(C) That all naval vessels not specifically built as fighting ships nor taken in time of peace under government control for fighting purposes, which are employed in fleet duties or as troop ships, or in some other way, other than as fighting ships, should be exempt from limitation provided they have none of the following characteristics:

    (1) Mount a gun greater than 5-inch calibre.

    (2) Mount more than four guns above 3-inch calibre.

    (3) Are designed or fitted to launch torpedoes.

    (4) Are designed for a speed greater than 16.5 knots.

    (5) Are armored.

    (6) Are designed or fitted to launch mines.

    (7) Are fitted to receive planes on board from the air.

    (8) Mount more than one aeroplane—launching apparatus on the center line; or two, one on each broadside.

(D) Certain existing vessels of special type to be exempted by mutual agreement.

London,
February 2, 1930.

Caro and I have just returned from lunch at Warren House, with Secretary and Mrs. Stimson, Secretary and Mrs. Adams, Senator and Mrs. Robinson, and Mr. and Mrs. Merrill, were the other guests.

After lunch, Stimson, Adams, Robinson and myself continued the discussion of how, now that the American first tentative proposition has reached its accepted form, it should be handled in our negotiations with the other powers.

JOSEPH T. ROBINSON

Journal as Ambassador to Great Britain

It was upon this that we were yet undecided until this afternoon. Secretary Stimson, as a wise and constructive leader, was resolved upon keeping the delegation united upon methods of negotiation, as well as upon the subject of them, and wished agreement upon these methods before he talked with MacDonald and the Japanese.

Knowing that Robinson had views upon the subject, which he had not yet generally expressed, and that he and Adams felt alike the desirability of maintaining until the proper moment the asset of our prior demand for 21, 8-inch cruisers, I suggested early in the discussion that Robinson state what position he would take if he were in Stimson's place. This he did in such a clear, straightforward way that the discussion soon closed with the matter settled by the adoption of Robinson's suggestion by Stimson and Adams, the latter expressing himself as fully satisfied.

Robinson suggested, in short, that we should ask at once for a statement of the English proposition upon all categories, which would then be made under the pressure of our old 21, 8-inch cruiser proposition. We could then present our proposition without having lost whatever advantage that pressure involved in the formulation of the British demands.

Our situation is now as it was last summer. We can probably meet, with due regard to our equal naval strength, the English minimum in all categories considered necessary for its national security.

As the rest of the delegation had already expressed themselves as being satisfied with any method of negotiation which might be decided upon, this discussion between Stimson, Robinson, Adams and myself settled the matter.

The discussion as to global tonnage now going on in the Conference, practically, though not nominally, in plenary session, was really intended to "mark time" and give better opportunity to come to grips on the more important propositions, through informal conferences between the leaders of the delegations. It is now possible to make progress in the settlement of more important differences all around, and more or less side-track the "global" discussions which are forcing minor differences to the fore in the public mind in a way which may become embarrassing.

Journal as Ambassador to Great Britain

Yesterday all the delegation and their wives were entertained at lunch by the Prime Minister at Chequers.

We met him by arrangement on the road to Chequers at 10:00 A.M. and from then to lunch time he led us through the by-ways of Anglo-American and English history to Jordans, where William Penn and his family are buried, and the Quaker sect had its beginnings, to the seat of the Earl of Buckinghamshire, who showed us through his old mansion full of the relics of the Hampdens and the Cromwells, to the church near by where Hampden is buried, to the cottage where Milton wrote a portion of *Paradise Lost* and to Beaconfield, where, in its church, we stood uncovered by the grave of Edmund Burke.

It was a wonderful trip, the Prime Minister with his historically equipped mind acting as our kindly and considerate guide.

This evening, Lord and Lady Inverforth dine with us. He was Andrew Weir by name before his elevation to the peerage. We two had a dramatic duel on allied supply methods during the war before the French Cabinet with Clemenceau in the chair, and I am looking forward to the reunion with him, which we both have been trying to arrange for some time.

London,
Tuesday, February 4, 1930.

This morning passed in a three hours' conference of the American delegation. Secretary Stimson and Senator Reed reported on the conference yesterday afternoon which they, with Dwight Morrow and Secretary Adams, had with the Prime Minister and Henderson. They made no concessions on the twenty-one 8-inch cruiser proposition.

The important question still is as to three 8-inch cruisers to the United States versus five 6-inch cruisers in their place, just as it has been for some time, but progress was made upon the other points discussed.

Admirals Pratt and Jones were called before us, and told the situation. Both were strong in their opinions—Jones that we should stand firmly for twenty-one 8-inch cruisers to make the fleet most effective—Pratt that we should stand for eighteen 8-inch cruisers, which will give us five 6-inch cruisers additional.

To this small difference has apparently been reduced the question of substantial parity of the two fleets, now aggregating about 2,400,000 tons.

The delegation as a unit decided finally upon the American stand which should be submitted to Great Britain and Japan, and this afternoon in conference prepared a cable to President Hoover.

If, after conference with the Admiralty, MacDonald does not alter his present attitude, the prospect of agreement upon our proposition, substantially as it is, seems very good.

Senator Reed outlined our proposition also to the Japanese.

In the intermission between the conferences of the delegation, I attended the funeral of Lady Reading.

London,
Thursday, February 6, 1930.

Last evening our tentative proposition was shown by Secretary Stimson to MacDonald and by Senator Reed to Wakatsuki. It was to be held as secret.

This morning the press seemed to have information that the proposition had been submitted, and critics were claiming that the United States had surrendered to Great Britain in the cruiser contention.

At a meeting of our delegation this morning, it was agreed by all that the time had come for a public statement by our chairman, Secretary Stimson, as to our offer. Secretary Stimson asked for a discussion as to what this statement should cover. My own view, strongly held and strongly stated, was that this was the one great opportunity to fix in the public mind, not only the insignificance of our cruiser difference with Great Britain, but the fair and sensible settlement of it which we propose. Delay would lose us the inestimable advantage of the first statement. The statement, if made today, with a detailed explanation of our cruiser offer, including figures, would reach the public in tomorrow's papers as a very conclusive argument, appealing to common sense and appearing simultaneously with and as an answer to the attacks for our not insisting on 21 cruisers, a course which would have wrecked the conference.

After I had stated my views, I had to leave the meeting for a half hour to meet the new Minister from Afghan who, by previous appointment, was to be at the Embassy at 12:30 P.M.

It seems that after my departure it was left with Senator Robinson to prepare a Press statement, but settled that it was not to include cruiser figures. This latter, it afterwards developed, was not Senator Robinson's idea; but he prepared a statement without figures as to cruisers, feeling he was under such instructions.

In the time elapsing before the meeting of the delegation at 4 P.M., I made a condensed statement of the cruiser offer, with figures, which was at the same time a simple explanation and a common-sense argument for it.

At the meeting when Senator Robinson and I handed in our two papers, it was agreed that the statement to the press should cover both. Accordingly, Secretary Stimson united them in his statement, changing them very little.

The inclusion of the cruiser argument, in my judgment, will be found to have greatly influenced the trend of editorial opinion. My desire to present this argument was heightened by the fact that Admiral Jones filed with the delegates a written copy of his views, adverse to our proposition.

My statement, as I handed it to the committee, was as follows:

The fundamental principle to be embodied in any naval treaty between the United States and Great Britain was agreed by both to be that of parity.

Although the gross tonnage of the two fleets to be equated in fighting effectiveness was 2,400,000 the Hoover-MacDonald negotiations last summer practically reduced the discussion to the comparatively insignificant one of a difference in their respective cruiser class tonnage of 24,000 tons and the equating of this small tonnage difference in terms of 8-inch and 6-inch cruisers.

To resolve this difference, the United States has now made a proposition under which, if accepted, the actual tonnage difference between the two cruiser fleets will be only 12,000 tons. In the large cruiser class, under this offer, Great Britain will have 15 and the United States 18, the United States being compensated for a reduction of three 8-inch cruisers by an increase of five 6-inch cruisers.

In connection with this offer, the United States makes this additional

Journal as Ambassador to Great Britain

proposition, to wit: (1) Great Britain shall have the option by reducing its number of small cruisers to increase its large cruisers from 15 to 18, so as to give it a total tonnage of 327,000 tons, the exact amount of tonnage which the United States now asks. (2) The United States shall have the option by reducing its large cruisers from 18 to 15 to increase its small cruisers so as to give it a total tonnage of 339,000, the exact amount of tonnage which the British now ask.

The following is the statement to the press, as issued by Secretary Stimson:

At the opening of the Conference, the United States delegation made no statement of its position of the needs of its country beyond the historical fact of the agreement in principle for parity between Great Britain and the United States. We are now in a position where we can go further. Following discussions among ourselves and negotiations with the British and Japanese which have clarified the limits of possible agreement, our delegation has made suggestions as follows:

(1) With Great Britain, immediate parity in every class of ship in the navy. The gross tonnage of these two fleets is substantially 1,200,000 apiece. The negotiations between President Hoover and the Prime Minister, Mr. MacDonald, last summer, practically reduced the discussion of parity between them to the comparatively insignificant difference in their respective cruiser class tonnage of 24,000 tons. We propose to settle this difference as follows:

Under our suggestion, the actual tonnage difference between the two cruiser fleets will be only 12,000 tons. Of the larger cruisers armed with 8-inch guns, Great Britain will have 15 and the United States 18, an advantage to the latter of 30,000 tons. Of the smaller cruisers armed with 6-inch guns, Great Britain will have the advantage of 42,000 tons. But beyond this, in order to insure exact equality of opportunity, the United States makes the suggestion that each country will have the option of duplicating exactly the cruiser fleet of the other. Thus Great Britain would have the option, by reducing its number of smaller cruisers, to increase its large cruisers from 15 to 18 so as to give it a total tonnage of 327,000 tons, the exact amount of tonnage which the United States now asks. On the other hand, the United States would have the option, by reducing its large cruisers from 18 to 15, to increase the number of its small cruisers so as to give it a total cruiser tonnage of 339,000 tons, the exact amount of tonnage which the British now ask.

In battleships we suggest by reduction in numbers on both sides to equalize our two fleets in 1931 instead of in 1942. At present the British battleship fleet contains two more vessels than ours. In destroyers and aircraft carriers we suggest equality in tonnage and in submarines the lowest tonnage possible. As is well known, we will gladly agree to a total abolition of submarines if it is possible to obtain the consent of all five powers to such a proposition; and in any event we suggest that the operations of submarines be limited to the same rules of international law as surface craft in opera-

143

tion against merchant ships so that they cannot attack without providing for the safety of the passengers and the crew.

(2) Our suggestion to the Japanese would produce an over-all relation satisfactory to us and, we hope, to them. In conformity with our relations in the past, it is not based upon the same ratio in every class of ship.

We have not made proposals to the French and Italians, whose problems are not so directly related to ours that we feel it appropriate at this time to make suggestions to them. A settlement of the French and Italian problem is essential, of course, to the agreement contemplated.

The United States delegates do not feel at liberty to discuss any further details in figures, and it is obvious that the announcement of hypothetical figures by others is calculated only to provoke argument.

Our delegation is in agreement on every item of our program, and we are in the most hopeful spirit that, in cooperation with the other delegations, the primary purposes of the Conference—namely, the termination and prevention of competition in naval armament and such reductions as are found consistent with national security—may be accomplished.

This is all that we deem it helpful to state until our suggestions have been considered by the delegations to whom they have been sent.

London,
February 9, 1930.

Sufficient time has now elapsed to make it possible partially to appraise the world reception of Secretary Stimson's public statement of the American position appearing in the papers of the morning of February 7th.

I believe it largely due to the explanation of the proposed adjustment of our cruiser differences which it contains that American public opinion seems to regard the offer as protecting the principle of parity between the American and British fleets. Our public had been educated to regard this cruiser question as pivotal; and thus, to have left it unexpressed and indefinite in the first statement of our position would have been, perhaps, a fatal error. The alternative to each nation of duplicating the other's cruiser fleet appeals in its fairness as much to the British as to the American public. It is chiefly responsible for a situation of public opinion which will make it extremely difficult for the big navy faction to make a mountain out of a mole hill of technical difference, for it answers their contentions with an argument which "the man on the street can understand."

144

ANDRÉ TARDIEU

Journal as Ambassador to Great Britain

The credit of the suggestion of the alternative to each country of the right of duplicating the other's cruiser fleet is conceded to Senator Swanson, of Virginia, a member of the Senate Committee on Naval Affairs. Our whole delegation in a cable to him sent by Secretary Stimson, expressed to him our sense of obligation at the time the statement was finished. M. de Fleuriau, the French Ambassador, called at the Embassy to say that Tardieu while surprised at the issue of the statement, saw no difficulties affecting the French suggested by it.

Morrow had unsuccessfully endeavored to see Tardieu the evening the statement was issued and show it to him before Tardieu left for Paris. Somebody else did show it to him, however, and Tardieu had expressed to MacDonald emphatically his surprise that Great Britain and the United States had agreed without consulting him. MacDonald explained that there was no agreement —that the statement was of the American proposition only and made because it was important that the public should have a right statement of it instead of a garbled one issued by the "leak" method which would otherwise appear in the press.

Stimson told me the above when I gave him de Fleuriau's message to me, and it explained de Fleuriau's purpose to let us know with Tardieu's authority, that he understood the circumstances which compelled the early issue of Stimson's statement.

Stimson has studied with care the technical naval questions involved. Because of this knowledge, gained through months of intensive investigation, as well as because he is a good tactician, he has placed the United States in a position of leadership in this Conference. He is patient and extremely considerate with his delegation. He keeps them all satisfied; but also keeps firmly in his hand the control of negotiations. In these he uses the members of his delegaion where they may be useful, but always directs and coordinates their activities.

He is a safe leader, not afraid to take individual responsibility where necessary, without hesitation, and yet wise enough to patiently explain all he does to his delegation. As a result, he has a united delegation behind him. As a body they are strong men, and only capable leadership would satisfy them. Their attitude toward him during all these difficult negotiations—composed as they are—is of itself a tribute to his unusual qualifications for his place.

Today we received the French tentative proposition, and yesterday, the Japanese. Both are extreme. And I am wondering if our battleship proposition made for "trading purposes" has not inspired a similar course on their part. When one makes a mistake, he should not fail to acknowledge it, and not add a weakness of character to an error of judgment. We should not have started in to trade in this matter. However, we have learned a lesson and will not make a similar mistake again.

I left at the office a new statement to be handed to Secretary Stimson this evening. Morrow, Robinson and I are agreed on it. This statement reads:

The informal discussions which are now going on are developing the differences which exist between us and are throwing light upon the form which the question covering them shall take so as to project them clearly in debate.

This is necessary to give the public a clear idea of what these differences are and what they involve.

This consideration of differences constantly tends to develop their comparative insignificance as related to the magnitude of the total quantity involved. Upon battleships as between Great Britain and the United States as in the case of cruisers, the progressive determination of the differences involves small quantities.

The battleships of Great Britain are now 20 in number, and the battleships of the United States are now 18 in number.

The present aggregate battleship tonnage of Great Britain is 606,450 and that of the United States is 532,400, both measured in Washington Treaty standard displacement.

This disparity in tonnage between the two nations is worked out by 1936 under the operation of the Washington Treaty, through the scrapping of ten old battleships by Great Britain and eight old battleships by the United States, and by the completion of five new 35,000 ton battleships by each nation. The Washington Treaty further provides for the beginning of five additional 35,000 ton battleships by each nation between now and December 31, 1936. These new battleships which it is contemplated by the Washington Treaty shall be laid down are for the purpose of replacing old battleships that go out of commission after 1936.

Assuming that satisfactory agreements can be made with reference to cruisers, destroyers and submarines, we propose that immediate parity in number of ships be reached by the scrapping now of five ships by Great Britain and three ships by the United States. If this is done, the respective fleets will be:

Great Britain, 15 ships, aggregate tonnage 472,550.
United States, 15 ships, aggregate tonnage 462,400.
Difference in favor of Great Britain 10,150 tons.

To cover this small difference of 10,150 tons in the respective tonnages the United States could either:

(1) Scrap another old ship of 26,000 tons and add one new ship of 35,000 tons, thus increasing by 9,000 tons our aggregate tonnage which will then be 471,400, or only 1,150 tons less than the fleet of Great Britain; or,

(2) Add approximately 3,000 tons each necessary to horizontal protection of five present ships, making a total addition of 15,000 tons, which would bring the total tonnage of the United States to 477,400 tons, an amount 4,850 tons in excess of the fleet of Great Britain. When Great Britain correspondingly modernizes two of her ships by adding 1,100 tons each, the tonnage difference between the two fleets would be reduced to only 2,650 tons.

It is believed that either of the foregoing alternatives would give parity in tonnage and fleet equality in effectiveness.

We have made two mistakes. The first one was when we included in the statement of our proposition which was handed to the other powers, the suggestion that a method of obtaining parity in the battleship class between Great Britain and the United States would be an option to the United States to scrap the *Wyoming* of 26,000 tons and build a new battleship of 35,000 tons, coupling this with a reference to equalling in fighting effectiveness the *Nelson* and *Rodney* of the British Fleet.

Our naval experts did not agree that this was necessary in order to give the fleets equal effectiveness, but in a preliminary informal conversation with MacDonald, when mentioned, he had then indicated no opposition to it. It was really inserted by us for trading purposes in order to fortify our contentions as to the other categories.

When the general proposition had been approved by the President and submitted to the other countries, Secretary Stimson made in general terms a statement for the press as to its contents, but including the detailed figures clearly explaining our cruiser position. As might have been expected, the propositions of the memorandum, although issued to the other Powers as a secret document, were later given in substance to the press. Immediately the *Wyoming* point, which we had regarded as a trading point, was severely criticized both in England and in the United States as being unfair and subversive of reduction.

The second mistake which was made then was not immediately to state our battleship proposition in the detail in which we had stated our cruiser position, so that the public could understand our whole position and not be led to believe that we had jeopardized agreement by standing alone upon what was stated to be an optional method. As a result, the Secretary is being criticized generally for poor management and the attention of the public, since it is uninformed as to the insignificance of the quantitative differences existing as compared with the total tonnage, which a proper statement would clearly have explained, is being diverted to a general discussion, not of our real battleship position, but to one we are assumed to have taken.

We have lost the great advantage of an immediate exposition of the real situation when the attacks first commenced. Every day's delay now in making this statement places us at an increasing disadvantage and increases also the confusion in the public mind as to the real issues. In all other preliminary negotiations, including those during the summer, which led up to the Conference, we have succeeded well in reducing differences to their simplest terms before making a public statement of them. In this way the insignificance of the quantitative differences, as compared with the total tonnage involved, was impressed upon the public mind. By Secretary Stimson's statement of the insignificance of these differences in the cruiser class, which is a critical question in the public mind, we have since had a clear demonstration that the public comprehends it properly. Editorial opinion in the United States is reported to us as being nine to one in advocating the justice and reasonableness of our cruiser position. If a proper statement of our battleship position was made now in the same relative form as Secretary Stimson's statement as to cruisers, our position would likewise, in my judgment, unquestionably receive the same general public support.

Emerson once said that "a man, to master an opportunity, must mount it on the run." We have lost by delay our best opportunity to properly impress the public mind with our battleship position. If we had not done so, our path would now be much smoother.

Such mistakes, however, involve methods and are annoying but not fatal ones. Many inferences which the press are drawing are very unjust to Secretary Stimson who had to bear the brunt of the mistakes of us all.

Journal as Ambassador to Great Britain

London,
Thursday, February 13, 1930.

The intricacies of a naval negotiation between five powers, each represented by a large staff, defy any attempt to detail them fully in contemporaneous notes. For the last few days, I have had a single-handed struggle with the whole delegation for an official explanation to the public of our battleship proposition similar to the one in which I engaged, with more immediate success, for a detailed statement of our cruiser proposition in Secretary Stimson's first statement. Today it seems that I am to succeed, though whether my statement, as revised in its technical references, will be issued tomorrow or later in a speech by Stimson remains to be seen.

It is most unfortunate, however, that so much time has been lost.

London,
Saturday morning, February 15, 1930.

Dictated at my office.

The statements now made by France and Japan regarding their naval requirements, considered with our own and that of Great Britain, indicate to my mind the probable course of negotiations. Each nation now has what it considers an irreducible minimum of requirements. This irreducible minimum renders impossible any agreement unless either an absolute break-up of the Conference or a public sense of the probability of it, establishes in the minds of the different delegations a new conception of what public opinion in their respective countries requires of them. In other words, the attitude of the different delegations toward their propositions is that each cannot safely make the concessions necessary to match the requirements of the others.

It is folly to waste time trying to persuade a delegation to reduce its minimum when we are unwilling to reduce our own. No spirit of compromise now governs this Conference, and it will not

149

govern it, in my judgment, until a break or the immediate prospect of one, when quantitative differences are so small, fires the indignation of the world.

From now on, until the real combat commences, the attempt to secure vital concessions necessary to agreement will fail, and time spent upon them is wasted. Only a little more time will be required for that exact statement by each delegation of its position which is necessary before the whole discouraging picture is developed.

I firmly believe that the longer we delay precipitating direct discussion between the delegations, even though it proves acrimonious, the worse we will make the situation. We should cease to camouflage present difficulties before the public. We should explain them. In international negotiations, attention can never be diverted from a mistake; and we have made one serious mistake affecting the future public attitude, which we have not, as yet, corrected by explanation.

Today's London *Times* indicates that an effort is now being made in the Senate of the United States to get the members to agree to oppose any treaty unless it provides that the British scrap a *Rodney* or we build one. Those making this effort know perfectly well that if that is to be our position, the Conference will fail. We have everything to lose by a delay in meeting this movement, by a statement of the facts and an explanation of the figures involved. As it is, our silence is an encouragement to the interested enemies of an agreement. This agreement is not going to be made if we proceed on the assumption that a naval technical argument is more appealing to the public of the world than a common-sense argument framed, of course, after a full consideration of both sides of any naval technical question.

We have a direct disagreement on the part of our naval advisers on our most crucial question, that of cruisers. The Japanese say they have a direct disagreement on the part of their naval advisers on the same question, to wit, the relative fighting effectiveness of the larger cruiser and the six-inch cruiser, and the numerical relation to each other which they should bear in a fleet properly organized for its best fighting effectiveness.

© *The Central News, Ltd., London*

THE DELEGATES TO THE LONDON NAVAL CONFERENCE OF 1930

Seated (left to right): Antonio Chiaramonte-Bordonaro, Italian Ambassador; Giuseppe Sirianni, Italian Minister of Navy; David A. Reed, U. S. Senator; Joseph T. Robinson, U. S. Senator; Charles G. Dawes, U. S. Ambassador; Henry L. Stimson, U. S. Secretary of State; Ramsay MacDonald, Prime Minister and First Lord of the Treasury; Arthur Henderson, Secretary of State for Foreign Affairs; Aristide Briand, French Minister for Foreign Affairs; Jacques-Louis Dumesnil, French Minister of Marine; Aimé de Fleuriau, French Ambassador; Reijiro Wakatsuki, Member of Japanese House of Peers; Takeshi Takarabe, Japanese Minister of Marine; Tsuneo Matsudaira, Japanese Ambassador.

Standing: Colonel Sir Maurice Hankey, Secretary-General of the British Delegation; Admiral of the Fleet Barone Alfredo Acton, Senator of the Realm (Italy); C. T. te Water, High Commissioner for the Union of South Africa; J. E. Fenton, Australian Minister for Trade and Customs; Dwight W. Morrow, U. S. Ambassador to Mexico, Charles Francis Adams, U. S. Secretary of the Navy, Hugh S. Gibson, U. S. Ambassador to Belgium, A. V. Alexander, First Lord of the Admiralty; Wedgwood Benn, Secretary of State for India; René Massigli, French Representative on the League of Nations, Henry Moysset, Director of the Office of the Prime Minister (France); Philippe Roy, Canadian Minister to France; T. M. Wilford, High Commissioner for New Zealand; Prof. T. A. Smiddy, High Commissioner for the Irish Free State; Sir Atul C. Chatterjee, High Commissioner for India; Matsuzo Nagai, Japanese Ambassador to Brussels.

These technical questions relating to five categories in each of the five naval fleets, with a question involving one category generally affecting all other categories, are responsible at the present time for a daily grist of conflicting expert opinions comparable only to a snow-storm and tending to completely befuddle the average mind.

It reminds one of the situation in which the statesmen and economists of the Reparation Commission had involved themselves when, in despair, they threw up their hands and appointed our First Committee of Experts. Our only advantage is that this Conference is not yet so enveloped in the arms of the technical octopus that it cannot disentangle itself and is still able, therefore, to exercise its common sense. However, to release it, there should be an early demonstration to the world of what is the fact, that the Conference is steadily getting farther away from agreement instead of approaching one. We are trading, not trusting. We walk around each other and measure each other and suspect each other, as if we were engaged upon a mission of war rather than one of peace. On the surface it may not look so, but this is the fact.

Now that the naval technicians have all been heard and each delegation has practically all the technical information on each side of a question which it, at any rate, can understand, it develops that no delegation is talking compromise unless propositions by which another is asked to concede something are camouflaged by that name.

To my mind, the obvious course in wisdom to pursue now is to develop immediately and strongly our differences in direct discussion, without seeking to withhold from the public a knowledge of our acute and dangerous position. A solution is to be reached through the public pressure behind a common-sense agreement, and a relegation of technical arguments involving in their complexity the methods of infinitesimal calculus. We will not get this public pressure until the public is aroused in the present situation.

We must finally come, if we are to succeed, to the discussion and compromise of quantitative differences which have been so developed and so reduced in their terms as to create in the minds of the world a sense of their relative insignificance as compared with the total tonnage of the navies involved, and the desirability of a peaceful and common-sense adjustment of them.

London,
February 16, 1930.

Caro and I attended a lunch given by Secretary and Mrs. Stimson to the Dominion delegates. After lunch, a discussion of the naval problem occurred. Secretary Adams was present. I expressed the line of thought of my yesterday's dictation at the office, and elicited sympathetic responses from James E. Fenton, of Australia, Charles T. te Water, of South Africa, and Timothy A. Smiddy, of Ireland.

Secretary Stimson suggested that I speak over the wireless tomorrow night on an American broadcast, but I decided that this was not the time. Stimson also read me a letter he was sending to the President which would indicate that the President is somewhat concerned about our publicity in the United States.

When I got home this evening, I called my stenographer and dictated the following memorandum which expresses my present views.

MEMORANDUM

The optimistic generalities incident to the speeches with which the Conference opened were useful as voicing a world attitude deeply concerned with the success of this Conference. But after one month of negotiations, largely informal between the delegations, in view of their results, this is no longer the time for optimism but the dispassionate review of the inherent difficulties of the situation which, in all probability, only informed public opinion can resolve.

For the most part, thus far in our informal conferences, we have been talking figures and trades, not peace pacts or their desirability. It has been necessary for us to walk around each other and measure each other much as if we were engaged upon a mission of war rather than one of peace.

The naval problem involves in each country a technical, economic and political question, with each of these three elements of the problem varying in their relative importance to each other in each country. Then each of the five navies of the Powers is divided into at least five categories of ships, and

152

Journal as Ambassador to Great Britain

in determining the fighting effectiveness of a fleet, each category must be considered in its relation to every other category. Each of the five Naval Powers also has different defensive home requirements, such as the policing of trade routes and the administration of colonial possessions, and these needs require consideration in the determination of the make-up of their fleet. All the three elements of each nation's general problem—the political, the technical and the economic—must be considered in connection with each of these other questions.

It is no wonder, considering the complex problem each delegation has had to consider in relation to its own navy, that such stated national requirements as have yet been announced by the delegations differ from the conception of them which other delegations had, for it must be remembered that the naval requirements of the Powers are relative and that each delegation, in determining the requirements of its own nation has been figuring on the naval requirements of the others as well. It is now evident that the attitude of the different delegations toward their respective propositions, so far as announced, is that each cannot safely make the concessions necessary to match the requirements of the others. The public sentiment of the world, as interpreted by the delegations, has not yet expressed its opinion strongly enough to assure any high hope of a final adjustment. That it will so express itself finally I have little doubt.

What has happened was to be expected, for the inevitable effect of the necessary methods followed in order to develop the final statement of national positions and define the differences in national requirements is to make the position of each delegation more nationalistic, and to relegate for the time being the inevitable contest to adjust these national differences into a plan of disarmament and reduction consistent with the spirit of the Paris Pact and world opinion.

Up to this time the controlling idea in each delegation necessarily has been the formulation of that compromise between the views of the big navy partisans and their opponents in its own country which, beside assuring national security, will be acceptable to its general public opinion. Thus formulated through this compromise within itself, the position of each delegation represents what seems to it now an irreducible minimum. These minimums in national requirements, as now expressed in the aggregate, have produced a present impasse in the Conference. Since all national naval requirements are relative, the final adjustment of the combined requirements to a world demand for disarmament and reduction is not impossible. This impasse is but the natural result of the first definition of the differences, and from now on the discussions of the differences should clarify the public opinion of the world as to their significance as a whole in relation to the total naval tonnage under discussion and the desirability of a settlement.

A general knowledge of the existence of this impasse which at present seriously endangers the success of the Conference is necessary to develop the real strength of public opinion in each country on the question of the world naval disarmament. Without the full development of public opinion there is little probability of any material change in delegation attitudes as to their present national propositions, determined as they are by present conceptions of the state of public opinion in the respective countries.

153

The present, therefore, is not a proper time to attempt to create an unjustified impression upon the public of the prospects of an agreement. Public opinion should not be lulled into inaction, but rather stimulated by clearly indicating the actual situation of the Conference, which is at present most discouraging, and will become more so without an additional impact of public opinion, which will come when the real seriousness of the crisis is understood.

The progressive simplification through informal conferences of the terms of difference between the delegates should soon make possible that simple form of statement of them which the Average Man demands and to which he is entitled. If these quantitative differences seem small, the perception of their relative insignificance as compared with the total tonnage of the navies involved, will fix the attitude of the Average Man everywhere for settlement and the attitude of the Average Man is what we call public opinion. He well understands that the issue at stake in this Conference is the cause of world's peace, and that the Conference was called to advance this cause, not to kill it. But whether these quantitative differences seem small or large, when a clear statement of them is made and the Average Man knows that the Conference regards them as insuperable, his authoritative voice will be heard. He will not be content with failure until this Conference, in words which he can understand and for reasons which he can grasp, expresses itself one way or another. If the first expression of the Conference is against world's peace, then, as has happened in international conferences twice in the present year, he will drive the delegations back for another effort. His is the power. The Conference but recommends to the nations. He decides for them.

London,
February 18, 1930.

The above memorandum was completed this afternoon—having been modified by me from time to time, to bring it fully abreast of the situation as I see it today.

Secretary Stimson has asked me to speak in his place at the Pilgrims' dinner for Sir Esme Howard on March 4th; and this evening I left this speech with Dwight Morrow to be handed to Stimson for comment. It represents my ideas of constructive instead of passive publicity and epitomizes what I have been trying to impress on the delegation for over a week. All say now they agree with the views, but they ask whether this is the time to express them. Already, by indecision, in explaining our battleship stand, we have armed our enemies with an argument which, in the future, we shall certainly have to confront.

After reading my speech, Dwight Morrow thinks it ought to be

154

made at the dinner of the Pilgrims, but Stimson, of course, must make the ultimate decision. The impasse will probably be the same then as now, and yet time alone will determine what it demands.

Yesterday, the French Government fell. Premier Tardieu, for the minute, is left hanging in the balance, but not before he had left the whole Naval Conference hanging in the balance by filing a statement of French naval requirements before he went to Paris. His figures are so high that Great Britain says, in effect, that if they stand they must raise the British figures to the hammering down of which our whole summer's negotiations were devoted. On the other hand, the impasse with the Japanese, while at present not so spectacular, is just as threatening, indeed, to my mind, much more so.

And so we go on talking figures, discussing two-power pacts, three-power pacts or no pacts at all, as alternatives, as if we, instead of events, were in the saddle. Only one man must be put in the saddle for a time—Mr. Ordinary Man, of Everywhere.

London,
February 22, 1930.

This is Washington's Birthday. The Conference having adjourned until next Wednesday on account of the fall of the Tardieu Government, diplomatic activities have lessened, although some informal talks between Stimson and MacDonald and between the Foreign Office and the Japanese have taken place.

At a long meeting of our delegation the other morning, the situation was reviewed. Apparently, the trend of things is toward a tripartite agreement between the United States, Great Britain and Japan as the outcome of the Conference. The attitude of France will largely determine this. If she holds out for the present program, it is this or nothing. And any agreement between the three greatest naval powers even then will be an unstable one, for Great Britain will feel obliged to keep its navy in proper proportion to that which France may hereafter build.

Journal as Ambassador to Great Britain

And yet, a three-power pact maintaining between themselves for the present, reasonable relations, will be an advance even though it contains a political clause under which the building by France will release Great Britain from the contract and, in consequence, the United States and Japan as well.

Such an agreement might produce a new *status quo* in French public sentiment, the effect of which cannot now be determined.

A menacing building program on paper is one thing. A menacing building in reality is another. The latter costs money, for instance; although, where nationalistic sentiment is aroused, this is but a slight deterrent. But after a three-power pact, involving the United States, Great Britain and Japan is put in force, there will be many considerations not now involved which might influence France to adopt a naval policy designed not to disturb it.

It is impracticable to cover in these notes discussions which daily change in their trends and subjects with changing events. It is events which determine our decisions. In international conferences nations generally act and talk like little children, until they are confronted with menacing facts.

There is no remaining difference of understanding between the United States and Great Britain of real importance; and if what we can agree upon did not depend upon what the other Powers will agree upon, we would soon be drafting details.

Since the arrival of the Secretary of State he has, of course, taken my place as the personal intermediary between the United States and Great Britain in the naval negotiations, that is between MacDonald and our delegation; but his opinion is as I state it above.

This week has witnessed the same series of distracting social activities as the last. Attended a banquet at Guildhall, given by the Government to the sponsors of the annual British Trade Exhibition, a lunch by the American Press Association to our delegation and a small dinner at Secretary and Mrs. Stimson's apartment before we went to a reception at Londonderry House, which was attended by Prince George, all the Conference delegates and the political, industrial and social leaders of Britain.

Today, as all our delegation is scattered, having seemingly ac-

BRITISH MUSEUM

quired the week-end habit, I spent the morning alone in that incomparable repository of man's achievements through the ages, the British Museum.

London,
February 25, 1930.

During the impasse in the Conference caused by the fall of the Tardieu Government, informal work of importance moves forward, and, particularly the conversations of MacDonald and Stimson which are ironing out the last small difference of 7,000 tons between the tentative positions of the United States and Great Britain.

Sunday evening, Alberto Pirelli, and his wife, dined with us at the Embassy. Pirelli is the valued economic adviser of Mussolini. After dinner, Dwight Morrow came and we discussed with Pirelli the naval situation and the Italian attitude toward it. It would seem that Italy has an opportunity to take a most helpful step at this juncture in forwarding the chances of a naval agreement.

Last night, at Henderson's dinner at the Foreign Office, Dwight Morrow and I had an interesting talk with Wakatsuki and Matsudaira. Wakatsuki's party in Japan (the Minseito) has just won a victory in the elections. While as yet nobody is receding from announced positions, the apparent impasse is inducing more thought of what a failure of the Conference will mean, and signs of a more general spirit of compromise are appearing.

The general attitude of pessimism which public opinion is assuming makes unnecessary, in my judgment, my speech designed to emphasize the discouraging situation in order to arouse the friends of disarmament; and I accordingly notified the secretary of the Society of the Pilgrims of Great Britain that in my speech I would propose the health of Sir Esme Howard, and, in speaking to it, would omit a naval discussion. This decision is my own.

Somehow I cannot but feel that France is not going to stand in the way of a satisfactory agreement, once she has made every effort to secure collateral security pacts. Briand will certainly make every effort to save the Conference which his domestic public sentiment does not absolutely forbid.

Last night I had an interesting talk with Lloyd George about Briand. "He is constructive," said Lloyd George, "but in this Conference he has his feet tied. In my post-war diplomatic negotiations with him, he would often take me aside and explain the handicaps of his situation. 'I would like to do as you wish,' he would say, 'for it is reasonable, but until my public opinion better understands, I cannot act.'" Lloyd George went on to say that Briand always told him the truth, and that he (Lloyd George) accepted at once and without argument his positions when explained as above.

Lloyd George, however, expressed to me his belief that this time the knot around Briand's legs is very tight. Whether this is so or not will be determined alone by French public opinion.

London,
February 25, 1930.

LATER. My wife and I have just returned from one of the most interesting dinners of our stay here, given by the Archbishop of Canterbury, at Lambeth Palace. There were present six guests besides ourselves—Lord and Lady Sumner, Goeffrey Dawson, the able editor of the *Times,* and Mrs. Dawson, and Mr. Pinckney and his wife.

After dinner, the Archbishop, with whom I have become well acquainted, at various functions, volunteered to take us through the older part of the palace. We went to the old crypt, of date 1180, where John Wyclif was tried the second time, passed the prison room of Essex, and wandered through the halls centuries old when Columbus sailed. With our cultured and intellectual friend, the Archbishop, as a guide, himself as impressive as his surroundings, this little journey of exploration will be a lasting memory to us.

This afternoon at 4:30, I attended the meeting of the Board of Governors of the Peabody Donation Fund, now in its 65th year, being, as Ambassador from the United States, an ex-officio member of this body. The Duke of Devonshire presided.

158

Journal as Ambassador to Great Britain

London,
Wednesday, February 26, 1930.

A long meeting of the delegation this morning.

Agreed that we favor going ahead without awaiting the outcome of the French Cabinet crisis. We discussed terms of possible agreement with Japan.

London,
Sunday, March 2, 1930.

The situation in the Conference is about the same, and will be for a time until the French parliamentary situation is resolved. As to the informal negotiations going on, the United States and Great Britain have now reached an agreement which, however, may be upset unless we both come to a satisfactory agreement with Japan, and unless Great Britain comes to an understanding with France.

London,
Wednesday, March 5, 1930.

A long meeting of the delegation this morning. The President, having inferred from the press reports received in America that France is determined to impede the agreement, has cabled the delegation suggestions as to procedure to forward a three-power pact. But at least until Tardieu arrives on Saturday, and the real position of France is better defined, no final decision as to wise procedure in this matter is possible. Procedure on a three-power basis must be determined when we know the effect on the British attitude of the final French position. Again, we have not yet settled our cruiser differences with Japan in agreement with Great Britain.

Walter Edge, our Ambassador to France, has arrived from Paris, firmly believing that France does not intend to block but rather to help things. Primarily, her efforts probably will be to get Great Britain into a Mediterranean Locarno and then, if unsuccessful, to get us to favor some kind of an addendum to the Kellogg Pact. But until Great Britain and France thresh their matters out more definitely, for us to abandon any hope for a five-power pact and to interject independent proposals looking to a three-power pact would probably result in no pact at all. Of course, when a five-power pact is demonstrated as unattainable, we must center on the effort for the three-power pact.

Things on the surface look discouraging, but the fact is we have now gotten to grips and the real battle for peace is on. The world is aroused to the danger of failure to agree on disarmament, and the pressure of its opinion is being felt in stronger degree by all the delegations here, pushing them toward decisions. Our delegation shows no sign of losing its head or being forced to decisions which will be permanent, by any phase of public opinion which may be merely temporary.

Ultimate public opinion, not temporary opinion, is what we must satisfy. We have first access to the facts, not the public. Ultimately, the public will have the facts as we have them now, and will hold us responsible if we do not take present responsibility in guiding our actions in wise accordance with them.

Last night, I attended and spoke at a Pilgrims' banquet in honor of Sir Esme Howard, the retiring Ambassador of Great Britain to the United States. The chairman was Arthur Henderson; and Sir Esme, Sir Ronald Lindsay, the new British Ambassador to the United States, and I were the other speakers.

London,
March 9, 1930.

Dwight Morrow has been with me at the house all the afternoon, and we have had a session of two on the situation of this Conference.

France wants a real security agreement or a large navy. We cannot involve ourselves in a purely European entanglement. Therefore we cannot give her a security pact. She does not need security from us, nor do we from her. It is for France and Great Britain between themselves to agree or not to agree on this se-

ARTHUR HENDERSON

curity pact for the Mediterranean. This will then fix the English position in the Conference and we will then be compelled, under the parity principle, to establish the equality of our fleet with the fleet that Great Britain regards as necessary to insure her security against the French fleet.

Obviously, we cannot reach an agreement with Japan until we finally agree with Great Britain or in other words until Great Britain agrees with France or decides not to agree. If Great Britain and France do not agree, then a three-power pact, with a political clause applicable to all, under which Great Britain can withdraw under a menace of French building, is the only constructive outcome of the Conference.

This seems to be the crux of the situation. But the real issue must now be forced. It is no longer the time to evade it. Our nation is ready to act; and if Great Britain and France do not soon settle their own differences, we must take some step which will precipitate the exact situation in the public mind. We must call on the last reserve—the pressure of the public opinion of the world when properly informed.

One feels the disadvantage of committees at such a time. Inaction now is above all dangerous. Once the facts are evolved, deliberation is all right but action is imperative. Only action causes events and only events will now insure public pressure.

If there had been between Great Britain and France before this Conference some preliminary diplomatic negotiations covering months, such as took place between us and Great Britain, with Japan fully advised, in my judgment it either would not have been called, or we would now be drafting an agreement.

But this is no time for excuses.

Yesterday (Saturday), together with three other members of the delegation—Senator Robinson, Secretary Adams and Ambassador Gibson—and a considerable party, including our wives, we took lunch with the Duchess of Norfolk at Arundel Castle. Sir Esme Howard and Lady Isabella were there.

Friday, I had a congestion of social tasks. After a morning devoted to the meeting of the delegation, I participated during the balance of the day as follows: (1st) In a luncheon given by Mr. Briand and the French delegation to the members of our delegation. (2nd) In a reception at 4:30 given to the delegates at the Middle Temple. (3rd) In a dinner at 8:00 P.M. in honor of the 80th birthday of President Masaryk, of Czechoslovakia, at which I spoke, as did Arthur Henderson, Ambassador de Fleuriau, Wickham Steed and others. (4th) And finally, at 10:30 P.M., in a reception to the delegates given by the Speaker of the House of Commons in Westminster Palace.

Last night (Saturday) came the sad news of the death of ex-President Taft.

This depressed me, for I greatly admired him. His public life was a triumph of principle and usefulness.

Down in the Dominican Republic there has been a revolution —apparently bloodless—which seems to have forced President Vasquez from office. Thus our new government business system and departmental reorganization there will probably soon be set aside. It has had, however, about ten months in which to demonstrate its beneficial effect in concrete results and sooner or later, if it goes by the board temporarily, some government should come back to it.

London,
March 12, 1930.

Secretary Stimson has wisely put an end to the discussion of a possible participation in a security or even consultative pact on the part of the United States by announcing to the press that it will not take place.

The United States desires to remain aloof from entanglements in European controversies. Even a consultative pact made by the United States, as an inducement to France to lessen her naval demands, would imply a naval obligation to France. Fair dealing demands a frank statement of national intentions at such a time as this. Without them, peace pacts themselves may contain the seeds of future international misunderstandings and controversies. Our country's stand should be a clear-cut one.

The Conference as a whole is at an impasse, so far as a five-power pact is concerned until the French break it. I find hope in the constructive purpose of Tardieu and Briand, and I trust that the expected statement of Briand will open the way for an agreement.

A correspondent in the London *Times* this morning says that Briand is thinking of proposing a "five-power pact covering technical points on which unanimous agreement can be reached and including a larger British-American-Japanese agreement, the tonnage figures in the five-power agreement to be the maximum demanded by the different countries, with the understanding they shall be reduced if and when some later arrangement on the political question can be made."

If this has any authoritative basis, it indicates that, as I expect, France will not try to block a three-power agreement, at least. In other words, I believe that France, in a spirit of sincerity, has stated what she believes she needs for her proper protection, and not with any ulterior motive of blocking any possible constructive outcome of the Conference as some are suggesting. We are still not agreed with Japan, but our differences are now too small not to be finally resolved.

Last night, I dined with the Japanese delegation and others as the guest of Sir Roderick Jones, the chairman of Reuters Ltd. Had a talk privately with Matsudaira after the dinner.

MacDonald's Government had an adverse vote in Parliament last night on the amendment to the coal bill. This, in itself, will not mean a resignation, but it is significant of the precarious tenure under which the present Government exists.

Our flag on the Embassy is at half-mast on account of ex-President Taft's death, and all social engagements of the delegation have been cancelled for the week.

London,
Thursday, March 13, 1930.

The delegation was assembled this afternoon to hear and ratify a report from Senator Reed, who has finally effected a tentative agreement between us and the Japanese. Stimson has taken this settlement over to show Henderson. It will no doubt be acceptable to the British. While it is not exactly what either the Japanese or we would like, it is near enough to what would suit each as to make it defensible before the public of both countries.

In large 8-inch cruisers, we take 18 and they 12. In destroyers we take 150,000 tons and they 105,000 tons. In submarines we come down to 52,000 tons each. In light cruisers we make them a reasonable concession.

Senator Reed deserves great credit for his ability and patience in conducting this long negotiation. He has not only technical knowledge but a remarkable gift of clear and condensed explanation of involved questions.

Briand, who was expected today to make a dangerous ultimatum, has again postponed it after being appealed to by Stimson and Morrow. Morrow had talked with me about the method he proposed to follow with Briand before he left for the visit, and in his report to me this evening of what occurred, the effectiveness of that method was evident despite Dwight's modest reference to it. It involved a suggestion that Briand, the Conference savior of the past, should now, as a leader, save this one.

Briand did not expect us to promise a security pact, nor did he resent our position in refusing it. He does expect Great Britain in some way to compensate France with added security for a diminished navy.

During MacDonald's visit to the United States, he and the President (October 9, 1929) issued a joint statement in which the following appears:

"The part of each of our Governments in the promotion of world peace will be different, as one will never consent to become entangled in European diplomacies, and the other resolves to pursue a policy of active cooperation with its European neighbors. But each of our Governments will direct its influence toward securing and maintaining the peace of the world."

To the principles thus announced, we are adhering; but Mac-Donald's attitude (which probably reflects British opinion) in refusing France a security pact is somewhat inconsistent with his statement above.

The crisis in the Conference, therefore, still continues.

Journal as Ambassador to Great Britain

London,
March 16, 1930.

Today MacDonald is entertaining Tardieu (just arrived yesterday evening) and Briand at Chequers; and the future of a five-power pact largely depends upon the outcome of their conversation.

For the moment, Stimson, having announced the American position as against a security pact involving America, awaits MacDonald's effort to modify the British-French *status quo*.

At present we seem assured at least of a three-power pact with political clauses. But by the position France finally takes will its form and the measure of relief in naval disarmament and competition be largely determined.

Spent yesterday morning with Secretary Adams at the British Museum. I am finding him a delightful associate with a fine sense of humor, and a solid possession of ability, character and common sense.

At ten o'clock this morning, the delegation met to hear reports from Secretary Stimson as to the present status of the preliminary negotiations between the heads of delegations and to discuss our own attitude as to methods of procedure at the plenary session tomorrow.

Tardieu having announced his intention to make a statement of French naval requirements on that occasion, the rest of the leaders of delegations, very mistakenly, in my judgment, accepted an arrangement under which the other delegation heads would make similar statements.

Stimson read a statement of our own requirements that he had prepared, and expressed doubts as to whether he should make it.

My own remarks were to the effect that this method of procedure would tend to put the whole situation back where it was when, months ago, we started our diplomatic negotiations in order to resolve differences instead of emphasizing them. I strongly advocated saying nothing at all, irrespective of the others, but urged an immediate attempt to get MacDonald and Wakatsuki to forego such speeches, which would leave the floor to

165

the French and Italian expositions. My statement only accorded with the sentiments of all others, including Stimson.

The latter made a telephonic engagement with Wakatsuki and MacDonald whom he saw within a short time.

I have not seen him since his return (this is written at 4:00 P.M.) but Arthur W. Page reports that both MacDonald and Wakatsuki are in somewhat of a quandary after Stimson's call; but are considering omitting their speeches.

Senator Robinson and I and Senator Reed (if he gets back to the office) are going to call on the Japanese delegation at 5:00 P.M.

This problem of procedure is most important. The arrangement which has been made, due to Tardieu, I have fought against right along and under instructions from our State Department. It will be a great mistake, in my judgment, if we abandon our methods.

London,
Tuesday, March 18, 1930.

From the Chequers conference, Tardieu professes encouragement, MacDonald the opposite. The latter says the talk was a warlike conference. But Tardieu has the final decision and thus is best qualified to interpret the situation. He has left for Paris but is coming back. In the meantime, the fate of the five-power pact is in the balance, and the ratification by the Japanese Government of the agreement between the Japanese delegation here and our own, has not yet been received. This is one of the "down" days; but in this kind of negotiation the "down" days are often in themselves the cause of "up" days. They induce reflection upon alternatives and inspire greater effort.

The amazing thing today is a report, apparently authentic, of efforts by the Admiralty section of the French delegation to persuade the Japanese to alter the terms of our agreement as to submarines.

Stimson came to my office for quite a talk yesterday. He is carrying a heavy load, but never shows the white feather or a slackening of effort because of discouraging circumstances.

Journal as Ambassador to Great Britain

I suggested to him, Reed and Morrow, this morning, that an effort should be made to get Mussolini, the Italian Premier, to come here. There are three European naval powers represented at the Conference. Great Britain and France are represented by their respective Prime Ministers, and Italy should be by its Prime Minister. I am sure of this: that, if between Italy and France the same direct and thorough methods of study and continued contacts were maintained such as we have maintained with Great Britain and Japan, an agreement upon a quantitative basis could be found between them which would compel the surrender of respective national pride to common sense.

This happened to Japan and to ourselves. When we stopped talking so much about ratios and commenced to talk tonnage and figures, we agreed, and only then.

Italy has been talking "parity" without giving figures. Like faith, "parity" without works is dead. Figures and facts are the best guide to common-sense distinctions. If Mussolini were to come, he would not, and could not, avoid them. The more powerful a centralized power, the less certain can it be of the wisdom of the advice of its delegates acting at a distance.

Power on the ground correctly measures its environment and its possibilities. Power at a distance never knows to what extent the timidity of its agents colors their reports. Before this Conference is allowed to fail in a five-power pact, an effort should be made to get Mussolini here.

The *New York Times* of Monday, March 10th, has reached me. It contains the text of the Prime Minister's speech, which, on March 9th, he broadcasted throughout the United States and Canada. A portion of it reads:

If you hear one day that we are in difficulty, another day that we have stuck, that may well be so; but do not then imagine that we are sitting in despair. Rather picture us thinking and planning, composing and arguing, trying to find ways out. We shall not give up until human ingenuity and patience have been exhausted, and that is a long way off yet.

I should like to take you back for a moment to that peaceful and sunny day I spent with President Hoover in the forest hollow on the hills of the Rapidan. We faced our difficulties which were as real, if not quite so complicated as those which we daily face among the problems of the Conference in St. James's Palace. While still in London, General Dawes and I talked of

167

troublesome programs. We had argued about guns and categories. We were never unmindful of national honor, security, needs which every now and again seemed to bring us into a rivalry which appeared to defy our good will. It was this Conference in miniature. We succeeded because we were determined to succeed and because we knew that there was more honor, more security, more peace in an agreement than in rival navies. Neither of us gave away a ton which was dishonorable or was a weakness.

Then I went to Rapidan and, on the 9th of October the President and I issued in the name of our two nations a statement of great historical importance, containing the following sentence: "The part of each of our governments in the promotion of world peace will be different, as one will never consent to become entangled in European diplomacies, and the other resolves to pursue a policy of active co-operation with its European neighbors, But each of our governments will direct our influence toward securing and maintaining the peace of the world."

This declaration has not been departed from in the transactions which have been going on here. It has been the basis of our cooperation, and our American friends may rest assured that we shall depart neither from the letter nor from the spirit of this pronouncement. We shall not agree to any treaty which may result in entangling military alliances, but we shall cooperate in securing and maintaining the peace of the world. Some of us will strive to secure as an essential part of the agreement a pledge of good-will and pacific intentions similar to that which was made by the President and myself after we had convinced ourselves that a naval agreement was possible.

London,
Friday, March 21, 1930.

The best way to forecast the position which a foreign nation will probably take in an international negotiation is to consider the position our nation would take under the same circumstances. A proper appraisement of probable consequences is the most important element in the formulation of wise procedure.

The above has been my text in recent important meetings, because growing irritation, with the position of those not yet agreed, has created a dangerous tendency on the part of those who are agreed, to break out in public criticism.

On Wednesday, after a meeting of our delegation all the morning, Stimson had a lunch at his hotel apartment at which MacDonald, Alexander, Morrow, Reed and I were present. The discussion largely concerned procedure. At first, MacDonald and Stimson advanced the idea of a plenary session to show the public our exact situation. The First Lord of the Admiralty,

Alexander, demurred somewhat to this, and I then entered the argument.

I said that such a course which could only be dictated by a desire to evade temporary press criticism would, in my judgment, be disastrous in the present status of our negotiations. It would not silence or answer press criticism, but only stimulate it. A plenary meeting at this time to air differences was a confession of an inability to resolve them before the possibility of resolving them was exhausted. It would set the world to debating questions without technical knowledge which they expected and appointed us to solve with technical knowledge and advice. It was a mass abandonment of leadership and would probably result in disaster to the Conference.

The only proper time for the next plenary meeting was when the Americans, British and Japanese were decided, first, upon the terms of a three-power pact between themselves, and second, after this decision, not until they had decided also that further negotiations for a five-power pact would be useless.

I pointed out that a plenary session now to outline the status of negotiations would not only destroy any chance of a five-power pact, but would place added power in the hands of the enemies of any agreement to destroy any chance of a three-power pact which now seemed not only a possible but a probable outcome.

After I was through, this view seemed to prevail, for the balance of the time was spent in considering more practicable steps. From this long meeting, consuming about two hours, I carried away two lasting impressions—one of the Prime Minister's breadth of view, common sense and wisdom, and the other of Dwight Morrow's wonderful mind, concerned this time with British and French naval figures and their relation to their relative fleet effectiveness.

The Prime Minister outlined his proposed statement to be given both to France and Italy as a suggestion of a "way out."

This morning, at a long conference, our delegation discussed procedure again, this time as to Japan. Our delegation agreed on a compromise, but this, while ratified by our Government at Washington, has not yet been approved by the Japanese Government. We wisely decided to await the Japanese answer, thus setting our course by the compass of common sense and not by the temporary gusts of press and public criticism.

Wednesday afternoon I spoke at the dedication of the new Nurses' Training School, given by the Rockefeller Institute for Medical Research to the University Hospital. Prince George presided.

Last night, Mrs. Masaryk, the daughter-in-law of President Masaryk, brought to me at the Embassy as a gift from President Masaryk, a large inscribed photograph of him in a silver frame, in recognition of my address on his birthday.

London,
Saturday, March 22, 1930.

The delegation met at Secretary Stimson's apartment at the Ritz for lunch and then attended the memorial service for Lord Balfour at Westminster Abbey.

At lunch the discussion related to the advices received from France to the effect that the French position is unchanged. This, together with the absence of both Tardieu and Briand, would seem to mean that we are to take the next step. I am far from regarding a five-power pact, even under the present circumstances, as unattainable. France has only stated her case as we would state our case were we in her position. After Locarno, especially, she views with concern Great Britain's attitude against a security pact, and feels if, in the future, she must rely only upon herself, that it is not unreasonable to decline to agree not to build the navy she feels adequate to her own protection. But in the form she states her position, she does not close the way to a three-power pact or indeed to a reasonable five-power pact from her standpoint. So, at least until we hear from Japan which will be next week, we must avoid public statements as to positions and procedure.

Even if most of the delegations of other nations have about given up hope of anything but a three-power pact and are doubtful about that, I am glad to say that is not the case with our own delegation.

Journal as Ambassador to Great Britain

London,
Thursday, March 27, 1930.

NOON.

I have just returned from the King's levee at Buckingham Palace where, with my staff, I passed, with the other diplomats, before His Majesty, and will try to outline the naval situation before going to my óffice.

So much has transpired recently that details have been submerged in my mind by the importance of the guiding principle which has now become dominant in the discussions, and upon the establishment of which, now likely, depends an effective and constructive five-power pact. This guiding principle is the recognition of the right of France to security.

The French are now assuming openly the constructive role I have long been expecting them to play, and Briand has made a speech in France (Tuesday afternoon) which, to use the expression of the London *Times*, "is interpreted as a suggestion that France's desire for security may be satisfied, not by an agreement to take military measures against an aggressor, but by taking such steps as would prevent war and so render military measures unnecessary."

Stimson issued at midnight of Tuesday a memorable statement, clearly defining the American attitude as to a consultative pact in a way to be helpful and to respond favorably to Briand's advances. I insert it here:

STATEMENT BY THE UNITED STATES DELEGATION

At the headquarters of the American delegation, it was stated at midnight last night that no change had taken place in the attitude of the delegation in regard to consultative pacts, and that its attitude remained as its spokesman gave it out several weeks ago.

At that time it was made clear that America had no objection to entering a consultative pact as such. On the contrary, the United States is already a party to a number of treaties involving the obligation of consulting with other powers.

It will not, however, enter into any treaty, whether consultative or otherwise, where there is danger of its obligation being misunderstood as involving a promise to render military assistance or guaranteeing protection by military force to another nation.

Such a misunderstanding might arise if the United States entered into

171

such a treaty as a *quid pro quo* for the reduction of the naval forces of another power. That danger has hitherto inhered in the present situation, where France has been demanding mutual military security as a condition of naval reduction, as appears from her original statement of her case last December.

If, however, this demand for security could be satisfied in some other way, then the danger of misunderstanding a consultative pact would be eliminated; and in such case the question would be approached from an entirely different standpoint. In such a case, the American delegation would consider the matter with an entirely open mind.

Yesterday afternoon, the British Cabinet held a meeting. While it is stated that: "The British delegation is as firmly opposed as ever to any new military commitments of any kind, it is authoritatively stated that the Government is prepared to amplify and to explain any part of the Covenant of the League of Nations, of the Locarno, or Kellogg Pact which may be obscure or uncertain in the mind of any of the other powers. It would be ready to give an assurance that Great Britain would do all in its power to make these instruments effective."

As a matter of fact, this attitude of Great Britain, together with that of Briand and Stimson, should favor a five-power pact, for the reaffirmation of British support of Articles 8th and 11th of the League and its agreements with Italy and France and other European nations, made in connection with the proposed protocol of the League of Nations, gives France all the security which she now asks without entangling the United States in European conflicts.

Today, Briand is here and at three o'clock this afternoon the heads of the delegations meet for conference.

Senator Robinson, as I have said before, is in a powerful position on our delegation, and he is a constructive statesman. His services cannot be over-estimated; for his agreement to the United States position, as stated by Stimson, was absolutely required. He has that important essential to real usefulness in international negotiations like this—a willingness to work for the substance of things quietly and effectively, never caring for that temporary and dangerous personal exploitation which comes from the seeking of concurrent credit and publicity.

A sense of modesty, either congenitally or intellectually acquired, is an asset, the value of which in the important junctures of life is seldom realized, but existing, is often the unsuspected cause of public reputation and enduring fame.

I believe the Conference is approaching a successful ending. For two months it has been at work. To the general public of the world, realizing, as it does, the vital importance of its success, and that in its hands primarily lies a present advance or retardation of the cause of the world's peace, its progress may have seemed slow. But when the work of the last two months is considered at this time, when the Conference is at last ready to take final decisions, it is evident that its work in preparation for this period of decision, has not been unduly prolonged.

Five nations meet at this Conference. The navy of each has five categories to consider, and each nation is involved with different economic, technical and political questions. It is under these difficult circumstances that the Conference has finally reached a position where each nation, through its representatives, is about to take its final attitude on agreement or disagreement, because it has now in its mind, expressed in qualtitative terms, substantially what readjustments must be made in its navy to make possible the five-power disarmament pact. Up to this point, of necessity, the discussion of technical naval differences has made the Conference resemble one of war instead of peace. But this has been only because up to this time it has been impossible for it, with a resultant naval position thus determined, to consider from the higher standpoint the advantages or disadvantages to each country of a disarmament agreement. Now, the practical completion of the process of progressive simplification of technical naval differences to their present form enables the nations to think in terms of high alternatives. Shall this decision be to forward the cause of world peace or world war?

Each nation knows substantially what will be the cost to it, in naval terms, if the Conference is a success. Each nation knows also that the cause of the world's peace is at stake in this Conference. Because of the smallness of these quantitative differences, which should be easily resolved, I believe that in this last and most important stage of the Conference the political differences accompanying them will be resolved as well.

Journal as Ambassador to Great Britain

London,
March 25, 1930.

Today, Caro and I attended the annual court of the Governors of the Royal Free Hospital. In my remarks on this occasion, I said:

And against the magnificent background of these inspiring figures there was one phrase painted in small letters, shining as a jewel in a setting of gold. It was "Without letters of recommendation." That little phrase indicates that in carrying out the great humanitarian purpose of its organization, this institution in determining whom it shall assist considers neither race nor position nor power nor personality nor anything but the actual needs of an individual, friendless, helpless and hopeless as he may be.

And in so doing, it is fulfilling in its way the mission on earth of the Lord Himself, Who, at all times and everywhere, looking only to the needs of men, took upon Himself the burdens of the heavy laden and the suffering.

London,
Sunday, March 30, 1930.

Much has happened since Thursday. On that afternoon I spent most of the time in conference with Morrow, Robinson and Reed. Stimson, in the morning, had asked suggestions upon the form of a consultative pact which the delegation could accept. Some work had been done on this, and when I joined the discussion the following form was under consideration:

If the naval security of any signatory is threatened, the high contracting parties shall communicate with one another fully and frankly as to what pacific means may be adopted; but neither the agreement nor any consultation thereunder shall imply commitment on the part of the signatories or any of them to employ military force or to take any other coercive action. The obligation of the United States shall extend only to an examination of the situation as it may affect the interests of herself and her nationals.

This may be considered the "Robinson-Reed" draft, excepting the last sentence which I was told had been suggested by Stimson. I give it herewith, not because it or what we finally evolved from it may be what is finally decided upon—the President in the meantime having cabled some suggestions—but as giving an

174

idea of that careful and exacting consideration which must precede any final phrasing of an international pact.

The final form was based upon this statement, and was agreed upon by all after discussion by all. The first form, however, must be regarded as involving the most work and as enabling the rest of us to assist in the easier task of its revision to arrive at a form most likely to have a favorable reception in American opinion and to interfere least with the reaching of an accord between Great Britain and France on the difficult question of the French demand for reassurance as to security.

The final form upon which we reached agreement read as follows:

All disputes between the signatories hereto shall be settled by pacific means. The high contracting parties shall consult with one another fully and frankly as to what measures may be adopted to maintain peace among them; but neither this agreement to consult nor any consultation thereunder shall imply commitment on the part of the signatories or any of them to employ military force or to take any other coercive action.

Of the changes in the final form, the new first sentence was suggested by Dwight Morrow. The suggestions made by myself, which were accepted, included the omission of the last sentence in the first form, and the omission of the words in the first form reading: "if the naval security of any signatory is threatened" and the substitution of the words: "shall consult with one another fully and frankly as to what measures may be adopted to maintain peace among them" for the words in the first form: "shall communicate with one another fully and frankly as to what pacific measures may be adopted."

Secretary Stimson arriving from another conference, we submitted the final form to him, and he approved it, saying he would submit it to the President.

At lunch Friday, Briand and I had a private talk, with de Fleuriau, French Ambassador to Great Britain, as interpreter. In answer to Briand's question as to what I thought of the situation, I informed him confidentially in general terms of what kind of a consultative pact we possibly could agree upon in our delegation, and, of course, followed in outline the terms of our last draft. He expressed himself as entirely satisfied with a pact in such terms on the part of the United States, and stated that he thought the Conference would succeed in framing a five-power pact and that he would go to every possible length to bring about this result.

Yesterday, the President made a public statement to the effect that he was standing firmly behind his delegation. From this time on the able and hard working Secretary of State should be left more peace from a critical press. However, as Dean Swift says: "Censure is the tax a man pays for being eminent."

He might devote, I think, more time to cabling details to the President promptly; but he is heavily over-burdened, and one cannot judge without knowing all the circumstances.

The last week has been a tiresome one; but I enjoyed making a speech on the naval conference situation, ex tempore, at the Armourers' and Braziers' Company dinner.

Last night we entertained at the Embassy all of the staff which came with the delegation from America, including the Marines, and all of my Staff at the Chancery, secretaries, stenographers and clerks. About 115 sat down at the dinner tables, and seemed to enjoy the evening.

London,
Monday, March 31, 1930.

Attended a meeting of the delegation in the morning. Talk was limited only to a general discussion, as it is the British-French "move" now.

Before going to it, I had a talk with Jacques-Louis Dumesnil of the French delegation who was disquieted by the reports in the morning press as to the British attitude toward the French request for a security pact.

By tonight, however, the atmosphere has considerably cleared, for MacDonald and Henderson have submitted terms to Briand during the day which the latter has indicated to Stimson that he can accept.

A plenary meeting of the Conference will be held Friday and if the Japanese cabinet at its meeting tomorrow ratifies the agree-

UNITED STATES EMBASSY AT LONDON

14 Prince's Gate.

HENRY DAWES, SECRETARY TO THE AMBASSADOR

ment between our two delegations it may be that agreement upon a five-power pact can be announced in general terms.

Senator Reed has suggested an improvement in our last draft of a consultative pact. It is to insert the words: "what pacific measures may be adopted to maintain good relations" in place of the words: "what measures may be adopted to maintain peace among them." This makes the draft now read:

All disputes between the signatories hereto shall be settled by pacific means. The High Contracting Parties shall consult with one another fully and frankly as to what pacific measures may be adopted to maintain good relations among them; but neither this agreement to consult nor any consultation thereunder shall imply commitment on the part of the signatories or any of them to employ military force or to take any other coercive action.

Tonight we gave a dinner at the Embassy in honor of Secretary and Mrs. Stimson, at which over forty guests were present.

London,
Thursday, April 3, 1930.

The plenary session for Friday has been postponed pending the continuance of the British-French efforts to agree on the wording of what they both now seem to regard as an understanding.

The Japanese Government has ratified (with moderate reservations) the Reed-Matsudaira compromise, on which our two delegations have agreed. While the Japanese Government makes reservations, they are practically what had been expected, and are satisfactory to us and to the British.

The various discussions now going on are at present dealing with the remaining questions in a common spirit of constructiveness and desire to agree.

In general, it may be said that there is a good chance of British and French agreement. This may not eventuate. But the most important development resulting from the new and better atmosphere in which negotiations continue, is that at least a three-power pact, with a friendly French and probably friendly Italian attitude toward it, is possible. Some time ago it would have been difficult for the United States, Great Britain and Japan to agree upon a three-power pact without grave danger of offense to France and to Italy, which would prejudice future negotiations for disarmament and friendly cooperation with them hereafter.

If a three-power pact now results, it will be possible to drop the consultative pact idea. This will be somewhat of a relief to the President, although the innocuous pact that we have been considering seems defensible from every standpoint.

Stimson's first statement to the effect that we would favor such a pact if it clearly eliminated any obligation upon us to become entangled in European conflicts, was what gave the real stimulus to the present effort on the part of all to get together. The "consultative" pact idea, therefore, will have been a great factor in any success that the Conference achieves. Its psychological effect in demonstrating the sincerity of the American desire for agreement was very great at a time when it seemed to others that we, with lesser difficulties to face, were hanging back.

Stimson does not hesitate to put things before the President as they are, but at times his delay in doing so has, in my judgment, embarrassed the President.

At the meeting of our delegation this morning, only a part of us were present, as Briand and Massigli called on Stimson just before our session. Stimson and Morrow are now in conference with them. We discussed the final details regarding the Japanese reservations, and accepted the proposals of Senator Reed whose guidance has been invaluable in the matter.

(LATER)

Dr. Smiddy's dinner at the Union Club was a most interesting one. Talked with the Prime Minister, Matsudaira and Craigie. From what MacDonald and Craigie said as to their negotiations with the French, it is evident that little hope is entertained by them for an agreement between them, let alone the French-Italian agreement.

Journal as Ambassador to Great Britain

On Friday night at the Armory, I spoke at the annual dinner of the Honourable Ancient Artillery. Lord Denbigh, Colonel-Commandant, presided. It was a jolly and brilliant assemblage, the members appearing in their dress uniforms with their red coats.

An off-shoot of this organization, which was founded in London in 1528, or thereabouts, was established before the Revolution in Boston by some of its members who had emigrated there. As William Dawes, my great great grandfather, had belonged to the Boston company, called "The Ancient and Honourable Artillery Company," I was given a review by the Company as Vice President of the United States at Boston on the 150th anniversary of the outbreak of the Revolution and made an honorary member. For this latter reason, on Friday night, I was made an honorary member of the London organization, and given the regimental salute which they call the "fire."

The principal speakers on the toast list were the Earl of Denbigh, Field Marshal Jacob and myself.

Was shown the historical relics of the Organization, and through the old building with its fine rooms. Field Marshal Jacob and I were asked to sign a book which they keep as a modern extension of their "vellum" book of the 16th century. The latter was exhibited to us with its inscriptions by the 16th and 17th century Kings of England.

As the Naval Conference is marking time until the British and French decide to agree, or disagree, Caro, Henry and I spent the week end at the house of Captain and Mrs. Sandys Dawes at Mount Ephraim, Kent. We motored down Saturday morning, meeting our hosts at Frinsted at noon for the Tickham Hunt "point to point" steeplechase. In the most important four of the five races, a Dawes horse finished second in each of them. Sandys, Launcelot and Ivy rode their own horses, and Mr. McKeever (Betty's fiancé) rode one of Betty's horses.

The most exciting race was the Adjacent Hunts Ladies Race.

Journal as Ambassador to Great Britain

In this there were seven entries, but all the attention of the crowd, numbering at least 3500, was from the first upon Ivy (Launcelot's wife) and Mrs. Heald—two famous riders, two famous rivals, and two splendid-looking young women.

The race covered about three and one-half miles, and all around the course these two seemed never over a length apart. They rode like mad, and it was only by a neck that Mrs. Heald won. All the rest were distanced. Ivy said afterward that the fences were too low for her horse, and trained especially for high jumps, he lost speed by jumping too high. This made his start-off after a jump a little slower than her rival's horse.

"Slotty" (Launcelot) as usual rode in perfect form. He is famous in this neck of the woods. Sandys disclaimed praise in favor of "Slotty"; but I could see little difference between them, as riders. We stayed all night with Captain and Mrs. Dawes, and came home this afternoon (Sunday).

London,
April 12, 1930.

Since I wrote last, the final agreement has been reached in our Naval Conference, and two committees, one of jurists and one of technicians, are at work drafting a treaty. By last Tuesday, it developed that a complete five-power treaty as first proposed was out of the question.

A five-power agreement, however, will be drawn, postponing until after 1936 the replacement of capital ships and providing for the scrapping of a total of nine ships by the American, British and Japanese navies, namely, five by Great Britain, three by the United States, and one by Japan. It will further define aircraft carriers and outline the method of calculating naval tonnage, and, on the basis of a definition, if accepted, of special and exempt ships. It will contain an agreement on the unit size of submarines, and an agreement for a more humane use of the submarine in warfare.

All this will be agreed to by the five powers. A three-power pact, included as a part of the five-power pact, will then cover

180

the agreement for limitation of tonnage between the United States, Great Britain and Japan, under which the approximate tonnage of the three navies will be as follows:

	United States	Great Britain	Japan
8" gun cruisers	(18) 180,000	(15) 146,800	(12) 108,400
6" gun cruisers	143,500	192,200	100,450
Destroyers	150,000	150,000	105,500
Submarines	52,700	52,700	52,700

There will be no consultative clause. It has been a difficult negotiation.

If our objective had been only a three-power pact, our conclusion would probably have been vociferously acclaimed. Since, however, we did not achieve a complete five-power pact, probably as much will be said about our shortcomings as about our achievements.

In the case of the First Expert Reparation Committee in 1924, all concerned wanted an agreement, upon the proper terms of which its members differed at the beginning of the work. But in the present negotiation, besides the natural differences among those who desired it to succeed, we had a portion of the naval contingent in each country who wanted it to fail.

In line with the principles which I outlined in my Pilgrims' speech, the United States and Great Britain kept naval officers off their delegations. Although at the time of my address Japan seemed to approve it, she placed a naval officer on her delegation as delegate, as did also Italy.

As to our own naval advisers, some of them headed by Admiral Hilary P. Jones, while agreeing in general on other things, made a direct issue with Admiral William V. Pratt on the 8-inch cruiser question. I may possibly do him an injustice, but I inferred from Admiral Jones' statement to our committee that when we reached the difference of only three 8-inch cruisers (30,000 tons in aggregate) between Great Britain and ourselves, he regarded this point as one upon which we should break the Conference rather than compromise with Great Britain. As we were then endeavoring to equate two fleets, each of 1,200,000 tonnage, this illustrates how strongly some of our naval people felt. And it was more or less so with the naval officers of other countries, who naturally did not wish to see their ships sunk. This is why a complete mastery of the technical questions involved made Dwight Morrow and Senator Reed such invaluable and influential members of our delegation.

A thorough examination of every technical naval objection was made by our delegation with a full hearing of naval officers on both sides. It is agreed by all, I think, that the constructive and able work of Admiral Pratt, the Admiral in command of the American Fleet, has been a tower of strength to us, without which our difficulties might have been insurmountable.

Dwight Morrow is chairman of the Committee of Jurists and Sir Maurice Hankey is Chairman of the Committee of Experts, engaged in drafting the form of the treaty. Of Dwight I can justly say that he can highly qualify both as a jurist and as an expert.

The work of drafting is exceedingly difficult. The Americans and British, for example, want to cover in the preamble the connection of the new treaty with the Kellogg Pact. The French, to the contrary, wish to imply its dependence on a future, more comprehensive, treaty of the League of Nations, on which the League's disarmament committee has been working at Geneva.

The difference between the British and American attitude on the one part and that of France on the other manifests itself at all times during the Conference, and what is not bridged in a five-power treaty bobs up again in the abridged form.

London,
Sunday, April 13, 1930.

Only two speeches and four social affairs last week. This social debauch, for it has almost reached that stage, although now giving signs of waning, is only the same treatment that we gave the visiting delegates at the Washington Naval Conference in 1921–1922. I suppose it was inevitable here. The Minister of National Defense of Canada, James L. Ralston, a brilliant and most engaging man, said to me the other day that Mr. Smurg might well have been a naval delegate to London. In Max Beerbohm's

ADMIRAL WILLIAM V. PRATT

Journal as Ambassador to Great Britain

Hosts and Guests which Ralston quoted, Mr. Smurg is referred to as one "whose gratitude was as boundless as his appetite, and his presence as unsought as it appeared to be inevitable."

One of my speeches was made at the Embassy Thursday at 3:45 A.M. (9:45 P.M. Chicago time) by radio to a meeting of the business leaders of Chicago, under the auspices of the Association of Commerce and the Chicago Better Business Bureau. I received cables about the speech next day from Owen D. Young, my brothers Rufus and Beman, the latter from his place in Florida, Rawleigh Warner and Mr. Wieboldt, who is the President of the Better Business Bureau. The cable from Wieboldt read:

Twelve hundred business men cheered your speech five minutes. Radio network carried all over country. *Tribune* streamer morning quote Dawes *via* sea cheers city unquote. Abel Davis, toastmaster, called attention introduction your civic spirit talking during sleeping hours. Accept sincere thanks. Signed Wieboldt.

After all this introduction, the speech itself may seem an anticlimax, but here it is:

In my invitation to talk to this great gathering of the leading business men of Chicago it was suggested that I might say something about what is known of the good side of Chicago abroad. I started to do so but from my subconscious mind came the constant thought: what matters the intermittent praise or dispraise of great cities by individuals at home or abroad? What does it matter to Chicago what past or present generations may say about it? What has it mattered as they grew to the great cities of the world what countless forgotten individuals of the past have said about them? Their past is history; and their future is determined by events which are larger than those in the hands of any single generation of their inhabitants. Their lives span the long centuries. When a city reaches the position in a nation which Chicago has, its history runs parallel with that of the nation; its present is in most ways a reflection of the nation; its future is the future of the nation. Chicago needs no defense. This generation may fail to do its duty to her and to contribute to her onward step, but the advance of Chicago, inexorable, irresistible and imperial, goes on and will go on through the centuries. Nor does this generation of Chicagoans need defense. Its spirit is in no whit different from the unconquerable spirit of its forebears who first mastered the savage wilderness in its settlement less than a hundred years ago; and when, thirty-eight years later, grown already from a forest clearing to a great city, it burned to the ground, rebuilt it within the short span of two years.

Compare in your minds the city that it was twenty years ago with the

Journal as Ambassador to Great Britain

city of over three million peoples which confronts you today. Consider its phenomenal advance, not only in population but in educational and artistic achievement, and in industrial, financial and commercial power during the last twenty years—an advance unparalleled in the world's history. Consider the majestic and battlemented front of Michigan Avenue overlooking the Lake, and then think of it as it was twenty years ago.

Recall to your minds that first plan of Chicago which you saw in beautiful outline upon the walls of Daniel Burnham's architectural office twenty years ago, pronounced then by the fainthearted as but a beautiful dream, but now, after two decades of strenuous endeavor, a far-flung and magnificent reality before your eyes and those of the world. And then as well, on the cultural side consider only some of the outstanding achievements of recent decades—the Field Museum, the Opera, the Art Institute, the Symphony Orchestra, and the wonderful and brilliant growth of our two great universities. Consider all this, you who are obsessed by the fear that the organization of a few contemptible un-American gangsters cannot be mastered and stamped out by this generation of Chicagoans once it is aroused. They are but hornets in the flank of a lion, yet they are stinging the lion into action. Their buzzing, while it may interfere with perspective at home, does not do so abroad. In an article on the Chicago gangsters, by Mr. Edgar Wallace in yesterday's London *Morning Post,* I find this about Chicago: "Some day it will be the greatest city in the world. It will certainly be the center of the American earth, ethically as well as geographically. Its trade has already reached prodigious proportions. It has a strange kinship with British Canada that New York does not know. It is the healthiest city in the United States. I am not so sure that apart from its gang shootings, it is not one of the most law abiding."

It is only because Chicago is larger than in the old days that the greater emergencies which arouse its unconquerable spirit are more slowly sensed. For this reason only, from time to time, we may hear the piping chorus of weaklings intimating that this generation has lost the birthright of courage. But Chicago has sensed this emergency. This great meeting is an evidence of that. For a brief time, organized criminals, in league with politicians, have harried this generation of Chicago's citizens. When Chicago calls, its people answer. Difficulties do not seem to discourage, but inspire them. I speak with knowledge of the spirit of Chicago.

When with you last fall for two weeks, one of them the week of October 24th when the stock market crashed, I went to forty citizens of Chicago and secured subscriptions for over $6,000,000 of the bonds of the Chicago "Century of Progress" Exposition, payable in cash on demand. And preceding that: through the genius of Stuyvesant Peabody, 120,000 of its rank and file citizens had paid over $600,000 for admission tickets to an Exposition three years off.

The answer of this generation of Chicago to the crime emergency has been given. It was given in the elections of two years ago. It has been given in the advance by its citizens of $74,000,000 within the past few months for the needs of Chicago. It has been given in the steady marshaling into the battle line behind law and order of civic organization after organization and of the best moral elements of our citizenship. It has been given by the ac-

184

tions of the Chicago Association of Commerce and your Better Business Bureau.

The movement has but started, but I say to you that this generation of our citizens will vindicate itself as have the generations of the difficult past, and in the glorious history of Chicago, itself not dependent upon any one generation, will be remembered not only as a constructive generation but as one which, in its bare hands, seized the venomous serpent of organized crime and choked it to death.

To you, the leading citizens of Chicago, I would say: You meet tonight in the real spirit of the city itself. You represent a generation craving only the leadership which you can give it in order to pay the debt of the generation to Chicago, the vast and dynamic city which has enabled each of us to become what we are—a city not dependent upon us but we dependent upon it. This is not a new day for Chicago—this city so dear to our hearts—for Chicago has had and will have many such days in a life which is measured not even in terms of years but of centuries. It is not a new day for Chicago. It is a new day for this generation of Chicago's citizens.

The other speech was an entirely unexpected one at a very large annual dinner of the Association of British Chambers of Commerce, Thursday evening, at the Hotel Victoria. There was a long list of speakers, including the Prime Minister who had, during the day, announced the naval agreement between the United States, Great Britain and Japan.

After the speaking was closed, and the guests at the head table were starting to leave, the audience set up a call for me, and I responded in a five-minute tribute to MacDonald's work in our conference.

In starting his speech, the Prime Minister said:

I have had a very busy day. The events of the day have been fast, and I think that they have been good. As I announced in the House of Commons, just before coming to join you, the United States, Japan and ourselves have come to a complete agreement. Owing to the very great and natural complexities, which nobody ought to be surprised at, it is to take a little longer while to make the Three-Power Agreement a Five-Power Agreement, but as the delegates from the United States and Japan who have been here for a long time, are required to get back—some, like Mr. Stimson, bearing, next to the President of the United States, the heaviest burden that a United States citizen can bear—and do not wish to remain here longer than their time can profitably be utilized, we have decided today to recommend that the Japanese and the United States delegates, having finished the work with which they were primarily concerned, might go back, whilst the French, the Italians and ourselves will pursue our search for a complete naval agreement. [Cheers] It is very happy that at a moment like this I should meet

Journal as Ambassador to Great Britain

again my old friend and colleague the American Ambassador, because the work which has reached another stage tonight was begun last June between General Dawes and myself on his arrival as Ambassador to this country.

Our dear daughter Carolyn arrived from home Friday. We are greatly enjoying her visit.

London,
April 14, 1930.

Attended first a meeting of our delegation and then a plenary meeting of the Naval Conference at St. James's Palace in the morning. The reports already wholly agreed upon by the first committee (the heads of the respective delegations) were unanimously adopted, and as the Prime Minister remarked "gave the raw material for the drafting of the treaty."

The adopted reports cover special vessels and vessels not subject to limitation, the unit size of submarines and their more humane use in war time, the disposal of over-age vessels, and replacement rules to cover ships not provided for in the Washington Treaty, the capital ship naval holiday and the disposal of surplus capital ships. The first report, dealing with the method of limitation of naval tonnage, had so many reservations to it that it was not then possible for the plenary session to adopt it.

It was announced that the treaty would not be ready for signature until Easter Tuesday, a week from tomorrow, when a final plenary session will be held. We are nearing the end of a ten months' effort. The *Leviathan* will be held twenty-four hours, next week, to enable our delegation to sail after signing the treaty.

London,
April 15, 1930.

We have entered another discussion in the naval negotiation. It concerns the clause to be inserted to protect any power, party to the three-power portion of the pact, if any nation not a party to that portion of the pact should engage in naval construction in a way materially to affect the requirements of the national

186

security of any one of the three contracting powers. Chairman Morrow, of the drafting committee, presented to our delegation yesterday morning the following suggested form:

> If, during the present term of the treaty, the requirements of the national security of any High Contracting Party in respect of naval defense, are, in the opinion of that party materially affected by any change of circumstances, that party shall have the right to communicate to the other Powers such change of circumstances and the alterations required thereby in its naval program. Upon serving such communication, such Party shall have the right to make the alteration proposed in which case the other Parties shall have the right to make a proportionate increase in the categories affected.

In the afternoon, Senator Robinson submitted an alternative form which has been favorably received by the British, and is now under somewhat disquieting consideration by the Japanese delegation. The Robinson clause leaves more teeth in the pact, and tends to relieve it of possible attack as being too easy to abrogate. It is as follows:

> If, during the term of the present treaty, the requirements of the national security of any High Contracting Party in respect of cruisers or destroyers are, in the opinion of that Party, materially affected by the construction programs of any Power other than those who have joined in Part III of this Treaty, that High Contracting Party will notify the other Parties to Part III as to the increase required to be made in its own tonnages within the categories of cruisers or destroyers, and shall be entitled to make such increases. Thereupon the other Parties to Part III of this Treaty shall be entitled to make a corresponding increase in the category or categories affected.

London,
April 18, 1930.

The Treaty is now all agreed upon. The safe-guarding clause, after much negotiation, was finally agreed upon in the following form:

> If, during the term of the present Treaty, the requirements of the national security of any High Contracting Party in respect of vessels of war covered by Part III of this Treaty are, in the opinion of that Party, materially affected by new construction of any Power other than those which have joined in Part III of this Treaty, that High Contracting Party will notify the other Parties to Part III as to the increase to be made in its own tonnages within the categories of such vessels of war, and shall be entitled to make

such increase. Thereupon, the other Parties to Part III of this Treaty shall be entitled to make a proportionate increase in the category or categories affected; and such other Parties shall advise with one another through diplomatic channels as to the situation thus presented.

The White Paper issued by the British Government gives a very clear and condensed statement of what the Treaty covers. It will be noted that at the time this White Paper was issued, the safe-guarding clause was omitted, as its form had not yet been agreed upon.

The following is the text—in which we have inserted cross headings—of the "Memorandum on the Results of the London Naval Conference from January 21, to April 15, 1930," issued yesterday as a White Paper (Cmd. 3547).

In a memorandum on the position at the London Naval Conference, 1930, presented to Parliament on February 4 last, His Majesty's Government in the United Kingdom took the view that if the strengths of national fleets were not to be a menace, they must be the subject of international agreement, the purpose of which should be to maintain an equilibrium which should form the subject of agreements made from time to time by the Naval Powers. His Majesty's Government believed that if such an agreed equilibrium could be established over a period of time, the sense of security of any power would be increased, and one of the most fruitful sources of fear and friction would be removed. Meanwhile, Governments could be engaged in strengthening the foundations of peace and paving the way for further measures of disarmament.

Proposals for achieving the above were set out in the Memorandum, and it will now be convenient to place before Parliament the measure of success which has been reached up to date at the London Naval Conference in giving affect to the aims of His Majesty's Government.

CAPITAL SHIPS

As regards capital ships, complete agreement has been reached between all the Powers represented at the Conference that they will lay down none of the replacement ships of 35,000 tons each which they were entitled to build, under the terms of the Washington Treaty, during the years 1931–36 inclusive. The British Commonwealth of Nations, the United States and Japan undertake to proceed at once to the reduction of their capital ships in numbers to 15, 15, 9, respectively, instead of waiting until the expiration of the Washington Treaty. France and Italy only reserve to themselves the right of constructing additional ships from the replacement tonnage which has been available for such use between the signature of the Washington Treaty and the present day, but which has not actually been used up to date.

188

Journal as Ambassador to Great Britain

As regards aircraft carriers, His Majesty's Government have not been able to obtain at this Conference a modification of the total tonnage and displacement limits laid down in the Washington Treaty. It was agreed that the matter should be left over until a conference in 1935, but meanwhile His Majesty's Government's proposal that aircraft carriers under 10,000 tons should be included in the aircraft carrier category has been generally agreed to, and the further provision has been added that the gun armament for these particular vessels should not exceed 6 inches in calibre, instead of 8 inches.

As regards other classes of vessels, it has not been possible yet to reach an agreement embracing all the Powers represented at the Conference. His Majesty's Government will continue conversations with France and Italy in the hope of arriving at a satisfactory adjustment.

THE POWER AGREEMENT

Meanwhile, complete agreement has been reached between the British Commonwealth of Nations, the United States and Japan on—

(a) The category system of limitation of capital ships, aircraft carriers, cruisers, destroyers and submarines.
(b) The figures within these categories, and
(c) The question of transfer between 6-inch cruisers and destroyers.

The figures for the agreement for cruisers, destroyers and submarines as between the three Powers are as follows:

British Commonwealth of Nations

		Tons
8-inch gun cruisers	15 units	146,800
6-inch gun cruisers		192,200
Destroyers		150,000
Submarines		52,700
	Total	541,700

United States

		Tons
8-inch gun cruisers	18 units	180,000
6-inch gun cruisers		143,500
Destroyers		150,000
Submarines		52,700
	Total	526,200

Japan

		Tons
8-inch gun cruisers	12 units	108,400
6-inch gun cruisers		100,450
Destroyers		105,500
Submarines		52,700
	Total	367,050

189

Journal as Ambassador to Great Britain

The United States undertakes not to complete more than 15, 8-inch gun cruisers before 1935.

The United States has the option to rest on this figure and to make a corresponding increase in its 6-inch gun cruisers from 143,500 to 189,000, in which case the total tonnage for the United States and the British Commonwealth of Nations will amount to 541,700. If it does not choose to exercise this option, it undertakes that its 16th 8-inch gun cruiser will be laid down in 1933, its 17th in 1934, and its 18th in 1935. In that event Japan will be free to advance a claim at the Conference in 1935 for an increase in its 8-inch tonnage.

This section of the Treaty, which will apply to the British Commonwealth of Nations, the United States and Japan, will contain a clause safeguarding our position in relation to the building programmes of other Powers.

OTHER DECISIONS

In addition to the above points affecting actual tonnage, a number of important decisions have been taken on the questions relating to the methods of limiting and defining naval material of war. The rules which have been drawn up relate to the following subjects:

The general principle of limitation (i.e., a satisfactory compromise between the systems of global tonnage and limitation by category); the definitions of the cruiser and destroyer; the unit size and armament of destroyers and submarines; the definition of exempt vessels; special vessels and aeroplane carriers; the rules for scrapping and replacement; the definition of displacement tonnage; and the prohibition of the construction of vessels which do not conform to Treaty limitations.

It has not been found possible to reach agreement on the abolition of the submarine, but as regards the three Powers a total submarine tonnage figure which shall apply equally to each of them has been arrived at, and His Majesty's Government has been able to insert a figure for destroyer tonnage which is appropriate if related to the three signatory Powers, and is less by 50,000 tons than the figure of 200,000 tons referred to in the White Paper of February 4th last.

It must be noted, however, that the figure of 150,000 tons of destroyers for the British Commonwealth of Nations must be conditional on an agreed destroyer and submarine strength of the European Powers represented at the London Conference. This will be the subject of further negotiations with the Powers concerned.

Further, although the submarine remains as a combatant naval vessel, an important agreement has been reached by all five powers strictly limiting its use and ensuring its compliance to the rules generally recognized to be applicable to all surface vessels. This is not so drastic as the Washington instrument but the latter Treaty, though ratified by us, never received the requisite unanimous ratification.

FINANCIAL SAVING

The immediate financial saving resulting from the Conference is the avoidance of expenditure for the replacement of battleships under the Washington Treaty. But for this agreement, before the end of 1936, Great Britain would,

190

under the Washington Treaty, have completed five new 35,000-ton ships and would have had a further five appropriated for and under construction. This might have necessitated the expenditure in the region of £50,000,000 up to the end of 1936. Further, the financial saving involved in reducing at once to 15 capital ships is estimated at about £4,000,000.

As regards cruisers, destroyers and submarines, the United States, Japan and the British Commonwealth of Nations, have overcome the difficulties which resulted in the failure of the Geneva Conference in 1927. The final British proposal at that Conference was for a combined total tonnage of cruisers, destroyers and submarines, including over-age vessels, of 737,500 tons. The comparable total agreed upon today is 541,700 tons. On a conservative basis, we have been saved a further expenditure in these classes of ships of some 13 million sterling.

Important as are these financial savings, a yet more important result of this first stage of the London Conference has been the elimination of competitive building in cruisers and auxiliary craft between the British Commonwealth of Nations, the United States and Japan, with all that this implies in the mutual improvement of their political relations. The figures of the agreement beween these Powers have been placed at a low level, and it is the earnest hope of His Majesty's Government that during the next stage of the Conference agreement may be reached with the French and Italian Governments at levels which will permit of their programmes and tonnage figures being incorporated in the agreement already reached between the other Powers.

After the signature of the Treaty, the Conference will adjourn in order to give further time for negotiations between the French and Italian Governments, with a view to the settlement of difficulties which, as yet, prevent a complete agreement. These negotiations may be prolonged, and it is unnecessary that the Delegations from distant countries, which are not so immediately concerned, should remain in London while the conversations are proceeding; it is for this reason that an adjournment has been decided upon.

Dwight Morrow has talked over with me from time to time the matter of the conflicting duties which seem to confront him, and whether he should return to Mexico, or take appointment as Senator from New Jersey immediately upon his return to America. Yesterday, he received word from Mexico that Rubio Ortiz was sending a confidential personal messenger to meet him on his return to New York, and requesting Dwight to remain on the ship after its landing until this man had a conference with him. This would seem to mean that Ortiz wishes to make an appeal to Dwight to remain as Ambassador to Mexico before Dwight sees his political friends and irrevocably commits himself.

Dwight feels it will be necessary to get David J. Baird, the present Senator from New Jersey, who is to resign in order that

Journal as Ambassador to Great Britain

Dwight shall be appointed in his place, to agree to stay and enter the primaries for the next election in November.

I think Dwight feels that whichever place he takes, it will look like running away from the other, but this is not his fault; and is only one of the consequences of being considered indispensable in two different places.

London,
Monday, April 21, 1930.

The Treaty will be signed at St. James's Palace at 10:30 tomorrow morning, the final copies having been distributed to the delegates.

Caro, Carolyn, Virginia and I spent the week-end with Lord and Lady Astor at Cliveden. A large party were present, including Secretary and Mrs. Stimson, Senator and Mrs. Robinson, J. Theodore Marriner, Arthur Page, Mr. and Mrs. Charles Dana Gibson, the Earl of Lothian (Philip Kerr), Admiral Hepburn, Mr. and Mrs. Brand, Brendan Bracken, member of Parliament and managing director of the *Economist,* Lionel Curtis, Mrs. Wantringham, Mr. Tennant, Mr. Appleton, and a number of others.

Was much interested in meeting Charles Dana Gibson. I remember well the first reception I ever attended in Washington at the house of Thomas Nelson Page, in March, 1897, just a third of a century ago, during President McKinley's first inauguration. I was there with Caro and a party of Chicago friends. I remember the interest of the other guests when Charles Dana Gibson and Richard Harding Davis walked in together—two famous, distinguished and handsome young men, then at the height of their vogue. If Gibson had not been an original artist, he certainly would have been a distinguished success in almost any other vocation.

Was with Robinson and Dwight Morrow this morning. Dwight just had a telephone call from Mrs. Morrow from New Jersey, saying that Colonel Lindbergh and his wife (formerly Anne Morrow) had just arrived at the Morrow home in New Jersey after a flight in one day from Los Angeles with only one stop on the way. Verily, the father-in-law of a daring celebrity like Lindbergh knoweth well the meaning of anxiety.

Journal as Ambassador to Great Britain

Now that the naval negotiations are through, I do not know how long I will continue in this office. My tenure is subject to the discharge of my obligations, deliberately incurred, to raise the funds for the "Century of Progress" exposition, and when that task calls I must go. For the ungrateful task of raising the money there are no volunteers and no "draft" law which can be invoked.

Except for the naval work which has now occupied ten months and in which there was a specific objective, there has been little work of importance in this position, and under normal circumstances the life of an Ambassador here seems largely a round of social events, public speaking on non-controversial subjects, and idle enjoyments.

My sister Bessie Hoyt and her daughter Nancy arrived this afternoon.

I will especially miss Secretary Adams, Senator Robinson, and Dwight Morrow when they leave for America tomorrow. Secretary Adams has performed a most essential work at this Conference. He is a combination of competency and affability, and his good judgment and equipoise in a situation, sometimes embarrassing to him as a representative of the navy in our delegation, have been recognized by all. He has loyally served the interests of his chief, the President, and our country, and is the fourth of the Adams family to represent our nation in Britain in important position and work. I have come to value him as a man and friend.

London,
April 22, 1930.

This morning, at St. James's Palace, the Naval Treaty was signed. The leaders of the delegations all made statements. Before the meeting and after the meeting, indeed, most of the day, was given to formal calls of delegations, photographers and farewells at the railway stations. The atmosphere seemed charged with peace, mingled with relief. From the lips of the speakers dripped the same generalizations about peace in the abstract that characterized the first plenary session, but this time they had an achievement to talk about as an addition.

Journal as Ambassador to Great Britain

Together in the afternoon our delegation called on the Prime Minister at 10 Downing Street, on the French and Italian Ambassadors at their Embassies, and upon the Japanese delegation at the Japanese Embassy.

Secretary Stimson and the delegation was presented by me to the Embassy staff at the Chancery, and late in the afternoon Stimson and I went also to the United States Consulate and met the American Consul General, Albert Halsted and his staff.

In the evening the whole family went to Waterloo Station to say "good-bye" to the American delegation, its experts and employees, who were leaving for home. I parted with my friends with regret. Dwight said he had sent something to me to hang on the wall as a memento. Secretary Stimson had already presented each of our delegation with a gold pen, with which we had signed the Treaty.

The Japanese delegation, representatives of the Foreign Office, the French Ambassador, and many others were at the station.

A delegation of British ex-Marines was on hand to bid farewell to the splendid platoon of our own marines who, in their natty uniforms, have added much, both to the appearance and the convenience of our delegation headquarters at the Hotel Ritz. Happiness was the order of the evening, but when the train pulled out those of us who had been left behind felt sober and a little sad. I told Dwight that a lot of water would have gone over the dam when next we met. I hope all things go well with him.

I wired President Hoover this morning as follows:

HERBERT HOOVER,
White House, Washington.

The Treaty has just been signed. The high purpose so near to your heart, the statement of which initiated these negotiations in which you have had such a commanding part, is thus translated into an enduring benefit to the world and its peace. The able and courageous leadership of Stimson has at all times united, coordinated and stimulated the activities of your delegation here, and he and those of the delegation who sail tomorrow have won the general respect and sincere regard of all with whom they have negotiated. I send you my congratulations.

CHARLES G. DAWES

Journal as Ambassador to Great Britain

Letter from the President
THE WHITE HOUSE, WASHINGTON

April 29, 1930

HON. CHARLES G. DAWES,
American Ambassador to England,
London, England.

MY DEAR MR. AMBASSADOR:

I have your kind telegram of April 22nd. I wish to take this occasion to express to you the deep appreciation I have for the foundations laid by you, which have contributed so much to make possible the successful issue of the London Conference. I am still uncertain as to whether we will need your great influence to secure its ratification by the Senate.

Yours faithfully,
HERBERT HOOVER

London,
April 23, 1930.

Was looking forward to a little season of quiet and relaxation, but am afraid I am to have no such luck. The President evidently wants me to come over for a time to help in getting the Treaty ratified.

Joseph P. Cotton, the Acting Secretary of State, has cabled me:

You will proceed to Washington as soon as possible for consultation. What we want you back for is to help in defending the Treaty in the Senate, and we regard the matter as important. We would like to have you as soon as may be. Is this reasonably possible? Please confer with Stimson if he has not left.

I answered:

Unable confer with Stimson as he sailed this morning. Personally feel doubt as to my usefulness in particular situation mentioned, but of course will gladly come if thought best. However, suggest that the Secretary, as well as Senator Robinson, whose judgment of the situation on the bill is so sound, be consulted. If it is best that I come, can sail Saturday on *Aquitania*, arriving May 2nd, three days after delegation. In this event, think announcement from Washington would be desirable as forestalling press speculation.

Rewired the cables to Stimson on the *Leviathan* asking his comment. If the answer comes to go I will miss the visit of my old friends, John T. McCutcheon and Tiffany Blake, and their

Journal as Ambassador to Great Britain

families, and Dan Wing and his wife, to which I have been looking forward for a year.

Will have to cancel the review of the Boys Brigade at Glasgow, at which I am expected to be the principal guest May 3rd, and will miss degrees from Cambridge University and from the University of Manchester, besides cancelling a large number of lesser engagements, all of which causes trouble to those who have made arrangements for them. But what I will most regret is missing the visit of my old friends who, like me I know, are looking forward to this reunion. "We will not pass this way again."

In the morning Caro and I went to the train to see Admiral and Mrs. Takarabe off. Afterwards, Mr. Wakatsuki called at the Embassy to say "good-bye."

Dwight Morrow sent me a fine old contemporary colored engraving of the fight between the *Chesapeake* and the *Shannon* off Boston on June 1st, 1813.

London,
April 24, 1930.

To my relief, I today received from Cotton, the Acting Secretary of State, the following message:

The President suggests that we await arrival of delegation and see what develops here during the day or two following. It is a certainty the Senate will be engaged for some days in examination before it comes to public debate on the question, so we should have time to advise you fully before taking final decision.

One can judge of the situation from here only with difficulty, but I do not think I will have to go. I do not believe that the Treaty is in any great danger from the Senate with Robinson, Reed and Morrow to fight the battle.

I received a good many callers at the Chancery today, where I am installed again, having had my office for the last three months with our Conference delegation at the Hotel Ritz.

Journal as Ambassador to Great Britain

London,
April 25, 1930.

Today, I sent the following cable to the President:

Much appreciate cable. The wisdom which you have shown throughout these negotiations from the beginning was never better exemplified than in your nomination as delegates of Robinson, Reed and Morrow, who will now sponsor and explain the Treaty in the Senate. Am sure not only that they need no reinforcement but that anything which even suggests it had best be avoided. Am quite sure you will not feel it necessary for me to come. However, you will know best about this. I cannot but feel that the reaction to the Treaty which everywhere in Europe, even in Germany, is increasingly favorable, will be the same in our own country. Affectionate regards and renewed congratulations.

DAWES

London,
Tuesday, April 29, 1930.

Am at last caught up with my mail. Saturday went with my wife, Carolyn and Virginia, my sister Bessie, her daughter Nancy, and Miss Decker to Colchester to see the Roman Walls and the Norman Castle built from the stone and brick of the oldest Roman city in England. From Colchester we went to Sudbury, the habitat of the Dawes forebears, returning in the evening to London.

Last night (Monday) all our family went to a dinner given by the Mr. and Mrs. Matsudaira at the Japanese Embassy, where they served us some of their native dishes with chop sticks instead of knives and forks. We were the only guests outside of the Embassy staff. We had a most delightful evening; but if I had to depend upon chop sticks exclusively to feed myself, I should die of starvation. My admiration for the Japanese as technicians was increased.

Sunday I made an inquiry by telephone to Chicago about the status of the "Century of Progress" plans. A twenty-minute conversation cost me sixty-four pounds, but the talk was worth it. However, if I had known the rate was about seventy-five

197

dollars for every five minutes, I think I could have condensed a little more.

Today I spoke at luncheon to the American Consuls of England, Scotland and North Ireland, given by the United States Consul General at London, Albert Halsted. In inviting them in my speech to "tea" at the Embassy, I said I understood that for the most part their wives had been left at home. I admonished them that the custom of taking their wives on these trips would be an admirable safeguard for the traditional American policy of "avoiding foreign entanglements."

I insert an account of the Gridiron dinner, on April 27, attended by President Hoover, as reported in the London *Times,* of April 28, 1930.

The Gridiron Club, whose members are the flower of the correspondents in Washington and the salt of whose dinners is a merciless flaying of persons and politics, turned serious for a moment last night and recalled how thirty years ago the United States Marines and the Royal Welch Fusiliers had together relieved Tientsin and clasped hands in friendship. A young American engineer named Hoover, who was among the beleaguered and is now President of the United States, and a young lieutenant of Marines, who received a wound and was carried off by Fusiliers, and is now Major General Smedley Butler, sat at the high table and watched the ceremony.

On the President's right was the British Ambassador, Sir Ronald Lindsay.

President Hoover in his speech recalled how, in the Boxer campaign of 1900, for weeks some 900 soldiers and sailors of 11 nationalities, with 300 civilians—a quarter of whom were Americans—had fought in the trenches and behind the barricades against tens of thousands of fanatical Chinese; how they had come to the point of exhaustion and to the edge of despair, when one morning the enemy firing ceased, the attackers melted away, and a few hours later the column of Marines and Fusiliers marched into the Settlement.

And there was a Club spokesman to tell how when the Marines had asked why the battles of the American Revolution were not embroidered as honours on the Colour of the Fusiliers, they were told that the regiment would never permit it because these "were fought against men of our own blood" and to recall how, when General Pershing and his staff had landed at Liverpool in 1917, the Royal Welch Fusiliers were drawn up as their escort.

So 500 men got to their feet when an American flag, carried by a Marine, and a British flag, carried by an Englishman in uniform, were borne on to a little stage, and the Marine Band marched stiffly into place behind them. Then John Philip Sousa himself, "The March King," as Americans call him, stepped to the conductor's stand, and led the first public performance of his latest composition: "The Royal Welch Fusiliers," the full score of which is to be presented to the regiment it honours by the American Ambassador in London.

The little ceremony was a touching and graceful tribute to an old comradeship and it was plain to see that the President was moved. So indeed was everybody else, and something of this stirring of heart was in the warmth of the reception given to Sir Ronald Lindsay when he rose in his place for a first introduction to the Club and its guests.

London,
May 10, 1930.

My friends, John T. McCutcheon and Tiffany Blake, and their families arrived May 2nd, and are visiting us at the Embassy. Their visit coming after the long siege of the naval negotiations and conference which had continued for the last ten months, found me with the leisure thoroughly to enjoy entertaining them.

I here insert a letter which I wrote to the Prime Minister and his reply which mark a pleasant conclusion of our mutual naval endeavors.

EMBASSY OF THE UNITED STATES OF AMERICA
April 28, 1930

MY DEAR MR. PRIME MINISTER:

The Treaty is signed and the heavy burden of responsibility which you carry at all times has been lightened for a few days any way. I cannot let the occasion pass without just a word in appreciation of those qualities of yours of natural leadership and personal character which have been the chief factor in the success of the Conference which now, after three months of difficult endeavor, has achieved an historic step in peaceful international relationship and mutual understanding. Long before the Conference met, knowing from contact your exacting environment and incessant work, I was anxious lest you break under the strain, and that you did not do so during these last three months, the most difficult of the ten, somehow makes me feel that the Lord in selecting His servants must give them the strength to do the work He intends. Under discouragement which would have completely upset and baffled the weak you have always persevered, showing only patience and tolerance and kindness; and then, in the final success, only humbleness.

You know already the respect and affection which my contacts with you have inspired, but I could not be content as the Conference ends without this expression of it.

Yours,
CHARLES G. DAWES.

199

Journal as Ambassador to Great Britain

To this letter, the Prime Minister replied as follows:

10 Downing Street,
Whitehall,
April 29, 1930.

H. E. GENERAL C. G. DAWES, C.B.,
4 Grosvenor Gardens,
S.W.1.

MY DEAR GENERAL:

Thank you so much for your letter of yesterday. I need not tell you how greatly I appreciate it. The work has been very interesting and has been most attractive for itself but, when, in days to come, I live over again these months in memory, nothing will give me greater pleasure than the thought of the friendship which it enabled to grow up between us. You have been a most delightful colleague and, but for you, the success which has been attained could not have been reached.

Further than that I am happy beyond words that the relations between the United States and ourselves have been so wonderfully changed. That alone, I think, is an achievement which means much for the future good of the world, and in that your part has been as big as mine.

I do hope that we are going to meet not infrequently now that the Conference has finished, and that business will not always be the occasion for bringing us together.

With kindest regards, I am,

Yours very sincerely,
J. RAMSAY MACDONALD.

The evening that John and Tiffany arrived, we three left for Glasgow where, on the next day (May 3rd), I reviewed the Boys Brigade, Glasgow Battalion, at their annual review.

This is the great day of the year in Glasgow, and ten thousand young Scots were in the parade. The organization dates from 1883 and, while on somewhat similar lines in general as the Boy Scouts, ante-dates them. It has been reviewed in the past on these annual occasions by the Prince of Wales, the Duke of Connaught, and a long list of distinguished Britons, and I was aware that my selection as reviewing officer this year was an unusual honor.

We were in charge of Sir Steven Bilsland, Battalion President, and the Right Honorable Lord Provost of Glasgow, Thomas Kelly. We were given a lunch by the Lord Provost at the beautiful Municipal Building and a dinner after the review by Sir Steven Bilsland.

Journal as Ambassador to Great Britain

Made two speeches, one for a few minutes to the crowd of officers who crowded around the reviewing stand after the parade, and one in the evening at their formal meeting.

The march past of 250 young bagpipers and drummers was to me the most unique and moving part of the parade. As best describing it and what occurred, I append a newspaper clipping.

By general consent the most picturesque element in the Boys Brigade inspection on the Queen's Park Recreation Ground, Glasgow, on Saturday afternoon, was the march past of 250 youthful pipers and drummers.

The kilt was worn by a few of them only, but the coverings of the pipes, representative of every clan in the Highlands and Islands, and the gay ribbons fluttering from the drones, went far toward providing a compensating quality of color.

There were all sorts and sizes in this imposing company—lanky lads, who twirled the sticks with grace as well as with dexterity, and little fellows, scarcely equalling in inches the biggest of the drums, which sloped rakishly across their left shoulders.

The port of all was admirable, and they swung along in widely spaced line, 14 abreast, with the braggart step of the traditional "hundred pipers" their fingers jumping nimbly over the chanter stops as the echoes for a mile or more were made to ring with "Highland Laddie."

Hat in hand, General C. G. Dawes, the American Ambassador to Great Britain, the Inspecting Officer, stood at the saluting base, obviously charmed with the spectacle and the inspiration of the slogan.

Earlier he witnessed the march past of the 12 battalions which constitute the strength of the organization in the Glasgow area, represented for the day by nearly 10,000 boys.

It was an impressive sight, with precision and steadiness marvellously achieved.

The occasion had its lighter side as well. This was provided under the heading of "displays." Between the march past, conducted in two portions, with six battalions taking part in each, a large party wearing gymnasium costumes tripped to the front.

The group occupying the center, earned the admiration of the spectators. A cricket match, one soon realized, was in progress. The various movements of real players were suggested with realism, the meeting between ball and bat being represented by a sharp click uttered in unison.

Football was next imitated. Numerous stages of an exciting game were simulated, and a delirously executed goal came by way of climax. This was followed by an assault at arms on the same mimic lines.

As the strains of the National Anthem, played by the brass bands, died away, there was a helter-skelter on the part of many to where General Dawes stood with the official party, which included Lord Provost Kelly.

A speech obviously was expected, and Sir A. Steven Bilsland, Bart., M.C., the Battalion President, lost no time in asking the distinguished visitor to address the parade.

Journal as Ambassador to Great Britain

"After your wonderful demonstration," said the General, "about the meanest thing I could do would be to make a long speech to you. To do so would be a very poor return for what has proved a wonderful afternoon, not only for me, but for everybody here.

"Yours is a distinctive organization. From it has sprung other great organizations of boys who are going to stand on the side of right and become men who, in their after lives, will stand for the right things.

"I have seen some of the boys' organizations, but I have never seen anything better than yours.

"You have one great distinctive element in your association here which none of us in other parts of the world has, that is your wonderful bagpipe band. They told me today that there were going to be hundreds of pipers, and they said to me further," added the General, "that sometimes all of them don't play the same tune at the same time. [Laughter]

"I have heard them play today but there was no discord, no flaw in their playing.

"It was a great honor that was done to me by the officers of your organization. I am very grateful to them and very thankful to you."

Three cheers were given the General by the boys.

Yesterday the battalion attended services in St. Andrew's Hall, City Hall, Queen's Park St. George's Church, Govan Town Hall, and St. Mungo Hall, when appropriate addresses were delivered.

That evening, after the dinner, John, Tiffany and I motored to Edinburgh, where we spent the next morning, reaching London in the evening.

During the last week, all of us and our families, went to a steeplechase race with the Daweses of Kent, who were fully as numerous as our own party. "Slotty" (Launcelot) made two beautiful races, coming second in one (on his own horse) and in the other leading all the way around to the last jump, over water, when the horse fell. The horse, a magnificent animal, deemed, when he started the race, as fit for the Grand National, strained his tendons, and probably is done for as a steeplechaser. Slotty was not hurt by the fall. The owner of the horse, who was present, was said to have declined an offer of three thousand pounds for the animal a short time before; but after the race sold him on the grounds for four hundred pounds.

On Friday, we gave a dinner at the Embassy in honor of Adolph Ochs, of the *New York Times*. There were thirty at this function, including the Prime Minister, Lord Allenby, and many other distinguished Americans and Britons.

Also on Friday, Major General Dobell, the Colonel command-

JOHN T. MCCUTCHEON

ing the Royal Welch Fusiliers (he was insistent that Welch be spelled with a "c" in accordance with their organization tradition) and Major Geiger took lunch at the Embassy, and we arranged the ceremony for the presentation of the United States Marine and J. P. Sousa Tribute to take place June 25th at Tidworth with a battalion of the Fusiliers present. The Fusiliers are most appreciative and are anxious to have the reception of the gift as impressive as was the announcement of it in America.

This will be a real Anglo-American occasion, the kind that stirs the blood, if we succeed in carrying out what we agreed upon, and provided—and this is a big if—it does not rain.

London,
May 18, 1930.

Will reconstruct this last week as best I may from my engagement book.

Last Monday (May 12th) was the "grand night" dinner of the Middle Temple and as "Master Junior" I re-echoed the Master Treasurer's toasts and "rang the bell." There seems to be something satisfying to the members of the Temple, distinguished barristers and judges of the English Bar, to see the American Ambassador "ring the bell." I much enjoy these Middle Temple meetings and am coming to feel quite well acquainted.

On the next afternoon (Tuesday) I accompanied Dr. Nicholas Murray Butler to the Middle Temple, where the benchers met to receive a gift from the Carnegie Foundation of the volumes, about 2000 in number, necessary to complete the American Section of the Law Library. Here I did not come last as Master Junior nor did I "ring the bell," but in my role as Ambassador. Tiffany Blake and John McCutcheon attended this ceremony with me.

This same evening I spoke at a reunion of the British Bar Mission to the United States, at a dinner at the Mayflower Hotel.

On Thursday I spoke at a luncheon given in my honor by the American Chamber of Commerce at the Hotel Victoria. The membership of this body, I was told, is about equally divided between Americans and British. About three hundred and fifty were present.

On Wednesday evening, occurred the first Court of the season at Buckingham Palace. Among others, Caro presented our daughter Carolyn and Mrs. Blake and Mrs. McCutcheon.

On Thursday evening, attended the second Court at nine o'clock. At these Courts, both the King and Queen received. The King, owing to his illness, did not attend last year's Courts. Before going to Court Thursday evening, I spent a half-hour at the reception preceding the Pilgrims' dinner in honor of Nicholas Murray Butler.

Friday and Saturday evenings, attended respectively a reception at the house of the First Lord of the Admiralty, and a dinner at the Atheneum Club, given by my friend, Sir Josiah Stamp, in honor of Dr. Butler.

At this point, I lay aside my engagement book, with the impression that its use hereafter will tend to diffusiveness. While what is written above does not indicate it, I have really done some work this last week—mostly on "Century of Progress" matters. Hungerford, Director of the Transportation Exhibit, is here. Took him to see Sir Josiah Stamp at Euston Station, and Stamp, dear friend that he is, promised to send us the Royal Scot train and engine, and whatever historic engines of the London, Midland and Scottish Railway we deemed would be of interest. He is going to America and will announce his promise to us there.

The McCutcheons and Blakes left Friday. We have greatly enjoyed their visit. Our friend, the Lord Mayor of London (Sir William Waterloo) stowed away young Jackie McCutcheon in his coach with him on an official ride through the city. Jackie was not visible to the crowds.

The Lady Mayoress has also been very kind to my daughter, Carolyn, during her visit. Melvin and Carolyn leave tomorrow for home, to our great regret.

Dwight Morrow has made an epochal speech on prohibition on opening his campaign for the Senate in New Jersey. After reading it, I cabled him: "For the first time in my life, I underestimated your capacity." I had in mind my advice to him not

Journal as Ambassador to Great Britain

to run for office this year. Even if he is defeated, the opportunity to make a speech like this is full compensation for it.

The city is filling up with American visitors, and a goodly percentage of my American friends are calling on me at the Chancery and Embassy. Their calls this week have prevented me from finishing up my mail and I have a stack of neglected letters to reduce tomorrow.

The papers announce that Fritz Kreisler is to play my piece at Queen's Hall next Tuesday evening.

Received a long letter from Senator J. T. Robinson, from which I quote: "Saturday night, Senator Walsh, of Montana, gave me a dinner which was attended by about thirty of my colleagues. I talked about two hours reviewing the history of the Treaty. The indications are that the opposition to the Treaty will disappear, and it will be advised and consented to within a short time, although I expect a number of witnesses to be called in explanation of its provisions."

London,
May 25, 1930.

The London Naval Treaty occupied me again for a short time this week. The State Department cabled me, asking me to present a note to the British Government, designed to clarify a point (and a very strained point it seems to be) raised by the Admirals opposing the Treaty in the hearings before the Committee on Foreign Affairs in the Senate. The Admirals suggest that the term *replacement* in the cruiser category agreement might be construed as allowing Great Britain, before 1936, to replace their obsolete 6-inch cruisers as they passed out with 8-inch cruisers.

This seems to me an unusual meaning to give the word *replacement,* but since all parties to the Treaty understand that the word applies to individual ships, rather than to the tonnage of the category, we expect no trouble in securing an exchange of notes to this effect between the Governments involved.

In my call on Henderson last Wednesday in regard to the matter, he said he anticipated no trouble about it. He will endeavor

Journal as Ambassador to Great Britain

to give me a definite answer tomorrow (Monday). As it is a Treaty matter, he must consult, not only the Cabinet, but the Dominions which takes some time.

The past week has been a busy one in the matter of functions as is generally the case during the summer, and what they call the "season."

On Monday evening, I attended a dinner of the Royal Geographical Society and afterwards a formal meeting of it when, in behalf of the American Geographic Society, I presented the Cullen Medal to Dr. John Hubert Mill, for his notable contribution to science.

Later, the same evening, Caro and I attended a musical given by Lady Corey, at her house in Belgrave Square, at which Fritz Kreisler was the artist. During the program to the surprise of some of my diplomatic colleagues who were present he played my composition and also played it the next night at his guest concert at Queen's Hall with an encore.

On Friday morning, Caro and I took the train for Manchester to attend the fiftieth anniversary exercises of the University of Manchester. We were entertained during our stay at the home of the Lord and Lady Mayoress of the city, most delightful hosts. The exercises in the afternoon, at which degrees were conferred, were most interesting and so was the convocation dinner in the evening at Whiteworth Hall, although the speaking program seemed a little long. In my response for the "Honorary Graduates," after receiving the LL.D. degree, I attempted a definition of the word "Wisdom" which, in his recent address at St. Andrews, Mr. Baldwin said was difficult. I hope it is watertight.

The Chancellor of the University, the Earl of Crawford and Balcarres, premier earl of Scotland, is the brother of Sir Ronald Lindsay, now Ambassador to the United States from Great Britain.

Those receiving the LL.D. degree were Philip Snowden, Sir Alfred Hopkinson, Arthur Henry Worthington, Sara Margery Fry (principal of Somerville College, Oxford) and myself. By inserting here a portion of the report of the proceedings in the Saturday issue of the Manchester *Guardian*, I can cover the part of them which concerned myself personally.

FRITZ KREISLER

Journal as Ambassador to Great Britain

Professor S. Alexander presented the honorary graduate to the Chancellor in these terms:

"Charles Gates Dawes (Doctor of Laws). No county in England is more closely bound in weal or woe to the United States than Lancashire, and his Excellency the Ambassador, whom I have the honor to present to you, graces the more this fiftieth anniversary of one of the Lancastrian Universities. He is famous for presiding over the committee of economic experts which, by the plan which bears his name for adjusting the debt of Germany, brought relief to distracted Europe. And as an envoy of peace, it is fitting that he is accompanied where he goes by the symbol of peace, indigenous to his own country. But peace with him is not languor. He leapt into the public eye by the vigor with which, in the face of general timidity, before America entered the war, he raised a loan for the Allies. The son of a General, he served in the war as a Brigadier General, and rendered great service to the American Army. No sooner did he become Vice President of the United States than he engaged in a battle with his own Senate. So strangely in his chariot is the tornado harnessed alongside the dove. And I trust that I overstep no limits set by diplomatic reticence if I add that under a tempestuous exterior and an unconventional address, brimming over into'picturesque expletives, none of which, however, he claims to have invented himself, he conceals the kindest of hearts and the most home loving of dispositions."

Brigadier General Dawes and Mr. Philip Snowden responded on behalf of the new honorary graduates.

By Mr. Dawes: "The early years of a university or college," said General Dawes, "are usually those in which they are engaged in a continued struggle, both for existence and growth. As the crises and difficulties of the early period lessen and the years go by, the anniversaries of the institution take on a new significance with the growth of what may be called a university self-consciousness. As with an individual as he grows older, so a university increasingly senses and weighs its growth of character. With ages these anniversaries do not, as in the earlier years, simply mark the ending of the year's collegiate work, but are occasions of university self-appraisement, of review of early struggles and decisions and purposes in the light of present accomplishment.

"Each university like each individual, like each community, like each nation, like each race, has its distinctive character—something peculiarly its own and which no other institution can exactly parallel—a character affected in its development somewhat by material environment but which is of the spirit alone. With age the character of each university becomes moie and more a fixed quantity sensed by the members of its organization, by its students, and recognized universally in public opinion. And upon this anniversary of the great University of Manchester, this community and the country

207

may well rejoice that it has developed a character which, if this were a convocation of the universities of the world to confer degrees, would entitle it to one of the highest.

"Yours is a great work. Although we often think of them as such, the university and college primarily are not so much the means by which knowledge is gathered as much as the means by which the student is given that mental training and discipline which enable him to acquire knowledge in his post graduate education in the school of life. [hear, hear] With his university training completed, the mind of the graduate is equipped with an added capacity to acquire knowledge rather than with added knowledge itself, and he goes into the world, other things being equal, better able to gather and retain facts—in other words to acquire knowledge which, while different from wisdom, determines the material with which wisdom must deal. A university education, therefore, opens the gate to the realm of wisdom. Wisdom may be hard to define, as Mr. Baldwin recently said, but its possession is demonstrated by any mind which, in its decisions, segregates and weighs and properly interprets correlated facts.

"In speaking on behalf of the honorary graduates, I am sensible that they have won their distinction at your hands because of a career in the world in which they have shown special facility and courage in speaking for themselves. [laughter] In voicing in their presence, however, their appreciation of the honor done by them by this famous University, I can speak with full assurance. These degrees today bestowed by the University are not simply university degrees, but, as well, degrees in the school of life. They are certificates that in that larger school we are thought to have been deserving. [applause] While the University, with a knowledge which comes from close association and supervision, confers its degrees upon the graduating student as an evidence of worthy work in his under-graduate life, we should not forget that the University, to some extent, at least honors us upon general and hearsay evidence. [laughter]

"I am sure we are all humble in porportion as we have the power of impartial personal appraisement, though this is a quality somewhat rare, even among minds otherwise sound [laughter] and when possessed, is difficult to exercise upon occasions such as this. But humility, where it exists, always deepens appreciation. To be thus honored today by the University of Manchester, makes it memorable in our lives, and for all of the honorary graduates, I express their genuine thanks."

Mr. Snowden. Mr. Philip Snowden said that while he appreciated very highly the honor of having been selected, with his friend General Dawes, to express the thanks of his fellow honorary graduates, he was glad that General Dawes had preceded him in the discharge of that duty.

"Already," he added, "any inadequacies on my part in returning thanks have thus been amply compensated. I wondered, until I heard the orator's speech today, why the University has sought to confer this distinction upon me; but I have learned that I possess virtues and qualities which hitherto I had never been aware of. We honorary graduates are a very varied selection. We have won fame, or notoriety, in very different spheres. I don't know whether General Dawes would regard himself as a politician. He has won distinction in so many spheres, statesman, soldier, international financier,

Journal as Ambassador to Great Britain

diplomat. But I think I should not be mistaken if I were to say that of all his achievements he is not the least proud of the work that he has done in bringing together in closer bonds of friendship the two great English-speaking nations of the world—whose friendship is the surest guarantee and the greatest hope of world peace.

"I alone, I believe, am a politician among my friends this afternoon. And it is no mean satisfaction to me that, as a politician, I received the recognition at the hands of the University, because it illustrates one of the finest traits of British public life—the toleration of opinions from which we may differ, and respect for public service honestly and fearlessly rendered. I am not, as the orator has remarked, a Lancashire man, but I did the next best thing by being born within a mile of the borders of this county and that, I suppose, is the reason why I can combine all the virtues and all the qualities of both counties.

"As colleagues, I have in this ceremony this afternoon a number of personal friends. If it would not be presumption on my part to say so, I think it is very worthy on the part of the University to honor those of their own people who have rendered great service to the University. I am proud to meet again Sir Alfred Hopkinson, who was among politicians but, I am afraid, never of politicians. [laughter] We were colleagues together for a time in the House of Commons, and I can say that his charm and his character won for him the high respect of all parties in the House of Commons. I am sure my friend, Tawney, will agree with me when I say that this distinction is not merely a distinction to him, personally, though he so worthily deserves it, but it is an honor conferred upon the Workers' Educational Association, to which he has devoted so much time and rendered such valuable service.

"There is just one other feature of this gathering to which I would like to refer, and that is the recognition of the services of women to social and educational work and to music. Miss Fry, apart from her educational work, bears a name which has long been distinguished in humanitarian and other phases of social service. I would not have ventured to refer to a rather distant association with Dame Ethel Smyth had it not been that the orator has had the audacity to mention it. But I knew her rather well in much more turbulent circumstances than those of this afternoon. [laughter]

"I can only express feebly in words the thanks of all of us whom you have honored this afternoon. We congratulate the University upon the attainment of its jubilee, and acknowledge the great work it has done. A most striking advance has taken place during the last fifty years. When I was a lad the chances of a poor boy going to a university were hardly existent. Now any lad of parts has few difficulties to surmount in going from the elementary school to the university; and it is universities like this in Manchester—those universities which we call the new universities—which have democratized higher education. They have done a magnificent work, but there is greater scope for their work in the future. There never was greater need than there is today for trained men and trained women in every sphere of industry, and every other walk in life. This University has done magnificent work of that kind during the last fifty years, and I am sure that it has before it a still greater career of usefulness to the community."

Journal as Ambassador to Great Britain

At noon today (Sunday) Caro and I went to Westminster Hall where 156 American "Gold Star" mothers, en route to France, where they will visit the graves of their sons who died in the war, and 116 veterans of the 27th Division A.E.F., were received on behalf of the British Government by Earl De La Warr, of the War Office, and Countess De La Warr.

Lord Jellicoe and Field Marshal Plumer were there, and I introduced to them many mothers whose sons had fallen by the side of their British comrades in the British Line. The 27th Division served under Plumer. Afterwards, we all accompanied the mothers as they laid wreaths at the grave of the Unknown Soldier in Westminster Abbey, and at the Cenotaph. It was an affecting and solemn occasion. I was very proud of the simple and unaffected way in which these fine and natural American women conducted themselves, and I could not but think how majestic was their naturalness as contrasted with some of their countrywomen who besiege me with requests to be presented at Court.

While standing near Lord Plumer, some one told us that one of the mothers present had lost two sons in the 27th Division. I told him that I would find her and present her to him. His answer was a request to go with me "to be presented to her."

London,
Sunday, June 1, 1930.

Again, the Naval Treaty. I was able on Friday to cable Stimson the form of the answer to his request for an interpretive letter clearing up the Admirals' objection referred to in these notes of May 27th. The British Government will probably act tomorrow (Monday). It seems to me entirely satisfactory, and as I have not yet heard from Stimson, it is probably so regarded in Washington. Japan has already answered satisfactorily.

This has been an extremely full week. Tuesday and Wednesday evenings we attended the Courts.

On Friday took part in the memorial services for our Americans who died in the war. They were held at St. Margaret's, Westminster. Accompanied by the Rectors and my aides, I laid a

LORD JELLICOE

LORD PLUMER

wreath at the grave of the Unknown Soldier in Westminster Abbey.

On Friday evening, with Sir Henry Cole and Rawleigh Warner, I went by boat to Antwerp, Belgium, to look at the "Belgian Village" in their exposition which Sir Henry thinks we can use as a basic idea, at least, in an exhibit at our Century of Progress. Was entertained elaborately and fully, but have not time to mention more than my appreciation of the value of Sir Henry's idea and the fact that my friend, Aloys Van de Vyvere, of Brussels, who was Belgian Minister of Finance during the War, came over to spend the day with me. We had a fine visit. Mr. Frielung's organization has achieved a very artistic thing in this "village" and, what is equally important, one that is attracting vast crowds of spectators.

On Thursday evening, Caro and I went to the home of Charles T. te Water (High Commissioner for the Union of South Africa) for dinner. Also, at 10:00 P.M., that evening, by arrangement, I talked over the telephone with the passengers in an aeroplane flying seven thousand feet above Los Angeles, said to be the first occasion on which such a thing had been done across the sea. They had just talked with Mussolini at Rome, so they telephoned. The Los Angeles Examiner initiated and carried out the project.

Between India, unemployment, Palestine, the safeguarding question, and an insecure tenure, necessitating the continual adjustment of a constantly shifting and indefinite alliance with the Liberal Party under Lloyd George, the Prime Minister is "Old Man Trouble's" own child just now.

S.S. Aquitania,
At Sea, June 8, 1930.

After an especially busy week, I am crossing the sea without working on a speech or any neglected matters. Prepared my statement on the Naval Treaty early in the week and cabled it in full to President Hoover, through the State Department, for his comment. In his answer approving it, he suggested two additional sentences at the beginning of the statement.

211

Journal as Ambassador to Great Britain

S.S. Aquitania,
At Sea, June 9, 1930.

Sir Henry Cole, and my secretary and nephew, Henry Dawes, are accompanying me on this trip.

I wrote last in these notes just a week ago (Sunday) in the morning. That afternoon, with Caro, my sister Bessie, Rawleigh, and Dorothy Warner, my niece Nancy Hoyt and Miss Decker, I went to Albert Hall where Toscanini led the New York Symphony Orchestra in a magnificent concert. The box assigned to us was next to the Royal Box, and at the end of the concert the King sent for me, and I talked for a few minutes with him and the Queen. The King said he regarded Toscanini as one of the greatest conductors in the world.

The same evening, Caro and I went to a dinner given for Mr. and Mrs. Toscanini by the Italian Ambassador.

The balance of the week is memorable to me not only for the visit to Cambridge and my lunch with the Imperial General Staff, but also for a visit at the Embassy from my life-long friend, Daniel G. Wing and his wife. It seems a long call back to our days in Lincoln, Nebraska, when Dan started his banking career and I started as a lawyer. He stuck to banking all through, and as president of the First National Bank of Boston is regarded as one of the leading financiers of New England. During all the long intervening years, he has been a faithful and helpful friend to me.

Was interrupted here by a call from the Captain of the Ship. We talked about his predecessor on this ship, Captain Sir James Charles, who carried our regiment over the sea in the *Carmania* in August, 1917, and who died, years afterward, at the end of his last voyage on the day of his retirement from active service.

During the week, the State Department, approving the proposed form of statement, the British Government joined in the clarification of the cruiser agreement of the Treaty.

Friday morning, a member of the Foreign Office called on me and gave me unofficially and confidentially a statement of the *status quo* in the Italian-French naval negotiations, supplementary to the Treaty (as he saw it). Dino Grandi has proposed that if the French will hold up the building of the 1930 program, the Italians will do the same—not laying any keels if the French do not. And if the French wish to lay down only a certain amount, the Italians will lay down only that amount. The French Government, so the press says, agree to this in principle.

But the trouble is that the French do not want to hold up their program indefinitely if negotiations are prolonged; and on the other hand they do not want to open negotiations at present because of Mussolini's recent speeches.

This delay in negotiations is unfortunate, for if France starts and continues her present building program, the British, in a year or so, will have to seriously face the question of a resort to the safeguarding clause of the Treaty, according to this official's idea. It is also most unfortunate because this delay probably will mean that the Preparatory Commission of the Disarmament Conference may meet in the fall with this demoralizing row on its hands.

During the week, confirmed with Vickers the arrangement which I made at Col. R. R. McCormick's request, to have the Schneider Cup winning aeroplane flown at Chicago at the air races this summer.

On Wednesday evening Caro and I attended a reception given by Lady Ward at which the Queen and Prince George were present. Lady Ward is the daughter of Mrs. Whitelaw Reid, and the latter, always interesting and charming, took us in charge.

On Thursday morning, Caro and I motored to Cambridge University, taking Mr. and Mrs. Arthur Henderson with us in our car. The occasion was the conferring of degrees, the presentation of medals to exceptional students, and the recitation of Prize Exercises, and, what was the most important, the installation of Stanley Baldwin as Chancellor of Cambridge in succession to the late Lord Balfour.

The following is the address of the orator to the Chancellor when my degree was conferred:

Americans have since first John Adams came to London, sent to us as their delegates such men as they knew most excellent among themselves, as given to liberal study, as conciliators of friendship, as most esteemed by their own people. It would be too long to recall so many illustrious names,

Journal as Ambassador to Great Britain

but with your unanimous consent I feel sure I may name Charles Francis Adams, the illustrious poet James Russell Lowell, and him whom the British recall with an unusual affection, Walter Hines Page. We, always attached to ancient custom, are very glad that the Americans preserve with the same piety such a good custom and to see among us a man whose name signifies in all Europe peace and good will, and whom his own citizens have elected President of the Senate. Who ignores that many discussions arise among us, who ignores that the gladiators of the daily strife bite one another's fists in enmity, as did the Shakesperian slaves? Who ignores, I say, the madness of the human species? We feel so much the more glad because such a man, consecrated to friendship between the nations, has been sent to us as a delegate.

I introduce to you Charles Gates Dawes.

Caro and I were entertained at the house of Vice-Chancellor, Dr. Arthur S. Ramsey and his sister. We attended the lunch at Caius College, at which the Duke of Gloucester (the King's son) delivered a sensible and witty address and also the garden party given at Dr. Ramsey's home, a most enjoyable and interesting gathering, in most beautiful surroundings emphasized by magnificent weather.

In the evening Caro went to a dinner given for the ladies by Miss Ramsey, and I went to the dinner at Trinity College, given to the new Chancellor, Stanley Baldwin and the recipients of honorary degrees.

The first speakers were the Master, who spoke of the new Chancellor, and Mr. Baldwin, who replied. The other two speakers were Viscount Sumner and myself, who responded for the Recipients of Honorary Degrees. My table companion was the Duke of Gloucester. He has a sense of humor and an amazing frankness of speech, combined with simplicity of manner. The Duke had me in laughter over his recounting of some extemporaneous orations he had heard as a student at Cambridge. This kind of conversation with the Duke proved an advantage to my speech. It resulted in my abandonment of the letter of the text and to a digression in which I spoke of the embarrassment incident to representing properly Professor Einstein, who sat near me.

I said of Baldwin and Henderson, "To me personally this occasion is made the more pleasant because the incoming Chancellor of the University, one of the great statesmen and leaders of his

214

PROCESSION AT CAMBRIDGE—TRINITY COLLEGE IN BACKGROUND

Induction of Stanley Baldwin as Chancellor.

time and at present the leader of the Opposition in this country, has seen fit to nominate for this honor Mr. Arthur Henderson, of a differing political party—a man for whom close official association has given me both friendship and high respect. Surely, the act evidences one of those qualities which have made Mr. Baldwin great and which, in estimating devotion to the highest interests of the country, overlooks the inevitable differences of opinion as to methods by which it may best be achieved."

At Sea,
Thursday, June 11, 1930.

Having received an invitation from a committee of passengers in another class of the ship, I went to them last night and, of course, had to make a speech but enjoyed it.

I seem almost to be taking this trip with Captain Charles, his memory is so treasured by the officers and crew of the *Aquitania*. They knew of my friendship with him, and are very kind to me. The old gentleman, McIntosh, who now is in charge of the reading room, and has served a full fifty years with the Cunard Company, shed tears when he talked to me about Captain Charles. Mr. Shipton, who was his valet, and now is in charge of the smoking room, told me that Charles, whenever the ship was rolling when he went to bed used to caution him about putting his wrist watch where it would not fall. Shipton said he greatly valued it. This was the watch I sent him from London in 1917 (after he had landed the 17th Engineers safely in England) inscribed to him "From the Under-Officer of the After-Wheel House."

Baltimore & Ohio Train,
En Route to Chicago,
June 17, 1930.

The *Aquitania* was delayed a full day in docking by fog until noon last Saturday, the day on which Dana graduated from Lawrenceville School. There are advantages, however, in being

215

Journal as Ambassador to Great Britain

an Ambassador, for having arrived at Quarantine on Friday evening, the customs officers, after their inspection, carried Henry and me on their launch through the fog to the dock. Five newspaper men had been on a boat waiting for us since 7:00 A.M., and they went back to the dock on the official boat also.

Dr. George Grant MacCurdy, the director of the American School of Prehistoric Research, was waiting for me at the hotel and we talked over Niebla and the taking up of the exploration work there.

Leaving for Lawrenceville, New Jersey, in the morning, my secretary, Henry Dawes, and I arrived there at 10:30 A.M. We spent the day with Dana and in attending the commencement exercises. Gus Hanna came over from Montclair and took Senator Walcott and me to Englewood, New Jersey, where I went in response to a radio invitation from Dwight Morrow.

At 1:00 A.M. Sunday, three hours after our arrival, Dwight arrived home, having made nineteen speeches on Saturday and eighteen the day before in closing his Senatorial primary campaign. Nevertheless, he insisted upon staying up until two o'clock in the morning. Had a most delightful visit Sunday with Dwight and his family, all of whom were there. In the afternoon a reception to war veterans was given and about 1800 of them and their families were present.

Colonel Lindbergh brought out the photographs he and Anne took of the Mayan ruins on their flight over the Central American jungles and we three spent most of the evening over them.

They expect their family (the Lindberghs) to number an additional member any day.

Dwight and Mrs. Morrow and John Marshall, who was there, all have been under a heavy strain, but all were as lively and as energetic as usual. Mrs. Morrow has been an active participant and invaluable aide in the campaign. It will be this week when they will feel the inevitable reaction from the incessant work of the past month. I expect a telegram on the train tonight as to the result of the primary which took place today.

LATER. The dispatch estimated his plurality at 300,000.

At 12:35, Sunday night, I took the train from New York for Washington, arriving there early Monday morning. Spent the

PHILIP R. CLARKE

morning with President Hoover and Secretary Stimson, and went to the Senate at noon, where I took lunch with Senator Joseph T. Robinson, and looked into the Treaty situation. Returned to the White House, where I am a guest, in the late afternoon. The President is alone, Mrs. Hoover being at Rapidan.

This morning, my brother Henry met me at the White House. He went with me during the morning, and we had a delightful visit. He left at 1:00 P.M. for New York, whence he sails, together with the Beaches, and Sarah Cutler, for London.

After lunch with the President alone, I left for Chicago at 3:15 P.M.

At Sea (returning),
S.S. Majestic, June 28, 1930.

I wrote my last notes on the train on the way to Chicago. At our last lunch on the back porch of the White House, the President summed up the situation of the administration at present which, as is to be expected, in times of general financial depression, is discouraging.

My visit to the Senate, which I mentioned in my notes of June 17th, was most interesting. I went to the Senate floor and seated myself on the Republican side. So many of my old friends among the Senators came to speak to me that I had to adjourn to the Vice President's chamber. There I greeted practically all who had been in the chamber, about forty in number. I had talked with Senators Dave Reed, Watson, Borah and Robinson, to get the status of the Naval Treaty and its prospects of ratification. Robinson says the maximum vote against the ratification, in the present outlook, is not over fifteen.

I left Tuesday afternoon for Chicago, where I arrived Wednesday morning. I spent the day with my brother Rufus, Major Lohr, Sir Henry Cole, and others interested in the Exposition. Am much impressed with Philip R. Clarke, whom I met for the first time. He is a man of genius and character combined. He unites energy with the power of quick decision and he enlisted in the Fair finance work in short order. He will be a great help, and my ability to get through my work in Chicago in a week is due to the fact that there is much I left him to do.

The other reason I finished so quickly was because of the splendid progress Rufus and his organization are making in the building of the Fair and the forwarding of their plans.

After five days of study, Sir Henry Cole (our technical expert) said that in his long experience he knew of no exposition which was so far advanced and so well organized within three years of the date of its initial start. After this, and my securing Clarke's cooperation in my financial work, I feel now that I will be able to serve out my time in the diplomatic service and raise the balance of the Fair funds during my regular leaves of absence.

They have the Transportation Exhibit Building plans so far advanced that a contract for the building will be let in the next two weeks.

Spent some time on personal business, but the most on Fair finances. Secured from present subscribers of bonds, who are also guarantors, their signatures to a contract to turn in their bonds when paid for to the Trustee to be stamped "without guarantee" in return receiving the cancellation of their guaranty agreement, corresponding to the amount of bonds stamped.

This did not take very much time; but by so doing, for the $3,850,000 of the $10,000,000 bond issue left to be sold, I have now about $5,900,000 of remaining guaranties, or a margin of over $2,000,000 which should make it easier to sell the bonds.

The $10,000,000 now assured will keep the work running until next summer, when I will come over again.

Lived at the Chicago Club nominally, but spent four nights at Evanston with my daughter Carolyn and her family. On last Sunday afternoon, went to Milwaukee to the Sacred Heart Sanitarium with Ross Bartley to see Francis J. Kilkenny who has been seriously ill, but is now recovering.

I left Chicago last Tuesday afternoon for Washington, less than one week from the time I arrived there, and three weeks before I had expected to be able to leave, when I sailed from England.

Journal as Ambassador to Great Britain

At Sea,
S.S. Majestic,
June 30, 1930.

Was met at the depot by a White House automobile and stopped on my way up town at the Carlton Hotel, where Dwight Morrow had just arrived. Stayed with him for a time, and then went to the White House and met the President. Returning to the Carlton, I took Dwight with me to the State Department, where we had a visit with Stimson. Took lunch and dinner with the President.

In the afternoon went to the Senate, but not onto the floor. Saw Jim Watson and Dave Reed and others. The favorable *status quo* of the Naval Treaty situation has not been changed. Dwight told me that during his call on the President in the morning he told him that at such time as the President would deem it most helpful to him, he would announce himself in the strongest terms for the renomination of the President. Had another visit with Dwight in the afternoon and left a memorandum with him *in re* Mexico's participation in the Chicago Fair which Rufus had given me.

In the late afternoon, Henry P. Seidemann called on me at the White House, bringing the finished balance sheet and quarterly operating statements of the Dominican Government. These I afterwards went over with President Hoover and left with him. He has not yet got around to this Government's accounting reform, but hopes to do so. If Seidemann could be put in charge of our national accounting, its new history should commence. To bring this about, a change in the present budget and accounting law must be enacted, taking away from McCarl, the present Comptroller of the Treasury, his accounting responsibility. For the accounting part of his present duties he is inexperienced.

After dinner at the White House, called on my way to the train upon Ruth Hanna McCormick and Sir Ronald Lindsay, the British Ambassador.

Today on the ship I went by invitation to the tourist section, where I met Dr. Ralph V. Magoffin, President of the Archaeo-

Journal as Ambassador to Great Britain

logical Institute of America. Uncle Will Mills and Horace Taft accompanied me. Dr. Magoffin is taking across 200 teachers on a "Vergilian pilgrimage" to go over the route which Vergil says Aeneas travelled. We are going tonight to hear him lecture.

At Sea,
S.S. Majestic, July 1, 1930.

Much enjoyed Dr. Magoffin's able lecture last night. It was entitled "Modern Makers of Ancient History." He explained how modern archaeologists, by their discoveries, have fixed the date of the founding of Rome at about 1200 B.C., when the Roman historians guessed it to be about 741 B.C.

London,
July 11, 1930.

The opponents of the ratification of the London Naval Treaty in the Senate have been trying to get possession, by resolution, of the confidential diplomatic correspondence between the State Department and myself covering the seven months prior to the convening of the Conference. They want it made public in order to make trouble and beat the Treaty. The resolution, as introduced, demanded that the documents be turned over to the Senate without reservation, but an amendment inserting the words "if such action is not incompatible with the public interest" was passed by a vote of 38 to 17, and the papers will, of course, not be given to the Senate.

Rumors of my embarrassment on account of a frank dealing with facts and personalities in them which would result from the publication have been rife for the last few days. Of course, in my messages, I gave all pertinent facts and opinions which I thought would be of value to our Government in the formulation of its policy and methods in negotiation and in the preparation of its positions; and did so freely as is the duty of an Ambassador. Their publication would be no more embarrassing to me than to other diplomats involved in the naval negotiations if the absurd course of making public such confidential communications to their respective Governments was followed.

I gave without hesitation all the facts I deemed valuable, and satisfaction with these dispatches was duly expressed by the President. If these cables had been made public, at least they would have shown that I exactly forecasted the antics in which certain Senatorial opponents of the Treaty are now indulging.

As to the last week: I arrived in London on the morning of the Fourth of July. The annual reception which we gave at the Embassy was attended by 2500 people, about the same number as last year. The Irish Guards Band, forty-two in number, furnished the music on the terrace at the rear of the Embassy, and refreshments were served in the garden. In the evening, after Caro and I had shaken hands with this multitude, we went to the annual banquet of the American Club at the Savoy Hotel where, as usual, I made a speech and also presided.

Lord Derby, Sir John Simon and Dr. Robert McElroy were on the toast list. About four hundred guests were present.

On last Monday, I attended a lunch given by the Master Mariners to Sir Thomas Lipton, soon to sail for America on his fifth attempt to lift the cup with a new yacht, *Shamrock V*. The Prince of Wales presided and made one of his happy and thoughtful extempore speeches. Sir Thomas replied. I was also called upon for remarks by the Prince and responded briefly. It was a rousing meeting. Had a talk with the Prince who had heard of Chicago's troubles with its gangsters. He was as fine as ever.

We attended Court Thursday evening—a brilliant scene. The balance of the week I have been busy catching up with my mail and entertaining American visitors and callers.

Arthur and Mary Beach (my sister) and Sarah Cutler (my cousin) are with us, as is also Uncle Will Mills and Dana. We are having a real family reunion.

Journal as Ambassador to Great Britain

London,
July 20, 1930.

The desperate fight of a small group in the Senate against the ratification of the Naval Treaty still goes on, but they are about worn out; and the Treaty should be ratified by the United States in the coming week. The few Senators who are speaking against it have made every effort to obscure the merits, and emphasize the short-comings of the agreement; but the only apparent effect has been to strengthen the public's sentiment favoring it.

Senators Joe Robinson and Dave Reed, who have been on the firing line in the Senate debate in behalf of the ratification, have done magnificently and should always be remembered for this final achievement. Their clear explanations and forceful presentations have cleared away all the smoke screens of the Senatorial opposition and have prevented the latter from confusing the mind of the average man and diverting it from the real issues at stake.

The following dispatch (July 11th) from its Washington correspondent, Willmott Lewis, published in the London *Times*, I append as further covering what has occurred:

SECRET NAVAL DOCUMENTS—PRODUCTION REFUSED
BY MR. HOOVER
(From our own Correspondent)
Washington, July 11.

President Hoover late this afternoon sent to the Senate a message in which he declined to transmit the documents and records relative to the Naval Treaty of London, on the ground that this would be a breach of trust. The message was a reply to the resolution of the Senate, passed yesterday evening by 52 votes to 4, requesting the President to send forward these documents if "this action would be compatible with public interest."

The President's decision, curiously enough, seems to dissatisfy nobody very seriously, least of all the opponents of the Treaty, who are left with their precious grievance. These last are, in fact, so completely convinced that full knowledge of the "secret documents" would help them not at all in their fight against the instrument itself, that they have been careful to refuse offers of a confidential examination which have been made to them. They would rather be left in continued freedom to make political capital of the issue they have created.

As for their colleagues, most of them were prepared in advance for the

222

sort of thing President Hoover said in his message. He pointed out that the Executive is in duty bound to guard the interests of the United States, to protect future negotiations, and to maintain relations of amity with other nations. He must not allow himself to become guilty of a breach of trust by the betrayal of confidences. To make public these documents would close to the United States those avenues of information which are essential for future dealings with foreign powers. The President has no desire to withhold any information having the remotest relation to the Treaty. All Senators, he added, were privileged to examine the documents in confidence and several had already done so. He gave his word finally that no secret or concealed understandings, promises or commitments had been made by the United States delegation to London.

"All nonsense," said Senator Johnson of California, when asked for his opinion of the message, and his associates in the opposition echoed him. But with the reading of the message, this tempest in a dispatch box died down for a time.

As to the occurrences here, the last nine days my friend Van de Vyvere, Minister of Finance of Belgium during the War, has been visiting us. We went together to a dinner last night at the Belgian Embassy. We talked much over our war-time experiences together.

Yesterday (Saturday) and a week ago Saturday we attended athletic contests. The first was with the Hendersons at the annual meeting of the athletes from Cambridge and Oxford universities of Britain with those from Cornell and Princeton universities of the United States. The second was a ball game between the midshipmen on our visiting battleships and a team of Americans and Japanese resident in London, which we attended again with the Henderson boys and also my brother Henry and his wife and daughter Mary.

Am putting in spare time on the study of Dr. MacCurdy's fine treatise on prehistoric man (*Human Origins: A Manual of Prehistory*) as I want to be more letter perfect when I visit the Dordogne region and Spain with him next month.

Called on Sir Auckland Geddes, chairman of the Rio Tinto Company Ltd., and had a long talk with him about the archaeology of the Niebla area and the Rio Tinto mine which we shall visit.

Houghton, Mifflin and Company have reissued here my *Journal of the Great War*. I am pleased with the long and favorable reviews of it in the London *Times* (Literary Supplement) of July

Journal as Ambassador to Great Britain

17th; in the *Daily Telegraph* of July 1st (written by Captain B. H. Liddell Hart) and in the *Spectator* of July 12th, as well as a short one in the *Observer* this morning.

Took Van de Vyvere the other afternoon to a lecture at University College by Dr. C. Leonard Woolley on his 1929 discoveries at Ur. It was fascinating. Had a long talk with him and with Sir Flinders Petrie, whose 50th anniversary as an archaeologist it was. The latter presided at the lecture.

London delights me with its opportunities for increasing my knowledge by personal contacts with first authority. Made my usual trip to the London Museum.

London,
July 22, 1930.

Today received the two following cables, dated yesterday:

The Senate has ratified the London Naval Treaty, and upon this happy culmination of the labors in which you bore so useful and important a part, I send you again my hearty thanks and cordial congratulations. You may well take a generous pride in your share in this great service.

(Signed) HERBERT HOOVER.

The Senate this afternoon ratified the Naval Treaty by a vote of 58 to 9. I send you my sincere thanks and congratulations.

STIMSON.

On my part I sent cables of congratulation to the President and to Secretary Stimson, and as well to each of my associates on the American delegation to the Conference. To Senator Claude Swanson, I sent a message congratulating him upon his speech in the Senate favoring the Treaty, which I had just read for the first time.

London,
Thursday, July 24, 1930.

Caro and I attended Their Majesties' garden party at Buckingham Palace this afternoon. About six thousand were said to be present. The arrangements for the Diplomatic Corps, as usual,

A. VAN DE VYVERE

MRS. CHARLES G. DAWES

were excellent. At the pavilion where the King and Queen met the diplomats, I had a talk with the Prime Minister who says that Parliament will ratify the Treaty next week. When Parliament rises he is going to Oberammergau, and then fly back to Scotland. Matsudaira told me that Japan will ratify shortly.

The King and the Queen were most kind. The former asked me about my recent trip to America and the Chicago Exposition, and then commented on the gangsters whose latest villainy in Detroit is exploited in this morning's papers. Verily, from the newspaper standpoint, good news is often bad news.

On Tuesday last, Van de Vyvere and I spent a wonderful hour with a wonderful man in a wonderful place—Sir Flinders Petrie, in the midst of his Beth-Pelet exhibit at University College. We spent most of our visit examining the neolithic implements he has found in and near Beth-Pelet.

London,
July 31, 1930.

The last week has been largely devoted to American visitors with whom we have had an enjoyable time. In the last month, Caro tells me that at lunch or dinner we have entertained at the Embassy about two hundred Americans.

On assuming this office, I determined that if I could help it, our visitors from home would never experience a "cold" Embassy such as I once encountered in 1897 during my first visit to Europe. Caro is entitled to the credit for the way we take care of people. She is a born executive, and with her perfect tact and kindly heart she keeps the Embassy, with its large staff of servants and a continual capacity load of transients and house guests, a place of comfort and happiness.

Nothing much is doing at the Chancery and I am putting in, without trouble, two hours a day in archaeological study, preparatory to my trip to France and Spain with Dr. MacCurdy in the latter part of August.

The King has signed the Naval Treaty, and the announcement of that fact will be made at 3:00 P.M. in Parliament today.

Journal as Ambassador to Great Britain

The sudden death in America of my army comrade and dear friend, General Henry C. Smither from appendicitis, has saddened me. He was a great soldier and a faithful ally. We worked together in the A.E.F., in the establishment of the United States Budget System, and on the Santo Domingo economic commission. I had him appointed Chief Coordinator of the United States when we established by Executive Order the present system of coordination in our governmental business. In this position, he served from 1921 to 1928, when he resigned to become an officer in the Indian Refining Company.

London,
August 9, 1930.

Caro, Dana, Virginia and Miss Decker left for a visit home this evening, sailing from Southampton tomorrow on the *Leviathan*. They will be gone about six weeks.

While my family is away, I will make the archaeological trip with Dr. MacCurdy to France and Spain. The *New York Times* wired the other day, asking about it. Mr. Seldon, the correspondent, made the following statement after a talk with me, which I append as self-explanatory. This will save waste motion hereafter with the reporters.

General Dawes, the American Ambassador, who is leaving during the month with Mr. Addison L. Green, chairman of the Board, and Dr. George Grant MacCurdy, the director of the American School of Prehistoric Research, for a two weeks' trip through the Dordogne region of France and other points in France and Spain associated with prehistoric man, was asked what he expected to find. He replied that he had no expectations, and that as far as he was concerned the trip was merely one of observation in company with high archaeological authorities. As to expectations, he said that the trouble with archaeological investigations carried on with a preconceived theory is that whether or not justified, the feeling is created that in such examinations facts are not impartially weighed.

"I admit I am interested," said the General, "in the study of prehistoric man and his accomplishments in the Mediterranean region and feel that the work now being done in this connection should be encouraged. In my judgment, what it now needs especially is that more detailed and coordinated study which will result from concurrent investigation in different sections with a specific objective. For instance, there are in the Museum at Candia,

226

Journal as Ambassador to Great Britain

in Crete, over a thousand clay documents written in the script of an unknown language which Sir Arthur Evans, who has been conducting archaeological investigations in Crete since 1893, believes to relate to the very beginnings of European civilization. Script differing in detail, but similar in its general nature, has been found in many other sections of the Mediterranean region.

"The great Megalithic remains of the Maltese Islands, of Niebla in Spain, and other Mediterranean sections, together with the evidences of the immense extent of prehistoric mining, all indicate that we have underrated the age, the intelligence, and the accomplishments of prehistoric man, and his industrial and social organization. All related objects, as much as possible, should be studied at one time and under one direction. This, I realize, is quite difficult in archaeology but this, it seems to me, is what the situation demands just now.

"The fascination of the later archaeological periods in the Mediterranean region, because of the closer similarity of the life of that time to that of our own age, perhaps has led to a comparative neglect of Stone Age study in that region. The Minoan, Egyptian, Grecian and Roman civilizations were all preceded by the civilization of the Stone Age man and from the evidences, many of them recently discovered, of the great extent and probable unity of the latter, it may well be considered as the most interesting of them all. Necessarily, much of the excavation in connection with the historic archaeology in the Mediterranean has been conducted in separate compartments where each investigator being interested in particular periods, is not always concerned with the importance of his finds as related to other periods. Again, so far as the paleolithic and neolithic periods are concerned, historic archaeologists are necessarily content with merely mentioning the fact that their excavations reached them.

"All archaeological study is, of course, a changing one. New discoveries constantly bring new conceptions, and form the basis for new deductions. As in other places, these discoveries are being made in the Mediterranean region. Dr. MacCurdy is one of the leading prehistoric archaeologists, and naturally adept at what I may call archaeological coordination. I plan to visit with him the Dordogne region in France, in which he has made such an extensive study of prehistoric man. We hope also to visit the Altamira cave in Spain, finally getting to Niebla near the Rio Tinto Mines."

Last night I took dinner at the Carlton Club where Winston Churchill entertained in honor of my friend, Bernard M. Baruch. About twelve guests were present. Among them, I remember the following: Sir Auckland Geddes, Worthington Evans, Brendan Bracken, a member of Parliament, said to be of great promise, Mr. Vickers, Lord Ashfield, and young Randolph Churchill.

A most interesting discussion was had. The question was over a British tariff policy and our international relations. Churchill looked upon the unsettled condition of China with its great markets as ominous for Anglo-American trade there, and hoped for a joint policy to promote the cause of peace in that country on the part of the United States, Great Britain and Japan. He was much concerned over the health of Lord Birkenhead, which is critical and commented on his public usefulness. It was an intelligent gathering and talkative as well.

London,
July 23, 1930.

The following is a letter to Mr. Thomas W. Lamont:

My Dear Tom:

This letter is not official, and is for your confidential information.

H. H. General Shahwali Khan, the Minister of Afghanistan, with whom I have become acquainted during my stay here, has called upon me asking to be advised of some American expert to whom his government could issue an invitation to come to Afghanistan to devise for them a proper banking and currency system. H. H. General Shahwali Khan is a very intelligent man. He is a brother of the present King of Afghanistan, and the brother-in-law of the deposed King. He assured me that they now have a stable government in Afghanistan.

Before writing this letter, I went over the matter with Arthur Henderson when he was dining with me the other night at the Embassy, and asked him if he saw any objection from the British standpoint to my recommending somebody for this work in Afghanistan. He replied that he saw no objection, saying that the relations between the British Government and the Afghan Government were most friendly and cordial.

If the Afghan Government should invite you to take charge of this work, would you be likely to accept? You could select that time of the year in which the climatic conditions of Afghanistan would be ideal and, providing of course you brought two or three associates who could stay to install your plan, I do not think you would need to spend a very great time on the work; possibly, as was the case with myself in the Dominican Republic work, only a month. The Minister tells me that you would be received in Afghanistan with all the honors and courtesies of their Government.

In case you are favorably inclined to the acceptance of the invitation, I suggest that you show this letter, confidentially, to Secretary Stimson, who can tell you whether there is any possible objection on the part of our Government to your action. The Afghanistan Government wants an American for this work, because such an appointment creates around the work an atmosphere of impartiality conducive to confidence.

To you, as it would to me, I think the work would have an appeal. Its successful accomplishment affecting, as it will, the lives of so many people,

228

AT FONT-DE-GAUME (DORDOGNE), FRANCE

Right to left: Mrs. MacCurdy, Mr. Kluckhohn, General Dawes,
Dr. MacCurdy, Mr. Addison L. Green, the caretaker.

THOMAS W. LAMONT

cannot but bring its full reward in self-satisfaction from a sense of duty done.

If you cannot yourself undertake the work, could you recommend anybody? He must have the qualities of a statesman and a friend-maker, as well as those of a financial and administrative expert. He should have a personality combining amiability, courage and firmness. You see, I am describing yourself.

Trusting that I may hear from you soon, and with affectionate regards,

Your friend,

CHARLES G. DAWES.

Mr. Thomas W. Lamont
23 Wall Street,
New York, N. Y.

North Haven, Maine,
August 5, 1930.

Ambassador Dawes,
American Embassy, London,
4 Grosvenor Gardens.

Many thanks your letter. Very interesting. Am here for months holiday after strenuous Mexican conference. Will discuss with partners immediately upon return stop. Feel can be of service either personally or by suggestion names. Writing fully. Best regards.

LAMONT.

August 14, 1930.

Motored from Blair Atholl, Scotland, over to Lossiemouth to see the Prime Minister, taking my friends with me for lunch with him, as he has suggested. These included John F. Harris, Charles A. Hanna, Mr. Glendenning, Mr. Church, Mrs. William Mitchell and her son. Mr. MacDonald took us with his son Malcolm and his two younger daughters to lunch at the Marine Hotel. His house "Hillocks" however, was our headquarters for our stay.

Had a private talk with him covering an hour. He is disturbed at the French military program, involving large appropriations for fortifications and aeroplanes and a large naval construction, planned to commence soon, although the latter is not as yet in the appropriation stage.

He has been unable to get Briand to agree to British and American participation in the discussion between Italy and France as to the naval settlement which they could not reach at the Naval Conference. He maintains that this discussion should be considered as an extension of the negotiations of the London Naval Conference and should be under similar methods and preparatory to the deliberations of the Disarmament Conference of the League of Nations.

They do not agree to this, or rather, France does not agree. And he regards this as discouraging and fears that France is going ahead with a naval program which will force Great Britain to follow. He said he would keep me informed of the situation.

Referring to the nervousness and unrest of the British and European peoples in the present business depression which exists almost everywhere except in France, he said that he was disquieted. As to the moot question of British tariff legislation, he intimated that it would not be difficult for him, if he deemed best, to reach an agreement upon policy with Stanley Baldwin. He seems to me to be clearly correct as to this, and that therefore in his hands is the power to fix present British policy.

I am wondering if it is not in his mind to do something along this line even though it will split off a portion of his party. All conditions over here—political and industrial, agricultural and commercial—have seemed to me for a long time to portend tariff legislation.

We returned to Lude House, Blair Atholl, by automobile in the late afternoon.

Lude House, Blair Atholl,
August 15, 1930.

In the course of his conversation yesterday, MacDonald, in discussing the situation in India, told me that Great Britain would at any cost maintain law and order and British prestige, which alone assures peace in India.

Lord Irwin's vague talk about dominion status has encouraged disorder in India, in my judgment, and aroused apprehensions in Britain that MacDonald and Henderson would not use the firm hand.

Relative to the efforts of the enemies of the Treaty in the

Journal as Ambassador to Great Britain

United States Senate to get hold of confidential diplomatic communications, MacDonald told an amusing story of another diplomat's nervousness over one of his (MacDonald's) expressions in a letter to him. If the letter was to be made public, this statement would be regarded as an indiscretion in this diplomat's opinion affecting public opinion in his country. After MacDonald's objection to having the diplomat alter the letter himself as suggested, MacDonald wrote him a new one in place of it, receiving the old letter back from him.

Gus Hanna and I have had a delightful visit with John Harris at this beautiful place. John is an ideal host. It seems queer that John, and Gus and I—friends forty-two years ago at Lincoln, Nebraska—should have this reunion in such a distant place and different environment.

August 17, 1930.

Arrived by train from Edinburgh this morning.

The visit to Blair Atholl was made all the more pleasant by the presence of Attorney General Mitchell with his wife and son. They will be there for several weeks.

London,
August 21, 1930.

For the last few days have had a delightful visit with my brother Rufus and his wife and two daughters, Helen and Margaret. Tomorrow, they, with Gus Hanna, leave for a few days' motor trip in England, and afterward they go to Sweden, and Gus to New York. As for me, I leave tomorrow on the "Golden Arrow" for Paris, the Dordogne region and Spain.

Went with Gus the other day to Mme. Tussaud's "wax works" to see my figure which had been erected—if that is the proper word—in the "American section" about a year ago. After viewing it, I realized I had not missed much by my delay.

Rufus has established a London office for the Foreign Exhibits

Journal as Ambassador to Great Britain

Department of the Century of Progress, for which as director he has selected Col. John S. Sewell, who will be associated with Sir Henry Cole.

Cable from my wife today saying they had arrived in Evanston and all were well.

Seville, Spain,
Monday, September 1, 1930.

I left London on this interesting trip on August 22nd and spent that evening in Paris. Left next morning for Périgueux, travelling with Mr. Addison Green, chairman of the Board of Trustees of the American School of Prehistoric Research, his fine son, Marshall, and Mr. Warren, of the *New York Times*.

At Périgueux, where we spent the night, we were joined by Dr. George Grant MacCurdy, the director of the School, and his wife, the latter also a trained archaeologist. The next day we all went through the Vézère Valley Caves (Dordogne) where prehistoric man made his home. The object of my visit was to see with my own eyes, aided by the expert minds of others, these famous places, the accounts of which have so interested me. In these notes, I will not try to go into archaeological details. It was for me a day of wonder and delight.

Les Eyzies is termed by Dr. MacCurdy as the center of Paleolithic cavedom, and besides our visit there, we went to Le Moustier, Cap-Blanc, Combarelles, Font-de-Gaume, Cro-Magnon and Laugerie-Basse. I stumbled and crawled along the deep limestone passages of Combarelles, and Font-de-Gaume, and saw in their inner depths—in Combarelles, two hundred and fifty meters from the entrance—the pictures executed by Paleolithic man twenty-five thousand or more years ago, under conditions of great personal discomfort. It seemed to me that he must have sought these more remote and difficult sections of the caves to indulge his artistic instincts, not so much because he was seeking a shrine for the pictures themselves as some archaeologists say, but a protected place where, if his enemies did find him relaxed, they could attack him only in one direction and then only after he had been put on his guard again.

Wide World Photos, Paris

AT PREHISTORIC MUSEUM, LES EYZIES, FRANCE

Left to right: General Dawes, Mr. Green, Dr. MacCurdy, the curator of the museum.

AT COMBARELLES, FRANCE

Left to right: Mrs. MacCurdy, Mr. Addison L. Green, caretaker's son, Marshall Green (at back), Dr. George Grant MacCurdy, caretaker of cave (in shadow), General Dawes, Mr. Frank L. Kluckhohn of the *New York Times*.

Journal as Ambassador to Great Britain

One cannot traverse the pitch dark and narrow cavern without making a noise unless he has a light. If an enemy either carried a light or made a noise in approaching the Paleolithic artist in the far portion of a cave he would warn him and, of necessity, he was compelled to do one or the other.

The Aurignacian man had his kind, and the world as well against him. Probably it was he who disposed of the Neanderthal man and the latter could have been no mean enemy. To me, the Aurignacian, or Cro-Magnon, man (whichever you wish to call him) is the most fascinating figure of all the different types of early man. Of an average height over six feet, with a brain capacity fully equal to that of the Caucasian of today, as definitely superior, at least, in superficial characteristics to the Neanderthal man as we would be were the latter still on earth, where did he come from? Archaeologists cannot answer.

Paris,
Thursday, September 4, 1930.

[Continuing the notes of September 1st.]

This day's work was strenuous. Notwithstanding it was very hot, we put in about eleven hours. The whole of the next day, August 25th, we consumed in automobiles, travelling to Hendaye, where we spent the night.

August 26th was devoted to a torrid ride of nine hours by railroad to Santander, Spain. August 27th (my 65th birthday) we spent at Santander, in the morning, in the archaeological museum with its curator, and in the afternoon, in the famous Altamira Cave nearby with its outstanding polychrome pictures by Magdalenian man. These brilliant pictures are an awe-inspiring sight. They surpassed my preconceived ideas in every way.

The Magdalenians were the last of the Paleolithic men having been preceded by the following cultures: Eolithic, Pre-Chellean, Chellean, Acheulian, Mousterian, Aurignacian, and Solutrean.

Then, after the Magdalenian man, came five succeeding cultures of Neolithic man (of the late Stone Age who ground his

233

Journal as Ambassador to Great Britain

flints instead of flaking them by percussion or pressure) before the Bronze Age or the Iron Age had commenced. At a rock shelter near Les Eyzies, France (Laugerie-Basse), the bed rock was just under the Aurignacian deposits. No man had lived there before the Aurignacian man, and yet the successive layers of his leavings and of Solutrian and Magdalenian man alone measured thirty feet.

Probably thirty thousand years were consumed in their gradual building up. I think here was where I best and yet but feebly visualized the stupendous and mostly unwritten history of this whole fight upward of the human race—terrible in its sufferings but majestic in its achievements.

From Santander we went to Madrid by train, arriving on the morning of August 28th, which we spent in the archives of the Indies, that great collection of as yet not thoroughly examined documents relating to the beginnings of modern civilization in the Western Hemisphere. It is here that Professor C. V. Clark, under the auspices of the Smithsonian Institution, has done much of his work in searching for a Mayan codex.* We examined one fine Mayan document here.

The Curator laid before us the original letters of Christopher Columbus, written in reference to his prospective voyage of discovery, and many of the official papers connected therewith.

When we returned from lunch, I had a telephone from the Infante Don Alfonso, whom I had met in the United States, and who had noted my arrival by the morning papers. He joined us in a visit to the archaeological museum (*Museo Arquelogico*) in the afternoon, and we took tea at his home. He invited me to visit at his place on the Mediterranean, where his wife is now staying, and to which he was to fly the next day.

When we arrived the next day at Seville (August 29th) his wife, the Infanta Beatriz, to whom he had telephoned, called me up, and said that she and her husband would come up to Seville on Monday after our trip to Niebla and the Rio Tinto Mines.

On Friday, August 30th, we went by automobile to Niebla,

* For an account of the researches of Dr. Clark which were carried on under a grant by Ambassador Dawes, see *Annual Report of the Smithsonian Institution, 1934*, pp. 6-8.

RÍO TINTO MINE—SECTION OF SOUTH LODE OPEN-CUT

RÍO TINTO MINE—ROMAN WATER-WHEEL

where we met Captain Timmis, of the Rio Tinto Company, who had come to show us that interesting region. We also met Mrs. Whishaw, an old lady in delicate health, who heads an archaeological school there. I had been interested in her contention that the great Niebla castle was partly of Neolithic origin. We climbed and crawled around the immense old castle most of the afternoon, but Dr. MacCurdy could not discover any evidence of Neolithic work.

The remains of ancient work—Roman and pre-Roman— abounded on every hand, but there seemed no tangible foundation for the claim that any of it was by the hand of the Stone Age man.

Likewise, at the wonderful Rio Tinto Mines, whose immense pre-historic slag piles had fired my imagination and to examine which I had asked Dr. MacCurdy to come here, we could not consider any part of them to be of Neolithic origin, as Mrs. Whishaw had maintained.

But we were more than repaid for our trip by the sights we saw, and our hospitable entertainment by the officers in charge of this great mining enterprise, including Mr. Hill, Captain Timmis and Mr. Gough—all Englishmen. We stayed the night with them and spent the next morning, a very hot one, in a somewhat strenuous tour of inspection.

For six hundred years, the Romans mined this section, starting, it is believed, about 200 B.C. The contents of the Roman and pre-Roman slag piles (probably Phoenician) are estimated by the Rio Tinto engineers at 30,000,000 tons, representing the smelting of 50,000,000 tons of ore. The copper thus obtained, they estimated at about 1,800,000 tons. Roughly, they thought that the pre-Roman slag comprised about one-fifth of the whole. At one time the Romans must have had 50,000 men at work in and around the mines. We were a little dazed at the indisputable evidence of the extent of the work done before the Roman exploitation.

We returned to Seville on Saturday evening (August 31st). On the trip from Madrid, Mr. Dubose, of the *Associated Press*, and Mr. Kluckhohn, of the *New York Times*, accompanied us.

On Saturday morning, Dr. and Mrs. MacCurdy, Mr. Green and

his son, Marshall, left by automobile for Gibraltar, from where they sail for America. I spent the day in Seville with Captain Timmis and the two newspaper correspondents, going in the afternoon to Itálica, an ancient Roman city, with a vast amphitheatre, and the birthplace of the Emperors Trojan, Adrian and Theodosius. The city is but partially excavated.

On Monday morning, I returned the calls of the Military Governor of the district, the Mayor of the city and others. At noon, Don Alfonso called on me at the hotel and took me to lunch with the Infanta Beatriz at the fine old home of their friend, the Marquesa de Yanduri, adjoining the Alcazar. The latter and Sir Charles Lewis, a young English friend of the Infante, were also at lunch.

Don Alfonso is in command of aviation in the Spanish Army, and a man of intense activity and industry. In mental attainments and personal attractiveness, he is most unusual. His wife is equally distinguished in personal and intellectual qualities and charming manners. I am told that they are as universally admired and respected in Spain as I know them to be in England and by those who met them on their visit a few years ago in the United States, where I became acquainted with them. I much enjoyed their entertainment.

I left for Paris the night of September 1st, arriving here Wednesday morning, September 3rd.

Paris,
September 6, 1930.

Arrived here morning of September 3rd and went to the Hotel Ritz. Jo Davidson, who had not yet completed my bust for the Senate Chamber, caught me soon after, and intermittently he had me every day at his studio, sitting while he chipped away at his marble.

Have lunched with Ambassador and Mrs. Walter Evans Edge and met many old friends during the last few days. This morning I went with Edge and the two United States Commissioners to the French Colonial Exposition, Bascom Slemp and G. L. Burke, to look over the Exposition grounds.

Journal as Ambassador to Great Britain

London,
Monday, September 8, 1930.

Arrived here from Paris Sunday evening. My brother Rufus and his daughter, Helen, and Attorney General and Mrs. Mitchell and their son, William, were at the Embassy, having arrived Sunday morning.

Today, I have been at the Chancery catching up with affairs.

In response to requests from the papers for a statement about my recent trip, I gave them the following statement:

We visited Les Eyzies, the center of Paleolithic cavedom in France and the surrounding points in Le Moustier, Combarelles, Font-de-Gaume, Cro-Magnon, and Cap-Blanc, where Dr. MacCurdy and his school of prehistoric research have been working for seven years. I was particularly interested in the cave at Combarelles. We stumbled and crawled along its deep limestone passages and in their inner depths, 750 feet from the entrance, viewed pictures executed by Paleolithic man twenty-five thousand years or more ago.

In most of the caves in France, where pictures are found, they are in the most inaccessible portions of the caverns and at times were made under conditions of indescribable personal discomfort. To draw some of them, the artist would have to lie on his back and make his pictures upon a wall only a few inches over his head. Evidently little thought of any future spectators was in his mind. He was an artist for art's sake. I am only a layman in archaeology and while, as archaeologists say, some of these inaccessible places may have been selected as a shrine connected with some religious belief, it would seem to me that in most cases the artist who lived in a time of perpetual individual warfare was seeking a protecting place where, if his enemies did find him relaxed and off his guard, they could attack him only in one direction and then only after they had put him on his guard again. One cannot crawl through this pitch-dark and narrow cavern without making a noise unless one carries a light. If an intruder either carried a light or made a noise in approaching the Paleolithic artist in the far portion of the cave, he would warn him and of necessity the intruder would be compelled to do one or the other.

As to the methods of search for the remains of prehistoric man, the thought came to me that if man could be as ingenious in seeking knowledge of the past as he is in creating wealth for the future, he could amplify present methods in a practical manner. For instance, some of the most remarkable caverns containing the remains of Paleolithic man and his art have been discovered by chance. In the thousands of years intervening between prehistoric man's occupancy of them and the present, the opening of the caverns, through rock falls, land slides, or other surface changes have often been obliterated and the caves rediscovered by accident—in one case through a rabbit burrow.

Journal as Ambassador to Great Britain

The limestone cliffs along the Vézère Valley and all through this general section are unquestionably honeycombed with caverns, whose former entrances are now covered up, many of which have been occupied by Stone Age man. Within the last decade, by the use of geophysical instruments, mankind searching for oil is able to locate a rock dome as deep as, or deeper than, three thousand feet below the surface. Surely by the use of a modified form of such instruments, or by rotary drills, near the top line of these cliffs, the shallow unopened and undiscovered caverns within them would be located and openings made into them from the base of the cliffs.

In accidentally discovered caves whose former entrances have been obliterated, such as the Altamira Cave in Spain, the very finest specimens of Paleolithic art have been found. Their cover of earth has protected the paintings from deterioration. There are no doubt other Paleolithic art galleries like Altamira awaiting discovery.

London,
Tuesday, September 16, 1930.

My brother Rufus was here until the 13th. He has been busy establishing the London headquarters of the Chicago Exposition, in which he has installed Col. John S. Sewell, as head, and Sir Henry Cole, as technical advisor.

On one evening I gave a dinner to Rufus at the Embassy at which about twenty-eight guests were present, including many of the officials of the British Government in charge of technical and research work of the Government, who are interested in cooperating with him. Rufus has been very active during his European trip, and over here as well as in the United States, he has Exposition matters moving with expedition and intelligence.

On last Friday afternoon, I left for Liverpool, where I was the guest of the city until last Sunday evening, having been honored by an invitation to open the Centenary Celebration of the Liverpool and Manchester Railway which ushered in the miracle of modern steam transportation. This was not simply a local, but a world occasion as well. I was treated on this visit with marked kindness and attention.

On Friday evening, the Lord Mayor of Liverpool, Sir Lawrence Holt, gave a dinner for me at Town Hall, at which about two hundred guests were present, and at which he and I spoke. During my stay, I was delightfully entertained at his fine home,

AFTER THE OPENING CEREMONY AT THE CENTENARY OF THE LIVERPOOL &
MANCHESTER RAILWAY

REPLICAS OF ENGINE "NORTHUMBRIAN" AND ATTACHED CAR
CONTAINING A BAND, AS THEY APPEARED IN 1830 AT THE
CELEBRATION OF THE OPENING OF THE LIVERPOOL & MAN-
CHESTER RAILWAY

At the left of the engine, wearing the chain of office, is the Lord Mayor of Liverpool,

Journal as Ambassador to Great Britain

where the Lady Mayoress was a most charming hostess, and the four young children very interesting.

The railroad exhibition, which is to run for a week, is a great spectacle. I was told that 3500 actors participate.

The program of the first opening of the railway a century ago by the Duke of Wellington was re-enacted. Replicas of the engines, "Northumbrian" and "Rocket," ran on the track before us —the former carrying passenger coaches built and decorated as in the year 1830, with their passengers dressed in the costumes of that year.

I insert here a copy of my Liverpool address.

I feel that on this occasion of the Centenary of the Liverpool and Manchester Railway, it would be futile to review at length the details of an accomplishment which, in its far-reaching consequences to mankind, may be ranked as one of the most important in the progress of world civilization. The Centenary of this railroad is not only a national event for Britain; it is a world event. In these surroundings, upon this railroad, a hundred years ago, there opened a new era for humanity—an era in which both the needs of mankind and the means of supplying them were immensely diversified and multiplied. It was this railroad which became the model for an immediate world imitation. Many epoch-making discoveries have had to fight their way slowly to that general utilization through which alone can come a change in the manner of life of the great multitudes. But the work of the two Stephensons and their associates, as demonstrated upon the Liverpool and Manchester Railway, took the world by storm.

With the development of great enterprises great men are always associated, and those who contributed a hundred years ago to the launching of the Liverpool and Manchester Railway were confronted by obstacles which, to the mediocre, would have seemed insurmountable. These obstacles, necessarily inherent in a *status quo* which represented not only the united achievements but the united traditions of a great and conservative people, required for their overcoming business and political leadership of the highest order. The financiers, business men and statesmen who carried this enterprise through its early stages have justly found an enduring place in history. But standing out before them all in the minds of the world are the two Stephensons and their little locomotive, the "Rocket", with its tubular boiler and its draught-creating steam blast.

When, upon this little railroad, were laid the foundations of successful steam transportation on land, there were laid also the foundations of changes in the social and business organization of the civilized world which have made the last century distinctive in its history. Great as have been the beneficial changes in the life of this Island which the railroad has wrought, the debt of distant countries to this achievement of British genius is even greater than that of the British peoples themselves.

239

Journal as Ambassador to Great Britain

When the railroad was built, the people of the British Isles were already a homogenous people. With a magnificent system of roadways and canals already centuries old, and with a large population in an area of comparatively limited extent, there had long been in existence in Britain those opportunities for extended human contact and cooperation which had created a trade not only Island wide, but world wide, and an industry which supplied in the higher essentials, not only its own people, but those of many other countries. But this condition did not exist in many countries for which you made the railroad possible, as in the United States. Here in Great Britain you increased contacts already possible. There you made possible contacts otherwise impossible. Here you tightened in bonds of mutual endeavor and the understanding which always arises from it, a people already homogenous. There you made possible earlier the homogeneity of a people of diversified origin scattered over an area so great that, without railroads, it might have been indefinitely delayed. Here your railroads were laid down to cities already old, and followed the course of a population which had pioneered centuries before. There, in the vast areas of an unsettled West, the railroads were themselves the most aggressive pioneers. Their far-flung extensions into uninhabited country determined the course of settlement and the location of cities yet to come. Here in 1830, your country was integrated, developed and settled in all its parts. There the great western half of the country was then practically a wilderness. Here your railroads but accommodated themselves in the first instance to conditions of an existing population. There in the West, transporting the settlers, they determined where the coming population could and would exist. They thus became formative elements not only in the commercial, agricultural and industrial development of the West, but in community and social organization as well.

There is a deeper meaning to all this. Sir Flinders Petrie, in his "Revolutions of Civilization", treating of the development and decline of six civilizations in Egypt during the last ten thousand years, estimates that in a period of six or seven hundred years after that first commingling of diverse bloods out of which alone a new civilization arises, there results a complete admixture of bloods, and that at the time of this complete admixture the new civilization commences its period of highest artistic and intellectual, and finally, material development. But all these older civilizations of which he wrote were developed ages before the railroad era in a period when the lack of transportation made slower the process of blood admixture. It is evident that the advent of the railroad which immensely multiplies the individual contacts of the populations which it serves, will tend to quicken the progress of a new civilization toward its period of highest achievement. Of the new and revolutionary influence of the railroad upon the development of the new civilizations of the western hemisphere, we have daily visible evidence in both North and South America but, remembering the great and accepted generalizations of Sir Flinders Petrie I doubt if our imaginations can grasp how profoundly it has changed what otherwise would have been the nature of their growth and life.

Today we are looking back upon the first century of railroading and the great miracle of modern transport. At the very beginning of the past century, Heckworth and Trevithick were experimenting with their crude early loco-

240

motives; in 1825, the people along the horse-operated colliery railroad operating between Stockton and Darlington were startled to see the Locomotive No. 1 making its slow progress over rails. Five years later—1830—witnessed the inauguration of the first public railway in Britain designed for steam operation—this Liverpool and Manchester—and the triumph of Stephenson's "Rocket."

The railroad gauge of the United States and Canada was set at an early day the same as that of England—four feet eight and one half inches—and this was largely because of the early importation of British locomotives into our country. As far back as 1825, the first locomotive turned its wheels upon American soil. This was the Stourbridge "Lion" which one of our most distinguished early engineers, John B. Jervis, had brought across the ocean upon a sailing boat. Others followed. A very early one was the "Herald" which arrived in Baltimore for the Baltimore & Susquehanna in 1829 and went at once into service. Still others followed. A good many of them went into New England; and some of these were doing active service thirty years thereafter. These engines formed to no small degree models for the development of our own locomotive building industry in America. On the Camden & Amboy, in New Jersey (now a part of the Pennsylvania Railroad) was operated in 1831, the British-built locomotive "John Bull."

In return, we have contributed something to the railroad progress of this Island. An American—Ross Winans, of Baltimore, was instrumental in developing the double truck car, and introducing it into Europe. At an early date, Philadelphia-built locomotives were coming over here—in some quantity. George Westinghouse, inventor of the air brake, received his first real encouragement here in England. And I do not have to remind you of the name of Pullman, which you see everywhere upon the fine trains of Great Britain and Continental Europe.

Three years ago the cordial feelings between the railways of Britain and those of the United States were heightened by the visit of one of your finest modern locomotives, the "King George V" to the Centenary of the Baltimore and Ohio—the "Fair of the Iron Horse"—at Baltimore. Daily this British-built and British-manned locomotive made its appearance in the pageant as a live actor and was acclaimed with vast applause by the crowds upon the grandstands.

In 1933, there will come to the United States at the "Century of Progress" Exposition in Chicago, the steam engine "Rocket," loaned by your Government for the first visit outside the British Isles.* Along with it will come the great "Royal Scot" train which will be sent by the London, Midland and Scottish Railway, the modern successor of the Liverpool and Manchester Railway. The "Rocket" at Chicago will be placed in the Transportation Building now under way, in the center of the greatest dome ever erected, around the circumference of which, and surrounding the "Rocket" will be placed the distinctive modern locomotives of the different parts of the world. By this we hope to symbolize appropriately at one and the same time the greatness of the gift of Britain of modern transportation to the world, and the full appreciation by the world of the debt it owes her.

* As originally intended the "Rocket" was not sent over for exhibition at the Exposition. The "Royal Scot" train came and was visited by millions of Americans.

Journal as Ambassador to Great Britain

I returned Tuesday from a four days' visit to Northern Ireland which was most interesting. My old war-time friend, Lieutenant General Sir Travers Clarke, now retired, but still the honorary colonel of his old regiment, the Royal Inniskilling Fusiliers, whose headquarters are in Belfast, was responsible for my going. He accompanied me throughout the trip, and for the most part we were guests of this famous old regiment, living with them at their barracks and enjoying a most lavish hospitality.

Sir Travers and I were met at the ship by Mr. H. M. Pollard, the Finance Minister of Northern Ireland, representing the Government, and by General Arthur Grenfell Wauchope and Colonel Rothwell, of the Inniskilling Regiment. The pomp and circumstance which surrounded us thereafter reminded me of war times. We reviewed the Regiment and their picturesque bag-pipe band which led them on their parade.

On last Friday afternoon, the day of our arrival, we went over the great Harland & Wolff Shipbuilding Yard. In the evening we attended the officers mess at which both the Prime Minister and the Lord Mayor of Belfast were present. We were also entertained at tea by the Prime Minister, Lord Craigavon, who had assembled his cabinet to meet us at Stormont Castle.

At dinner and after, we were delighted by the military band of the Inniskillings, as well as by the bag-pipers, who played for three Irish dancers from the Regiment.

At lunch on Saturday, which the Lord Mayor of Belfast gave in my honor at the City Hall, I made a prepared speech.

On Saturday afternoon, we motored to Barons Court, where we were the guests of the Governor of Northern Ireland, the Duke of Abercorn. He is the head of the famous Hamilton family, and is an able and cultured man. Finding him "well-up" in prehistoric archaeology and, indeed almost every subject in which I was particularly interested, I had a wonderful two days with him. The Duchess also was extremely well posted, and the stay at Barons Court was most delightful.

ROYAL INNISKILLING FUSILIERS, BELFAST, SEPTEMBER 26, 1930

Front row: Battalion Major R. G. S. Cox, M.C.; Battalion Major H. A. Allen, D.S.O.; Major-Gen. A. G. Wauchope, C.B., C.M.G., C.I.E., D.S.O. (G.O.C., N.I. District); Battalion Lieut.-Col. W. R. Meredith, D.S.O.; the American Ambassador, Brig.-Gen. C. G. Dawes, C.B.; Lieut.-Col. W. E. Rothwell, D.S.O., O.B.E.; Lieut.-Gen. Sir T. E. Clarke, G.B.E., K.C.B., K.C.M.G., Colonel of the Regiment; Major T. H. Cockburn-Mercer; Mr. Raymond Cox, First Secy., American Embassy; Capt. R. M. Vaughan, M.C.; Lieut. and Adjutant R. E. Moody.

Middle row: 2nd Lieut. J. C. O'Dwyer; Lieut. R. A. Heard, M.C.; Lieut. F. L. Webb; Lieut. W. H. E. Cotter; Lieut. and Quartermaster T. V. W. Roberts, M.B.E., M.C.; Capt. E. A. G. Atkins; Capt. E. K. Walkington, Royal Irish Fusiliers; 2nd Lieut. J. R. Filmer-Bennett; Lieut. J. W. A. Hayes; 2nd Lieut. D. G. Moore.

Back row: Capt. H. McBoyle, M.C., Royal Irish Fusiliers; Lieut. F. S. Marchant; Lieut. H. C. G. Stewart; Capt. M. P. L. Cooper; 2nd Lieut. H. S. P. Barstow, Royal Irish Fusiliers; Lieut. R. W. H. Scott; Lieut. B. J. Mahon; Lieut. B. J. H. Boyle.

BARONS' COURT, ULSTER, SEPTEMBER 28, 1930

Left to right: Lieutenant General Sir Travers Clarke; Colonel S. R. McClintock; Lord Craigavon, Prime Minister of Northern Ireland; Duke of Abercorn, Governor of Northern Ireland; Duchess of Abercorn; the American Ambassador.

Journal as Ambassador to Great Britain

The Prime Minister and Lady Craigavon were also guests at Barons Court, and Raymond E. Cox, the first secretary of the Embassy, who came with me, General Wauchope, Colonel Rothwell, and of course, Lieutenant General Sir Travers Clarke. Everything possible was done for us. The Duke who is a many-sided man, was a member of Parliament for thirteen years.

On last Monday morning we inspected the depot of the Inniskillings at Amergh.

My friend, Charles A. Hanna, on his recent visit, knowing I was to visit at Barons Court, gave me a set of his books, *The Scotch-Irish or the Scot in North Britain, North Ireland, and North America*, to present to the Duke of Abercorn because they contained so much material regarding the early Hamiltons. The Duke has written him expressing his appreciation.

When we left London, my friend, Sir Josiah Stamp, saw us off. We had his private car, which was attached to the train both going and coming from Liverpool, and also one for which he had arranged from Barons Court to Belfast both ways. We found also he had looked after our quarters on the ship in the crossing from Liverpool to Belfast.

Monday evening, when I arrived at Belfast, I found Prime Minister Craigavon at the train to take me in his motor car from the train to the ship.

Altogether it was a fine trip, of which the splendid fellowship of the Inniskilling officers was a large element. I was delighted to be with General Sir Travers Clarke in the environment of the early part of his distinguished military career, and with his old Regiment.

London,
October 5, 1930.

This morning, the R-101, the largest air-ship built, which left Cardington last evening to fly to India, crashed on a hill near Beauvais, France, and burst into flames. Fifty-three people were on board and only seven of them escaped death. Among the dead are Lord Thompson, Secretary of State for Air, and Sir Sefton Brancker, the Director of Civil Aviation. It is an appalling tragedy. The last time I talked with Lord Thompson was at his office during the flight last year of the sister-ship, the R-100, to Canada. He had been receiving radio messages from the ship reporting progress from time to time which he read to me with pride. He discussed his coming trip to India on the R-101 with enthusiasm. Now he lies dead.

The progress of transportation of all kinds and in all times has ever been marked by tragedy. Always side by side with pioneers has marched Death. But to their very fearlessness and daring, not to say recklessness, humanity owes a debt.

Aviation which is here to stay is still in its early development. Such trips as have been made by the large dirigibles, after all, have been largely experimental. Progress is an inexorable law which cannot be withstood. But I wish there were more safeguards, for instance, in the licensing of pilots for aeroplanes. No plane is safe without a safe pilot. And yet, few talk of the dangers of aviation, and many of its safety.

In my younger days, about 1911, when I flew with Walter Brookins, the first of the Wright pilots, in an early Wright bi-plane, the same arguments as to safety which we hear now I heard then. But today, aviators tell me a different story of the safety of those first machines. Later, when non-inflammable helium gas becomes generally available for dirigibles, we will probably get from aviators a different appraisement of the safety of the hydrogen gas air-ships.

The Imperial Conference is now in session and many problems confront it. We are living in a fast changing world. The general reaction from the War in the last twelve years has been favorable to the adoption of various international agreements maintaining peace, not the least important being those which resulted in the re-establishment of German economy. But at the moment, there seems almost everywhere to be a reversion toward a more aggressive nationalism. This is one of the embarrassments of the Imperial Conference, as well as of the Preparatory Commission for the Disarmament Conference.

Perhaps a contributing cause to it is the present world-wide business depression. As in adversity a man is stimulated to look better after himself and feels less confident of the good intentions of others toward him, so also it may be with nations.

At any rate, during this period of the Imperial Conference, which meets for the most part in executive session, one hears more current talk about the interest of the individual states in the Empire than about the common interests of them all as an Empire.

The island kingdom of Britain is being inexorably driven toward the policy of protection and away from that of free-trade. It has been interesting to watch the growth of public sentiment in this connection. But as protection is not yet Britain's policy, the position of the British Government in the Imperial Conference, where all the Dominions are committed to it, is a most difficult one.

There is little important business at the Embassy these days. Am expecting to see the Prime Minister tomorrow and to complete arrangements, if possible, for the international broadcasting of speeches by the President of the United States and the Prime Ministers of Great Britain and Japan at the time the American and Japanese ratifications of the Naval Treaty are deposited in the Foreign Office in London.

London,
Thursday, October 9, 1930.

Called on the Prime Minister at 10 Downing Street this evening in regard to arrangements for a ceremony at the time the American and Japanese ratifications of the Naval Treaty are deposited. This consumed little time and the Prime Minister talked of other matters at length. The terrible disaster to the R-101 and the loss of his intimate friend, Lord Thompson, have greatly depressed MacDonald. He suffers much from insomnia. I do not wonder at his sleeplessness for we live in a depressed and disturbed world, and the Prime Minister is confronted by problems arising from every part of it.

While he did not mention it, I think that the straightforward and detailed proposition of the Canadian Premier, Richard Bedford Bennett, made at the Canadian Conference yesterday for preferential tariffs on British exports to Canada in return for preferential tariffs on Canadian exports to Britain, puts the Prime Minister in a very embarrassing position, for the proposition involves a tariff in Britain on wheat and other food stuffs. On this question, the Labour Party will split. The Conservative Party is more likely to favor it with more or less internal friction. Bennett has forced a clean cut proposition easily understood into the minds of a people already subconsciously receptive. MacDonald cannot meet him even half way without involving himself in a fight with Snowden and a large element of his own party.

The tariff question and its relation to the respective Dominions in their business with Britain is evidently the subject first in the minds of the Dominion representatives at the Imperial Conference. Their direct proposals, however, are met, so far, with indecision and evasion on the part of Britain. Sooner or later Britain must settle this policy and the sooner the better for her relations within her own Empire. From the failure to settle it comes the great embarrassment of the Prime Minister.

London,
Saturday, October 18, 1930.

International broadcasting arrangements these days involve diplomatic activity, especially when the broadcast is to cover countries as widely distant as the United States, the United Kingdom and Japan.

Matsudaira and I have had many conferences (one of them being with the Prime Minister) relative to the broadcasting of speeches by the President of the United States and the Prime Ministers of the United Kingdom and of Japan, at the time of the deposit of the ratifications of the Naval Treaty by their respective countries. At present we seem likely to fix "on the same time" which, it seems strange to say, will be in England at 3:00 P.M., October 27th, in the United States at 10:00 A.M., and in Japan, at midnight of the same day. Technical discussions of the three radio organizations must be coordinated with those of the diplomatic officers of the three nations and conformed thereto.

As Hugh Gibson once said—a remark attributed by the press to me—"Diplomacy is not hard on the brain, but it is hell on the feet." It has proved so here this week. Stimson cables details of his conversations with the Japanese and British Ambassadors at Washington.

Since the French seem about to publish their naval program for the next year, without further outside consultation, he fears this procedure will jeopardize the preservation of the levels instituted by the London Naval Treaty, as it is likely to lead France and Italy to embark on a naval discussion at the meeting of the Preparatory Commission of the Disarmament Conference on November 6th, and thus still further complicate an already unfortunate situation. He suggests that the three great naval powers which have already ratified the Treaty each make representations to France and Italy that they forego their efforts toward diplomatic victories with respect to parity and postpone that issue until 1936. He is seeking to avoid having Article 21, the escalator clause of the Treaty, brought into play.

President Hoover is confronted here with what seems to be a well-nigh "irrepressible conflict" between France and Italy, but, as in the past, he is preserving initiative. With him, trouble means renewed activity. He is not ignoring either the difficulties with which the present business depression in our country surrounds him, but he bravely and wisely faces them and does his best to deal with them.

During the past week, I went to two dinners, one of them being by Sir Roderick Jones for General James B. M. Hertzog, the South African Premier, with whom I had a most interesting conversation.

My talks with Sir John Simon, Lord Reading, and Reginald McKenna—with the first two about India, and with McKenna about the world business depression—also contributed to make this dinner an instructive one to me.

The other dinner was one given by the English-Speaking Union to Lord Grey, who spoke. Lord Reading presided and John Drinkwater responded to one of the toasts.

Journal as Ambassador to Great Britain

London,
Sunday, October 25, 1930.

Stimson says that the British Government replied to his suggestions which I outlined in my last notes, that under the circumstances it is feared that anything in the nature of joint representations at the present moment might do more harm than good. He added that joint representations were not his suggestion but rather independent representations. This was clearly evident from his former explanatory cable to me, covering his conferences with the British Embassy at Washington. Sir Ronald Lindsay, however, being ill was not present. He said that the President and he were deeply disappointed and asked me to consult the Prime Minister and express the regret of our Government.

When I went over the matter with MacDonald, at 10 Downing Street, he said that he could not understand the attitude of the Foreign Office and that the matter had never been explained to him in the way I outlined it on the basis of the State Department's cable to me. He promised to see Henderson and directly, instead of through others, to look into the matter with him. As Henderson was out of the city, I will not know until tomorrow whether we will have succeeded in getting the British Government to alter its present attitude.

The situation on the Franco-Italian parity dispute is a grave one, in the mind of the President; and he feels the British should act while there is still time to preserve the levels set by the London Treaty. He feels also they are too optimistic about the French attitude. He believes that the influence of outside public opinion clearly expressed is all that can save the Latin negotiations from developing into failure.

This appeal through this Embassy to the Prime Minister over the head of the British Embassy at Washington and the Foreign Office, indicates how strongly Hoover feels on the subject.

The time for the international radio broadcast has finally been adjusted, and the time of starting the broadcasting simultaneously in the three countries will be 10:00 A.M. in the United States, 3:00 P.M. in London, and 12:00 M. in Tokio.

The Japanese act of ratification has arrived, and the ceremony of depositing the ratifications will take place tomorrow noon in the Locarno Room of the Foreign Office, when I will deposit the ratification of the United States.

In the broadcast, the speeches will be in the following order: (1) Premier Hamaguchi of Japan, speaking in Japanese at Tokio, (2) President Hoover in Washington, (3) Premier MacDonald in London and (4) Ambassador Matsudaira in London, who will read Hamaguchi's speech in English.

Caro and I have just returned this evening from a week-end at Hinchingbrook with the Earl of Sandwich and his family, and with Mr. and Mrs. Henry Field.

London,
Monday, October 27, 1930.

The British Government reversed its position concerning which I conferred with MacDonald on Friday evening. It cabled to its Washington Embassy that it had done so and instructed its Ambassador to notify our Government. Immediately after Mac-Donald had had his interview with Henderson, upon his return, instructions were given to the British Ambassadors to France and Italy to make to these Governments the representations regarding their naval controversy which the President had suggested.

Answers were received by the Foreign Office this morning from these Ambassadors that this had been done yesterday. I was informed of all this by MacDonald, Henderson and Craigie this noon at the ceremony of depositing the ratifications of the Naval Treaty at the Locarno Room of the Foreign Office. I cabled the State Department accordingly.

In some way the President's request clearly expressed to the counselors of the British Embassy at Washington, had not been clearly presented to the Foreign Office.

The ceremony of depositing the ratifications of the Naval

249

Journal as Ambassador to Great Britain

Treaty at the Foreign Office consumed only a quarter of an hour. MacDonald presided, with Henderson by his side, in big red chairs. Around the table sat the Dominion Premiers of Canada, Australia, New Zealand and South Africa and the High Commissioner of India, and Matsudaira for Japan and myself for the United States. Ireland not yet having ratified was not represented. The French and Italian Ambassadors were present, but sat as onlookers a short distance away.

MacDonald said a few words and then we at the table signed the *process verbal* and all was over.

The attitude and appearance of de Fleuriau and Bordonaro, the French and Italian Ambassadors, appealed to their own and our sense of humor. The scene was like that of a small school room, the good little boys sitting at their desks doing their sums dutifully under the eye of an approving teacher, and the two little bad boys sitting all alone. We all laughed about it with de Fleuriau and Bordonaro who appreciated the ludicrous appearance of their isolation.

There were very few present at the ceremony and all of them were diplomatic officers or attachés. The press was not represented.

Together with my friend, Owen D. Young, who is here for an international radio conference, I listened at the Chancery in the afternoon to the broadcasts of Hamaguchi, Hoover, MacDonald and Matsudaira. The addresses all came over the air finely. This was the first time the Japanese Government had broadcast internationally.

London,
Tuesday, October 28, 1930.

This morning, with the rest of the Diplomatic Corps, I attended the opening of Parliament in the House of Lords. It was a brilliant spectacle. The King read the speech from the throne. From the time of his arrival in the House of Lords to the time that he left was only about a quarter of an hour.

As always, upon a state assembly here, the curious existing

compromise between the representatives of a power which has passed and the possessors of present power was evident. It would seem on these occasions that with certain exceptions real power must take the back seats.

The floor, for instance, is occupied largely by the Peers, while members of the House of Commons have the poorest seats or rather standing room in the galleries. And yet the speech which the King read was in reality neither his own nor that of the House of Lords, but of the House of Commons, which is representative of victorious democracy.

The fact that the semblance of power so often attaches to those who have lost its substance, and the substance to those who do not envy the trappings of semblance, is due after all, to the power of tradition affecting all classes of the British people and constituting one of the great bulwarks of British stability and solidarity.

But it seemed curious to me that from the vantage point of the diplomatic seats which are but a short distance from the throne of the King and Queen, I could not see MacDonald, Baldwin, Lloyd George, Churchill, Henderson, Thomas, Snowden, Alexander, Chamberlain, Beaverbrook, and others in whose hands, at the present time, the formulation of British policy chiefly lies. Nor did I meet or see any one of them during the morning. There were, of course, many men of great influence and power in the immediate audience of the King; but the leaders of present public thought and the active administrators of governmental power, both of the United Kingdom and of the Dominions, were farther away in the hall. The Dominion Premiers were in the gallery. In a ceremony acclaimed and approved by the whole British people, this seems curious to newer peoples and newer governments.

The prohibition issue in the United States is politically about in the condition of the tariff issue here. However, they both later will become clear-cut.

Journal as Ambassador to Great Britain

London,
Sunday, November 3, 1930.

The business depression seems deepening almost everywhere. It is producing its usual repercussions politically. Here in the United Kingdom political affairs are in a state of flux. The young men seem to be turning against the old leaders. They are no longer docile but are demanding a clearer precipitation of the protective tariff issue than the leaders of the three parties seem inclined to give them.

In the United States, the election next Tuesday bids fair to be one of many surprises. Impatience is apt to scorn reason, and the ballot box register protest instead.

London,
November 4, 1930.

I have always been an admirer of the energy and resourcefulness of Herbert Hoover of which I had so much evidence in the period immediately following the Armistice in France. He has not changed. His initiative and energy in this time of general discouragement is only characteristic; but its continuing exercise in the naval disarmament situation is noteworthy. Through Gibson, who may be justly described as one of our ablest diplomats, he is now taking hold of the French and Italian impasse. Of the details of this procedure, the State Department keeps me informed.

Gibson, as the United States representative on the Preparatory Commission of the Disarmament Conference of the League of Nations, is, as a consequence, in a position to discuss naval matters with France and Italy with official prestige and without incurring the resentment often created by unsolicited and unwelcome advice involving domestic political situations in other countries. At present, Gibson seems to be making some progress in his talk with the French, but little, or none, with Italy.

Today is election day in the United States.

In the morning *Telegraph* there appears the following notice of

252

Journal as Ambassador to Great Britain

a speech by Winston Churchill. One may remark in connection
with it that the big whales in American politics are in much the
same situation as the British species. The troubles of the American
whales, however, are encountered in the sea called "prohibition",
while those of the British whales are in "protective tariff"
waters.

The Sharks of Politics
Mr. Churchill and a Jolly Picture.
Appeal for Party Unity.

Mr. Winston Churchill, addressing his constituents at a meeting at Waltham
Abbey in the Epping Division last night, said: "There is a disquieting
but growing sense of the inadequacy of Parliament and the party system to
cope with the sombre and urgent economic problems which confront us.

"Powerful newspapers have succeeded in discrediting all political leaders
and in weakening the machinery of our political life without having the
capacity to put anything effective in their place.

"This, above all others, is the time when the Conservative or Unionist
party, representing the most solid and strongest elements in the nation,
ought to be united, courageous and wise. Unhappily, we ourselves are disturbed
by faction and unrest.

"In the southern constituencies, the Beaverbrook-Rothermere Press, and in
the northern constituencies the taxation of the staple foods, will impose an
enormous handicap upon our candidates. These evil tendencies are not getting
better; they are getting worse.

"The kind of spectacle presented in South Paddington last week was calculated
to repel rather than to attract the enormous unattached mass of
voters without whose aid and sympathy no strong government can be established.

"Unless the Conservative Party can lift its ideas to the national level, and
rise like a massive rock out of a sea of confusion, nothing but disaster lies
ahead. What is that disaster? Let us sweep away the illusions and soft words.

"The disaster which I conceive may well be imminent, is that the general
election, which may come at any time, should result in no great change of
parties, but should leave us for a further and much longer spell of deadlock
and uncertainty, with another Parliament as futile, as hopeless, as born-tired,
as spendthrift, as this one."

Mr. Churchill said he would give them a picture of the present political
situation.

"Three big whales named Baldwin, Lloyd George and MacDonald, are
busy fighting each other in a somewhat exhausted condition. At the same
time each whale is himself being attacked by two sharks.

"The names of the two sharks attacking the Baldwin whale are Rothermere
and Beaverbrook. The names of the two sharks attacking the Lloyd George
whale are Runciman and Maclean. The names of the two sharks attacking
the MacDonald whale are Moseley and Maxton.

Journal as Ambassador to Great Britain

"Quite a pattern. A jolly picture, isn't it? of the central affairs of a great Empire struggling with adversity. I think I shall send it to the Royal Academy next year with the title 'British Politics in 1930' or 'All Against All.' If it was 'All for All' it would be hard enough to come through our difficulties. You can imagine what will happen if we go on all against all."

LATER:

I took General Harbord to the guest-night dinner of the Middle Temple this evening, which we both enjoyed. The guest of honor was Prime Minister Bennett, of Canada. There was no speaking.

London,
November 5, 1930.

9:00 P.M. Enough of the American election returns are in to show there has been a Democratic victory. Tonight the Senate seems to stand Republicans 48, Democrats 47; Farmer Labor (Shipstead) 1. The Democrats claim a majority of the House of Representatives, although the returns are not all in.

Dwight Morrow is reported elected by a large majority. At breakfast this morning I was informed that he was endeavoring to get me by long distance telephone, but in a half-hour was notified that the call had been cancelled. As he was calling about 3:30 A.M. from New Jersey, he probably decided to go to bed and let the papers notify me of his success.

Ruth McCormick, although she had won a great victory in the primary battle, was defeated for the Senate in Illinois. As I remember, the Republicans have a majority of about 100 in the present House, and a nominal (but not actual) majority of 18 in the Senate.

There has been a big turnover. Hard times and prohibition went hand and hand to beat the Republicans. There is no occasion to philosophize. Events are in the saddle. Prohibition cuts squarely across the old party lines. As a result of the election, two new leaders stand out—Governor Franklin Roosevelt of New York as a wet Democrat, and Dwight Morrow, of New Jersey, as a wet Republican. Morrow's victory is recognized as a tribute both to his ability and to his character. I sent appropriate cables to him and to Ruth McCormick. The latter made a great fight,

254

RUTH HANNA MCCORMICK
(Mrs. Albert G. Simms)

greater than any woman ever before had made in America, both for the nomination and at the election, but the fates were against her.

Today's reports indicate that Gibson has made real progress with Italy as well as France, and the naval conflict between the two countries may at least be postponed.

LATER: Dwight Morrow cables that his estimated majority is about 190,000.

London,
November 9, 1930.

The American election leaves both the Senate and the House of Representatives nominally divided about equally between the Democrats and the Republicans; but as a matter of fact both the Senate and the House are controlled practically by a coalition of Democrats and insurgent Republicans—a condition which already existed in the Senate alone.

The press is belaboring the President unjustly. Whenever possible, the public seems to delight in holding individuals responsible for uncontrollable events, good or bad. After a great disaster, there is usually talk of some captain or engineer or mine superintendent who might have averted it. The grand jury sometimes indicts for negligence. After a while, however, the agitation subsides and subconsciously all know that the criticism has been generally unfair.

Yesterday, General Harbord and I took lunch at Electric House with the directors of the British Marconi Company. Marchese Marconi, himself, was present, together with Lords Inverforth and Inchcape, Frederick Kellaway, Sir Basil Blackitt, and other leaders of the international radio business. Mr. J. H. Thomas, also a guest, was a brilliant and instructive entertainer whose talk was enjoyed by all.

At 4:00 P.M., I attended a meeting of the Trustees of the Peabody Foundation at which J. P. Morgan was present. In the early evening, I attended the dinner of the University College Hospital, at the Mansion House. Prince George presided and the sum of about 6,000 pounds was raised for the hospital.

Journal as Ambassador to Great Britain

At. 11:00 P.M., Caro and I attended a reception at India House where the High Commissioner for India, Sir Atul Chandra Chatterjee, introduced us to the India Maharajahs who are here for the Indian Conference.

During the day, I conferred with Owen D. Young. I had received a personal and confidential letter from Carston Nielson, the editor of the *Dawes Way* at Berlin, to the effect that Dr. Brüning, the Chancellor of the Reich, would appreciate a purely personal interchange of ideas with Young in neutral territory, at Basle or thereabouts, and asking me to arrange the meeting which was to be strictly confidential. I cabled the substance of the letter to Stimson adding that I had shown it to Young and was transmitting it with his knowledge. I said also that if he saw any objection to Young's going and so indicated to me, it would govern Young's action, and that in any event Young would not decide the matter before Tuesday, the 11th.

London,
November 9, 1930.

In re Dr. Brüning's desire to have a confidential talk with Young, Stimson thinks that it seems a purely personal matter for Young to determine by his own wishes and conveniences. He sees no reason of policy why Young should not accept the invitation as he would be acting in a purely personal capacity and feels that the talk suggested may well be helpful to the Reich Chancellor.

I telephoned the substance of this to Young without mentioning names, and he is coming to the Chancery tomorrow to talk over the matter and let me know his decision.

The Sunday English papers are full of comments upon the important governmental policies which, in these critical times, are demanding decision while they are met only by indecision. If MacDonald only had a free hand, he might find an opportunity in the situation, but he is unwilling—or feels it useless—to split his party in the endeavor.

In this world-wide and serious business depression, the majority of the public in most of the countries thus affected seem in oppo-

Journal as Ambassador to Great Britain

sition to their governmental administrations. The reasoning of the average man everywhere is simple. He wants a change of things, so why not start by changing administrations? In time of adversity he will generally regard any action, good or bad, wise or unwise, on the part of an existing administration, as wrong. In other words, his attitude is determined by his feelings rather than by his reason.

Existing administrations everywhere, however, while probably doomed to early defeat, may have a chance to come back into public favor later if they act courageously, but not if they fail to act. If they act wisely, posterity, which ignores popularity in forming its judgments, will applaud them. Posterity will even condone an unwise act if it is sincere and courageous, but for indecision and inaction in a time of crisis, it has only condemnation.

London,
Friday, November 14, 1930.

The last four days have been much occupied by ceremonies. Monday evening was taken up by the Lord Mayor's banquet at Guildhall. Tuesday was Armistice Day, which was observed by the impressive ceremony at the Cenotaph, when the King laid a wreath in memory of the British dead of the war in the presence of an immense and silent crowd.

That afternoon, Caro and I attended the Page memorial lecture given by Lord Howard, of Penrith, with Sir Austen Chamberlain in the chair. General and Mrs. Harbord and Mrs. Owen D. Young accompanied us.

In the evening, by invitation of the Prince of Wales, Caro and I sat with him in the Royal Box at Albert Hall, where the Remembrance Festival of the British Legion was held, and as a part of the exercises the Prince spoke. The others in the box were Lord and Lady Jellicoe, Lady Spencer Churchill, two officers of the Legion, and the aides of the Prince. Eight thousand were in the audience. The massed bands led the soldier audience at one time in their singing of the old war-time songs with wonderful effect. It was an inspiring event. The greeting of the Prince by

Journal as Ambassador to Great Britain

the audience evidenced his wonderful hold upon their esteem and affection.

During the day I had wreaths placed at Brookwood, the American military cemetery and at the Cenotaph.

On Wednesday, at noon, Caro and I attended the opening of the Indian Round Table Conference at St. James's Palace, at which the King spoke. This was the first of such conferences attended by the Indian Princes, to be held in London. The other conferences have been in India. It was a most important occasion. The conference is a most momentous one. Here will be discussed by the representatives of the King-Emperor and his Government, the Princes and other representatives of the vast population of India, the method of meeting the demands of the majority of the Indian people for a government with dominion status.

The problem is similar in its complexity to that which, in the future, may confront our own country in the Philippines. That India could, in its own interest and that of the world, be given a self-governing dominion status seems impossible. Its population is divided by castes, religions, traditions and conditions thousands of years old. That the removal of the strong hand of Great Britain would not result other than in civil war and anarchy seems evident. What is the greatest concession (if any is possible in existing circumstances) along the line of eventual self-government but short of it, which can be made consistent with continuance of law and order?—that would seem to be the question in the minds of the Conference as indicated by the speeches at the opening of their sessions, one of which was by the Prime Minister.

The Dominion representatives of the Imperial Conference were there. No foreign diplomats other than myself were present.

That evening (Wednesday), I attended the annual banquet of the British Travel Association at Grosvenor House. This association is quasi-governmental receiving the support of the Government in its work to increase tourist travel to England and Scotland. Lord Denby presided. The other speakers were the Duke of York, and the Right Honorable John Robert Clynes, and myself.

258

GENERAL J. G. HARBORD

Journal as Ambassador to Great Britain

Owen Young has decided it is impracticable and unwise for him to go for a conference with Brüning.

London,
Saturday, November 22, 1930.

General and Mrs. Harbord spent the week with us at the Embassy. On Tuesday afternoon, Lord Derby organized his Committee of British Participation in the Chicago Exposition. It took place at the Chancery where I called in a few friends to meet him, to wit: Sir Robert Kindersley, Sir Felix Pole, Mr. Francis Powell, Sir Campbell Stewart, Sir Henry Cole and Colonel Sewell. Lord Derby will be a tower of strength in this matter. He is a natural leader of men, and his great prestige in the country is to be attributed in great part to his high character, ability and personal charm.

Last Tuesday we went with the Harbords to a family dinner with Lord and Lady Inverforth.

Wednesday evening Captain (our naval attaché) and Mrs. Galbraith, gave a dinner at which the four Sea Lords of the Admiralty were present. This was a most enjoyable dinner, though I had to leave early to make a speech at 10:00 P.M. at the opening of the Eastman Dental Clinic at the Royal Free Hospital, and then later leave there for a few minutes at a reception at the Argentine Embassy.

London,
Saturday, November 29, 1930.

On Tuesday evening, Major General John E. B. Seely and his wife took dinner with us at the Embassy, and we then went to the Club House of the English-Speaking Union where I introduced the General who gave a lecture on the "Spirit of Adventure in the Anglo-Saxon." The General was a cavalry commander on the western front in the Great War, and described how some of our engineer troops at first armed only with picks and shovels, with which they were working when the attack came, entered and stayed with his troops through a terrible fight entirely of their individual volition.

Thursday was Thanksgiving Day. On that afternoon, I went to Parliament and listened to Stanley Baldwin and J. H. Thomas debate Imperial preference. They befogged somewhat the real issues at stake between them by the interjection of political sparring. In my judgment, the protectionists will make real progress and much quicker if they do not mix arguments for tariff framed to extend their Dominion markets with arguments for tariffs solely framed to regain their own home market.

If they follow the example of their Dominions, which have already protected their home markets, and first protect their own home markets, they will fare better in their negotiations with the Dominions hereafter, to say nothing of faring better economically at home.

England is being crippled, as is the rest of the economic world, by the falling off in international trade, but it is being ruined by the loss, under free trade, of its own home market and the resulting unemployment. Besides this protectionists are confusing and dividing their own supporters by arguments relating to two objectives which would best be taken up before the public and reached in succession, not together.

In the debate the other day, the speakers kept referring to the tenets of Cobden. I wonder if any of them have ever read the wonderful "Report on Manufactures" by Alexander Hamilton. Forced by events which are deaf to human precedents and traditions, Britain is being forced in self-preservation to the policy of a protective tariff. Why, therefore, do its leaders not read Hamilton, the greatest exponent of that policy? I have asked this directly of Winston Churchill, and of Stanley Baldwin, but neither had read Hamilton's famous report to Congress.

Thursday evening, I presided at the annual Thanksgiving Day dinner of the American Club.

Journal as Ambassador to Great Britain

London,
Sunday, December 7, 1930.

Last Monday evening, I attended the 268th anniversary dinner of the Royal Society, given in the Hall of Lincoln's Inn. It was a notable occasion. There were present the leaders of science from all parts of this country, and many from elsewhere. The eminent biologist, Sir Frederick Gowland Hopkins, the discoverer of vitamines, presided. The leading speakers were the Prince of Wales, the Prime Minister, Sir Gowland Hopkins, and Sir Ernest Rutherford.

The speeches of the Prime Minister and Sir Gowland Hopkins were especially noteworthy. I have never heard them excelled as examples of intellectual extempore after-dinner speaking. My seat at the table was between the Prime Minister and Sir Austen Chamberlain and their companionship added to my enjoyment of the evening.

On Tuesday afternoon, Caro and I went to an exhibition of early American silver at the American Woman's Club which I opened formally in a short speech. That same evening, I went to a dinner at the Mercers' Company, one of the oldest and richest of the London Guilds, dating back in its organization about 800 years and afterwards chartered by Richard II in 1393. The dinner was most elaborate and given in a hall considered as one of the most beautiful in the city.

To my surprise, I found myself seated by the right of the Master (the Chairman) and to my greater surprise was told during the course of the dinner that he was to propose a toast to me to which I was expected to respond.

The Master, Squadron Leader Robert Charlton Lane, then gave me a unique introduction which was witty, quite pointed and good-naturedly provocative.

Referring in my reply to his catalogue of short-comings in American character and history, while I declined to admit them, I countered by showing if they did exist, it was because of inherited traits from over-seas.

On Wednesday evening (this was the week of functions) Caro

Journal as Ambassador to Great Britain

and I went to a dinner at the Italian Embassy, given by Ambassador Bordonaro for ex-Minister of Finance Volpi, and on Friday evening to a dinner given for us by Colonel and Mrs. Thomas.

Last night (Saturday), Caro and I were guests at the birthday festival of Toc H in London, held in the Albert Hall. This was its fifteenth anniversary of the founding of Talbot House, Poperinghe, France, in 1915, near the Ypres sector on the western front. We were taken to the Royal Box with the officers of the organization, including the Lord Bishop of London, Padre Clayton ("Tubby") the founder, and Lord Wakefield. Over 8000 people were in the audience.

The program of singing, especially that part in which the whole audience joined, led by the band of the Welsh Guards, was most inspiring. But the supreme moment of the evening was when the great hall was darkened and the ceremony of lighting the little lamps of remembrance for the dead was enacted. With Lord Wakefield and one or two others, I was given a lighted taper and, walking through the ranks of those silently holding the unlighted lamps, assisted in this solemn rite.

I was glad it was dark for I was in tears as probably was most of the audience.

London,
Sunday, December 14, 1930.

Last evening, attended the International Celebration of the 300th anniversary of the recognized use of cinchona (quinine) by Europeans, given at the Wellcome Medical Museum. The Netherlands Minister, Jonkheer de Marees van Swinderen (who married the daughter of Charles Glover, of Washington, D. C.), presided and I was one of the several speakers.

Tuesday, Silas Strawn, of Chicago, called at the Chancery and I have seen much of him this week. I know of no private citizen in America of our time who ever rendered to his home city a service at once as difficult and important as that which Strawn rendered Chicago when, through his initiative and virile leadership and that of Philip R. Clarke, the city bridged the crisis resulting from the failure to collect its regular taxes for over a year.

262

Journal as Ambassador to Great Britain

If he works as hard in his own interests as he does (without apparent appreciation) for his community, he would receive high official recognition, but the kind of work he is doing makes him bitter enemies among politicians. The American Bar Association, however, elected him its president, and this is more of a distinction than most public offices in our country.

The people of the whole world seem more or less immersed in lethargy. I am afraid this is especially true over here where eight hundred thousand young men died in the Great War who, if here now, would be in their most active period of life.

And then there is the dole which cannot but sap to some extent the energies and initiative of a people in the same way that inherited wealth does that of families. If the dole was abolished, however, one shudders to think of the suffering which would result, to say nothing of a possible revolution. It must stand.

England, our mother country, is in a crisis. If one did not sense the indomitable "spirit of the breed", which is still alive, he would despair of her future. The laws of human reaction are inexorable, and as mass attitudes are responsible for the desperate present, so their change will as surely bring improvement later. Yet that change will be slow in coming. Everything points to that everywhere.

I am prompted to note a conversation I recently had with a major diplomat from a country not indebted to the United States or directly involved in her national debt question, because of the suggestion made as to a possible recourse by Germany to the moratorium clause in the Young Plan, notwithstanding its dangers to the present stability of European economy. This would be for the real purpose of precipitating immediately the question of debt reduction. This diplomat was Erik Kule Palmstierna, formerly Finance Minister of Sweden and now Swedish Minister to London.

The information he gave me was not conveyed officially or during a call at the Embassy for that purpose, but was repeated to me at a lunch last Tuesday given by the Maharajah of Alwar at the Hyde Park Hotel. He stated that influential European discussion of the international debt question, as related to the present economic depression with the consequent large increase in the purchasing power of gold, is trending toward a conclusion that the present is the psychological time for precipitation of an effort for debt concessions from the United States. The form of the suggestion would not be in terms at first of drop reduction in the debt burden due to the increase in the price of gold. Parenthetically, this is substantiated by the unsuccessful effort by resolution, to put this matter to the fore at the meeting of the Council of the International Chamber of Commerce last week in Paris.

The discussion, he said, is also as to whether the question would not best be precipitated by immediate recourse by Germany to the moratorium clause in the Young Plan and that, outside of Germany, European financial as well as official authorities were engaged in it.

The more I have considered the above information, the more it seems that there may be a possibility that Germany is considering seriously the policy of early recourse to the moratorium. I cannot believe that there is anything at present in her present financial or industrial condition which would justify this. Left by the War, however, with less of a resulting financial burden than any of the Allies, she is instituting budget and revenue reforms which, given political quiet, with greater rapidity than in the case of any other European government, should, when a general upturn in business comes, restore a sound condition not only in German government finance but also in German industry and commerce.

This fact might lead those in charge of Germany's economic policy to decide upon early recourse to the moratorium. She cannot but contemplate that if she insists upon a moratorium in later prosperous times, if such come, she will be justly denounced as false to her former professions of the will to pay. She might decide, too, that any appeal to American public opinion cannot wisely be made as long as the interest on her foreign debts is being paid, since the public mind generally assumes a continuing capacity to pay what is being paid, and while payments continue would probably never uphold a national policy of debt concessions. Germany might assume that the only possible way in which the attitude of the American public could be changed would be through changing their conception of the condition of their debtors.

If, following Germany's recourse to the moratorium, other European debtor governments failed in consequence to pay us their annuities, the question in the American mind might be changed from "How long will our debtors continue to pay their annuities?" to the question "Will they ever commence again?" It is possible that Germany may consider the question of reparations reduction as practically one of "now or never" and act accordingly.

London
Sunday, December 21, 1930.

Business here and in our own country shows no sign of betterment. The New York bank failure (the so-called "Bank of the United States" with $200,000,000 deposits), the failure of eight or ten little banks every day, some of them not so little after all, the decline of commodity prices, the decreased car loadings, the falling gross and net earnings of general industry and trade—all combine to make this a critical winter in the financial and business history of the United States.

Unemployment and consequent suffering are widespread. Much "whistling to keep up courage" is going on, and one feels that such a universal condition will right itself but slowly.

I have been studying the last *Budget Report* of the United States which Colonel Roop, the Director, has sent me. He has improved it in many ways. The pages are reduced in number from 1504 last year to 704 in this Budget. This resulted from placing the body of the Budget in double columns and eliminating the old columns on the right-hand side of the page. Budget statements, Nos. 1 and 2 cover in the same table appropriation receipts and expenditures, thus better emphasizing the difference between expenditures and appropriations.

On Tuesday evening, I heard a notable speech by the Prince of Wales at the dinner of the Incorporated Sales Managers Association at Guildhall, on the subject of promoting British trade.

Journal as Ambassador to Great Britain

The Prince is the best salesman the Empire possesses. He told me afterward how he disliked to stick so closely to his notes, but considered the subject too important to do otherwise. The speech made a great impression on the country.

London,
December 29, 1930.

We celebrated Christmas day (Thursday) at the Embassy with a Christmas tree in the morning for the family and the servants. At dinner, at 1:30 P.M., we had as our guests Dr. and Mrs. Harry Garfield, of Williams College, Francis B. Loomis, and Mr. and Mrs. Gary, formerly of the Embassy staff.

At 6:00 P.M. that evening, Caro, Virginia, Henry and I went to Cliveden, where we were the guests of Lord and Lady Astor until Saturday at their family gathering. During this time, at intervals, there were other additional guests, but I should estimate the permanent number outside of the large family circle at about ten. Among those guests who dined were Dr. and Mrs. Garfield and the Gaekwar and Maharanee of Baroda. Among the "permanents", so to speak, were Thomas Jones (Lloyd George's old secretary, now secretary of the Cabinet), Sir Lionel Curtis, Sir Hilton Young and Brendan Bracken, the latter two rising members of Parliament, and all very able and interesting men.

In the course of a discussion of different methods followed in the writing of history, upon which I expressed some ideas formed from the reading of the classics, Jones suddenly extended me an invitation to make one of the annual lectures at a Welsh university (the name of which I did not note) taking this subject for it. He said he had been asked by the Chancellor to ask me to speak there, but had not delivered the invitation. This was timely, because I have often planned to write something of this kind, and I now have plenty of time. So I told him that if I would not be held down to a specific date I would accept.

As a result, I have spent most of this day with Loeb's Classical Library which I have, and as I write I have by my side Appian's *Roman History*, Thucydides, Dio Cassius, Julius Caesar (*Gallic Wars* and *The Civil Wars*), Strabo, Plutarch and Suetonius. To

LORD ASTOR

prepare this lecture is going to be a delightful task. Measured by the standard of academic lectures, it may not turn out to be very good, but at least it will be different.

One never knows, who reads with an open mind, to what conclusions history will lead him. These will differ somewhat according to the age in life at which one reads history, and his life's experience up to that time. This I know: that my present conclusions will be sounder than any I could have formed before my war experience. War, more or less, is a postgraduate course in human nature. Dio's long and absurd amplifications of the speech of Julius Caesar to his troops who were in a panic at the approach of Ariovistus puts into Caesar's mouth this sentence: "These laws, not drawn up by man, but enacted by Nature herself, always have existed, do exist and will exist so long as the race of mortals endures." But Dio, a citizen, clearly demonstrates in his history that his understanding of these laws was infinitely inferior to that of Caesar who was not only a citizen but a warrior as well.

In an emergency a great leader never thinks or acts as would the ordinary man. This is one reason why historians so often fail entirely to comprehend the motives and acts of a leader in emergency. As a rule, the historian's life is one of observation, investigation and literary production. His is not the "battling" life. He has not experienced that of which he writes, and if he had, his natural reactions would not be those of a leader. His literary reactions, however brilliant, are based on the only interpretation of human nature possible to him. He will ascribe to his subjects whenever the facts make possible—in other words not ridiculous —what he imagines would have been his course of action and reasoning under the circumstances. This does not work out well under analysis.

London,
Friday, January 8, 1931.

A week ago Monday my family and I went for a visit to Paris, returning this last Monday. We stayed at the Hotel Ritz and had an interesting time, especially Virginia for whose pleasure the trip was primarily planned.

Journal as Ambassador to Great Britain

We were entertained by Ambassador and Mrs. Edge and others, and met many old friends, some of them my old associates of the French army. During our stay, Marshal Joffre died and, together with General William W. Harts, I called at his hospital as a tribute of respect. Here in London I attended the Requiem Mass in his memory at Westminster.

As an old friend and comrade of General Pershing, I have been awaiting the publication of his book with expectancy. I am writing this before I have even seen the book, much less read it, but I venture to predict it will bear the imprint of certain characteristics of General Pershing which account not only for his success but for his enmities; not only for his present popularity among the rank and file of the A.E.F. but for the bitter criticism of some of these same men at the time of their demobilization after the War.

General Pershing had one specific objective in the war—the doing of his full duty. It was impossible for politicians to realize then, as it is impossible for them to realize now, that in war a man like Pershing cannot even conceive of such a thing as yielding to outside pressure. Nor can any but those who were closely associated with him in the war realize how impossible it was from the inside to influence him to change any attitude determined by him in cold blood as essential to the best interests of his army. Just as the courageous attitudes of public men which made them unpopular in their lifetime often become, with posterity, their chief claim to statesmanship, so with this army commander history will assign as evidence of his greatness some of the very acts in time of emergency which set his contemporaries abuzz with indignation.

These characteristic qualities which enabled General Pershing against enormous pressure to maintain the independent functioning of the American army were manifested continuously in similar but less critical situations. For instance, the difficulties of the Commander-in-Chief of the A.E.F. during the post-armistice sojourn in France and Germany are little realized, and reference to them will well illustrate General Pershing's attitude toward the politician. The men who had emerged from over forty days of terrible fighting in the Argonne, and indeed all the army in France, realizing that the war was over and won, naturally tended to resent the degree of discipline, the maintenance of which the Commander-in-Chief of the A.E.F. deemed absolutely necessary as a matter both of wisdom and of duty. With the coming of the Armistice, there had been loosed upon France like a swarm of locusts a great number of well-meaning Americans, including politicians who, forgetful that the field was already covered by our civil and military war-time organizations plunged themselves into various activities, including oratory, which, for want of better terms, I may describe as designed partly for the social relaxation of the American soldier and partly for his over-praise. In speeches and public interviews they were telling the soldiers of the great debt the nation owed them, and that when they came back to the United States our citizenship would sit at their feet as constituting its real leadership.

Individuals and organized minorities of every kind were pressing upon the authorities and officers of the army for preferential treatment for individuals and troops in the matter and method of demobilization. One of these individuals, who afterwards came not only to recognize and confess his error, but to defend General Pershing at home, protested that it was an undignified and wrong thing to compel the American dough-boy to work for the restoration of certain French roads in accordance with war time inter-army agreements. He regarded this work as something insulting to them and to their service. A very considerable part of our army, of necessity, never handled anything but spades and other implements of hard work in the war, and they did their glorious work with them. It was not their fault that they were not at the front. They were the same kind of men as the rest of the army, and when the German break through came on March 21st, 1918, some of these engineer soldiers working near the British line had thrown down their spades and taken the rifles from the dead on the battle field, and joined in a desperate counter attack with the British troops.

This particular individual, far from resenting an insult to the American army, was himself insulting a considerable section of it who had spent practically all their war service in digging ditches, building railroads, erecting hospitals, and procuring and moving

269

supplies and munitions. He was unwittingly encouraging insubordination in a military organization at a time when a natural reaction made the maintenance and discipline unusually difficult.

Another man published critical interviews based upon American complaints as to the alleged non-delivery or loss of army mail sent during the war to the soldiers and received at a time when the troops were in action, under conditions impossible to properly visualize.

I mention these two instances because the men in question—two powerful American politicians—were called by me before General Pershing who set forth the natural consequences of encouraging insubordination and trouble in the American army at such a critical time of natural restlessness. These men were honest enough and sensible enough to realize the force of facts of which they had not known and the reason for the attitude of General Pershing.

On their return to America, they immediately became powerful defenders of the honor and record of the American army and its Commander-in-Chief at the very time when the so-called investigation committees were starting upon their quest with the fool idea that they could exploit themselves and their political interests by throwing muck upon American military achievement.

Our great war President, Woodrow Wilson, and his able Secretary of War, Newton D. Baker, had protected the American army from political mischief-makers. Thank Heaven and them, the Commander-in-Chief was spared this kind of trouble during the war itself. He did not then, like the generals of our Civil War, have political assassins firing at his back when he was facing the fire of the enemy.

Nobody knew better than General Pershing that his refusal to grant the generally demanded relaxation of the discipline of our army during the post-armistice period was making him unpopular for the time being among his own soldiers. But he knew that he owed it to them, and to our country, to take no risks by granting indiscriminate leaves of absence, for instance, and to send his men back as he did—an army upon whose conduct during their entire stay in France there had been no spot or stain, and who

GENERAL JOHN J. PERSHING

Journal as Ambassador to Great Britain

left a memory not only in France but in the world which is a glory to our nation and its history.

General Pershing's closest associates in the War remember no act or decision in matters relating to the welfare of his army and the carrying out of his duty to it and to our Government in which he seemed unduly influenced by his own personal interest.

In these days of wide-spread political cowardice and playing to the crowd, it is well to point out that eventually General Pershing has been rewarded for his performance of duty, not only by general public respect and high appreciation, but by the love and devotion of his noble comrades, the rank and file of the American Expeditionary Forces, whose real interests were ever nearest his heart.

On Wednesday evening, I attended a dinner at Fishmongers Hall, given by my friend, Sir Robert Kindersley, to celebrate the issue of one thousand million savings certificates which occasion brought together a large number of British financiers and industrialists.

The Prince of Wales was the principal speaker. As my seat at the table was at his side, we had a long talk. He will leave on a South American trip this month. He expressed disappointment that his route had been so changed that he could not stop in Havana. The Foreign Office is in receipt of such disturbing news as to the existing political conditions in Cuba that they changed his routing. He told me the British Embassy at Havana had reported that a large banquet given either by or to our American Ambassador to Cuba had been broken up by tear bombs. The Prince said that he himself thought it would be all right to go. The press has not as yet published this Havana banquet incident, the censorship probably preventing.

London,
January 13, 1931.

Yesterday morning, I attended, with other members of the Diplomatic Corps, the memorial services in the Chapel Royal, St. James's Palace, for the Princess Royal, the King's sister. Owing

Journal as Ambassador to Great Britain

to the smallness of the Chapel, each country was represented only by its Ambassador or Minister. The audience was mostly official, the Cabinet, the Dominions, the High Commissioners, and the Indian Princes being present. Two members of the Royal Family attended, the rest being at the burial ceremony at Windsor.

Attended the Marlybone Presbyterian Church this morning and heard a good sermon. This evening, I have been thinking over what to say at a dinner to be given Tuesday evening, the importance of which I only realized this morning, when I read Atherton's memorandum about it, as follows:

Dinner on January 13th.

Chairman: The Aga Khan.

The Guests are: The American Ambassador, the German Ambassador, the French Ambassador, Mr. Stanley Baldwin, the majority of the British ruling Princes, and the majority of the British Cabinet, including the Prime Minister.

The Speeches will be: The Aga Khan, offering the Loyal toast, followed by Mr. Sastri, who will propose "Our Guests"; which will be answered first by the Prime Minister; second, by the American Ambassador; third, by John Drinkwater; and fourth, by Mr. A. P. Herbert, Editor of *Punch*, representing the British press.

R. ATHERTON

London,
January 18, 1931.

The Indian Round Table Conference is drawing to a close. Tomorrow the Prime Minister will read to it the British statement of attitude. I have not commented much on the Conference, but not because I have not kept in touch with it.

Everybody talks to the American Ambassador, apparently without reserve, not, I think, because of his personality, but because of his country's attitude of impartiality and because his country is subconsciously always in mind over here, either as an example or a force.

As among the other Ambassadors, I have found myself singled out frequently during this Conference at public occasions, as at

272

the large dinner given by the representatives of British India, Tuesday evening at the Park Lane Hotel, where I spoke; at the lunch of the Royal Institute of Public Health yesterday, when three Maharajahs were made honorary members; at Sir Roderick Jones' dinner to certain Indian delegates last week and at the opening of the Conference when the King spoke.

For this, I think the Indian Princes are somewhat responsible. In their talks with me they always refer to the United States, to their admiration for its institutions and to their desire to visit it. They do not hesitate to talk over their Conference difficulties nor their individual position in it with the utmost frankness. On the other hand, as always, the British are both confidential and explicit.

Thus I hear all sides of the question as actually discussed privately beneath the comparatively calm surface of the proceedings at the plenary meetings. I am impressed by the fact that internal division is equally rife among the British and the Indians. The situation is not one of a united Britain against a united India, but of a divided Britain and a divided India. And it is a very grave situation—much graver than the world outside realizes.

As they express themselves to me, there is as much pessimism among the Indian Princes and commoners as among Britons as to the outcome of the Conference. While some maintain that real progress has been made, all admit that the crucial problems are unsolved, including those of Hindu versus Moslem, and those involved in the possible granting of a responsible Indian government supported by an Indian Parliament with a reservation to a British Viceroy of responsibility for law and order and public safety.

As J. L. Garvin has said of the latter: "Dual responsibility of this strange kind, much less on this vast scale, has never been known in the affairs of mankind." But while Garvin, representing one section only of British thought, accepts dual responsibility as a lesser evil and "as the only way out, at least, or the only way forward," not so for instance, with Winston Churchill and Lord Rothermere representing another section. Rothermere in the *Despatch* this morning, claims that the Indianization of central authority in India means the ruin of the British Empire and the collapse into primitive barbarism of the 320,000,000 Indian people. With Churchill, he feels that even its present discussion is immensely dangerous.

Last Friday I took lunch with Brendan Bracken (member of Parliament), the other guests being Winston Churchill, Frederick William Leith-Ross, and Lord Ivor Churchill. If the Prime Minister's statement to the Conference tomorrow seems to commit the British Government to a new policy, Winston Churchill says he will immediately go before the public to combat it and to call attention to the inability of the Government to impose the policy without parliamentary ratification.

All the above will serve to explain the feeling of apprehension over the whole situation. India itself, at present, is a tinder box. A spark may set it off. In such a time of crisis as now exists in India anything may happen at any time. In Britain, the vital public discussion is just commencing. In India it has been at fever heat for two years. Will events in India await prolonged discussion?

These are indeed dark days in this country. The unemployed now number over 2,600,000, not counting the Lancashire cotton spinners who have just struck. The dole indebtedness mounts steadily. Somehow the country seems dazed, as indeed the whole world does.

London,
Wednesday, January 21, 1931.

The Round Table Conference has adjourned—and the Prime Minister has spoken—ably, as he always does.

Progress is said to have been made, but whether it is forward toward orderly self-government for India, with reservations, or backward toward chaos, without reservations, time alone can tell. All hope for the former, all fear for the latter. But certainly, pledged in his policy by former governments and by events, as well as supported now by leading representatives of all political parties of Britain, the Prime Minister has done his part well—better perhaps than anyone else could have done.

There is at least hope that a *modus vivendi* has been attained, and that the extremists of India, now practically in revolution, may pause to reason. The future of India is problematical. Differences such as have divided its population internally for ages—differences of race, religion, custom, classes and government—cannot be resolved "en masse." Left to themselves, are the Indians ready to grant each other what, in terms conveniently general, they unitedly ask of Great Britain? And do they unitedly really ask the same thing? So far neither they nor others seem able to answer.

On Monday morning, desiring to hear young Arthur Henderson as a barrister address the Court of Criminal Appeals, presided over by the Lord Chief Justice of England, Hewart, with whom I have become acquainted, Henry and I went to the Law Courts. We were first conducted to the chambers of the Lord Chief Justice, who introduced us to his associates, Justice Avery and Justice McNaughton, and then we were given seats on the bench with the justices. Here we witnessed an unexpected and terrible scene, one which will ever be to me a distressing memory.

This newspaper clipping describes it:

MURDERER FAINTS IN APPEALS COURT,
THE LORD CHIEF JUSTICE'S FATAL WORDS.

The real story of life and death from the Court of Criminal Appeals—that court where so many condemned murderers have listened to the words that blotted out their last hope of escaping the scaffold.

In the dock sits a young man of 26. For five weeks now he has been under sentence of death for murder—a murder committed last July. And he has come to the Court of Criminal Appeals to make his last bid for life.

His counsel has said his last word; and the young man stands up as Lord Hewart, the Lord Chief Justice, begins to announce the decision of the court.

There is an utter stillness, broken only by the grave measured syllables of the Lord Chief Justice, as he says:

"How can we interfere with the verdict of the jury?"

As the man at the dock hears these words, he falls unconscious to the ground.

The Lord Chief Justice stops. In the silence the wardens lift the man from the floor and carry him into the cell beneath the dock.

"We will wait until the prisoner is prepared to return," says Lord Hewart.

Ten minutes later the man is brought back into court. He stands with his hands on the rail of the dock, supported by the wardens. He passes his handkerchief repeatedly over his face to wipe the tears away.

"You may sit down," says the Lord Chief Justice.

Then he continues his judgment. It ends with the words: ". . . the appeal will have to be dismissed."

The man in the dock hears it impassively. He stands up and walks quietly out of the court, with wardens supporting him on either side.

PUNCTILIOUSLY IMPARTIAL

The man's name is Fred Gill. He was sentenced to death at Leeds Assizes for the murder of Oliver Preston, an elderly money lender, in his office at Keighley.

He was sentenced to death by Mr. Justice Talbot, who told him:

"I cannot hold out any hope that the sentence will not be carried out. Your time is short, and I would tell you to prepare yourself for that end."

The ground of appeal was that the verdict of the jury was against the weight of the evidence, having regard to the fact that Gill was convicted wholly on circumstantial evidence.

Lord Hewart, giving the judgment today said: "The case stands in this way. On the pure question of fact the mass of evidence offered by the prosecution and also evidence offered for the defense was fairly laid before the jury.

"As to the summing up of the learned judge, there can be no doubt that it was punctiliously impartial. In these circumstances, it seems that it is not possible for this court to interfere. It was admittedly a question of fact for the jury to decide."

When once I realized that the condemned man was in the prisoners' box everything seemed to photograph itself on my consciousness—the mental agonies of the prisoner, as shown by his countenance, the calm and unanswerable summing up of the Chief Justice in his red robes, his low and clear voice saying: "How can we interfere with the verdict of the jury?" and then the crash to the floor of the condemned boy, for he seemed little more than that.

The case against him was clear. He had killed a usurer with an iron bar, with premeditation, rendered desperate by his own poverty and the exactions of his victim. He had committed robbery also at the time of the murder.

I pondered over the case after court. In America, at least in the average state court, where an able attorney would have emphasized the provocation, and where the judge on the bench does not, to the same extent, as here, guide the jury during the progress of the trial, this prisoner, in my judgment, would have received only a limited penitentiary sentence. The average listener

SIR WARREN FISHER

at the trial might have regarded justice as having then been done. But what about such "justice" in its effects upon crime and upon law and order?

I got the figures as to the number of murders committed in the United States in 1926 and in Britain in 1928. In the case of our own country, they were 2249, and in Britain they were 136. That answered the question and quieted my natural misgivings. English justice better protects the community.

London,
Sunday, January 25, 1931.

This last week, which I have already partly covered, has been a busy one. One interesting experience was a long interview on the British and Treasury Control System, so called, which I had with Sir Warren Fisher at the Treasury. He is the Permanent Secretary to the Treasury—a very able and outstanding man and a power in the Treasury operations. My purpose in calling on him was to get authoritative information in connection with the preparation of an address at the annual dinner on February 13th of his Majesty's "Civil Service" at which he is to preside, and at which I am to be the "guest of honor"—a marked distinction I am told, for the usual custom is to have a member of the Royal Family in this position, and it will not be followed this time since the Court is in mourning because of the death of the King's sister.

I am more or less in a quandary over this speech. All the more since this interview with Sir Warren, I feel disposed to make a real "non-ambassadorial" address in which I outline the underlying principles of the system now in operation for over eight years which was imposed in the United States under my direction as Director of the Budget for the executive control of governmental expenditures. The more I study the principles of the British Treasury control, the more I see where they are lacking. Can I, or not, make a helpful exposition of what is needed now in the modification of that system at least for this time of great emergency, here and elsewhere in governmental finance? That is the question.

Journal as Ambassador to Great Britain

Of such a course I well understand the risks of possible misunderstanding. I am not yet decided what I shall say, but I am at least going to prepare, and, indeed am preparing, carefully and with much thought what some one ought to say. If, after more consideration, it seems unwise for me in my official position to say it, I will address an extempore speech which the audience will prefer and incorporate the result of my mature conclusions in a memorandum.

During the week, with the Prime Minister at his office at the House of Commons, I had a conference at the request of Secretary Stimson to go over with him the reasons why our Government will not sponsor the selection of an American as President or Vice President of the coming Disarmament Conference in 1932. These reasons Stimson had set out in a letter to the British Ambassador at Washington, but he wanted to be sure that they came directly to the attention of the Prime Minister.

Owing to the stand of the Preparatory Commission of the Disarmament Conference in favor of budgetary limitations of armament, as well as because none of the nations are making the long and careful preparations for the coming general Disarmament Conference, with its more complex and larger problems which the United States, Great Britain and Japan found absolutely necessary as preliminary to the Naval Conference, Stimson believes that the Conference is doomed to failure. He also points out that the most complex problems of the Conference, directly concern Europe alone, and, while the United States is sympathetic toward the effort for their settlement, it cannot properly assume a responsibility for its outcome whether a failure or a success.

I found the Prime Minister frankly pessimistic about the outcome of the Conference. He sees no progress in the French and Italian naval situation. Neither does he look happily on the attitude of France and Germany toward the coming Disarmament Conference. He fears Germany may end in simply using it for the purpose of making a declaration against the Versailles Treaty.

He made no demur to Stimson's reasonings. Incidentally the press reports from Geneva this week stated that the German Minister of Foreign Affairs, Curtius, representing Germany at Geneva, and some of the other European national representatives

Journal as Ambassador to Great Britain

there were favoring my selection as president of the Conference. It was finally stated that our Government would not sponsor the selection of any American. I have no information as to this except from the press and some of the correspondents here.

During the week I prepared a tribute to the memory of my dear friend, General Henry C. Smither, for the annual publication of the West Point Graduates. General Harbord has been asked to write of his military career, and I have covered his work as Chief Coordinator of the United States, to which place I appointed him.

Friday evening, I had a most interesting time at the grand dinner of the Middle Temple. Rode home with my old friend, Sir Walter Lawrence. He is an authority on India because of his long experience there, and I was privileged to listen to the conversation between him and Sir John Simon, in which the latter outlined his coming speech in Parliament upon the outcome of the India Round Table Conference.

I also append to these notes the able "summing up" in this morning's Sunday *Times* of the Conference conclusions and what partially they involve, by Earl Peel, formerly Secretary of State for India and a Conservative member of the Conference. The article from the Sunday *Times* (January 25, 1931) read:

The Indian Conference—And After. Building up a New Constitution. Responsibilities of the Governor General. Hindu-Moslem Relations. By the Right Honorable Earl Peel, Secretary of State for India, 1922–4 and 1928–9.

The Conference has come and gone after ten weeks of continuous session. What have the eighty delegates contributed to the Indian Constitutional Question? It was in some ways unfortunate that the Conference trod so closely upon the heels of its Imperial predecessor. Had a few weeks intervened between the two Conferences, the government might have had time to make more preparation or to provide the delegates with some of the material that was rather lacking in the early stages of our discussions.

It may be said that almost at the beginning the Conference baffled the prophets and started on an unexpected course. It is quite true that the Simon Commission Report laid the foundation of a Federal scheme of which the ruling Princes might in time form part, but many of their recommendations dealt with the old order, and their central Legislature was little more than an enlargement of the present Assembly and Council of State. The despatch of the Government of India which followed the report had looked upon a treatied Federation as a far-off divine event, but not as an urgent, immediate problem. It was the attitude of the Princes that shook the kaleidoscope of Indian affairs into a new setting when they declared their readiness to enter the Federation as constituent elements rather than an aggregation of states entering into relations with the other great unit of British India.

A Momentous Decision

It was this momentous decision that made a real federation possible. The Princes, no doubt, ran great risks, and may possibly have to incur great sacrifices. It is quite true that they insisted throughout that their internal authority in their states must remain unimpaired. It is also true that they would not permit any interference from a federal government with those dynastic and other relations over which the Viceroy, the representative of the King-Emperor, was retaining his control. By entering the federation, the states would, no doubt, exercise a strong influence over matters of common concern to all India, while the Princes themselves would be the authority for carrying out federal orders in their own states. Still, the general experience has been that the powers of the central government, however closely guarded or narrowly defined, have, in fact, grown at the expense of the authority of the constituent units.

Doubts Dispelled

Nor, again, were all the representatives of British India at first converted to the change. They foresaw an alteration in the character, or perhaps its abolition, of that assembly in which they had played an active part for the last ten years. They feared that the new federal conception might obscure the glory of that Dominion status which had become the formula of political aspirations. They had misgivings as to the way in which the new tendency might be regarded by their superiors in India or by those sections of opinion in Congress which had denounced their acceptance of the invitation to attend the Conference. Some of their opponents, indeed, in India declared that the British Parliament, with its Satanic tendencies, was merely ready to transfer power from its bureaucrats to arbitrary rulers as a way of checkmating the democratic movement. Nevertheless, the idea of a United States of India, combining in one government, ultimately united in the same company, enthusiasts and sceptics.

It was only by steps that the true federal idea was reached. At first, the present assembly was to remain the central authority for British India and, with an executive of its own, was to deal with subjects which were confined to British India, such as law and order, criminal and civil law, and other matters. The Federal Legislature was to restrict itself to specific federal subjects common to all India which might be assigned to it. But the difficulties and confusion of two legislatures and two executives proved too great, nor could anybody establish the exact relations between them.

One Legislature

It was seen that such a proposal was too elaborate, and that there could only be one legislature to deal with federal affairs and with British India central subjects. This decision, while avoiding one set of difficulties, naturally gave birth to others. Were the representatives of the Princes to take their part, either by speech or vote, in the affairs of British India? If not, what was to happen if a government was defeated on a British India question while retaining the confidence of the legislature on all-India questions? Was the legislature to have two aspects, one British and one all-India? Those who can remember Irish Home Rule controversies are aware of the difficulties of the in and out clauses.

Perhaps the distinction between unitary and federal governments was not always held closely in view. The idea of an executive responsible to the legislature had strong adherents, while the conception of an executive and legislature with separate and closely defined authority, rather on the American or Swiss plan, was never closely examined. Yet it is clear that the transfer of authority from Parliament to India is perfectly feasible on either scheme.

Method of Election

No doubt an assembly of eighty delegates was not a suitable body for drawing up the precise details of a constitution. They could do no more than sketch the general outlines, while leaving many details for future settlement. But, of course, many of these details, were of the highest moment for the working of the constitution, and the conservative delegates were fully justified in withholding their assent to a scheme until these matters could be settled and a more general view of the whole picture obtained.

For instance, the method of electing or selecting representatives from British India to the two houses of the legislature has still to be laid down, though a strong preference was expressed for direct election to one of the chambers. It may well be that, when the vast areas of the new constituencies have to be settled, practical considerations, at any rate, will point to the necessity for indirect election. Again, the proportion of members which the states are to contribute to both houses is not yet settled, while the equality of the two houses was assumed, but was not clearly expressed. Again, neither the federal government nor the states and provinces were assigned as the home of those residual powers so dear to the constitutional lawyer, while the control of the federal government over the new provincial authorities was discussed but was not settled.

RESPONSIBILITY OF THE EXECUTIVE

In Sir Tej Sapru's proposals the responsibility of the executive to the legislatures was carefully limited. He was evidently anxious to secure his cabinet against the fluctuations of opinion in the legislatures and accidental or snatched votes. His plan that a government should only be turned out of office by a two thirds or three quarters majority of both houses sitting together seemed to give a fine measure of security to a skillful minister. But it was not clear how an executive, which had come scathless through the ordeal, should secure the assent of its day to day proposals without the certifying powers of the Viceroy which had been so freely denounced.

281

Journal as Ambassador to Great Britain

The Viceroy's Role

Perhaps the problem of the executive was an even greater tax on the ingenuity of the delegates. Certain subjects, like the army, foreign affairs, and relations with the states, were to be reserved to the Viceroy; and over other matters, such as finances and law and order, the Viceroy was to exercise powers of control. Were the ministers in charge of the transferred and reserved departments to sit together, to listen to each other's remarks, but to decide on their own responsibility, or were the reserved departments to be quite separately administered and the Viceroy or Government General to be the connecting link between them? Was the Governor General to preside over the Cabinet and thus make himself responsible for decisions when his ministers again were responsible to the legislature. Was he to remain apart and, if so, how was he to be informed of the operations of his cabinet, or to be equipped for the exercise of those special duties of control or interference which were to be reserved for him in the Constitution?

Again, how precisely and by what machinery was the Governor General to exercise his protective duties over minorities or to defend the wide range of British commercial and manufacturing interests in India from unfair or unequal treatment? Without question, if such a scheme as was outlined at the Conference is to be carried through, the different authorities and duties of Governor General and of Cabinet, of machinery for maintaining the safeguards or protecting the minorities must be laid down with the utmost precision in a Statute so that there may be no disputes or quarrels about the limits of authority.

No doubt all these intricate problems could not be settled in ten weeks, but it is a great advantage that these difficulties have been brought into clear relief and have been publicly debated. While it is true that agreement has not been reached on so many parts of the structural design, it is fair to say that none of them have been shirked or evaded in discussion.

Capable Officials Essential

I should like to call attention to one problem that may affect the services in the future. The need for capable and highly-trained officials becomes more essential than ever for the safe working of the new governments both in the provinces and in the center. But a majority of the services committee decided that there should in future be no civil branch of the Indian Medical Service, but that the provincial governments should recruit their own medical services, although they were enjoined to recruit a number of European doctors to meet the requirements of the Army and of the British Officials in India.

The evidence before the Lee Commission showed how important it was for the well being of British officials in India that they should be able to have access for themselves and their families to European doctors of high standing. If they are deprived of this right, there is the risk that they may be too ready to leave the service and retire on proportionate pensions. I agree with the fears expressed by Lord Zetland and Sir Edgar Wood that, under the scheme, neither the provincial governments nor the Indian service would secure medical officers of the type required. When we consider the

282

Journal as Ambassador to Great Britain

immense burden of work which will be thrown upon officials by the remodelling of government in the provinces and in the great series of changes to be worked out in the center, it is surely of the highest moment that every effort should be made to use the experience of all these highly qualified officials.

No doubt, it would have been far wiser, first of all, to establish self-government in the provinces, and then to make use of the advice of ministers in the provinces to determine the details of the new federal constitution. But the majority of the delegates were very insistent that the remodelling of both systems should proceed at the same time. Nevertheless, it may be found when the work is to be done that the character of the constituent units must first be settled before the central government can take its new form.

Moslem and Hindu

But whatever form the new constitution may ultimately take, its success can only be assured and harmonious working established if a reasonable accommodation can be reached between the great religious communities. It is well known what efforts have been made to reach a settlement during the course of the Conference. Sometimes the gap seems to widen, sometimes it seems as if a phrase only might turn the scale. Suggestions have been made that these differences should be settled by a panel of arbitrators, but it is doubtful whether the relations of the two great parallel civilizations can be settled by these devices, or whether, even if the leaders can compromise, the millions of their followers could feel assured that their interests had not been sacrificed. But while the great Hindu-Moslem differences hold the foreground, the leaders of the depressed classes insisted that, unless it was practicable so far to extend the franchise as to give their numbers full weight, they would demand that they must themselves have their own rights as a minority fully secured.

The result would seem to be that separate electorates must be maintained though, of course, the percentages of representation for the different communities have still to be settled. But it remains true that the great communities themselves would have to make their own agreements. No settlement imposed from without could bring peace. Such a settlement might draw upon the head of the unfortunate arbitrator the fires of all the communities, but could not even then establish internal harmony. The governments have no doubt wisely decided that they cannot take upon themselves this dangerous and thankless task.

What Will India Think?

It is of course too early to judge how far the outlines of the new constitution may be acceptable to political opinion in India, or whether some large section at congress will leave the barren wastes of non-cooperation and crown with garlands their returning delegates. The members of the Conference have much to do to expound and explain the bearings of the new federal scheme. They will at least be able to tell their fellow countrymen when they return that they have had the fullest and freest opportunity of stating

283

Journal as Ambassador to Great Britain

their views on the problems of Indian political advance and development before the people and the parliament of Great Britain. They can justly claim that they sat at this Conference on a footing of perfect equality with the representatives of the British parties.

Any lingering resentment that Indians were not to be found on the Simon Commission must surely disappear. Feelings of distrust, of suspicion, must, in the general atmosphere of good will, have lost their force. Representatives of British India have freely acknowledged the welcome that they have received and the perfect equality that has been accorded them. Let us hope that they will be messengers of peace to their brothers in India.

London,
Saturday, January 31, 1931.

I have put in this week with intensive and hard work and study, both day time and evening. As I progressed in my examination of the British Treasury Control and Accounting System, of which my prior knowledge had been but general and academic, I suddenly realized that certain of its defects were so vital and so easily corrected by informed and determined executive power: first that to expose them in my address before His Majesty's Civil Service as an American who had both experienced and corrected them in his own Government, would tend to make it more difficult for the executive power of the British Government to deal with them; and second that it was my duty quietly and without publicity to prepare for the confidential use of the Government an exposition of the defects and my methods of correcting similar defects as the first Director of the Budget of the United States.

My study has shown me that the budget law of the United States, which was handed to me as the Director of the Budget to enforce, was simply a copy of the British Treasury Control and Accounting System. Because of my experience in the creation and administration of executive and coordinating army control systems in the War, I knew immediately that as it stood it would not help me to reduce immediately the expenditures of government and proceeded to form, by executive order, a separate organization to work parallel with it. With these two organizations in my hands, we could and did reduce government expenditures.

As a result, I am now able to present what I consider an unanswerable case—outlining incontrovertible principles, definite methods and results in terms of cash.

Yesterday noon I took lunch with my close friend Sir Josiah Stamp at the Atheneum Club, where I outlined my case and proposed procedure. He immediately recognized the importance of it. Incidentally, he said at this time that, urged thereto by financial necessity, he was forming an internal organization in the London, Midland and Scottish Railway, responsible to him as Chairman, based upon the same principles and paralleling the methods of the present functioning organization for economy and efficiency that I had set up in our Government in 1921–22.

Since I will incorporate my memorandum for the British Government, when finished, in these notes, I will not further discuss it here. Its preparation is an exacting task, involving considerable consideration of public and personal repercussions. My first dictation included twelve thousand words. I have reduced it to six thousand words. In another week I will have it down to four thousand words, if possible.

Have ceased thinking about my speech on February 13th to His Majesty's Civil Service.

For permanent record, I append a copy of my recent correspondence with David Lloyd George.

London,
January 22nd, 1931.

My dear Mr. Lloyd George:

First let me congratulate you upon your birthday, which finds you in such vigorous health and active life. You are so busy that one hesitates to intrude upon your time, but when you have a little leisure I hope you will examine the books I am sending you herewith.* When I last saw you, you said you were writing of the war days, and I mentioned to you the work of the Allied Board of Military Supply during the last four months of the war, to which was delegated the power of issuing direct coordinating orders to the armies for the unification of supply movements, etc., in the allied rear in the zone of the advance, to match the military unification at the front under Foch. You may have forgotten it, but it was your own cooperation which made this Board possible. While it only operated for the last four months of the war, that was long enough to demonstrate that it embodied a new principle in the art of fighting allied armies as one army is fought. Until

---

* *The Report of the Military Board of Allied Supply,* in 3 volumes.

it was created, Foch had no control over any army line of communications except the French line. His power of making inter-army shifts of troops in emergency was extremely limited in consequence. This Board alone made possible and assembled for Foch's use a motor reserve of 10,000 camions which, if the war had continued a little longer, would have been used as flying cavalry columes were used in old-time military operations. It did many other things as the report shows. It was a new device which will be adopted by allied armies hereafter from the beginning.

Because of the great emergency in which it was formed, the Military Board of Allied Supply probably represents in organization and method of operation the farthest advance in allied military supply coordination possible to obtain in the present development of civilization—in other words, considering the present state of human nature. As I say in the preface to the three volumes of this official report which I send you, it was a machinery by which this coordination in the rear of the armies could be attempted by a voluntary agreement without a vital cession of independent national or army authority. It provided the means of immediately securing the information and general outlining of the common situation in the rear of the armies which gave independent authorities the opportunity to clear away their misunderstandings and develop all the issues of any question upon which a mutual agreement was possible. Then, and most important of all, it provided the means for immediately enforcing the agreements through army orders. Acting as the Board did in time of active military operations, its agreements were formed and its orders issued without delay.

I was the member of the Board representing the American army, and being old enough to appreciate the value of preserving records for future use, I secured the issuance of orders by the Board to the Staffs of the allied armies in the Franco-Belgian theatre of the war as of October 31, 1918, and for a report of their supply operations from the beginning. It took five years after the war for these volumes to be compiled by the staffs of the allied armies, but the work was finally finished. We kept the Board alive for that time. It was probably the last inter-allied Board to go out of existence. These volumes comprise one of the most unique works in military literature and are now used, I think, in most of the army staff colleges, including our own.

I am sending these to you, not with the idea that you have time to go over them in detail, but because in the formation of the Military Board of Allied Supply you took a commanding part. You will remember, no doubt, that General Pershing took this matter up with you at the same time that he did with M. Clemenceau and that, having agreed to the plan in principle, you sent General Cowans, Sir Andrew Weir (now Lord Inverforth), Sir J. W. T. Curry, and General Crofton Atkins to Paris for a conference. This conference having failed, I came to England and called upon you at No. 10 Downing Street, where you told me you would call a meeting of the Supreme War Council the next day, before which Cowans and I could appear, and that you would then thresh the matter out and give us a final decision. You also told me that the only objection was coming from the Quartermaster General, Lt. General Cowans, and that if before the meeting of the Council I could secure his agreement, the matter could be regarded as settled. This

DAVID LLOYD GEORGE

I was able to do, because our proposition had been modified from the former proposal for a French Commander-in-Chief of the Rear so as to cover General Cowan's valid objection, and because it was known that you had taken hold of the matter. Consequently, the meeting of the Supreme Council was not held and I took back with me next day the agreement of the British government which, added to that of M. Clemenceau and General Pershing, established the Board.

I am also sending you a copy of my book "A Journal of The Great War." In Volume I of this book, on page 100, you will find what General Pershing said about your attitude when he presented the proposition to you. There is also a reference, on page 105, to the desire of yourself, Clemenceau and Pershing to dodge the details and discussions of the Allied Council and get started as soon as possible; and on pages 120 and 121 a reference to my interview with you. In writing of this interview, I regret I did not make it plainer that it was by understanding with you that I met Lt. General Cowans and was told that if his objection was removed we could consider the matter favorably settled.

With best regards,

Yours sincerely,

CHARLES G. DAWES.

21 Abingdon Street,
London, S.W.1,
30th January, 1931.

MY DEAR MR. AMBASSADOR:

It was exceedingly kind of you to send me those valuable books on the war. They will be a most helpful addition to the library of war literature I am accumulating, and which I hope to utilize when I come to writing my own story. I have a vivid recollection of the incidents you refer to and know what a pleasure it was to me to meet someone whom I recognized at once as a person who possessed the real magnetic and driving qualities which are essential in order to achieve any great purpose.

Once more thanks and with kindest regards, ever sincerely yours,

D. LLOYD GEORGE.

His Excellency,
General Charles G. Dawes, C.B.

London,
Sunday, February 15, 1931.

On Friday afternoon, after a month of hard work upon it, I handed to the Prime Minister at 10 Downing Street, my monograph upon the British Treasury and Accounting Control System, its defects in principle and method, including a detailed

287

Journal as Ambassador to Great Britain

description of a collateral system for improving it. The latter was an exposition of my organization under Executive authority, for a control for the coordination and the forwarding of economy and efficiency in the routine business of government. For over two weeks of the last four I have worked both daytimes and evenings upon it. I had hoped to confine it to about 5,000 words. When I finished it was about 8,500 words, but I had condensed it out of 25,000 words on detached manuscript and dictated notes.

Since it was to be considered by the Prime Minister and the Chancellor of the Exchequer of Britain, it had to be carefully written so as to better answer, as it went along, any subconscious unfavorable repercussions it might excite. In writing it, I considered in perspective for the first time, my own work in the Budget of the United States. When I wrote of it contemporaneously that was impossible.

Monograph on British Treasury Control

1. Everything which is said herein, including that as to the executive power invoked and methods followed refers essentially only to a device for the more correct routine business functioning of a corporation or of a government—a device which is entirely impartial and non-political, affecting in no way the general policies of either the corporation or the government but designed only to assure that the money appropriated for carrying out those policies be spent in the most economical and effective manner.

2. Faults in routine business systems of private enterprises are generally soon corrected or resulting financial difficulties force those enterprises out of existence. Faults in routine business systems of government often remain uncorrected indefinitely, as governments depend upon taxation for their essential revenues and not primarily upon efficient operation from a business standpoint.

3. Countries, whatever may be their government or the political party in power, suffer equally at times from disadvantages which are inherent in faulty systems of routine business and not in their faulty administration. Routine business under any government or private business system generally speaking will be as good as the system makes possible.

4. Proper business organization must insure not an intermittent and outside, but a continuing and internal executive control, concerned always and only with proper routine functioning and unconcerned with general policy save economy and efficiency. Outside control may occasionally stimulate efforts for economy and efficiency in routine functioning but its effects are only temporary.

5. In general, governmental routine business machines work poorly or

288

well according as their internal adjustments resemble those which experience has demonstrated as essential to good routine functioning in private business organizations.

6. The question I am considering is the relative operating efficiency and economy of governmental routine business under the British Treasury and audit control system, the central authority exercised in which was evolved through concessions by independent departments, as compared with that of a routine business system operating under executive control imposed by higher authority.

The British Treasury Control System as Applied in the United States

The budget and accounting act of the United States became effective June 10th, 1921, and on June 23rd I assumed the duties as Director of the Bureau of the Budget, to organize a budget system. It will be remembered that in 1921, when this law was passed, an acute and general financial and business depression existed, as at present, in the United States and all over the world. There was naturally a great and general demand in the United States for economy in governmental expenditures, as there is today both in that country and Britain. In this country at that time, in response to this demand the Geddes committee was formed. Both the President of the United States and the country expected me, as the first Director of the Budget under the new law, immediately to engage myself in the work of reducing governmental expenditures through greater economy and efficiency in governmental business. The reason for this expectation was the nature of my work on the administrative staff and under direction of General Pershing, Commander-in-Chief of the A. E. F., in France, which was known to the country and had consisted of building up and operating systems of executive and coordinating control over certain decentralized service activities of the army, including supply procurement and other lines of work.

To cope with my immediate situation and the pressing demands for economy in governmental expenditures I had at my disposal as Director of the Budget what in effect was the British Treasury Control system, for the new budget act authorized the formation of an organization which was simply an embodiment of it. My powers under it resembled many of those now exercised by your Chancellor of the Exchequer, but unlike him, who is responsible to a Cabinet, the act made me responsible to one man, the President, just as in the formation and operation of my Army organization in France I had been responsible to the Commander-in-Chief.

My intensive study of the British Treasury control system at this critical time, as a potential agency to be used in effecting immediate government economy, was made under strained conditions and involved the careful weighing of grave alternatives. Because of my Army experience, I recognized immediately and instinctively the defects of the British Treasury control and cooperating audit system as an exclusive agency to secure economical routine business functioning. Accordingly, while organizing and operating my office practically in accordance with the British Treasury control system, I used in my methods and work, in addition to the powers created by the Budget Act, other powers derived from the President to correct certain defects of the British system. Your Chancellor of the Exchequer, under an appropriate grant of power from the Cabinet, would be in a position to do the same. I will discuss farther on the defects, the method of correcting them, and the economic principles involved, and concern myself in the first instance with the immediate course of action I followed and its results, made possible only through the exercise of these additional powers, not conferred by the budget law but by executive delegation.

Let me again refer to the situation which I confronted on June 23rd, 1921, the day I assumed office. On June 30th—a week later—all the governmental departments and independent establishments of the United States were to start spending the money which Congress had appropriated to carry them through the fiscal year then commencing. In this emergency, neither the President nor the public nor I could be satisfied with anything but an immediate reduction in operating expenses below existing authorized governmental appropriations. Sir Edward Hilton Young in his book: "The System of National Finance", in discussing your Treasury control system says: "It is at the time when they (the estimates) are being discussed and formulated in detail in the departments that economies can be made in his (the taxpayer's) interest; when they are being passed in Parliament in blocks and undiscussed it is too late. Once the estimates have been published by the departments which draw them up the taxpayer's fate is sealed."

It is evident, since our appropriations at this time not only had been published as estimates but established in law, that if Sir Hilton Young is right, unless I could devise a system differing in its methods and results from the British Treasury control system, not only the taxpayer's fate would be sealed but my own as well.

In emergency nothing but immediate action avails. At my request, the President called a meeting, held six days later (June 29th), of the business organization of the United States Government consisting of the President, the Cabinet heads of departments, and from 1200 to 1500 bureau chiefs and others representing all sections of the routine business operating staff. This meeting, besides visualizing for the first time in our history the business organization of the United States Government, gave the President and myself, as his agent, opportunity to appeal for cooperation in the effort to reduce government expenses to the esprit de corps and loyalty of a great and powerful organization, whose officers and rank and file up to that time had functioned with but little sense of their individual responsibility to the government as a whole as compared with that they felt to their own particular department of it. As explaining the nature and the practical result of the meeting, I quote two extracts from my speech on that occasion: "The President says—and his word goes because he is the head of this governmental business corporation for which we are all working—that none of us is now allowed to assume that our congressional appropriations already made—I am talking now as a bureau chief—none of us is allowed to assume that the amount of those appropriations for the year commencing this July 1st, or any other year, necessarily constitutes the minimum of expenditures during that year."

In closing my speech, quoting from the stenographic report, I said: "Fellow Bureau Chiefs, are you willing, after hearing what I have said, that I

290

should now represent you in addressing myself directly to the President of the United States with an assurance of your cooperation in his request for a reduction of governmental expenditures? If you so agree, if you are willing, will you indicate it by standing?" (The entire audience arose. The President of the United States arose, followed by applause. The Cabinet and other officers on the platform also arose.) "I wish to say to you, sir, that the men before you realize the cares and perplexities of your great position. They realize that at this time the business of our country is prostrated, that men are out of employment, that want and desperation stalk abroad, and that you ask us to do our part in helping you to lift the burden of taxation from the backs of the people by a reduction in the cost of government. We all promise you, sir, to do our best—to do our best." To which the President of the United States responded: "I thank you all for your presence and your commitment to this great enterprise."

At the time of this first meeting, June 29th, of the routine business system of the United States, presided over by the President, the heads and bureau chiefs of the forty-three departments and independent establishments of the Government there represented had been authorized through appropriations already made by Congress to spend for the fiscal year 1922, upon which they would enter two days later, the sum of $1,834,865,762.01. As a result of this appeal to them as a united organization, after less than three weeks of consideration and revision of what they had formerly regarded as their necessities, they had promised to save $112,512,628.32 out of their appropriations, which amount at my suggestion they set up on their respective departmental books as a saving reserve for the year. This amount of savings under appropriations was increased steadily all through the fiscal year under a new system of internal executive control, made up without additional expense from the existing body of governmental employes, which I almost immediately established.

I have at hand the figures of savings under appropriations as they existed in March, 1922, representing the results of the effort for only the first eight months of the fiscal year, 1922. At this particular time this saving reserve under appropriations had increased from $112,512,628.32 to the sum of $143,171,816.63. In other words, of the amount appropriated for them to spend in 1922, as a result of the new system, they saved 7-8/10% in the first eight months of its operation. This amount of appropriations saved, however, large as it was, only represented the smaller portion of the total reduction in the cost of the routine business operations of government for that year, which chiefly resulted from the inauguration of the new system of executive control. We afterwards estimated and itemized in an official report to Congress, covering 170 ordinary book pages, the final savings for the year as amounting to $250,134,835.03.

Many of the improvements in methods of business functioning resulting from the inauguration and operation of the new system of executive control during that first year, which were very productive of large savings in later years, are described in the itemized report for the first year opposite comparatively small sums in the column of savings realized. On the other hand, under the better methods of a proper business system, there were effected certain savings that first year, as for instance in the operations of the United

States Shipping Board, which, for exceptional reasons, were much greater than in any succeeding years under the same improved business system. Again, the greater the preceding inefficiency, the more impressive always will be the beneficial effects of the institution of proper business functioning.

I quite agree that the present business functioning of the British Treasury control system is the best possible under a system of conceded central control by independent departments, as distinguished from executive control, and that the business system of the United States up until the year 1921 was by comparison very defective. Nevertheless, these results obtained in the United States government during the first year that a proper system of executive business control was put into operation, reducing the expenses of routine business by $250,000,000, are extremely significant. They would seem to demonstrate that instead of being measured in fractional percentages of former expenditures, the possible reduction incident to the instituting of a proper executive control here would be very considerable.

The Defects in Principle of the British Treasury Control System, with its allied and cooperating Audit System, as an Exclusive Agency for Securing Economic and Efficient Functioning in Governmental Routine Business

The joint and cooperating control of the British Treasury under the Chancellor of the Exchequer and the Audit Department under the Auditor General over other British governmental departments is limited in its effectiveness when it comes to the matter of their economical and efficient routine business functioning, and does not properly accord with the customary devices of private business for the same purposes. In his book, "The System of National Finance", Sir Edward Hilton Young says: "Naturally, and perhaps inevitably, with the increase in the volume, intricacy and technicality of the business of the great spending departments, the external control of them by the Treasury has weakened. It has passed into other hands. As Treasury control has weakened, the Admiralty and War Office have had themselves to undertake control and surveillance of themselves in matters of finance. The necessary work of parallel and independent restraint on the spending of the Admiralty and War Office, which the Treasury used to do, is now done to a large and increasing extent by their own internal financial branches. As the adviser and helper of the executive spending branches of an office, a well-organized internal financial branch has great advantages over an external power like the Treasury. It has more intimate association in daily intercourse with the spenders, and it has the detailed and technical knowledge of their work, lack of which has been the chief reason for the enfeebling of Treasury control. On the other hand, it is at one great disadvantage in comparison with an external power, that it is not wholly independent."

In a radio address broadcast January 28th, in referring to the work of the British Audit Staff as affecting economy and efficiency in routine business functioning, Sir Hilton Young further pointed out that the organization of the Auditor General with its staff of auditors examine every government office to see that "the offices spend the money they get on the purpose for which the Commons appropriated it, and not otherwise." Again, using his words, "This system of audit provides you with a splendid engine to ensure legality in expenditure, but it is equally clear that the whole of this magnificent machinery of audit has not anything very much to do with enforcing economy." "The Auditor General," he said, "is encouraged by the Commons and the Treasury to report any cases of waste, and much good work is done by the audit staff in that way. But this economy-audit is not their first business and, you see, it is done after the expenditure has been incurred. It is a *post mortem*. It is too late to save the money that time."

I will quote finally sections 2, 3, 4, 5, 6, 29, 30, 31 and 32 of the statement of Sir Warren Fisher, Permanent Secretary to the Treasury, made December 17th, 1930, before the Royal Commission of the Civil Service.

In this connection I desire to say that this statement and the testimony of Sir Warren given with it constitutes one of the ablest, clearest, and most complete expositions of a technical subject I have read. It may justly be considered the most authoritative exposition existing of the British system of Treasury control, its principles and its methods, not only because it is recent, but because it is based upon a long and distinguished connection with Treasury functioning as Permanent Secretary to the Treasury. Sir Warren treats of the system as it now exists and operating under Cabinet authority as now exercised, saying: "(2) It will not be disputed that the maintenance of the *quality* of the Services of the Crown is a matter of supreme interest to the country; and this is the criterion I propose to apply to my observations.

"(3) Until relatively recent years the expression 'Civil Service' did not correspond either to the spirit or to the facts of the organization so described. There was a service of Departments with conditions of service which in quite important respects differed materially; Departments did not think of themselves as merely units of a complete and correlated whole; and in the recognition by each department of the existence of others there was, from time to time, an attitude of superiority, of condescension, of resentment, or even of suspicion.

"(4) Such departmentalism is, of course, the antithesis of a 'service.' And clearly, for the efficient conduct of the country's business, an isolationist and capriciously disposed set of entities could not compare with a service inspired by a larger esprit de corps and cooperative sense, and informed by the spontaneous interchange of experience and knowledge.

"(5) The evolution of a Service conception in contrast to the merely departmental one has of late years progressed some distance. Status, remuneration, prestige and organization throughout the departments have been assimilated. There is an overgrowing team sense in all ranks; it pervades the whole conduct of public business, though it happens that the simplest evidence of it is to be found in the realm of sport owing to the recent introduction of a Sports Council for the Service and the new custom of service sides entering for matches with the three other Crown Services. For the principal posts in the Departments the field of selection is now the Service, and not the individual Department; and cooperation between the permanent heads is continuous, understanding and informal.

"(6) This development of a 'service' is by no means yet completed, and the inherent condition of sub-organization by Departments tends to obscure recognition of the process and to militate against rapid realization. But, if the country is to go on getting in requisite measure the service it needs from the civil establishment of the Crown, the ideal of a service must be fostered and supported in all ways possible and thereby traditions and experiences be broader and deeper based . . .

"(29) A phrase in common use, viz: 'Treasury Control', sometimes leads to the impression in the public mind that expenditure, to which exception is being taken in one quarter or another, might have been prevented if the Treasury were exercising its authority properly; it is timely therefore to re-affirm the fact that the Treasury (by which I mean the Departmental Treasury) is not a separate power behind the throne and that it has no intrinsic authority of its own. Its members are officials of the Board of Treasury and they derive their authority from that Board. The pre-eminence of the Chancellor of the Exchequer in finance interests him in the expenditure of all Departments, and the issues that thus arise fall roughly into three categories. There are questions of such importance as to involve at some stage if not from the outset discussion between the Chancellor and the Ministers of other Departments in the effort to reconcile divergent aspects of the public interest. There are questions similar in character but less in importance where Treasury officials and officials of other Departments will engage in similar discussion. Finally, there is the continuous search for shorter and more economical processes in giving effect to policies already settled. Both in the second and third of these categories it will be the case that Treasury officials are frequently engaged in lively and vigorous discussion with other officials. These discussions derive their authority from Ministers on either side. Instead of 'Treasury Control' it is right to speak only of the Chancellor's control of finance; and nothing in that is inconsistent with the view that, so far as the service is concerned, his purposes may most fully be achieved, not by a body of watchdogs with orders to bite, but by a Service animated by a common understanding of the objectives of its Government including the objective of economy, and by a common desire to attain those ends.

"(30) Moreover, it should be borne in mind that in major spheres policy, and therefore expenditure, is ultimately decided by the Cabinet; and, while it is an important function of Treasury officials to point out the financial implications of proposals before the Cabinet and to collate them so that not only the Chancellor of the Exchequer, but through him the Administration, may have a bird's eye view of the picture as a whole, the 'control' is necessarily in the body where the responsibility for reaching the final decision resides, viz: the Cabinet.

"(31) It is not only members of the public who have been misled by the phrase 'Treasury Control'; there have been times when even officials of the Treasury have, to its solemn refrain, conjured up a picture of themselves as the single-handed champions of solvency keeping ceaseless vigil on the buccaneering proclivities of Permanent Heads of Departments. A not unnatural result has been an attitude of mutual suspicion tinged in the case of Departmental Heads by a faintly ironical impatience with this apparent assumption by the Treasury of a peculiar righteousness and of a corresponding omniscience. Happily this state of affairs is fast becoming a memory; and I only refer to it here to express the sincere hope that it may be finally relegated to the limbo appropriate to shibboleths.

"(32) Earlier in this note I have, in connection with the idea of a service, quoted from the letter appearing as Appendix A. As that quotation is also relevant in considering the position of the Treasury as the General Staff in this conception of a Service, I should like again to refer to it as a whole and to conclude this note by adding one more excerpt: 'The real truth is, in my judgment, that the possibility of the Departmental Treasury securing economy as regards advice on policy and administration alike depends on two conditions. The first—and obviously the principal one—is the attitude and practice toward expenditure of the House of Commons and of the Government for which the House stands. That is, of course, a matter outside and above the sphere of a Civil Servant. The second condition cannot, if I may say so, be better expressed than in the language of the Public Accounts Committee report, which I have already quoted earlier in this letter. "It is essential that the heads of departments should work together as a team in the pursuit of economy in every branch and every detail of the public service" (par 43) and "if they are able to act together as a body, under firm guidance, they may, while in no way relieving Ministers of their overriding responsibilities, have an importance and influence second only to that of Ministers in accomplishing the most critical and difficult task that lies before them' (par 44).'"

The British Treasury control, as it has evolved for over a century, of necessity has been primarily determined as to its method of functioning by financial considerations rather than by its secondary duty, by advice or indirect compulsion, to secure more efficient functionng in collective routine business operation. Other things being equal, a continuing organization like the Treasury Department, concerned primarily with the general balancing of the budget of the Government and only secondarily with securing economy, will, in its efforts to secure economy, tend to spurt in times of financial distress and relax in prosperous time. Financial troubles and burdens are most distracting. It is for this reason that private business organizations as a rule do not put in their treasury departments any degree of responsibility for the efficient and economical business functioning of the other departments of the business.

The most striking evidence that the British Treasury control does not properly concern itself with economy and efficient functioning is its apparent attitude toward appropriations when once made by Parliament. Whether a department can be encouraged to operate upon less than its appropriation made for the fiscal year is a question which does not seem to receive proper consideration.

As Sir Hilton Young says in *The System of National Finance:* "The manner in which the estimates are prepared is therefore of the greatest concern to every taxpayer. It is at the time when they are being discussed and formulated in detail in the departments that economies can be made in his interest; when they are being passed in Parliament in blocks and undiscussed it is too late. Once the estimates have been published by the departments which draw them up the taxpayer's fate is sealed."

Conditions affecting the necessity of expenditures naturally change in the course of each year. No private business organization could afford to assume that the minimum amount which one of its departments will spend during a fiscal year will be the full amount of its appropriation. In properly organized private business, the amount appropriated for the expenses of a department at the beginning of the year is always considered the maximum amount, not the minimum amount which it will spend. Without the prompting of an internal, informed, and alert executive authority continually exercised, as is customary in private business organizations, not only the heads of subordinate departments of Government but the rank and file of the employes thereof will tend to assume as proper the complete expenditure of an authorized appropriation within the fiscal year.

The above would seem to apply to the defects of the British Treasury control system in such cases as it is able to exercise even a limited control. In all the inter-departmental relations, however, under the laws of human nature, it is necessarily affected by the repercussions on the attitudes of the other independent departments and services of the lack of a fixed and unassailable basis of executive authority for an attempt to exercise any firm and adequately effective control over them. This is the compelling reason for Sir Hilton Young's statement: "The eternal control of them (the spending departments) by the Treasury has weakened. It has passed to other hands. As Treasury control has weakened, the Admiralty and War Office have had themselves to undertake control and surveillance of themselves in matters of finance."

A conceded central authority over the methods of routine business functioning as distinguished from true executive authority, as exercised in ordinary private corporations, is far better of course than no central authority at all, but short of proper authority. What is needed is not conceded central authority but central executive authority.

Differences in the fundamental principles upon which functioning systems are based are certain to manifest themselves in the relative efficiency of their operations. Napoleon's sixty-fourth maxim of war, "Nothing is more important than a central command under one chief" is the principle upon which all successful private business systems are based. The present business functioning of the constituent governmental units affected by the British Treasury control system resembles that of a coalition instead of a single army, and for the same reasons.

Executive Control as distinguished from a Conceded Central Control encourages Voluntary Cooperation

You have here a general system of supervision of routine business functioning, admittedly one of voluntary cooperation. In my judgment you should have a system of control involving power to coerce cooperation when necessary. The fact that, if necessary, you can secure cooperation by coercion does not mean that under such a system you will not have cooperation without coercion. It means indeed that you will have more and better voluntary cooperation because the knowledge that the power of coercion exists creates in the minds of the members of a loyal organization an added sense of the importance of its objectives, and stimulates their search for opportunities for voluntary cooperation. The experience of all private business organizations demonstrates this truth. Economy never becomes less fashionable when extravagance becomes more dangerous. Note: Thiers said:

Journal as Ambassador to Great Britain

"An order given without supervision of its execution is given in vain. (*Un ordre donné dont on ne surveille pas l'exécution est un ordre vain.*"

Esprit de corps

The routine business personnel of the Government is of necessity divided and separated among the different departments. While his Majesty's Civil Service as a whole has its fine *esprit de corps*, the respective departmental organizations also each have their *esprit de corps*. These two examples of *esprit de corps* are related things—sometimes offsetting and sometimes supplementing each other—but they are not the same thing. Only organizations with visible and functioning leadership, properly empowered, are those which develop *esprit de corps* in its fullest effectiveness. Informal conferences between the heads of separate departments representing different interests cannot properly inspire an *esprit de corps* nor can such department heads successfully substitute their individual efforts in place of executive leadership. Your governmental routine personnel scattered among the departments have collectively certain powers to forward economy and efficiency in routine business operations, especially in matters involving better coordination of co-related activities of separate departments, but they belong collectively to no separate organization with executive leadership, formed to make possible the useful exercise of these powers. This organization when formed will possess its own *esprit de corps*, inconsistent with no other existing *esprit de corps*, and properly stimulating it in its distinctive work for economy and efficiency.

Conclusions. Form and detailed Functions of Suggested Organization

In this Government, the cooperating Treasury and audit staff have visualized the needs of its routine business activities and with all the power they possess and in a most creditable way they have sought to meet them. There has gradually been evolved a voluntary system of coordination and cooperation which, for a voluntary system, is without question the best of its kind.

Had the Treasury possessed the proper executive power, in my judgment, it would long ago have made the modifications in its present control methods and organization which would perfect it.

The power of the President of the United States, inherent in his position, to issue executive orders coordinating and improving routine governmental business methods and organization I assume is here inherent in the Cabinet, at least until modified by act of Parliament. Under its delegation of power to the Chancellor of the Exchequer, or by its issuance of executive orders upon his recommendation, the Cabinet could enable the Chancellor to remedy the defect which now prevents your Treasury system from operating with its greatest possible effectiveness.

As our government paid a deserved tribute to the British Treasury control system by embodying it in our budget and accounting law, where in greater part it has determined our budget methods, I would suggest that the form and methods of the independent organization which was set up in the United States under the Director of the Budget and in his office, framed in accordance with the principles which I have discussed and established to supplement and make more effective a system there which was in effect

Journal as Ambassador to Great Britain

your own Treasury system, be given due study. This organization was formed under the authority of the budget law, but under powers derived by the Director of the Budget from the President of the United States, similar powers to which can be delegated by your cabinet to your Chancellor of the Exchequer. It is a device which for nearly eight years now has worked in complete harmony with all the departments of Government, as similar devices work universally in private business. It functions so quietly in fact that the public has forgotten it exists. In their routine operations it has brought about economies in all the departments and independent establishments, including the Treasury Department itself. It has added little or nothing to the cost of government, made up as it is from an existing body of employes. In guiding the rank and file of the personnel of Government in an organized and distinctive kind of work for economy and efficiency, it has given them in this association that *esprit de corps* which comes from the continuing contact with intelligent executive power. From its beginning to the present, it has saved immense sums in the expenses of the routine business of the United States Government. It has taken its firm place as one of our politically unmolested, useful and actively functioning permanent national institutions.

Considering the fact that the matter of possible economies in the functioning of the present routine business system of the British Government can never be adequately determined until the executive control test is applied, at least for a time; considering that the present system—good as it is—may be improved in a simple way, without additional legislation, by a cabinet grant to the Chancellor of the Exchequer of certain powers not affecting general policy and dictated alike by common sense and the universal experience of private business corporations as being necessary to efficient routine business functioning; considering also that the test involves no radical disarrangement of existing functioning methods but only the means for an additional stimulus to their effectiveness in functioning in their present form; and considering that if this test of efficiency and economy is made, neither the initiation of additional executive control, its continued operation, or after-abandonment involves in consequence additional cost to the Government, it would seem proper that it receive consideration.

The Chancellor of the Exchequer said in his speech in the Commons on February 11th relative to your spending departments that "apart from policy there is no doubt small economies are possible. They are always being examined."

Increased executive control over routine business functioning will enable him in these examinations to determine by the last test what is that added increase of economy, if any, which lies beyond the independent power of the departments in the expenditure of money appropriated to them separately for co-related purposes, and what will be the effects of an organization under his executive leadership in stimulating in the departments their constant independent search for means of more effective and economical functioning. A similar influence to the latter we found in the United States to have an important and productive effect. His agents under this special organization, not concerned with financial obligations, but devoted alone to means for economy and efficiency in routine departmental functioning, would not be distracted by the constant consideration of the relation of

298

GENERAL HENRY C. SMITHER
Chief Coordinator, U.S.A.

Journal as Ambassador to Great Britain

possible savings to budget balancing. The question of economy and efficiency in routine business functioning is related to budget balancing only as economy is achieved or not achieved. It is a question involving only constant attention to methods of procurement, disposition of property, specification of general and technical material, advertising, warehousing, employment, travel of persons, transportation of property, disbursements, real estate, and such other ordinary business transactions as may from time to time give indication of a need of coordinated and executive supervision.

The general impression which exists that the administrative expenses of the British Government, including its staff services, are so small that further economy in them must necessarily be of little importance in its relation to the balancing of the Budget, may prove to be correct. There is no doubt of the fine internal organization and executive control of departmental business and a good measure of effectiveness in their outside Treasury control. But everywhere in times like the present no economies are so small as to be unimportant, for in their aggregate in a great system they may be unexpectedly large, and every opportun'.y for small economies should be meticulously explored.

It is of course quite impossible for any one to exactly estimate the savings which will ensue from a new kind of control over the routine functioning of an enormous business system which alone spends over 200 million pounds per year on the Post Office, Imperial Defenses and Tax Collections.

Nature of Organization in the Office of the American Director of the Budget, established in 1921 to increase Efficiency and secure Economy in the Routine Business Activities of Government

The Chief Coordinator and the personnel of the service of coordination are appointed from the body of Governmental employes by the Director of the Budget. By executive order of the President they are detached from their former departments, and thereafter serve in the new organization as directly responsible to the Director of the Budget, and through him to the President.

Duties of Chief Coordinator

1. It shall be the duty of the Chief Coordinator, under the Director of the Budget, to supervise co-related affairs of Government for the support of which moneys have been appropriated by the Congress.

2. Subject to the supervision and direction of the Director of the Budget, the Chief Coordinator is authorized from personnel drafted from departments and establishments to form such coordinating groups as in his judgment may be necessary in order to bring the full powers of government to bear upon the conduct of its ordinary business affairs. Such persons so named by the Chief Coordinator shall, upon call from him, furnish information to him and assist him in the performance of his coordinating duties, and their compensation shall continue to be paid by the departments from which they were respectively selected. Each person so selected to participate in joint coordinating undertakings shall as to such matters only be subject to the Chief Coordinator, in all other respects his usual relation to the department from which he was selected shall remain unchanged. The decision of the Chief Coordinator as to any matter involving coordination shall be transmitted to the department or instrumentality concerned and shall be final,

299

subject only to the right of such department or instrumentality to appeal to the Director of the Budget within ten days after the receipt of such decision; and, if such appeal be determined adversely to the appellant, to appeal to the President of the Republic within five days after such determination. Every decision not so appealed from, or if appealed from and sustained on appeal, shall in all respects be binding and shall be observed.

3. The Director of the Budget and the Chief Coordinator, with the approval of the Director of the Budget may respectively, from time to time, make, modify and repeal standing regulations covering matters within their respective jurisdictions, and such regulations shall be binding on all persons. Such regulations shall before becoming effective be approved by the President of the Republic.

4. It shall be the duty of each Secretary of State or other Cabinet Officer to furnish or cause to be furnished without delay to the Director of the Budget and to the Chief Coordinator all such information as they may respectively request appertaining to matters within their respective jurisdictions.

5. The service of coordination is an official agency of the Government. Its purpose is to secure an added measure of economy that lies beyond the independent power of the departments and establishments in the expenditure of sums of money appropriated to them separately for co-related purposes.

6. The Chief Coordinator shall have direction and control over the organization and activities of the service herein established. Through the coordinating service he shall exercise supervision over the business activities of the governmental organization, with particular attention to methods of procurement, disposition of property, specification of general and technical material, advertising, warehousing, employment, travel of persons and transportation of property, disbursements, real estate, and such other ordinary business transactions as may from time to time give indication of a need of coordinated supervision. He shall impose unified policies involving departmental cooperation, and he may formulate plans for the guidance of joint undertakings.

7. The Chief Coordinator is authorized and directed to prescribe rules and regulations which he deems necessary to safeguard property and facilities capable of rendering service from being wasted, withheld from useful employment, from being exposed to avoidable deterioration, and to avert ill-advised disposal of property below its real value under cover of authority granted by permissive laws to sell or lease idle property.

8. The Chief Coordinator, being an arm of the Executive, is responsible through the Director of the Budget only to the Executive, and his acts may not be questioned save by appeal as herein provided for. His decisions in all matters of coordination shall be reduced to writing immediately upon request by the head of a department or establishment.

9. Within ten days after a decision has been rendered or instructions have been issued in writing by the Chief Coordinator appeal therefrom may be taken to the Director of the Budget and should the appeal not be sustained by the Director of the Budget, the appellant may then appeal to the President of the Republic within five days thereafter.

10. Nothing herein contained shall be construed as relieving heads of departments or subordinate officials in any degree from responsibilities already imposed upon them by law or by executive order.

11. On the contrary, the Chief Executive reposes full confidence in the tact and judgment of the Chief Coordinator in the expectation that he will exercise the powers delegated to him, to securely establish harmonious and effective joint relations in the interests of economy and efficiency in the Government's routine business.

12. The pursuance of this object is essentially an aid to departments and establishments and they shall share in its maintenance.

13. The Chief Coordinator may call at will for such assistance as he may require of specially qualified personnel detailed to confer jointly and report upon any subject that may be assigned them by the Chief Coordinator and such aid shall be forthcoming whether the assignments be of a temporary or continuing nature.

14. All persons designated or detailed to perform continuous duty under the Chief Coordinator or in connection with any agency of his creation shall be regarded as serving under the orders of the President of the Republic and when so declared by the Chief Coordinator they shall be exempt from control of any kind by the department or establishment upon whose rolls they are carried until such time as they shall have been released from this exemption by the Chief Coordinator.

15. Subject to the general supervision by the Director of the Bureau of the Budget, the Chief Coordinator handles all questions of coordination arising through the application of the policies of the President and of the Congress to the routine business activities of the executive power of the Government.

16. Until such time as the need of the Chief Coordinator of representation outside the seat of the Government shall have assumed proportions justifying the permanent detail of personnel to the coordinating service, he will deputize from time to time as necessity therefor arises, persons to act for and in his behalf in addition to their other duties.

Duties of Coordinators

(a) To establish contact and confer with every branch of the Executive Government within the area, to impress upon them the need and policy of coordination, and to instruct them in the use of the coordinating machinery. It is not the function of the coordinator to assume any duties for the performance of which other officials are now responsible, but it is incumbent upon him to point out where savings may be made by coordination, cooperation, or combination, and to insist that the several officials concerned take positive steps to effect the desired result or show conclusively that it is impracticable.

(b) It is intended that the rule of reason should apply to these instructions, that the duties laid down are to be performed as far as facilities permit, and that primary attention be given to the larger activities, others to follow in order of importance. Reports to the Chief Coordinator are only to be made where remedy appears desirable and cannot be arranged between the coordinator and the branches concerned. Reports to the Chief

Coordinator with respect to deficiencies in any branch made include the coordinator's recommendation as to remedy and a statement that the matter has been considered by the branches concerned (giving names of the officials) and no satisfactory action taken by them or by their superiors. Each report to the Chief Coordinator should in general relate to one subject only. All official correspondence with the office of the Chief Coordinator should be addressed to the Chief Coordinator and not to any individual officer attached to the office.

(c) Coordinators are authorized to confer directly with the immediate heads of activities being inspected without the necessity of adhering strictly to the rules of procedure of the branch concerned. It will be the duty of the official concerned to advise his seniors in the premises. Coordinators will realize that a great deal depends upon their tact in these matters and deference should be paid to the rules and customs of the various departments so far as they do not interfere with the prompt and direct conduct of business. Controversy is obviously inimical to coordination and must be avoided except as a last resort. Every effort will be made to establish direct personal contact with other national officials and, in so far as is practicable, to transact matters of non-routine business by personal interview.

(d) Purchasing. (1) To inspect all government purchasing offices, to see that sound practice and government policies are carried out and that methods are enforced to ensure the substitution of new or used material on hand in the same or other departments before purchase is made (this will often require tracing back by the purchasing office to the office certifying the requirements); (2) to suggest substitutions to the branches concerned and to report action in this respect to the Chief Coordinator unless convinced by the branches concerned that such substitution is impracticable; (3) to direct the postponement of purchases when no emergency exists and when it appears that the desired material may be obtained from another branch of the government, making special report in such cases to the Chief Coordinator; (4) to report improper or inefficient methods to the Chief Coordinator; (5) to recommend combining of functions whenever it may appear practicable.

(e) Stock on hand. (1) To inspect accumulations of material on hand; (2) to ascertain if it has been inventoried, if inventories were accurate when taken, if they have been kept up to date, if a stock record is kept, if they have been reported to an office whose duty it is to declare all or part of it surplus, if such declarations have been made, if the descriptions on inventories are sufficient for identification for sales purposes, if sales or transfers to other departments have been made, if physical deliveries are being made, if proper facilities exist for the same, if the stocks are properly cared for to prevent deterioration or loss, if new stock is being issued when serviceable used material is available; (3) to report any stocks found which have not been inventoried and reported, and any which, although reported and not declared excess, are, in the opinion of the coordinator, in excess of local requirements and available for transfer or sale.

(f) Reserves. To ascertain if any items of such reserves consist of articles which will deteriorate rapidly or become obsolete if not made use of within a reasonable time or for which spare parts will be no longer obtainable; if any articles are being maintained in the reserve, suitable substitutes for which are in daily commercial use for general consumption, and which could, in the event of an emergency, be obtained without delay or without crippling industry or interfering with the normal life of the community from which drawn.

(g) Property in use. (1) To inspect real and personal property in use or installed for use, including grounds, buildings, machinery, equipment, furniture, etc.; (2) to ascertain if it is in continuous or in part use, if it has been reported as available for transfer or sale, if it is required to be retained by law or departmental order, if it is being properly used or preserved; (3) to recommend any discontinuance or disposition.

(h) Operations. (1) To inspect government activities and operations; manufacturing, repairing, agricultural, transportation, educational, or otherwise; (2) to report duplication, waste, or inefficient use of material, equipment, or personnel.

(i) Transfers. (1) To inspect activities in connection with the transfers of material between different branches of the government; (2) to verify the actual necessity for the material on part of the receiving branch; (3) to ascertain that the physical transfers of material are economically made; (4) to report any deficiencies in the above respects to the Chief Coordinator; (5) to determine the price at which transfers shall be made in case of disagreement between the branches concerned, which price shall be current market price, with proper differentials for carrying charges (not government storage) and with reasonable depreciation for used or deteriorated material.

(j) Sales. (1) To inspect activities in connection with the sale of surplus material; (2) to see that sound practice and government policies are followed; (3) that the expenses of the sale are reasonable; (4) that improper charges are not made against proceeds; (5) to report any deficiencies in the above respect; (6) to postpone any sale when it appears that it is not to the financial interests of the general government for it to continue, making immediate report in such cases to the Chief Coordinator.

(k) Adjacent Areas. To keep in touch by correspondence with the coordinators of adjacent areas with a view to effecting economies by interchanging material between areas when such transactions would be to the financial interest of the general government.

(l) Record. To maintain a brief record of the movements, duties performed, and results obtained by himself and staff, forwarding copy of same to the Chief Coordinator on the last day of each month. This report will be historical only and is not to contain recommendations or requests requiring action. Such should be made the subject of separate correspondence.

During the first years of the existence of this organization, the number of men detailed by executive order to serve under the Director of the Budget in the coordinating work and forming the nucleus of the organization in his office, including the Chief Coordinator, was only eleven. As coordinators operating in different sections of the country, there were nine additional, making twenty in all. The Chief Coordinator then drafted from departments and establishments a personnel to form such coordinating groups as in his judgment were necessary to bring the full powers of the Government to bear upon the conduct of its ordinary business affairs. Such persons so named by the Chief Coordinator furnished him upon call information to assist him in the performance of his coordinating duties. Their compensation continued to be paid by the departments from which they were respectively selected. The persons so selected to participate in joint coordinating undertakings were, as to such matters only, subject to the Chief Coordinator. In all other respects they maintained unchanged their usual relations to the department from which they were selected.

The coordinating boards thus formed were: The Federal Purchasing Board, a chairman and members representing seventeen different departments; the Federal Board of Hospitalization, a chairman and members representing eight separate departments of hospital work; the Federal Liquidation Board, a chairman and members representing six different departments; the Federal Traffic Board, a chairman and members representing twenty-four different departments and establishments; the Federal Specifications Board, a chairman and members representing twenty-three different departments and services; the Interdepartmental Board of Contracts and Adjustments, a chairman and members representing thirty different departments and establishments; the Federal Real Estate Board, a chairman and members representing eighteen different departments and establishments; the Permanent Conference on Printing, a chairman and members representing thirty-four different departments and establishments and one coordinator for Motor Transport in the District of Columbia.

(NOTE) These boards met at the call of their respective chairmen from time to time, to examine the situation, whenever necessary, of any co-related activity of the departments represented for the benefit of the Chief Coordinator in devising proper coordinating orders framed to improve and make more economical the coordinated functioning of that particular activity.

London
Thursday, February 19, 1931.

Have had two interviews already this week with the Prime Minister. The first one was to discuss a prospective international conference on the silver question, especially as it concerns the present business situation in India and China. This idea apparently originated in the United States Senate. Stimson sent me a cable to submit it tentatively to the Prime Minister. The latter has since discussed it with the British Cabinet and will submit his matured views shortly.

The second interview was this morning when the Prime Minister called me to 10 Downing Street and told me when I arrived I could not guess what he wished to see me about. I could not, naturally, and he then outlined a projected plan of action in case Craigie gets a tentative agreement between France and Italy on their naval differences which thus far have made section 3 of the Naval Treaty a three-power instead of a five-power pact.

Journal as Ambassador to Great Britain

The plan is as follows. If Craigie, of the Foreign Office, who has been acting as an intermediary between France and Italy, informs him after visiting Rome that the scheme that he (Craigie) now has in mind is the best he can get the two Governments to accept, the Prime Minister proposes to communicate the scheme to Matsudaira and myself, with a request for us to ask our Governments to agree to a meeting of the adjourned Naval Conference which, as chairman, he would then summon to consider it.

He does not regard Craigie's tentative figures as satisfactory, but in order to avoid recourse to clause 21 of the Naval Treaty (the so-called escalator clause) he would hope to get a declaration regarding their temporary character and other safeguards from the Conference. He would then be able to state that although building by Great Britain on the program submitted would, in the ordinary way, compel her to raise article 21 of the Naval Treaty, in view of the forthcoming Disarmament Conference, she would not do so but would trust to further negotiations, preparatory to that Conference enabling Great Britain, France and Italy to come to a complete understanding which would then be embodied in the London Naval Treaty, thus making part 3 a five-power treaty.

We are vitally interested in this matter, of course, since, if the French contention on submarines is agreed upon, an increase in British destroyers is necessary to keep equilibrium which again would necessitate an increase in United States destroyers to maintain her parity with Great Britain.

We had a long session on the matter, and then about noon I called on Henderson at the Foreign Office, who had asked me to come. He had another subject to broach—that of our attitude toward the Disarmament Conference in 1932, and our views on proper procedure in the matter of the preliminary negotiations. This I will not attempt to cover here; but incidentally I asked Henderson how Craigie was getting along. To my surprise Henderson told me that Craigie felt that he was "about at the end of his rope" and did not really expect to get a tentative agreement between France and Italy. This seemed much at variance with the views as to the expectations of Craigie which the Prime Minister entertained.

Journal as Ambassador to Great Britain

The Prime Minister said my Treasury Control memorandum is now in Snowden's hands. He told me he had no objection to my showing the memorandum to Stamp.

This noon, accordingly, I took lunch with Sir Josiah Stamp at the Atheneum Club, and gave it to him. Stamp read it over at lunch and has taken it home for study. He wants me to be an expert witness before the Parliamentary Committee on improvements in governmental business methods in the interest of economy, and make the statement there which, in his opinion, is unanswerable. I told him that I could not do this without the Prime Minister's consent, which naturally meant that of Snowden also. Told him also that the Prime Minister seems entirely sold on the memorandum but that it belongs in Snowden's department.

Am very busy, but as luck has it, am snowed under this week with engagements which I made when business was slack. Monday night I went to the banquet of the British Industries Fair at Guildhall; Tuesday, to a delightful dinner given by Lord Beauchamp at his home, at which only the University of London professors were present; Wednesday (last night), to the annual dinner of the British Royal Warrant Holders Association at Connaught Rooms. Monday, I went to a Pilgrims' lunch for Sir Henry Armstrong and on Wednesday (yesterday) we gave a lunch for forty guests (mostly Americans) at the Embassy for those associated with the Persian Art Exhibit. Lord Reading and Lady Asquith were among those present. For the balance of the week, I face another lunch and dinner to Captain Malcolm Campbell. It reminds me of Washington.

London,
February 22, 1931.

Quite busy on diplomatic matters the last week. Conveyed a request from Henderson to the State Department requesting the American views on the methods and plans which should be followed in the preliminary negotiations leading up to the Disarmament Conference in 1932. I think Stimson's comments on the situation, when Lindsay approached him relative to an American becoming President or Vice-president of the Conference, have aroused Henderson's apprehensions somewhat.

This evening, de Fleuriau, the French Ambassador, called upon me to inquire as to whether the United States would be represented on the League Committee on slavery in Siberia, in London next Friday. It will be represented. This gave me an opportunity to inquire whether de Fleuriau had heard how Craigie was progressing in Paris. He replied that this morning (Sunday) he received word from there that the British position as then outlined by Craigie was not acceptable to France, and that Craigie had been told that in consequence it was useless for him to proceed to Rome.

He stated that yesterday's publicity of the scheme in Paris was, he was afraid, intended to make trouble. I gathered from him that Paris regarded the British Admiralty as responsible for the check to the program. This did not surprise me, as MacDonald, in outlining his plan, said he did not regard it wise to appear at first too acquiescent to the Craigie scheme. Since de Fleuriau also said that France did not care to what extent Great Britain increased its number of destroyers, it seemed to me that MacDonald's program so far is progressing very well along the lines he intended. So I guess, and it is but a guess, that Craigie will go right on to Rome.

This week I will take up with its Minister in London the matter of the formal recognition by the United States of the Kingdom of Hejaz and Nejd, and its dependencies, and tell him that subject to certain assurances the United States will act favorably upon it.

On Friday noon, Caro and I took lunch with Lord and Lady Willingdon. It was a small party, among whom were Mr. and Mrs. Stanley Baldwin and High Commissioner Ferguson of Canada and his wife.

Lord Willingdon, who is to go to India as Viceroy, is facing his difficult task with his usual calmness and common sense. As someone has said: "Under him in India the British flag will not be flaunted but it will not be furled."

On Friday night, Caro and I attended a large dinner at the Mayfair Hotel, given by the British Racing Drivers Associa-

Journal as Ambassador to Great Britain

tion to Captain Malcolm Campbell, who has just broken the world record, driving an automobile at Daytona, Florida, at the rate of over 245 miles an hour. Earle Howe presided and proposed the toast to Captain Campbell, which I supported, and to which Campbell most appropriately responded.

London,
Sunday, March 1, 1931.

Naval matters moved fast this last week. Craigie, instead of going to Rome from Paris, came back to London last Sunday, and on last Monday, Henderson, Alexander, and Craigie went to Paris. At Paris these three met Briand and the French naval representatives and reached a tentative agreement to be submitted to Rome. They then went to Rome, where they secured Italy's acceptance in principle. They are now in Paris, where they hope to reach a final settlement between Great Britain, France and Italy which will then be submitted for approval to the United States and Japan.

We have been notified of the terms of the first tentative agreement at Paris, but I will wait and incorporate in these notes the final agreement, if reached, which will be submitted to us and Japan. The outcome indicates the importance of the time element in disarmament negotiations—something which no one understands better than Briand and Henderson. If all comes out well with these negotiations now so far advanced, the naval race of the world will be checked, at least until new negotiations are had hereafter. Craigie and Massigli are entitled to much credit for their work, which I believe Hugh Gibson should fully share.

On Tuesday, February 24th, I received a letter from Snowden, saying that the Prime Minister had given him my memorandum on the Treasury Control system which he would have carefully studied.

Journal as Ambassador to Great Britain

London,
Sunday, March 8, 1931.

In the settlement of the French-Italian naval differences, the submarine arrangement provides that France keeps her present submarine tonnage under construction and already built. This gives her approximately 82,000 tons as against 100,000 tons she demanded at the London Conference. This concession was made in addition to an agreement not to build 8-inch gun cruisers.

Both countries agreed to limit battleships to 23,300 tons. France retains the right when she completes the second 23,000 ton ship (about 1935) to retain the *Jean Bart* which, under the Washington Treaty, she would be bound to scrap. This latter agreement apparently makes it necessary for the five nations to revise the Washington Treaty, allowing France and Italy each an addition of 6,000 tons in the battleship category.

Stimson does not believe that this slight increase in the battleship tonnage for France and Italy will, in its necessary ratification by the parliaments of the five powers, meet with much difficulty, and I believe he is right. He desires an agreement or joint declaration on the part of the three powers (Great Britain, France and Italy) as to the auxiliary craft which would simply be brought to the attention of the United States and Japan, and an exchange of notes between the whole five powers as to the alteration of the Washington Treaty in regard to battleships. Under this arrangement, only the note as to the battleship tonnage would require submission to Congress. The arrangement between Italy and France regarding submarines brings about a cessation of competitive building between them, whereas, under the London Treaty, they may now engage in such competition since they are not parties to part 3 of the Treaty. Great Britain, of course, remains bound by the London Treaty to the 52,700 submarine tonnage, along with the United States.

On Friday, I notified Sheik Washba of the Kingdom of Hejaz and Nejd, minister of that country to Great Britain, that the United States was willing to recognize the Kingdom of Hejaz and Nejd and proceed to the ratification of the appropriate treaty defining relations. This action was taken by the State Department through our Embassy, since the present Minister Sheik Washba had been at a conference at which the matter was discussed in Egypt a year or so ago. The Department asked me to make a preliminary inquiry as to the propriety of recognition which I did at the Foreign Office and elsewhere, the reports as to the Hejaz Government being found satisfactory.

On Wednesday, I attended a dinner given by the Pilgrims to Lord Willingdon, at the Hotel Victoria. The speakers were Sir John Simon, Lord Willingdon and myself. Lord Desborough presided.

London,
March 10, 1931.

Today, I sent the following letter to President Hoover:

MY DEAR MR. PRESIDENT:

Distance gives perspective—just like time—and away from detracting local occurrences as I am over here I think my views of what you have achieved during the last session of Congress may be of interest to you and Mrs. Hoover. I have not often written personally to you as apparently some past ambassadors over here have written to their chief (possibly for publication after his death) for which you are no doubt grateful.

But if you were neither my friend nor I your appointee, I would write to you at this juncture as an American citizen to a great President of the United States. You have successfully endured the severest test of statesmanship during the past few months. No other President since the War has experienced during his whole term the difficulties and crises you have met during the last six months. Where some of these situations were in general similar, yours were always the more acute. To veto a bonus bill in a time of national prosperity is both commendable and courageous. To veto one during the worst of an unprecedented business depression, at a time when the bill prompted by demagogism could be represented as one to relieve suffering, is an heroic thing—as well as being commendable.

Your steadfastness—when so many from whom it was not expected have weakened—in defense of our American system of relief as distinguished from the dole principle and of private, as distinguished from Governmental ownership of utilities, was all the more difficult for the same reason. Your opponents were able to use a public calamity as an excuse for the violation of a fundamental principle of good government. When public opinion was distracted by conditions temporarily very adverse, you stood for a principle when you knew you would go down with it for the time. From now on you

310

Journal as Ambassador to Great Britain

will come up with it. From such things only does greatness come. Whatever the future holds from now on—whether or not you are re-elected—whether times get better or worse—you have stood the test, and have "won out." Your name will always be respected and revered as one of our greatest Presidents.

It is upgrade every way from now on. As is always the case, the reaction in your favor in time will be proportioned in its strength to the injustice, bitterness and misrepresentation of the recent criticism you have braved.

Mrs. Dawes joins me in best remembrances and greetings to you and Mrs. Hoover. Am planning my next trip to Chicago some time this summer or next fall.

Yours,
CHARLES G. DAWES.

London,
Sunday, March 15, 1931.

The past week was memorable to me for one of those happy accidents which gave an unexpected impetus to the chances for the inauguration on this side of the ocean of the American system for the executive control and coordination of routine governmental business in the interests of economy and efficiency. Caro and I have had a pleasant acquaintance with Lord and Lady Willingdon, formed when, as Governor-General of Canada, he visited Washington. We have met them several times the past two weeks but I have never thought of the fact that as the new Viceroy to India, soon to go to that country, he would possess the power in the administration of governmental routine business there that the President possesses in our own country, and could inaugurate our system there by executive order.

When I was preparing last month my monograph on the British Treasury Control system, now being considered by the Government, I had mentioned it to my friend, Sir Walter Lawrence, and had promised to show it to him confidentially when it was finished.

On Friday, Lord and Lady Willingdon, and Sir Walter, who is their old friend, took lunch with us at the Embassy. I had brought from the Chancery a copy of my monograph to give to Sir Walter, and as I handed it to him in Willingdon's presence, I suddenly realized that Willingdon, of all men in the world, was

311

at this particular time in a position where he had the power personally to inaugurate the system to his own credit and to the benefit of the business system of a government of 300,000,000 people. I gave the monograph, therefore, to him instead of to Sir Walter, accompanied by an hour of verbal exposition to the disaster of the lunch as a social function. Lord Willingdon's reception of it and his immediate comprehension of it and its importance was most satisfactory.

With it I gave him a copy of my book, *The First Year of the Budget,* and of the report of our Dominican Commission covering the installation of the system in the Dominican Republic. He questioned me most intelligently. My hope that he will adopt the system for India is based upon my knowledge of his ability and discernment, as well as upon what he said to me in that connection.

That evening, Caro and I attended a reception to him and Lady Willingdon at India House. He told me there that he was already studying the report, and Lady Willingdon added that he insisted in carrying it in his pocket, duly transferring it when he changed his clothes.

Dwight Morrow arrives tomorrow for a visit.

London,
Monday, March 16, 1931.

An extremely active day. Much concern is felt both by the State Department and Japan as to the form which the draft of the Franco-Italian Naval Agreement will take. As at present understood, the agreement covers nothing not permissible under both the Washington and the London Naval Treaties, except the granting of the right to France and to Italy eventually to retain 6,000 tons of overage tonnage in capital ships in excess of the total of the Washington Naval Treaty.

Were it not for this particular exception, the agreement could be made between Great Britain, France and Italy which would then be merely presented by them to the United States and Japan for information and record. No Senate or Privy Council ratifications by the latter two nations would then be necessary.

Journal as Ambassador to Great Britain

Stimson has discussed this problem with such members of our delegation at the London Conference as are in Washington and especially with Dwight Morrow, who is now on his way to southern France. On Stimson's receipt of letters from Ambassador Lindsay at Washington (dated March 10 and 11) asking that the United States be represented on the drafting committee along with representatives of the other four nations, he cabled Morrow who was on the *Leviathan,* at sea, to stop off here and discuss these matters with Henderson and myself before he decided it. Dwight will arrive tomorrow, and I have made an engagement for him to meet Henderson at 5:00 P.M.

The immediate questions are now: Can the agreement be supplemented in such a way as to eliminate any conflict with the Washington Treaty battleship tonnage provision, and shall the United States accept the invitation to be represented on the drafting committee?

In the meantime, last evening de Fleuriau, the French Ambassador to Great Britain, called on me at the Embassy. In discussing the battleship matter, he said that it would take over three years, in his judgment, for France to complete the second 23,000 ton battleship under the proposed Franco-Italian agreement.

I asked why France then could not delay completion of this second ship until the expiration of the Washington Treaty in 1936, thus obviating any necessity for the present revision of the Washington Treaty. Japan had already suggested that the *Jean Bart* (the French battleship whose retention after the building of the new 23,300 ton battleships in the proposed new agreement would create the extra six thousand tons over the French Washington battleship allotment) be converted into a trade ship. This suggestion of Japan, de Fleuriau said, was not approved by his Government. But he personally thought the matter of delaying the construction of the second battleship worthy of consideration.

This afternoon he again called on me at the Chancery. He stated that he had consulted his naval attaché who was of the opinion that France even in the ordinary course would not have the second battleship completed until 1936, and that he (de

313

Fleuriau) would make the suggestion to his Government that the present problem presented by the Washington Treaty provision be solved by delaying this completion until the Treaty had expired.

This afternoon, Matsudaira also called on his way to the Foreign Office and left me a copy of the statement from his Government which he was taking to Henderson. In this statement the Japanese Government asked that the proposed meeting of the drafting committee should be held when a feasible scheme for the adjustment of the capital ship question shall have been found after a further exchange of views in regard to the Japanese proposals concerning at least capital ships. It also stated that Japan had heard nothing as yet from the British Government with regard to these Japanese proposals. Thus Japan is maintaining what is our own attitude at this juncture.

Considering all the above, it does seem that this final tangle in the long drawn out naval negotiations should be straightened out some way without any considerable delay. Certainly with Dwight Morrow here, with his unrivalled resources, matters should progress rapidly.

Saw Lord Willingdon at lunch at Lady Astor's today. He seems to be progressing in his appreciation of the American system of executive control of government expenditures. He told me he was looking for a chief coordinator. I am afraid Mr. Snowden's illness is dangerous. He will be operated upon this evening.

London,
March 17, 1931.

Saw the Prime Minister at 10 Downing Street in the morning and posted him on the present situation in the Franco-Italian naval matter. The Japanese attitude had not been brought to his attention. From experience, we have found that he is always a factor when it comes to unravelling a diplomatic tangle, and Matsudaira and I agreed last night that he had best be advised of things as they appear now from our standpoint.

Then, at 4:00 P.M., I met Dwight Morrow at the train and,

Journal as Ambassador to Great Britain

after going over the Washington cables at the Embassy, we called on Henderson and Alexander at the Foreign Office.

Herbert Malkin and Robert Leslie Craigie (the Foreign Office experts) joined us for a part of the conference. Henderson and Alexander, and Malkin and Craigie, as well, promised every effort to get the Franco-Italian agreement in such shape that the revision of the Washington Treaty battleship allotments will not have to be made.

At 6:30 P.M., Morrow and I called on Matsudaira and posted him as to the progress. We then went to the Chancery, and sent two short cables to the State Department, and at 7:30 returned to the Embassy.

The Prime Minister, as I had arranged in the morning, met us for dinner at the Embassy, and afterwards the three of us had a long talk over the situation.

So far everybody seems to think a way out will be found. Mac-Donald's statement of the sudden impasse a short time ago on the Franco-Italian agreement and his part in its equally sudden settlement, which had heretofore been unknown to us, was most interesting. Dwight had already suggested to Stimson, I find, the very solution which de Fleuriau and I had talked over Sunday night and yesterday and concerning which I had cabled Washington. That, for the moment, seems the first thing that will be tried out.

I marvel at Dwight's resourcefulness. He is in a class by himself. Tomorrow we meet Henderson and Alexander at 10:30 A.M., but the real work will commence when Dwight and Malkin and Craigie at this meeting tackle the naval figures, with one specific object this time—to get this agreement within the limits set by the Washington Treaty without changing the Treaty.

We will soon know whether the agreement which, by the way, is still incomplete in some other details, can be brought about on terms not inconsistent with the Washington Treaty. If so, we should not be represented on the drafting committee and will be misunderstood and misrepresented if we are. If not, we may have to be represented and will then not be misunderstood. When we later told Matsudaira this he was pleased.

During the day, Sir Josiah Stamp telephoned me about the

progress of my monograph on Treasury control. He has ascertained that the Treasury is studying it and it is being passed around for opinions. It will soon come to Sir Warren Fisher, who is likely to have the last word. When it does, Fisher will discuss it with him, so Stamp thinks. Stamp said also that yesterday he appeared before His Majesty's Civil Service Commission at their request and had broken the ice by calling attention to the American system, and agreeing to put in a report on it. He asked permission to attach my monograph to his report or at least quote from it.

> Memorandum to the Royal Commission on the Civil Service, by Sir Josiah Stamp, upon Methods of Adding to the Efficiency of Organizations which are Departmentalized by Functions.

---

1. It is common ground that general services, where uniformity of standard and specialized knowledge are desirable, can well be given by independent departments which, while contracting to order, only do so on standards of their own and with rights of independent judgment and criticism. For example, we now have the supply of property, offices, furniture, etc., by the Office of Works; stationery, printing, paper by the Stationery Office; personnel by the Civil Service Commission. The present question is whether the same idea is not capable of considerable extension without further elaborating permanent departmental organizations. The desirability and possibility of extension arises because office and operating functions that were formerly regarded as everybody's business and "something that every gentleman ought to know by the light of nature" are emerging as worthy of separate scientific study and specialization. Not many years ago, except in one or two departments of the State, statistical and economic intelligence were regarded as the province of any of the staff, quite interchangeable, and generally given to the weaker end, or fool of the family. Nowadays it is recognized that a high degree of natural aptitude, specialization and outside coordination are the truest economy.

2. Whenever I have enlisted the services of the National Institute of Industrial Psychology for ad hoc investigations, they invariably include in their reports a great deal of matter of this hitherto general character, and make comments on an aspect which is obvious enough when it is once pointed out, so that people exclaim that any decent works manager ought to have seen to it himself long ago. These questions include the position and height of desks, benches, lathes, etc., particularly the position, color and intensity of lighting, the movement and position of objects, papers, waste, etc., and many other semi-physical, semi-psychological surroundings or adjuncts.

The Managers of Departments or areas rarely like these reports at first; they seem to feel in them some reflection that they themselves ought to have

SIR JOSIAH STAMP
(now Lord Stamp)

Journal as Ambassador to Great Britain

seen these things, or say that they involve the expenditure of money and anyone could have made propositions of this kind; but without the pseudo-scientific backing of such a society no such expenditure would have been welcomed by the management. Somewhat similar remarks apply to vocational guidance both before and after entry of workers. Experience of ad hoc investigations of this kind lead one to consider the wisdom of having a systematic and standardized control going through all departments in place of expecting each works management or department to acquire this specialized technique for itself. The supreme management, therefore, must increasingly override the natural desire of the head of a department to manage its own affairs in such particulars as these, and put in, by committee or official, a special inspection or agency of criticism and change. External judgment by figures is generally by itself powerless to show whether all is perfect or not.

3. My experience in connection with a large industrial combine was that the continual transfer of small matters, considered only of general interest, to an overriding technical or special service department, with powers of inspection, control and initiation, was at first accompanied by considerable friction. The head of each department or locality felt that he was being robbed of his own autonomy—he became a mere producer to order, and not a general manager—but as the good effects of these transfers, made with due regard to the human factor, and to the susceptibility of position, were seen, this feeling died down. The amount of generalized experience open to the "invading" authority was so much greater than the head of the department himself had time to obtain, that he saw the wisdom of suffering the incursion and even of welcoming it, and he began to confine his opposition merely to the supply of his own local and special conditions which might modify the application of a general principle, rather than fight either the principle, or the introducer of it.

4. A further experience of a very striking and successful kind has come to me in the field of "forms"—psychology of those who fill them up and those who use them; their make-up physically, and the objective representation of real functions behind them. I have come to the conclusion that no highly diversified institution of considerable antiquity can move faster than its forms allow it; that accumulations from the past clog its progress and that overhaul from within has rarely the qualities of objectivity and of "looking at familiar things as though they were strange." Where a single function of Government or trade activity affects a large number of departments, there is from first to last a long chain of forms entailed by a "case" and this chain, owing to its complexity, and the way it dives in and out of the different departments concerned, is nobody's business to look at as a single action. The forms involved are rarely in fact put in a line and related to each other and criticized with an outside view. Departments naturally consider that they ought to be masters in their own house and know far better than anyone outside can tell them by their long experience what forms are necessary and how they should be worked. They will suffer experts to buy them as a common function of all departments, but criticism of them is another matter, particularly on the creation of new forms. By the introduction of a specialist over a large number of departments I succeeded in two years in halving the stationery bill, a very large number of forms vanished completely from ex-

317

istence—the mere fact that an investigation was in prospect sufficed to produce an automatic and silent reduction; the different types of paper that were required had much closer regard to the total usage in each case and length of storage. The highest economies were secured from reducing the classes of paper, the sizes of the cuts; and the general scrutiny of long series covering a number of different departments begins to yield its results in cutting out functions altogether. Such an agency cannot easily achieve success if it is not personally responsible to the head of the whole concern. Heads of departments are assured that no functions are to be interfered with in work for which they are held responsible, without their consent, but they are put on their defence when criticized. They have no power to come to decisions in favor of their own view unless in the first place they can convince the critic or inquirer.

5. The great objection to all such methods is the old theory that "if a man is chosen to be the head of a department, he must either be trusted, or not, and if he is not, he ought to go." This doctrine, with all deference, is sheer nonsense. Trusted he must be, upon all the main activities of, and operations for, his department, but he cannot be regarded as an expert in the hundred and one matters that are now emerging for special experience, experiment or judgment. Nor should he pass a layman's judgment upon experts' reports dealing with the special aspects of actions and subsidiary organization of his subordinates, for this judgment will vary with the different heads of departments, and a lack of uniform stringency results. The head of a department is so busy with his major functions that reports of what is actually happening in detail at the circumference are generally drawn by the relatively subordinate, and frequently are unconsciously directed to justifying the status quo, because they might reflect on past management and decision by seniors, and a "man never knows where the whirligig will put him in relation to those criticized." Criticism must be made by someone outside the department, who is not subject either to fear or favor, with the knowledge that the judge in the case of difference of opinion will be beyond the department itself.

6. Another example of an over-riding criticism or supervision that has been highly profitable in its results is an independent back checking or audit of the results of new ventures and expenditure, made direct to the head of the concern by people with high technical qualifications, independent of the department.

Departments have been responsible for putting forward proposals for capital expenditure, the justification for which has been certain economies or increased earnings. When these proposals have been finally given effect to it is of prime importance to determine accurately whether they have been justified by events. Should the department be relied upon to make its own reports, bury its own mistakes and do its own criticism?

The results of independent audit with technical criticisms have been very profitable. In the majority of cases they have justified the care and accuracy of the original prognostications. But in a minority of cases they have thrown up a number of side-lights in the course of criticism and explanation of differences which have been of immense value in future enterprise and which had not been observed by the people actually working the machine. In one or two instances they have unearthed and brought bad work to book.

7. The methods of job analysis and time studies have two characteristics. There are certain general principles and comparative methods which extend beyond the confines of any departments. There are certain particular applications which can only be understood departmentally. A combination of the outside guidance and coordination and criticism with the inside specialized knowledge is essential to produce good results.

8. For all these reasons, and to avoid the multiplication of permanent standardized departments with rights of entry and too great a subdivision of labor, a "flying arm" of coordination and criticism attached to the office of the supreme control, with rights of entry to the departments and criticism and examination at any point, is likely to have important psychological and critical value. If the head of a department is assured that no changes can be made without full rights of representation and reference, the question of his dignity and autonomy are met.

9. What is the application of all this theory and experience to the problem of Government? I have made some study of what has been achieved in the United States by the method of Budgetary Control, originally initiated by the present U. S. Ambassador to this country. The general principles underlying that control are as follows, in the words of General Dawes himself: —"Everything which is said herein, including that as to the executive power invoked and methods followed, refers essentially only to a device for the more correct routine business functioning of a corporation or of a government—a device which is entirely impartial and non-political, affecting in no way the general policies of either the corporation or the government but designed only to assure that the money appropriated for carrying out these policies be spent in the most economical and effective manner.

"Faults in routine business systems of private enterprises are generally soon corrected or resulting financial difficulties force those enterprises out of existence. Faults in routine business systems of government often remain uncorrected indefinitely, as governments depend upon taxation for their essential revenues and not primarily upon efficient operation from a business standpoint.

"Countries, whatever may be their government or the political party in power, suffer equally at times from disadvantages which are inherent in faulty administration. Routine business under any governmental or private business system generally speaking will be as good as the system makes possible.

"Proper business organization must insure not an intermittent and outside, but a continuing, internal executive control, concerned always and only with proper routine functioning and unconcerned with general policy save economy and efficiency. Outside control may occasionally stimulate efforts for economy and efficiency in routine functioning, but its effects are only temporary.

"In general, governmental routine business machines work poorly or well according as their internal adjustments resemble those which experience has demonstrated as essential to good routine functioning in private business organizations." He tells the story of the original inspection—"To cope with my immediate situation and the pressing demands for economy in governmental expenditures, I had at my disposal as Director of the Budget what in effect was the British Treasury control system, for the new budget act authorized the formation of an organization which was simply an embodiment of it. My powers under it resembled many of those now exercised by your Chancellor of the Exchequer, but unlike him, who is responsible to a Cabinet, the act made me responsible to one man, the President, just as in the formation and operation of my Army organizations in France I had been responsible to the Commander-in-Chief.

"My intensive study of the British Treasury Control system at this critical time, as a potential agency to be used in effecting immediate government economy, was made under strained conditions and involved the careful weighing of grave alternatives. Because of my Army experience, I recognized immediately and instinctively the defects of the British Treasury control and cooperating audit system as an exclusive agency to secure economical routine business functioning. Accordingly, while organizing and operating my office practically in accordance with the British Treasury control system, I used in my methods and work, in addition to the powers created by the budget act, other powers derived from the President to correct certain demonstrated defects of the British system. Your Chancellor of the Exchequer, under an appropriate grant of power from the Cabinet, would be in a position to do the same. I will discuss further on the defects, the method of correcting them, and the economic principles involved, and concern myself in the first instance with the immediate course of action I followed and its results, made possible only through the exercise of these additional powers, not conferred by the budget law but by executive delegation.

"Let me again refer to the situation which I confronted on 23rd June, 1921, the day I assumed office. On 30th June—a week later—all the governmental departments and independent establishments of the United States were to start spending the money which Congress had appropriated to carry them through the fiscal year then commencing. In this emergency neither the President nor the public nor I could be satisfied with anything but an immediate reduction in operating expenses below existing authorized governmental appropriations. Sir Edward Hilton Young in his book "The System of National Finance," in discussing your Treasury control system says: 'It is at the time when they (the estimates) are being discussed and formulated in detail in the departments that economies can be made in his (the taxpayer's) interest; when they are being passed in Parliament in blocks and undiscussed it is too late. Once the estimates have been published by the departments which draw them up the taxpayer's fate is sealed.'

"It is evident, since our appropriations at this time not only had been published as estimates but established in law, that unless I could devise a system differing in its methods and results from the British Treasury control system, not only the taxpayer's fate would be sealed but my own as well. In emergency nothing but immediate action avails. At my request the President called a meeting, held six days later (29th June) of the business organizations of the United States Government, consisting of the President, the Cabinet Heads of Departments, and from 1,200 to 1,500 bureau chiefs and others representing all sections of the routine business operating staff. This meeting, besides visualizing for the first time in our history the business organization of the United States Government, gave the President and myself, as his agent, opportunity to appeal for cooperation in the effort to reduce government expense to the esprit de corps and loyalty of a great and powerful organization, whose officers and rank and file up to that time had functioned with but little sense of their individual responsibility to the Government as a whole as compared with that they felt to their own particular department of it. As explaining the nature and the practical result of the meeting, I quote two extracts from my speech on that occasion.

" 'The President says—and his word goes because he is head of this governmental business corporation for which we are all working, that none of us is now allowed to assume that our congressional appropriations already made—I am talking now as a bureau chief—none of us is allowed to assume that the amount of those appropriations for the year commencing this 1st July, or any other year, necessarily constitutes the minimum of expenditures during that year.'

"In closing my speech, quoting from the stenographic report, I said: 'Fellow Bureau Chiefs, are you willing, after hearing what I have said, that I should now represent you in addressing myself directly to the President of the United States with an assurance of your cooperation in his request for a reduction of governmental expenditures? If you so agree, if you are willing, will you indicate it by standing?' (The entire audience arose). The President of the United States arose, followed by applause. The Cabinet and other Officers on the platform also arose. 'I wish to say to you, Sir, that the men before you realize the cares and perplexities of your great position. They realize that at this time the business of our country is prostrated, that men are out of employment, that want and desperation stalk abroad, and that you ask us to do our part in helping you to lift the burden of taxation from the backs of the people by a reduction in the cost of Government. We all promise you, Sir, to do our best—to do our best.' To which the President of the United States responded: 'I thank you all for your presence and your commitment to this great enterprise.'

"At the time of this first meeting, 29th June, of the routine business system of the United States, presided over by the President, the heads and bureau chiefs of the forty-three departments, and independent establishments of the Government there represented had been authorized through appropriations already made by Congress to spend for the fiscal year 1922, upon which they would enter two days later, the sum of $1,834,865,762.01. As a result of this appeal to them as a united organization after less than three weeks of consideration and revision of what they had formerly regarded as their necessities, they had promised to save $112,512,628.32 out of their appropriations, which amount at my suggestion they set up on their respective departmental books as a savings reserve for the year. This amount of savings under appropriations was increased steadily all through the fiscal year under a new system of internal executive control, made up without additional expense from the existing body of governmental employees, which we almost immediately established. I have at hand the figures of savings under appropriations as they existed in March, 1922, representing the results of the effort for only the first eight months of the fiscal year 1922. At this particular time this savings reserve under appropriations had increased from $112,512,628.32 to the sum of $143,171,816.63. In other words, of the amount appropriated for them to spend in 1922, as a result of the new system they saved 7-8/10ths per cent in the first eight months of its operation. This amount of appropriations saved, however, large as it was, only represented the smaller portion of the total reduction in the cost of the routine business operations of Government for that year, which chiefly resulted from the inauguration of the new system of executive control. We afterwards estimated and itemized in an official report to Congress, covering 170 ordinary book pages, the final savings for the year as amounting to $250,134,835.03.

"Many of the improvements in methods of business functioning resulting from the inauguration and operation of the new system of executive control during that first year, which were very productive in large savings in later years, are described in the itemized report for the first year opposite comparatively small sums in the column of savings realized. On the other hand, under the better methods of a proper business system there were effected certain savings that first year, as for instance in the operations of the United States Shipping Board, which for exceptional reasons were much greater than in any succeeding years under the same improved business system. Again, the greater the preceding inefficiency, the more impressive always will be the beneficial effects of the institution of proper business functioning."

10. A more detailed application of the American Budgetary Control System to the Departments it is not for me to give, but I am acquainted with their general methods and find them in principle singularly parallel to those that I have referred to as having a valuable application in business.

11. It is not for me to say how far the British Treasury Control System is in itself perfect and renders such methods of extra-departmental criticism unnecessary or superfluous. Nor do I care to enter into a constitutional discussion of the extent to which any such methods are impossible in the British Civil Service owing to the doctrine of Ministerial responsibility. I apprehend that if these methods keep clear of policy and deal only with functioning and coordination, they need not be repugnant to that doctrine. Nor should I care to say whether the independent arm of criticism should be responsible to the Head of the Treasury or to the Prime Minister. Very much would turn upon the scope of their rights of inspection and criticism. But I am perfectly clear from my past inside knowledge of Government Departments that there are still objects of expenditure which are regarded as being a part of the scope of general management, but which could with profit be made the object of specialized criticism of an ad hoc character. The very fact that the Head of a Department, or its immediate subordinates, have lived all their lives in that department and in discharge of those functions, conscious of the etceteras, but never focussing upon them, is in itself a prima facie reason for wondering whether objective criticism would not be of considerable assistance to the Heads of Departments.

12. It may be of interest to state the duties of coordinators under the American system, as given by General Dawes:

Journal as Ambassador to Great Britain

"To establish contact with and confer with every branch of the Executive Government within the area, to impress upon them the need and policy of coordination, and to instruct them in the use of the coordinating machinery. It is not the function of the coordinator to assume any duties for the performance of which other officials are now responsible, but it is incumbent upon him to point out where savings may be made by coordination, cooperation, or combination, and to insist that the several officials concerned take positive steps to effect the desired result or show conclusively that it is impracticable.

"It is intended that the rule of reason should apply to these instructions, that the duties laid down are to be performed so far as facilities permit, and that primary attention be given to the larger activities; others to follow in order of importance. Reports to the Chief Coordinator are only to be made where remedy appears desirable and cannot be arranged between the coordinator and the branches concerned. Reports to the Chief Coordinator with respect to deficiencies in any branch must include the coordinator's recommendation as to remedy and a statement that the matter has been considered by the branches concerned (giving names of the officials) and no satisfactory action taken by them or by their superiors. Each report to the Chief Coordinator should in general relate to one subject only. All official correspondence with the office of the Chief Coordinator should be addressed to the Chief Coordinator and not to any individual officer attached to the office.

"Coordinators are authorized to confer directly with the immediate heads of activities being inspected without the necessity of adhering strictly to the rules of procedure of the branch concerned. It will be the duty of the official concerned to advise his seniors in the premises. Coordinators will realize that a great deal depends upon their tact in these matters and deference should be paid to the rules and customs of the various departments so far as they do not interfere with the prompt and direct conduct of business. Controversy is obviously inimical to coordination and must be avoided except as a last resort. Every effort will be made to establish direct personal contact with other national officials and, in so far as is practicable, to transact matters of non-routine business by personal interview."

Ambassador Dawes goes on to enumerate various subsidiary illustrations of his principle:

"Purchasing.—(1) To inspect all Government purchasing offices, to see that sound practice and Government policies are carried out and that methods are enforced to insure the substitution of new or used material on hand in the same or other departments before purchase is made (this will often require tracing back by the purchasing office to the office certifying the requirements; (2) to suggest substitutions to the branches concerned and to report action in their respect to the Chief Coordinator unless convinced by the branches concerned that such substitution is impracticable; (3) to direct the postponement of purchases when no emergency exists and when it appears that the desired material may be obtained from another branch of the Government, making special report in such cases to the Chief Coordinator; (4) to report improper or inefficient methods to the Chief Coordinator; (5) to recommend combining of functions whenever it may appear practicable.

"Stock on hand.—(1) To inspect accumulations of material on hand; (2) to ascertain if it has been inventoried, if inventories were accurate when taken, if they have been kept up to date, if a stock record is kept, if they have been reported to an office whose duty it is to declare all or part of it surplus, if such declarations have been made, if the descriptions on inventories are sufficient for identification for sales purposes, if sales or transfers to other departments have been made, if physical deliveries are being made, if proper facilities exist for the same, if the stocks are properly cared for to prevent deterioration or loss, if new stock is being issued when serviceable used material is available; (3) to report any stocks found which have not been inventoried and reported, and any which, although reported and not declared excess, are, in the opinion of the coordinator, in excess of local requirements and available for transfer or sale.

"Reserves.—To ascertain if any items of such reserves consist of articles which will deteriorate rapidly or become obsolete if not made use of within a reasonable time or for which spare parts will no longer be obtainable; if any articles are being maintained in the reserve, suitable substitutes for which are in daily commercial use for general consumption, and which could, in the event of an emergency, be obtained without delay or without crippling industry or interfering with the normal life of the community from which drawn.

"Property in use.—(1) To inspect real and personal property in use or installed for use, including grounds, buildings, machinery, equipment, furniture, etc.; (2) to ascertain if it is continuous or in part use, if it has been reported as available for transfer or sale, if it is required to be retained by law or departmental order, if it is being properly used or preserved; (3) to recommend any discontinuance or disposition.

"Operations.—(1) To inspect Government activities and operations; manufacturing, repairing, agricultural, transportation, educational, or otherwise; (2) to report duplication, waste, or inefficient use of material, equipment, or personnel.

"Transfers.—(1) To inspect activities in connection with the transfers of material between different branches of the Government; (2) to verify the actual necessity for the material on part of the receiving branch; (3) to ascertain that the physical transfers of material are economically made; (4) to report any deficiencies in the above respects to the Chief Coordinator; (5) to determine the price at which transfers shall be made in case of disagreement between the branches concerned, which price shall be current market price, with proper differentials for carrying charges (not Government storage) and with reasonable depreciation for used or deteriorated material.

"Sales.—(1) To inspect activities in connection with the sale of surplus material; (2) to see that sound practice and Government policies are followed; (3) that the expenses of the sale are reasonable; (4) that improper charges are not made against proceeds; (5) to report any deficiencies in the above respect; (6) to postpone any sale when it appears that it is not to the financial interests of the general Government for it to continue, making immediate report in such cases to the Chief Coordinator.

"Adjacent areas.—To keep in touch by correspondence with the coordinators of adjacent areas with a view to effecting economies by interchanging material between areas when such transaction would be to the financial interest of the general Government.

"Record.—To maintain a brief record of the movements, duties performed, and results obtained by himself and staff, forwarding copy of same to the Chief Coordinator on the last day of each month. This report will be historical only and is not to contain recommendations or requests requiring action. Such should be made the subject of separate correspondence."

13. I put my summary of this question no higher than this: Departmental division by main function must pay regard chiefly to the excellent and fit discharge of that function, which is distinct from the main function of operating or thinking in every other department. But associated with it are (1) methods, principles, adjuncts and minor functions which are similar or general through many departments and (2) matters for coordinated research. In these, excellence in main functions connotes no necessary special fitness or experience. These questions are too general, casual or occasional for permanent additional departmental interference. There is scope for the evolution of a new type of useful interference and assistance, which may differ according to the Governmental or business setting. It is an exterior audit, not of figures, but of efficiency.

It is not unreasonable to suggest that the evolution of business and governmental functions is throwing up matters for specialized treatment in such a way that the old single principle of departmental autonomy plus permanent specialized service departments, is no longer adequate for all purposes, and that a new type of auxiliary control, criticism and ad hoc special service as an addition to that principle, is now justified, not in any way as a criticism of the past, but as required to meet the developing needs of the future.

Excerpt from the report of the Royal Commission on the Civil Service recommending adoption of the American system.

"594. One witness suggested to us that provision should be made for a small section of highly trained staff whose duties should comprise independent criticism and coordination of the machinery of Government. (Question 22,457.) In the view of this witness the problems of management had become so specialized that they required to be studied by officers specially selected and trained for the purpose. This suggestion was based upon a scheme in operation in the United States of America where a small section of public servants is engaged upon these duties under the immediate control of the President.

"595. We think that provision should be made for the continuous overhaul of the machinery of Government by a small specially trained staff recruited from the Service generally, and we recommend that steps should be taken with this end in view. We recommend that this staff should be borne on the Treasury Vote; that the necessary surveys should be carried out jointly by members of this specially trained staff and of the Department for the time being under review; and that reports should be submitted both to the Treasury and to the Head of that Department.

"596. The Treasury is already regarded as a clearing house for questions concerning improved organization, labor-saving devices and the like. This recommendation is, therefore, only a further development of the functions already in part performed by that Department. We attach importance, however, to these surveys forming part of a systematic and periodic overhaul of the whole of the machinery of Government, whether or not proposals involving increased expenditure in the Department concerned have been submitted to the Treasury.

"597. In recommending the creation of this machinery we aim at promoting efficiency and economy by securing that problems of departmental organization are studied by minds specially trained in dealing with them. We consider that officers should normally be seconded for these duties for a period of a few years only.

"We do not intend by this recommendation to suggest any arrangement which would detract from or diminish the authority or responsibility of heads of Departments in the management or direction of their Departments." [1, 2, 3, 4]

London,
Wednesday, March 18, 1931.

Dwight and I met Malkin and Craigie at the Foreign Office at 10:30 A.M. The conference lasted over three hours, until 2:00 P.M.

Craigie and I called on Matsudaira to report our proceedings and consult him as to the form of the statement inserted below, which was issued later to the press by the Foreign Office.

Dwight and I spent the rest of the afternoon at the Embassy

---

[1] The members of the Royal Commission on The Civil Service were Lord Tomlin, Duchess of Atholl, Sir Christopher Needham, Sir Henry Sharp, Sir Percy Jackson, Sir Assheton Pownall, James Black Baillie, William Cash, Frank Walter Goldstone, Barbara Gould, Mary Hamilton, Eveline Lowe, Thomas Naylor (resigned), Percy Pybus, Robert Richards, Margaret Wintringham, John Bromley (in place of Naylor).

[2] This Federal coordinating service created in 1921 by Executive Order had functioned in our own governmental business system during the debt reduction period of 1921 to 1929, and until 1933, when it was abolished on June 10th of that year by an Executive Order of the President.

In my judgment, the reinstatement of this system, either by Executive Order as before, or by new legislation, is imperative as a needed improvement in our present governmental routine business system.

For the convenience of those who may be interested in this question, I will recapitulate briefly what appears in detail in the text of the Journal.

In January and February 1931 I made a study of the British Treasury Control and Budget System and wrote a memorandum recommending as an addition to it the system of executive control of expenditures which I had created as the first Director of the American Bureau of the Budget in 1921–22 and which, seven years thereafter, was then still in active functioning existence in the United States.

Upon the completion of the memorandum I gave it to the British Prime Minister and it was circulated by Mr. Snowden, the Chancellor of the Exchequer, among officials of the various British Services for study.

on a cable setting out for Stimson the conclusions reached tentatively at the conference as to the relation of the probable form of the agreement to the battleship provision of the Washington Treaty. A large delegation of American press men was received at 5:30 P.M.

From the technical discussion, the conclusion was that in all probability a slight revision of the Washington Treaty will be necessary. The press statement by the Foreign Office was as follows:

Statement by the Foreign Office.

The first meeting of the committee for drafting in final form the basis of agreement on the naval question which resulted from Mr. Henderson's and Mr. Alexander's recent conversations in Paris and Rome will take place on Thursday, March 19th. The Committee will be composed of the legal advisers and other representatives of the governments of France, Italy and Great Britain. The draft, when prepared, after consultation with the Dominions concerned, will be submitted to the governments of the United States and Japan.

The conversations on naval questions between General Dawes, Mr. Dwight Morrow, Mr. Henderson and Mr. Alexander were continued at the Foreign Office this morning. The matter has been similarly discussed between Mr. Matsudaira and Mr. Henderson.

Mr. Dwight Morrow is now planning to proceed with his holiday which was interrupted to enable him to enter into direct contact with the representatives of His Majesty's government in the United Kingdom who recently visited Paris and Rome.

Dwight's mastery of the technical side of the problem is the admiration of all. Besides that, he is a conciliator and friend

---

Sir Josiah Stamp, to whom with the Prime Minister's approval, I had shown the memorandum, favored its submission to the Royal Commission on the Civil Service —a Parliamentary body. He personally took up the matter with the Commission and on August 19th, from County Kerry, Ireland, wrote me as follows: "As far as I could learn your memorandum on organization got safely buried in the Treasury amongst the officials as I expected. But just after you left for the States I had an opportunity of getting it (or partly) on the table when I gave evidence before the Royal Commission on the Civil Service and they asked me to put in a memorandum which I duly did, incorporating a lot of yours. If you will get the report now published you will find the Commission made a definite recommendation mentioning the U.S.A. experience and my evidence. Then if the evidence itself is now available you will, I expect, find my memorandum printed in it. But I have not seen this yet. I know it would interest you and certainly it is the most effective thing that could happen at the outset to your memorandum to get definitely into a Royal Commission recommendation."

maker. He is talking with Massigli of France this morning. I was delighted to have him tell me that he is preparing in the Senate to take up the fight on the Senate rules. He is as outraged by them and their consequences as I was. As a Senator on the floor, he has the power to force this reform which a Vice President in the chair lacks. He has the courage and the ability, and I cannot visualize his failure. He is making his usual thorough preliminary study of all sides of the subject. I am greatly enjoying his visit.

London,
Sunday, March 22, 1931.

Dwight Morrow and his wife and their friend, Miss Aldrich, left for Sicily on their interrupted trip this morning. It was fortunate that he was available to assist the experts of Great Britain,

[3] Established by the President for the Coordination of Government Business

Supervised by The Director of the Bureau of the Budget

FEDERAL COORDINATING SERVICE

OFFICE OF CHIEF COORDINATOR
Washington

June 30, 1933.

MY DEAR GENERAL:

Thinking that you, who assisted at the birth of the Federal Coordinating Service, may be interested in the demise and obsequies of this organization, I am sending you a copy of a communication recently addressed to the Budget regarding these events.

A valuable Federal agency will now disappear. Never noisy—always it has sought to divert attention from itself and, during the term of its existence, it has saved Uncle Sam many millions. But experiences of the past two years have made me more or less a pessimist, and I have become convinced that human institutions in general do not live without noise.

Insofar as coordination is concerned I am hopeful that, as a result of the "new deal", in some other form the difficult but very important work of this office which was established under your direction may be continued. I think that such will be the case, but probably we may see the Federal pay roll increased through the employment of civilians to do the work now carried on by those enrolled in the Army and the Navy.

With good wishes, always,

Faithfully yours,

T. T. CRAVEN,
Rear Admiral, United States Navy.

General Charles G. Dawes
Chicago, Illinois

328

France and Italy to make a statement of their agreement on battleships as would be, not only clear to themselves, but also in a form which would not be misunderstood in the United States and Japan.

Malkin, of the Foreign Office, submitted the final form to Dwight and myself yesterday afternoon. We afterwards consulted with Shigeji Kuriyama, the Japanese legal expert, who regarded it, as we did, as satisfactory.

The experts of Great Britain, France and Italy will probably be another week in settling the technical statement of their agreement on the subsidiary classes of ships, but Japan and ourselves were primarily concerned only with the capital ship feature. Of course, only the legal experts of Great Britain, France and Italy have agreed on the capital ship statement; their principals have yet to approve it. But this, probably, they will do. The agreement, when completed, will be in the form of a joint declaration consisting of two parts made by France and Italy, and another declaration by Great Britain and the Dominions, the important part of which to us is that the battleship agreement made by France and Italy does not call for any observations on their part as signatories of the Washington Treaty. Great Britain and the Dominions also agree that not later than the Conference in

July 7, 1933.

[4] MY DEAR ADMIRAL:

I am grateful to you for your interesting letter of June 30th regarding the demise of the Coordinating Service set up by Executive Order during my administration of the Budget Bureau during the first year of its operations.

It is unnecessary to write you, who have so ably administered its work in recent years as Chief Coordinator, of its effectiveness in increasing the efficiency of governmental business operations with large resulting economies in expenditure.

I note with satisfaction that unlike some others in past administrations you are not predicting dire disaster to the "new deal" so far as it involves an effort in some other way to continue the work which you have done. I cannot bring myself to believe that the present Director of the Budget, of whom I have such good reports, will fail to preserve the principles underlying the Coordinating Service which have justified themselves in all business experience, both civil and governmental, from time immemorial. Your surmise may be correct that the work now carried on by Army and Navy officers detailed away from their Departments and made responsible directly to the President, under the present Coordinating Service will be carried on through the employment of civilians. I certainly hope the Director of the Budget will not make that mistake, for a knowledge and experience in the actual operation of the Departments themselves is an indispensable element in the proper administration of the work. However, we shall see.

1935, they will consult with France and Italy with a view to proposing to the other nations (the United States and Japan) any modifications of the London Treaty to give ultimate effect to the agreement of France and Italy expressed in the two paragraphs of the Franco-Italian declaration.

When completed, these declarations will be transmitted to the United States and Japan. Expert opinions differ as to whether the agreement in regard to the battleships is strictly within the powers granted by the Washington Treaty. That is a matter of the interpretation of the agreement. But the quantities involved in the question—only three or four thousand tons at the utmost— are so insignificant from a practical standpoint, that the probability is that the United States and Japan will take no exceptions to the declaration. It is not necessary, apparently, for these two countries, even formally to accept it. Considering that the effect is to stop the imminent race in naval building between France and Italy, which, if engaged in, might compel England to take advantage of the escalator clause in the London Conference, which in turn would compel us to do so, it should be difficult to make trouble for the agreement in the United States.

Dwight and I have had a great visit. Last night we had time to talk over home matters. He means business on the Senate rules, and of course that was a subject of much mutual interest.

As you leave your office I want to congratulate you upon the power and influence for better governmental business administration which you have exercised. In modern business, as well as in warfare, the unnecessary appearance on the battle field of those in command always attracts hostile artillery, and your modesty has been a constructive element in your success. It is a tribute to the Chief Coordinators that a new system, not authorized by law but established by Executive Order involving changes in method and the location of authority, has operated for over a decade without serious challenge and has been indirectly recognized as a permanent institution by Congressional action.

I wish you all success as you go back to the sea again and am very hopeful that your destination will be a western port, which will enable you to stop off at Chicago and see the Century of Progress and myself.

Your friend,
(Sgd.) CHARLES G. DAWES

Hon. Thomas T. Craven
Rear Admiral, United States Navy
Washington, D. C.

Journal as Ambassador to Great Britain

London,
March 24, 1931.

The draftsmen of the Franco-Italian naval agreement are still having their serious trouble among themselves.

The unexpected announcement this past week of a proposed customs-union between Austria and Germany has set Central Europe and France "by the ears." Considering this matter which is arousing much ill-feeling, especially in France, and the other extremely difficult questions which are sure to arise if the Disarmament Conference is held in 1932, and which are not having proper preliminary examination, it may be wise to postpone the date for the Disarmament Conference. Time will tell.

London,
Sunday, April 5, 1931.

There has been another serious "flare up" between the experts of Great Britain, France and Italy during the drafting of the Franco-Italian naval agreement, well illustrating how rough and difficult is the way to a peaceful international naval understanding.

It was assumed by the British and Italians that the "Bases of Agreement" between France and Italy containing the words "those provisions (of Part 3 of the London Naval Treaty) which are of general application" would be held to include the last sentence of Article 19 of the London Treaty which reads: "Nevertheless replacement tonnage may be laid down for cruisers and submarines that become *over-age* in 1937, 1938 and 1939, and for destroyers that become *over-age* in 1937 and 1938."

The inclusion of this last sentence would automatically regulate, as in the case of Great Britain, the United States and Japan, the amount of tonnage which France and Italy could have under construction on December 31, 1936.

Craigie explains the trouble as follows:

"When the French representatives reached London, it became clear for the first time that they interpreted the "Bases of Agree-

331

ment" as regulating only construction to be completed by the year 1936 and that, failing agreement at the 1935 Conference as to the additional tonnage which France and Italy might be allowed to construct during the years 1935 and 1936, these powers would have a free hand for construction in those years.

"To the Italian Government, the French thesis is quite unacceptable because the principal advantage of the agreement from the Italian point of view had been stabilization of building programmes and the reduction in expenditures which they had foreseen from the spreading over six years of the tonnages available for new construction. These advantages would, however, in the Italian view, disappear if the programmes were not only to be compressed into four years but also the probability of increased building programmes in 1935 and 1936 had to be considered. The French interpretation of the "Bases of Agreement" was also entirely unacceptable for His Majesty's Government, first because it is in their view entirely at variance with the principles upon which the agreement had been negotiated, and second because admission of the French claim would mean in practice that while the members of the British Commonwealth of Nations remained bound for six years, France would only remain bound for four years, and might afterwards resume complete liberty of construction."

I am hopeful that the difficulty, like so many others in the past, will be resolved. The principles are now in diplomatic correspondence over it, and in the meantime the drafting committee is resting on its oars.

London,
Saturday, April 15, 1931.

I have neglected these notes for some time, not because of the lack of "happenings" but because these were so many.

Taking them in inverse order of their time of occurrence, King Alfonso of Spain has left Spain without conceding his rights however, and a provisional Republican Government has been set up there. In leaving Spain he was accompanied by his cousin, the Infante Don Alfonso and the Duke of Miranda. The Queen and the other members of his family left Spain by a different route. They are now together in Paris. So far the provisional Spanish Government has maintained fairly good order, with protection to life and property. The Communists so far have been unable to precipitate anarchy as they naturally desired. France has already recognized the provisional Government. Great Britain will do so on Monday, and is now only awaiting the confirmation of the Dominions to whom it has communicated its intention. I have cabled the State Department regarding the status of the British procedure toward recognition this morning after a visit to the Foreign Office.

Unquestionably, on receipt of this cable, the State Department will immediately recognize the provisional Government of Spain. I expect to see the announcement in the press this evening or tomorrow morning. To the superficial, this might seem actuated by the thought of acting before Great Britain with a view to pleasing Spain; but there is nothing of this involved. Robert Vansittart and I—he in giving and I in hastily transmitting the information as to the British procedure—both recognized the desirability of the speediest action possible on the part of both Governments, in order to assist and strengthen morally the provisional Spanish Government in its effort to preserve law and order in Spain in this critical period of its existence. I therefore notified our Government that our immediate action would not create any embarrassment here.

The status of the Franco-Italian naval difference remains as outlined in my last notes (April 5th). The quantitative differences are small considering the importance of the issue involved—the cessation of a competitive race in naval construction which, through the "escalator" provision of the London Treaty may involve eventually the United States, Great Britain and Japan, as well as France and Italy.

The drafting committee is again in session. I have kept the State Department informed through frequent but intermittent contact with informed members of the committee as to the situation.

Journal as Ambassador to Great Britain

Considering the really minor nature of the difference which has created the present *impasse*, I am inclined now to believe that it is but a reflection of a change in the general attitude and policy of France in the matter of disarmament. If this is true, it is partly because the announcement of the proposed customs union between Germany and Austria has revived again the question of security in the minds of the French Government and people. Again, if this latter is true, while a definite and final rupture of these naval negotiations will probably not occur now, France may propose a truce in further competition between Italy and France until the proposed Disarmament Conference meets in 1932, and leave the settlement of the question there. This is far better than nothing at all. It means another year of rest in the race, but it will result in adding to the large pile of other difficulties confronting that Conference. However, it is idle to speculate.

Met Sir Warren Fisher, the Permanent Secretary to the Treasury, at the dinner of the British Olympic Games Association at which I had to speak the other evening. He says my monograph, on the British Treasury Control System and its defects, is passing through the various departments of the Treasury, and will soon reach him with their reports thereon.

Stimson is planning a trip this summer to Britain and various other European countries. In answer to his inquiry as to my opinion of this, I wired that in my judgment it would offend none of those countries but please all. The short distances involved on this side of the ocean enable the frequent contacts of those first in authority in the different governments which contribute greatly to their common understanding of international situations.

Such contacts are as valuable and important to our Secretary of State as to others in similar authority and for the same reasons. This custom is the distinguishing mark of the "new diplomacy" or rather of my conception of it, as I outlined in my address at Washington University.

Journal as Ambassador to Great Britain

This evening my friend, the Infante Don Alfonso, who had arrived from Paris this morning, called upon me at the Embassy. Of all living representatives of the famous old-time families of Europe, whom I have met during or since the war, none is more virile and energetic. He does not need the background of the Orleans and Bourbon names. His personality and intellect would command him attention anywhere. His account of what happened in Madrid last week was most interesting. The decision of the King to leave was taken at 6:30 P.M. At 8:45 P.M. the party started from the palace in five automobiles. In the first car were King Alfonso and the Infante Don Alfonso and in the second were the Duke of Miranda and a Spanish Admiral. The distance to the sea coast was about 240 miles. The first gate of the palace yard they found locked. Don Alfonso said it took two and one half minutes to get it open, and every minute counted, for the mob was gathering. The three men who accompanied the King were heavily armed, and Don Alfonso said he carried his revolver in his hand. He was apprehensive of blockades and wires across the road but they found none.

The plates on the cars had not been painted over as Don Alfonso had ordered, and it was evident to everybody they passed that they were in the royal automobiles. They feared trouble at a narrow bridge some way out of Madrid but had none since the people had all flocked to the city. They got out in the nick of time from the city, and as their route to the Mediterranean had been kept secret, they arrived at port safely.

The Infanta Beatriz (Don Alfonso's wife) stayed with the Infanta Isabella (his aunt), who was 80 years of age and paralyzed, and managed to get her to Paris. The Infanta Isabella died there this afternoon and Don Alfonso is leaving to take charge of the funeral arrangements. He has been with the King this afternoon. The latter, Don Alfonso said, was a man of unflinching courage and strong character, which seems to be the general impression everywhere. Don Alfonso will return here from Paris next week.

This afternoon I attended a little ceremony at All Hallows Church, presided over by Padre Clayton of Toc H ("Tubby" Clayton, its founder). Two representatives of the War Office and the Foreign Office were there, and presented the flags from the British Army Council to the representative of St. Paul's Church, Hoboken, New Jersey, for their battle cloister. Clayton took us over this venerable and historic church which was erected on the ruins of an old Roman building of large size. We went down into the remains of the Roman structure under the church and found the most interesting relics both of the Romans and of the later Saxons. The church stands near the extreme western end of what was the old Roman city of Londinium.

Last night spoke at the annual dinner of the Railways Officers and Servants Association, a charitable organization. Lord Cromer, the Court Chamberlain, presided.

Yesterday the retired Spanish Ambassador, the Marqués de Merry del Val, called at the Chancery to say "good bye."

London,
Saturday, April, 25, 1931.

The French have made a proposition to Great Britain and Italy regarding the Franco-Italian naval difference. The text has been given to us. In effect, it proposes that the tentative "Bases of Agreement" which formerly were regarded as being settled between the three nations and regulated the building programs in subsidiary craft of France and Italy until December 31, 1936, when the London and Washington Treaties expire, be modified so as to cover a lesser period to July, 1935. This is now under discussion, not by the experts of the drafting committee but by the three Governments.

Transmitted to our Government an invitation from Sir George Ferguson, chairman of the Conference of Wheat Exporting Countries, which met in Rome, to send a representative to the next meeting of the Conference which will be held in London on May 18th. Ferguson is the High Commissioner of Canada at London, but the invitation is not issued by him in that capacity but as chairman of the Conference.

Grover Cleveland once said, "A surplus is more easily dealt with than a deficit." From Sir George's account of his experiences at Rome, I am inclined to think he would regard this as debatable.

Have asked for a month's leave of absence and plan to sail for the United States on May 5th. I have personal business to attend to but my principal purpose is to sell some of the balance of the Exposition bonds, thus financing that enterprise into the year 1932. It is now financed to November 30th.

In view of the almost unparalleled business depression, I find myself wondering how we have done as well as we have in Exposition matters.

London,
April 26, 1931.

Snowden will present the national budget in the House of Commons tomorrow. There is a general feeling of hopelessness about the situation of the national finances and the business prospects of the British people. If, as is not expected, Snowden would sponsor a "right about face" in tariff policy, which would give British industry and British workmen the protection in supplying their own home market, which other nations, including the British Dominions, give their respective industries and labor, he would lay the foundation for a revival of hope and business activity.

But he will not do so, and for probably another long period the dumping of foreign surpluses at prices below the cost of production will go on here, increasing the unemployment, disorganizing industry, still further lessening government revenues and threatening national solvency.

It is a grave crisis. It is inconceivable that a change of national policy will not come, but how soon? And will it come in time? Trade and industrial statistics are most alarming. But I cannot lose faith in the coming to power eventually of British common sense in the formulation of governmental policy. These are depressing times everywhere, especially so here.

London,
April 27, 1931.

I must confess it looks discouraging just now for the settlement of the Franco-Italian naval difference. I received today the answer to the recent French naval memorandum of the British Government and its memorandum sent to the Italian Government relating to it, which I cabled to our Government for its information.

Ambassador de Fleuriau has been to see me and is still hopeful that after a time, when the French presidential choice is made and politics there simmers down, negotiations can be resumed with some hope. He had been talking with Briand over the telephone. But the British have little hope that Italy can see its way clear to a compromise with the present French position. The effort is now to delay matters and let them cool off.

Dwight Morrow is here and this evening he and the Prime Minister dined with us at the Embassy; and we three have had a two hours' discussion of the situation. Dwight arrived from his Sicily trip yesterday afternoon and I spent that evening with him.

Called on the Prime Minister at 10:30 A.M. at 10 Downing Street.

This afternoon Dwight and I were in the House of Commons and heard Snowden, who is weak from a severe illness, present the budget. He made a good impression.

Lord Reading, whom I saw there, thinks the new budget will be favorably received by the "City" as the best which could be expected under the circumstances.

Journal as Ambassador to Great Britain

Dwight Morrow sailed last Wednesday. We have had a delightful visit from him and his wife. He returned from his trip to Sicily and Italy much rested and in his best form.

Wednesday evening I attended the dinner of the Foreign Press Association at the Mayfair Hotel. On that day also I attended Parliament to hear Winston Churchill's brilliant speech on the budget.

Today I spoke as the guest of the Green Cross Club at the American Women's Club. My friend Sir Hilton Young was the other speaker.

The Infante Don Alfonso spent Tuesday with me. He is looking about for some occupation, now that his family are in practical exile from Spain.

Italy answers the French note on their naval differences, accepting the British suggestion for a compromise. It is expected that France will not reply until after the election of the French President and perhaps later.

Am now planning to sail about May 22nd.

London,
Sunday, May 3, 1931.

To keep our State Department informed as to the progress of the constantly changing naval negotiations between Great Britain, France and Italy requires the American Ambassador to perform similar functions to those of an informed press correspondent conveying confidential news not for publication but for use in the determination of policy by those charged with responsibility for it. The information must be exact and authoritative, clearly expressed and condensed in form as far as possible.

An inquiry was received yesterday from Stimson as to whether, in considering the tentative "Bases of Agreement" between Great Britain, France and Italy there had been discussed here in London a rewording to provide for the limitation of the *laying down* of tonnage instead of limitation of *completed tonnage,* the entire agreement being made to end in July, 1935. He did not wish me to offer this suggestion, but to inquire about it. This was rather a clever way to secure its consideration if it had not already received it, without running the risk of giving offense by an undue appearance of "mixing in." It gave me an opportunity, however, to get what I have long wanted, not only for the information of the Department but of myself, a statement from the Admiralty itself as to its reasons for regarding the present French proposition for a 4½ years' agreement for limitation of building as not better than no agreement at all.

In order to indicate the bearing of this statement, I will first summarize the present situation in the British, French and Italian negotiations.

It is accepted by all under the "Bases of Agreement" that France could lay down a total of 165,000 tons. The British Government, however, and the Italian Government as well, holds that this agreement was to limit construction according to Part 3 of the London Naval Treaty during six years up to December 31, 1936, at the rate of 27,000 tons yearly. The French Government maintains that while it will agree not to start any additional new construction over the 165,000 tons before July, 1935, the "Bases of Agreement" allows them to compress the building of the 165,000 tons into four years, 1931 to 1934 inclusive, at the rate of 41,000 tons yearly.

France also claims that the agreement limits only the amount of construction which France and Italy may *complete* before December, 1936, and leaves open the amount of tonnage which they may have *under construction* on that date. Thus she could *lay down* replacements in 1935 and 1936 for other over-age tonnage in addition to the 165,000 tons allowable under the provisions of Part 3 of the London Treaty, while Great Britain, bound by that part of the Treaty cannot do so until December 31, 1936.

This additional over-age tonnage replacement would be about 67,000 tons. To this claim the British, with Italy in agreement, have now made a counter proposal to France that the construction program of France and Italy will remain limited for six years

340

as originally proposed according to the British and Italian interpretation of the "Bases of Agreement," but it must remain for the Naval Conference of 1935 to decide whether any additional naval construction will be allowed Italy or France.

The reason why I desired authoritative Admiralty comment on the French proposal was because from other experts that I consulted I had not been able to understand—and this was possibly my fault—just why, apart from any political considerations, from the standpoint of Great Britain and therefore of the United States and Japan, the acceptance of the French 4½ year proposition would not be an improvement upon the present status. It would result apparently in a postponement, at least until 1935, of the necessity for Great Britain's resort to the "escalator" clause of the London Treaty, which France can now precipitate at any time by building in her subsidiary classes, which are not covered by Part 3 of the Treaty.

Stimson's cable arrived yesterday morning. As it was Saturday, it was not until 8:30 P.M. that I located Alexander, the First Lord of the Admiralty at a football dinner at the Hotel Victoria, where he was on the toast list for a speech. I called him out and (kind friend that he is) he told me that he would hurry up his speech, summon his deputy with the necessary papers from the Admiralty, and meet me at the Embassy.

He duly arrived at 10:45 P.M. accompanied by Vice-Admiral Frederic Dreyer, the deputy Chief of the Naval Staff. From them I learned that if there was a 4½ year agreement they would consider that Great Britain would be at the disadvantage (a) of entering the next five-power conference with the French construction a *fait accompli*, and therefore (b) in the event of having to invoke Article 21 (the escalator clause) they would have to face too large a building program in too short a time. They maintain that if it is inevitable that Article 21 must be operated, it would be much preferable to spread the incidence of such operation rather than compress it into 1935 and 1936.

This was the gist of the Admiralty's opposition as they gave it to me, and which I transmitted to Stimson. I can well understand, of course, Italy's objection to the agreement. She is concerned chiefly with "parity" with France.

341

Journal as Ambassador to Great Britain

These technical naval building considerations which the British Admiralty has in mind, may be compelling, but I hope the political situations which, in the three countries directly concerned are now working for a delay in negotiations will clear up and that then these naval objections may be given most careful reconsideration. They would seem to need it. It will be most unfortunate if failure to agree among these nations upon technical points which now seem to involve only 67,000 tons of possible construction destroys an opportunity for what would be in its effects equivalent to a five-power pact limiting competitive building until July, 1935, between nations possessing navies with an approximate aggregate tonnage of 3,600,000.

London,
Sunday, May 10, 1931.

After writing my notes last Sunday evening, I went over to the "Dorchester House" hotel and heard my friend Fritz Kreisler give a wonderful concert. I saw him for a time after he had finished. After one has heard a beautiful piece of music rendered once or twice by a master it is apt to keep ringing in his ears for a long time. It has been so with me this week, and the piece on Kreisler's program was "La Fille aux Cheveux de Lin" by Debussy.

The week was made especially pleasant by a visit of my old friend Thomas W. Lamont. On Friday evening I gave a dinner at the Embassy in his honor. Among those present were the French and Belgian Ambassadors, the High Commissioner from Canada, Lord Reading, Lord Cecil, Sir Josiah Stamp, Sir Robert Kindersley, Sir John Simon, Walter Lippmann, Samuel Insull, E. C. Grenfell, Vivian Smith and C. F. Whigham (these last three being the London Morgan partners), Robert L. Craigie, Sir Roderick Jones, of Reuters, Charles D. Hilles, Ray Atherton and Raymond Cox, of the Embassy staff, and last, but not least, my cousin C. H. Bosworth and my old Marietta College classmate, Dr. W. W. Boyd.

On Friday afternoon I presided at a lecture at the University of London given by Professor Edward O. Sisson of Reed College, Portland, Oregon, on "Lincoln's Lost Causes."

Journal as Ambassador to Great Britain

On Thursday evening, as the guest of Sir John Simon, the Treasurer (President) of the Inner Temple, I attended a dinner at the Temple which, like the Middle Temple dinners, is most interesting from many standpoints. One absorbs history at them since the Masters in pointing out the objects of interest in the Temple must continually recount it.

I have been reading this week General Pershing's book, *My Experiences in the World War.* It is thoroughly characteristic of him as a soldier, administrator and man; and it is just the book I expected him to write. It gives the public an opportunity to visualize properly the American effort in France, and to measure the real stature of the Commander-in-Chief of the American Expeditionary Forces, the only Commander-in-Chief to last through from the beginning of his assignment in France to the conclusion of the War. It is not full of personal praise and sticks to the facts. Considering that it was finished so long after the War, the book is all the more trustworthy because he has written it with continued resort to his official contemporaneous documents in order to be exact in his statements. It is worthy of him in every way.

In the *New York Times Sunday Magazine,* the other day, I read a criticism of the book by Captain Liddell-Hart. Pershing is there condemned by a foreigner for the very thing that will redound justly to his fame in his own country—his protection of the entity of his American army which the allied Governments and commanders tried so hard to destroy. Events have justified him. Had he yielded, he would now be condemned by his countrymen and pitied by his foreign critics. In the copy of the book—or rather the two volumes—which John sends me, he writes: "For Brigadier General Charles G. Dawes with appreciation of his distinguished service in the World War, and with affectionate regards from his life-long friend, John J. Pershing."

Hugh Gibson is spending the night with us, passing through London on his way to America for a visit and to consult his physician. He is not very well and I am worried about his health.

343

Journal as Ambassador to Great Britain

London,
May 17, 1931.

These are full days, not so much of business as of receiving callers from America, many of whom have requests to make. The tide of American tourists is rising. Caro, who is proving herself, as usual, an ideal home executive and hostess, told me today that in the last two months we had entertained at the Embassy over two hundred and fifty people at lunch or dinner and one hundred and forty at her teas. These latter affairs I do not attend. Many distinguished Americans have been included in these numbers.

On Tuesday I presided at a dinner at the American Club in honor of Lord Reading. He spoke on his American experiences as High Commissioner and Ambassador to the United States during the War, abandoning the topic he had selected because he was moved to do so, as he said, by my introduction of him. He made a most eloquent and moving address.

The world business depression seems to deepen. To go to America just at this time to try to sell bonds for the Exposition is no trifling expedition; but self-confidence, perhaps unjustified, has stifled my apprehensions.

Briand's resignation as Minister of Foreign Affairs menaces the success of the Disarmament Conference and of other European efforts for peaceful adjustments for the time.

At Sea, S.S. Bremen,
Saturday, May 23, 1931.

Had a long interview Thursday with the Prime Minister at his office in the House of Commons at 5:00 P.M. We discussed the state of depressed things in general, and also the best way to secure proper international consideration of international economic problems like that of silver particularly and many others generally.

Much pressure is being brought on the different Governments

LORD READING

concerned and in particular on our own Government, Great Britain and Japan, to call an official international conference on silver. Each Government expresses willingness to join such a conference, but each desires some other Government to take the initiative in calling it. MacDonald frankly expressed himself to me as believing that an official international conference on silver would be a mistake.

The trouble is that the problems of world over-production of silver, wheat and practically all basic commodities seem humanly insoluble. Time as well as the law of supply and demand, at least in this stage of the world's civilization, must be relied upon. To call a conference of the nations upon silver when some nations are silver users and want low prices for silver and some nations are silver producers and want high prices for silver is simply to have a row and then adjournment. For myself, I see even advantages in this process and believe we will only progress by trying out things. But the Governments naturally desire to avoid the responsibility of initiating a conference which in its immediate results is doomed to fail.

What I am proposing informally to our Government, to the Prime Minister, and to Ambassadors Tsuneo Matsudaira and Alfred Sao-ke Sze (China) is to have these economic conferences started upon private initiative in the different countries, in the same manner as the present wheat conference.

Private initiative with prestige like that, for instance, of a national producers' association in each country can bring about a conference which will command world attention, especially if Governments should have "unofficial" observers in attendance. The result would be a discussion by free delegates not embarrassed lest what they say on an economic question is not acceptable politically to their Governments.

Such a discussion would be of more real value than the discussions of an "official" conference, for the latter would be controlled by political considerations in each Government represented. Such an "unofficial" conference would demonstrate whether it would be worth while for the Governments to call an official conference later.

Again it would satisfy a justified and general demand of the world's public to have common international problems receive common international attention.

Sailed yesterday (Friday) morning from Southampton.

At Sea, S.S. Bremen,
May 24, 1931.

Governor Franklin D. Roosevelt, of New York, sent a note by his son Elliott, inviting me for dinner last night at his stateroom. No others were present. Roosevelt's service in Washington was under President Wilson as Assistant Secretary of the Navy. As I seldom visited Washington in those days, I had never met him to my recollection, though he said we had met at Bordeaux, France, during the War.

It was a regular Rooseveltian evening—both delightful and strenuous. I do not know when I have enjoyed an evening more, and we both were surprised, being still fresh and in the full height of conversational activity, to find we had consumed 4½ hours when we separated or rather when I left his room. With common experience as civil servants, common experience during the War, common friends and acquaintances by the score, we forgot any political differences, which after all, are never real barriers and naturally forgot to look at the clock.

Roosevelt is only 49 years of age. After this evening's visit, I feel that if he is the next President of the United States, he will serve with honor to his country and credit to himself. He seems to have strength and equipoise, clarity of mind with soundness of judgment, and to steer his course by the compass of common sense.

At Sea, S.S. Bremen,
May 25, 1931.

Am meeting many people on the boat and find all soaked with business pessimism. Coming into this business atmosphere from which the diplomatic territory in which I have lived is more free, I am endeavoring not unduly to imbibe it.

Journal as Ambassador to Great Britain

Received a radiogram from President Hoover yesterday asking me to stay at the White House when in Washington. Dwight Morrow also radioed that his car would meet me at the dock to take me to his home at Englewood, New Jersey. Received a number of other messages.

Dined again with Governor Roosevelt at his stateroom last night, and we had a session until midnight, and a fine time.

The press reports indicate clearly that business in the United States is growing worse. With unerring but not premeditated accuracy I manage to select the worst possible times to go home to raise money for the Exposition. However, as I came out all right in the panic month of October, 1929, I will not prejudge the possibilities. It is 1893 over again. Business and people then and now seem dead on their feet.

I hear much criticism of President Hoover for his unquestionably useful efforts to mitigate the evils of the situation. It is to his great credit that he is being criticized for doing too much instead of too little. In such times the public, resentful beyond possible control, take melancholy comfort in assailing their leaders. Little for the present that the President can do, however meritorious it may be, will be the occasion for anything but abuse.

Englewood, New Jersey,
At Senator Morrow's Home;
Saturday, May 30, 1931.

Landed at New York Wednesday noon. From my landing until now, I have lived in a whirl. I was greeted by Charles A. Hanna, Major Lohr and Col. Frank Knox who met me at the dock.

Stopped at General Harbord's apartment which, being out of the city, he left at my disposal, and went over Exposition matters with Lohr and then went to Englewood, New Jersey, to Dwight's home, where I am visiting.

We dined at Tom Lamont's house in New Jersey on Wednesday evening. Went to New York on Thursday and Friday.

The atmosphere of business gloom is unmitigated. As a matter which I have come to consider as one of course, the stock market made its lowest dip of this major depression. And it has remained "dipped." However, went right to work on the Fair bonds.

I may be mistaken, but I see a prospect of about $500,000 sales of World Fair bonds as a result of the two days' preliminary work. It is a good deal like working in a morgue, but occasionally one comes across financial life where he expected death.

In the meantime, I am much enjoying this fine visit with Dwight and his family. He and I stay up talking until morning hours, and wander around the beautiful place, almost too busy to see it.

The house is run much like our Embassy at London so far as the number of guests is concerned. Guests come and go in numbers all the time. There were about twenty at lunch today. Charles and Anne Lindbergh and the baby are here. The better I know the Lindberghs the more I admire their naturalness. Anne got her pilot's license Thursday, one of the requirements of the examination being to spiral down from an altitude of 2000 feet. Dwight is a philosopher and his wife likewise, but I can see signs of worry about a tentative airplane trip to Asia by Charles and Anne "by the northern route with short hops" now being confidentially discussed.

Among the callers here, I have met some young parlor socialists, my first experience with these curious, well-meaning, but inexperienced children, who defend vigorously the retention of their own inherited wealth but are full of plans entailing self-sacrifice or slavery upon the part of others. Their discussions are like those of "A" with "B" as to how to get "C" to do something for "D."

MRS. DWIGHT W. MORROW

Journal as Ambassador to Great Britain

B. & O. Railroad,
Thursday, June 4, 1931.

Spent Monday in New York, coming in from Dwight's in the morning. Took lunch with the editorial staff of the *New York Times*. In the evening had a few friends at dinner at the Union League Club. At 10:00 P.M. met Owen Young at his apartment and stayed with him until time to take the midnight train for Washington. Young had just arrived from Van Hornsville. He feels that his wife is making headway in her illness.

At Washington went to the White House, where I stayed while in the city. The President, despite reports I have heard, seems in good form. Hugh Gibson was also a visitor at the White House.

Tuesday and Wednesday evenings I spent with the President. He went over with me the first draft of his coming Indianapolis speech. Told him I thought that his speech in its present lengthy form was too good, and was like the Sextette in Floradora, it contained enough different themes to supply a whole opera. With Gibson and me he went over his ideas as to the European situation which were ably expressed and well conceived.

My time in Washington was spent largely at the State and Treasury Departments. Met many old friends. Called on Sir Ronald Lindsay, the British Ambassador, who says he is having a fine time.

Had two long and interesting visits with Secretary Mellon. One thing especially I note in this terrible business depression, undoubtedly the worst in the country since 1873, is that even the richest men are worried. All have been met by very large and unexpected demands for money to salvage their speculating friends and to assist in meeting past commitments of their enterprises. Mellon is one of the richest men in the United States; but just as I found with every great business leader in New York, his face was "sicklied o'er with the pale cast of thought."

Tomorrow I reach Chicago. There, added to the other troubles incident to the depression, is a bankrupt city government already in default on city obligations, and so far unable to get the remedial legislation from the State Legislature which would enable it to help itself. It cannot even raise money to pay the city employees. The banks are unwilling to take on more of the city obligations until, through the enactment of new legislation, they see a chance of being paid back.

Our municipal political system, combined with the indifference of the city voters, has put mediocrity almost always in the saddle, and with it at times, chicanery and thievery. What has happened in Chicago I am afraid will happen in most of the great cities of our country, unless people take the franchise more seriously.

My Brother Henry's Home,
Evanston, Thursday, June 18, 1931.

I left Monday night for Marion, Ohio, to attend the dedication of the Harding Memorial by President Hoover at exercises presided over by Ex-President Coolidge. I had received a telegram from President Hoover asking me to go with him from Marion to Springfield, Illinois, as he had important matters to talk over with me.

Carl Sawyer met me at the train at Marion, in the morning, (Tuesday) and I stayed at his home until the arrival of the Presidential train. Joined the President's party and attended the exercises in the afternoon. As a friend of President Harding, I was grateful to President Hoover for his fine memorial address. President Coolidge's tribute was also a just and fine tribute to Harding. A great crowd was in attendance. My seat was next to the Coolidges on the platform, bringing back recollections of the old Washington days.

On the train going to Columbus, Hoover went over the financial situation in Europe, which is critical. At that time, he expected the National Bank of Austria to fail, as the relief measures under negotiation seemed likely to fall through. We were reassured on this point, however, by a telephone call from Stimson which was received at the State Capitol. If the Austrian bank failed, it was expected that the Reichsbank would be compelled to take a moratorium. This would precipitate a world financial crisis, affecting our own country materially, as the New York banks alone were reported to have $500,000,000 of German acceptances.

The New York bankers had been telephoning Hoover before he left Washington, requesting governmental assistance in the European difficulty. In this situation, as generally outlined, Hoover was considering what he could do to relieve it. His present thought was to suggest a reparations moratorium all around for one or two years, funding the payment due to the United States for that time. France in this case would have to forego receiving reparations, at present amounting to more than she is paying the United States. Hoover could not propose such a plan without being assured by the leaders of the opposition in the Senate that his proposal would be ratified by the Senate next December.

He asked my opinion on this course, and if he took it said he wished to call me to Washington to help in securing Senatorial agreement. I approved the plan, but urged that the period be made two years instead of one.

European finance is tottering, but this plan might help in tiding things over.

Meanwhile the Bank of Austria's gold reserve, like that of the Reichsbank, is becoming dangerously low, and the recalling of short time loans by America, and our favorable balance of trade, continues to draw the life blood from European finance.

In our own country banks are closing every day, and money is being hoarded in safe deposit boxes. Conditions here approximate those of 1873 and 1893.

After reviewing at Columbus a parade of the survivors of our Civil War, now pitifully few in number, the President and his party left for Springfield. We were met at the train there the next morning by Governor Emmerson, Speaker Shanahan, and others and went first to the Governor's mansion. In the forenoon we attended a joint meeting of the two legislative houses of the State, held in the Armory, where a great crowd was present. The President spoke, and his immediate party, including myself, were introduced. After a small lunch at the Governor's mansion, we attended the rededication of the tomb of Abraham Lincoln, by the President. After this we went back to the Governor's Mansion again for some two hours where I again had a talk with the President.

He and his party left at 4:30 P.M. for Washington, and I took the 5:50 P.M. train for Chicago, arriving about 11:30 P.M. last (Wednesday) night.

Cabled my wife that there was no likelihood of my being able to leave before August, and suggested that she come over earlier than July 19th, which is her present plan, so as to be here with me a part of my stay.

Barrington, Ill.,
Sunday, June 21, 1931.

Spent yesterday morning at the house of my brother Henry and the afternoon, until 5:00 P.M., at Glenview. Arriving at Barrington at 6:00 P.M., I found that President Hoover had called me twice by telephone. The telephone operators were evidently waiting for me, for I got into telephone communication with the White House within two or three minutes.

Hoover said that he had consulted with a sufficient number of Congressional leaders and was about to announce his foreign debt proposal. He said he was giving my name as a sponor of the plan in his official statement. He wanted me to see R. R. McCormick of the *Chicago Tribune* and insure, if possible, his favorable attitude. Accordingly, after looking into the matter, I wired him about half an hour later as follows:

Herbert Hoover,
White House,
Washington, D.C.

R. R. McCormick in Ontario. Editor in charge says he personally strongly favors proposition, but being unable to consult McCormick will withhold editorial comment tomorrow.

CHARLES G. DAWES

Shortly after, I received a telegram from the President asking me to give the press a supporting statement, which I did. This morning the press carried the President's statement. General press comment is entirely favorable.

Wide World Photos, Inc.

DR. HJALMAR SCHACHT

Journal as Ambassador to Great Britain

The Reichsbank situation is critical, but there are indications that the situation is better in hand—the reserve of the Bank of England having suddenly risen owing to the flight of capital from Europe. Verily, these are momentous times.

Evanston, Ill.,
Monday, June 22, 1931.

Hoover's proposal for the United States in the reparations debts postponement matter thus far has been most favorably received here and in Europe save for France, which is non-committal. The stock market here and abroad reacted favorably. In the strained condition of things, time only can tell as to results, but the move was at least good psychologically speaking, and after all that may prove to be of lasting beneficial effect.

The United States is giving up much more than France is asked to do and the latter must face a heavy responsibility if she alone stands out against the arrangement. As the result of the mention by Hoover in his statement of my approval of the proposal, I received from Berlin the following cable from Dr. Schacht, the former President of the Reichsbank:

"Again you have shown your usual wisdom and courage by supporting President Hoover's most helpful message. Please accept feelings of greatest admiration.

(Signed) DR. HJALMAR SCHACHT."

Evanston,
Thursday, June 25, 1931

France is suggesting difficulties in regard to the Hoover debt proposal, seeking to protect the status quo in reparations as fixed by the Young Plan. She suggests payment of the unconditional part of reparations payments (660,000,000 marks) by Germany into the International Reparations Bank to be reloaned by the Bank to the Reich.

Under this proposal, as under Hoover's, Germany will be

saved the money drain without endangering, to so great an extent, the Young arrangement. But this difference is difficult to adjust, especially as in the case of France, parliament, now in session, must acquiesce. The Reichsbank is having its depleted gold reserve reinforced to the extent of $100,000,000 by other central banks, including the Federal Reserve Bank of New York.

The European financial situation, while improved, is still precarious.

I received a long cable which I append from Jean Parmentier, the leading French delegate on both the Dawes and Young Committees, which, coming from him, undoubtedly states authoritatively the French governmental reaction. I telephoned the contents to Lawrence Ritchey, the President's secretary at the White House, for the President's information.

Paris,
June 24, 1931.

GENERAL DAWES,
Chicago.

President Hoover's most generous proposal is likely to check the present crisis and to prevent redoubtable events. It may however profoundly modify the financial settlement of the war and I feel myself to be personally responsible in part of the said settlement in which you have taken so great a part. Allow me to call your attention on the following points:

A. A total suspension of the payments during one year so profoundly modifies the whole agreements that it may be doubted whether it will be possible to bring them again to life after such an interruption. The greatest precautions must be taken for resuming after that delay the normal working of the agreements.

B. If these precautions fail and the payments resulting from war debts and reparations remain interrupted, each of the allied and associated nations will keep as its own and definite charge, its war expenses including the financing of war supplies manufactured on its own territory and used by associates. On this item there would be only to be deducted the net sums already received on that account, and which are unimportant as far as France is concerned, from the whole amount of damages to persons, the burden of which is heavier to France than to other associates, in that this country incurred proportionally the most important losses in men.

The reconstruction advances made to other countries, said advances are for the main part supported by the United States. Material damages due to invasion of Belgium in violation of treaties having converted the north of France into the principal battlefield, the devastation by all belligerent armies of its industrial territory has caused damages infinitely more considerable than those sustained by our other associates. For repairing the damages the French treasury has had to pay with interest at 6%, more than 10 billion dollars in gold value. Presently the total amount of the sum received by France in reparations account is less than 1 billion 500 million dollars. Even if the capital value of ceded American war stocks is added to said sum the total arrived at is less than 2 billion dollars, namely one fifth of the sums actually expended. Admitting that annual balance of 420 million gold marks should be received by France during the whole period provided for by the Young Plan, the present value computed at 5% interest and 1% redemption fund of these collections would amount to 7 billions of gold marks viz. 1 billion 670 million dollars.

In fact, even if the positive balance which is assured to France by existing agreements continues to be paid, this country will keep as its own charge two-thirds of the necessary reconstruction expenses of the battlefield. Said burden will be borne partly as a deprivation of income in gold value inflicted upon the holders of reconstruction loans by the depreciation of the franc and partly by debit interests supported by the budget.

C. Remembering our old association and friendship, I don't hesitate to ask you to bear in mind these facts, which you know of old, in the discussion you will certainly have in the present circumstances. Thanking you in advance for all you will be able to do for me, I send you my most friendly and faithful greetings.

PARMENTIER.

Evanston,
Sunday, June 28, 1931.

The heat has been terrific the last week and still continues. Spent yesterday and last night at my daughter Carolyn's house out at Barrington, and am now back at Henry's.

The Hoover proposal is still hanging in the balance on account of French reservations. The precarious financial status of the Reichsbank, and the interest of all other nations in preserving German credit, is resulting in great pressure for the adjustment of differences. The financiers of the different countries could easily agree but respective political differences, which also must be adjusted, are not easily resolved.

Put in much of yesterday studying Theodore Burton's book on *Crises and Depressions* published in 1902, and had my opinion strengthened that substantial business recovery is still several years distant, especially in steel and iron.

Journal as Ambassador to Great Britain

Evanston,
Friday, July 3, 1931.

Nearly a week has passed since I wrote in these notes—an interval in which the immediate financial crisis in Europe in all likelihood has been resolved. It has been achieved by President Hoover's statesmanship—a statesmanship which combined courage with competency and initiative.

In a state paper, commenting on the French attitude, Hoover made such a clear exposition demonstrating that the interest of France was subserved by acceptance, with minor modifications, of his original proposal that it changed completely the French attitude. It made clear to the French public that the adverse first reaction of their Government to the proposal occurred because the Government had over-looked in the situation the effects of a certain provision in the Young Plan requiring a deposit by France in the Bank of International Settlement of about $125,000,000 as a guarantee fund in case Germany takes a moratorium on the conditional portion of her annual reparations payments. As Germany is sure to do this, then, if Hoover's proposal is not accepted by France, this amount, plus the amount France would have to pay on her debts to the United States and Great Britain during the year would over-balance by about $100,000,000 what France would receive as her share of the unconditional reparations payments.

This "put the shoe on the other foot." The effect was the immediate reversal of French attitude, and I have little doubt that the papers tomorrow will carry the news of a successful settlement of the French differences.

If so, it makes a great American achievement. It demonstrates, too, how entirely self-interest determines the attitude of nations in real emergency. What first moved Hoover to immediate action was the fear of the collapse of the Reichsbank and German credit, which would affect adversely the immense American holdings in German securities, especially in short time German bank credits, about $500,000,000 of which were held by the New York banks.

HERBERT HOOVER   CHARLES G. DAWES

France's attitude changed as her understanding of what was to her real interest changed. Likewise, the attitude of all the other countries was determined by their estimate of what represented their self-interest.

In these days of commercial and financial inter-nation interdependence, no great nation is immune from the effects of a credit collapse in any other great nation. That always involves a possible world-wide credit collapse. That is why the world now rallies to the cause of German credit relief. If the Hoover settlement is made, as now seems so likely, much sentimental stuff may be written about altruistic motives.

But the great credit which is due Hoover is because in a world emergency, he alone being in a position to make it possible, had the courage and the wisdom to suggest an acceptable plan commonly beneficial to the nations.

My friend, Dwight Morrow, has been with him at the White House during the critical part of these negotiations, and I know he must have been of invaluable assistance.

After all, luck, or, perhaps I had better say Providence, played its great part. The emergency being so sudden and the necessity for action being so urgent, I have no idea that Hoover, when he outlined his contemplated proposal to me on the train between Marion and Springfield, had considered the possible effects of the "guarantee" provision of the Young Plan. Certainly France at first over-looked it when the Hoover proposal was made. And, yet, in my judgment, that provision was used to furnish the last unanswerable argument which brought France to terms.

Barrington, Ill.,
July 5, 1931.

As is generally the case in financial negotiations between nations, the actual closing of the agreement between the United States and France is continually delayed. Nevertheless it is due to come on Monday. After it, there must be further negotiations between Great Britain and the European nations concerned, to settle their divergent interests. In emergency—both in war and finance—a prospective common calamity brings nations to an almost immediate agreement "in principle." This term, in effect, generally means only that the nations agree that later agreement is made mandatory by their common extremity.

The details of settlement then consume an immense amount of time and work. In this particular situation, the agreement between France and the United States means that in time all other nations concerned *must* agree upon final details, and, in the meantime, Germany's financial load, heavy now almost to the crushing point, will be somewhat lightened. The situation at the Reichsbank is still so critical, however, that it is a question whether the collapse of German credit can be averted.

Yesterday (July 4th) the annual public reception was given at the American Embassy in London. My wife, assisted by Ray Atherton, officiated. For myself, I spent a quiet day at Barrington. In the evening Carolyn drove me over to Albert Lasker's house where he gave a small dinner in honor of Vice-President Curtis.

Evanston,
July 8, 1931.

France has agreed in principle to the Hoover proposal, and the moratorium, despite agreements, still to be made upon details by Great Britain and the European powers, is an accomplished fact. Germany is still in credit straits but probably can maintain its credit structure. As for the United States, Hoover's action, which was unavoidable, has brought it face to face with prolonged negotiations looking to debt reduction. This was bound to come sooner or later, and this readjustment, when made, will be an important contribution to better world business conditions and relations. But it will be made only with extreme difficulty.

Everybody seems to regard Chicago's bankrupt condition as an unmitigated misfortune. As a matter of fact, it seems to me that it affords the real opportunity for proper business reorganization of the city affairs. As the city, through reckless political control and extravagance, is unable to pay all its employees, they are necessarily reduced in number. Necessity lowers the pay rolls and reveals what is the real minimum number of employees essential to efficient municipal functioning.

The strength of the political machine is such that notwithstanding the courage and sincerity of Mayor Anton Cermak, which one cannot doubt, the superfluous employees could not all be discharged if there was any money which could be raked up to pay them.

The future will show that Chicago, as a city government, has benefited by its present distress. As with a reckless and profligate individual, adversity brings a city to its senses. Hard times work for civic fiscal reforms.

Evanston,
Wednesday, July 18, 1931.

The past week has only intensified the European financial crisis. Germany has declared a bank moratorium. Poland, Roumania, Hungary and other countries are in credit straits. In our own country, business depression deepens, though the banking situation is, for the moment, more tranquil. Confidence, which is the basis of credit, is gone in Germany, and sums which might have allayed general distrust, if loaned her a month ago, would prove inadequate now. She is fighting now to save the mark by restrictions on the sales of foreign exchange, by an embargo on gold shipments, and by bank credit restrictions while waiting for a relief loan by the four central banks—the Bank of England, the Bank of France, the Federal Reserve System and the Bank of International Settlements. Their action is delayed, however, by political conditions imposed by France as the price of cooperation. Such chaos is teaching its lessons. Among these are that of the inter-dependence of the European nations upon each other, and that no nation can permanently prosper economically upon the calamities of another.

It is also evident that public opinion here and elsewhere is changing its attitude somewhat on the whole question of reparations and debt payments. If they can be settled on a basis reasonably satisfactory to all concerned, so that they no longer can be used by nationalistic politicians as a basis for creating ill feeling between neighboring peoples, the prospects of continuing peace and more effective disarmament will be greatly improved.

The present world-wide economic crisis has reduced these questions everywhere—here and in Europe—from a matter of public discussion to one of public feeling. In this is some hope, for when the public feels it acts.

Europe, however, is at the cross roads, and one of them leads to the ruin of its present social structure.

Spent Sunday and Monday at Coleman Lake, Wisconsin, as the guest of George Scott. My brother Rufus and Col. Frank Knox were members of our party. Caro, Virginia and Miss Decker arrive from London tonight.

Evanston,
Friday, July 19, 1931.

This morning, William R. Castle, Under-Secretary of State, telephoned me from the White House that the President, who was with him, desired me to return to London as soon as possible to be there while the German loan negotiations between the representatives of the nations concerned were taking place. He stated that the President said that in view of my reparations and financial experience he thought the earlier I got back to London the better, that the situation was very serious because of conditions likely to be imposed by France, and that he feared the negotiations would be prolonged over several weeks.

I had expected to return long before this, but the local financial crisis here, now apparently over, had prevented. I asked Castle to reserve me accommodations on the first boat, which he did, and I sail on the *Mauretania* next Wednesday, the 22nd, stopping off on the way in Washington to see the President.

My family is here, and we have opened our Evanston house. Caro will remain here with Virginia for about a month.

Secretary Stimson and Secretary Mellon are in Paris, and will go to London for the International Conference on German relief, which the President desires me to attend.

OGDEN MILLS

Journal as Ambassador to Great Britain

Am stopping at the White House en route to New York, having arrived this morning. The President had also summoned Dwight Morrow, who reached here this morning.

The President arrived from his camp at Rapidan shortly after and we spent most of the morning at his office during which he was in telephone communication with Stimson in London. Castle, the Under-Secretary of State, was present.

At lunch, Ogden Mills joined us, and practically the balance of the day was consumed with the discussion of the next step which the President was considering. He had read us the cable correspondence of the last few days between himself and Stimson at Paris and London. By cable last Friday to Paris he had made certain suggestions for Stimson and through him for Mellon, to submit to the International Conference of Ministers at London to the effect, in brief, that for the time a stabilization of German credit at the present level should be maintained without additional loans at present from the Central Banks. The action of the German Reich and the Reichsbank in the matter of credit and exchange restrictions in effect has already stabilized German credit at the present level.

The President proposes, in effect, a moral support of Germany in this position, and the encouragement of foreign bank creditors, including our own, to cooperate in helping Germany to maintain it.

While France, at present, suggests a loan, it does so without making, as yet, a satisfactory statement of its conditions. The consensus of opinion of American, British (we are informed) and even of French bankers, seems to be that a loan of $500,000,000, for instance, will be entirely insufficient to restore normal German credit, whatever may be the form the loan may take, and even if the American banks were willing to join in making it, which they are not.

As a matter of fact, therefore, there can be no agreement reached at the London Conference for a specific form of relief, other than the President's suggestion, and this suggestion is made possible only by what Germany itself has done in stopping the outgo from Germany of gold and exchange.

At this juncture, it seems plainly evident that when other specific methods of relief through either long or short time loans are proposed at the Conference, they will be rejected. We know this, for we know the United States Government cannot be committed to a loan participation by the President for he lacks the authority of Congress, and we know, also, as I said before, that the American banks will not participate. The White House is kept authoritatively advised in these matters.

How, then, to assist in the situation so that public confidence may not be unnecessarily shaken by the inability of the Conference to take some definite step which will soon develop?—that is the question. Public expectation has been unavoidably, but unduly aroused.

The outcome of the Conference, in my judgment, can only prove constructive if it confines itself to peaceful resolves and generalities, avoiding the inevitable impasse which detailed propositions will involve, and adjourns quickly and coincident with this that, through a statement of the President of the United States, general confidence in the continuance of the present coerced stabilization of German credit at the present level can be preserved.

Mills, Dwight and I, between us, worked out a form of statement which we thought appropriate, based on a preliminary draft given us by the President. The matter ended in the President's preparing an entirely new draft of his own, better suited to the purpose than either of the former ones, which will be issued tomorrow morning.

During the discussion, the President was kept informed by Stimson over the telephone of the developments of the day at London.

After dinner, the general discussion of the situation was resumed between the President, Dwight Morrow and myself. We spent practically the whole day with the President in his office.

Journal as Ambassador to Great Britain

White House, Washington,
Monday night, July 21, 1931.

So much has transpired this busy day that despite its great importance I can note but the salient things.

Ogden Mills and I had strongly urged the President to cable yesterday the statement to which I refer in the latter part of my notes of yesterday, but Stimson in London demurred over the telephone when the President suggested it. It was then decided to send it tomorrow (this) morning. But when morning came, we were confronted in the headlines of the papers by a statement that MacDonald had persuaded the German Chancellor, Dr. Heinrich Brüning, not to ask for a loan. This was but the first of a continuous flow afterward by telephone of a series of conflicting and confusing reports from Berlin, London, New York and elsewhere, as well as from the London Conference, which was evidently floundering as expected, only more so.

The President then decided that the statement should not be sent, but that the proposal which he had sent in detail to Stimson at Paris last Friday, from which he has not since deviated in his instructions, should be forwarded as an official statement and guide to conference action and given to the press. This was done. The proposal was as follows:

STATE DEPARTMENT

For the Press   July 21, 1931.

American Proposal as sent to Secretaries Stimson and
Mellon at London.

(This is practically a repetition of the proposal cabled by Hoover to Stimson at Paris last Friday.)

The essence of the problem is the restoration of confidence in Germany's economic life, both in Germany and abroad.

1. On the political side the United States hopes that, through mutual good-will and understanding, the European nations may eliminate all friction so that the world may rely upon the political stability of Europe.

2. On the economic side, the present emergency is strictly a short term credit crisis. Fundamental pressure upon German economy during the period of depression has been relieved by the joint action of the creditor powers in suspending all payments upon governmental debts during the period of one year. But Germany has financed her economic activities to a very great ex-

363

tent through the medium of short term foreign credits. There is no reason to doubt the soundness of the basis upon which these credits rest, but the general uncertainty which has prevailed for the last few weeks resulted in such a loss of confidence that the German banking and credit structure was subjected to a very severe strain. This strain took two very definite forms, both of which resulted in a drain of banking resources and the depletion of German gold and foreign exchange holdings.

In the first place there was a flight from the mark within Germany. In the second place there was a withdrawal of foreign deposits and a curtailment on the part of foreign banks of outstanding lines of credit.

Fundamentally, there is nothing to justify these movements and if, through cooperative action, they can be arrested, there is no reason why the present emergency cannot be immediately and definitely surmounted,

(a) As to the first, namely the internal flight from the mark, this can be and is successfully being combatted by the vigorous action of the German Government and the Reichsbank. Once unreasonable fear has been eliminated, it is certain that the patriotism of the German people can be relied on to prevent the destruction of the credit of their own country.

(b) As to the external credits, we believe that the first approach to the problem is the development of a program that will permit the maintenance for an adequate period of time of the present outstanding lines of credit. In this connection it is our understanding that this volume of credit together with the freed reparations and the natural gain from the allayment of the panic should be adequate to meet the needs of the German economic life for the immediate moment. On the other hand, it must be apparent that, unless provision is made for the maintenance of these credits, an attempt to provide new ones, whether of a short or long term character, would be ineffective. In the development of such a program, the governments of the countries having principal banking centers, including the United States, Belgium, France, Great Britain, Holland, Italy, Japan and Switzerland, and other important banking centers, might well undertake to encourage their bankers so to organize as to permit the maintenance for an adequate period of time of present day outstanding lines of credit to Germany. The responsibility for working out the details of such a program and the methods of making it effective with due regard to the protection of the banks and the needs of German economy should be left to the banking communities of the respective countries and the central banks could, we believe, be relied on to furnish the necessary leadership, cooperation and direction.

Such voluntary arrangement should be supplemented, for the time being, by strict control of all foreign exchange transactions by the Reichsbank so that the integrity of the program can be maintained and the banks that are participating can be assured that there would be no arbitrary withdrawal either from within or without Germany.

3. It is our belief that if such a program could be made promptly effective, it would result in an immediate restoration of confidence, and that in a comparatively short time the necessity for restrictions of this character would disappear and normal conditions would once more prevail. There is all the more ground for faith in such a result in view of the fact that the United States debt suspension program has now become effective and that the

events which succeeded the announcement of that program clearly demonstrate that relief from payment of intergovernmental debts established in the minds of the business world the basis for renewed confidence.

4. A committee should be selected by the B.I.S. or created by some other appropriate method to secure cooperation on the following question:

A. In consultation with the banking interests in the different countries to provide for the renewal of the present volume of outstanding short term credits from those countries.

B. In making an inquiry into the immediate further credit needs of Germany.

C. In the development during the course of the next six or eight months of plans for a conversion of some proportion of the short term credits into long term credits.

July 21, 1931.

The Acting Secretary of State was asked about reports from abroad to the effect that the President had made proposals to the London Conference. Mr. Castle said that the proposals of the President, conveyed to Messrs. Stimson and Mellon, were, briefly, as follows:

Germany has been greatly assisted by the relief from reparations payments for one year, aggregating about $400,000,000. Her trade balances are favorable and increasing. The flight of the mark has been stopped and the internal banking situation has been regularized by the courageous action of the German authorities. The next step is to stabilize and assure the continuance of the volume of short term credits now held by foreign bankers and institutions which amount, it is estimated, to $1,400,000,000. The President's proposal is simply that the bankers and institutions in all countries should in aggregate in each country maintain present volumes of credit and that the German Government, through the Reichsbank and otherwise, should enforce strict and complete control of all foreign exchange so there will be no preferential or arbitrary withdrawals and that will enforce the maintenance of the total volume of credits from each country. Such a system of cooperation, supplemented by the action of the German authorities will stop the drain on Germany from abroad and by the restoration of confidence, enable Germany to secure in the normal course of business such additional credits as she may require.

This proposal is not in the nature of a moratorium but merely the maintenance of the large volume of credits to Germany which now exist. It permits the world to return to normal conduct of business by assuring stability in the German credit structure. This is a necessary first step to give time for the development of any plans for long term loans in substitution for short term obligations. The interest France has taken in the provision of such a long term loan is ample evidence of her desire for cooperative solution of the situation.

Journal as Ambassador to Great Britain

All this only started the day. Continuously the telephone rang. Mills carried on conversations with George L. Harrison, president of the Federal Reserve Bank in New York, and with Secretary Mellon in London. The President talked with Stimson in London at one time for an hour. Harrison, at New York, was in direct communication with Montagu Norman, Governor of the Bank of England in London and would report from him. Direct word was had through these sources from Dr. Hans Luther, president of the Reichsbank in Berlin.

Only first authority was consulted by the President and his immediate staff as affording proper information to justify his own conclusions. The President had with him in his office Ogden Mills (Under-Secretary of the Treasury), Castle (Under-Secretary of State), Eugene Meyer (chairman of the Federal Reserve Board), Senator Morrow and myself.

When he would finish a telephone conversation, he would summarize it to us for our observations. All information that he received only strengthened him in his original position.

I believe no one concerned with the whole situation in Europe had at his command more authoritative information than did the President. He had not an idle moment during the day except for lunch. His clearness and quickness of comprehension, his equipoise and calmness, and his command of knowledge of every element in this diversified and world-important problem were remarkable. He was always the alert, competent and compelling Chief Executive, and at the end of the day nothing had shaken his confidence in the soundness of his original position and views.

Stimson, who had attended the meeting of the London Conference of Ministers, endeavored to get authority to agree to a loan by the Central Banks, saying that France and England stated that they could join. Hoover replied with direct word from Norman, through Harrison, that the Bank of England would not participate notwithstanding what was said at the Conference of Finance Ministers. As to the suggested participation of the United States, he said he spoke with the direct assurance of the chairman of the Federal Reserve Board.

He thought Stimson should suggest a more thorough canvass by the Ministers of their own banking authorities. He said that

EUGENE MEYER

he had word, coming direct from Dr. Luther, that the Reichsbank itself considered an additional loan at this time unwise. The President felt that Britain and France should share the responsibility for the only decision possible and not endeavor to place it on the United States alone.

France suggested certain reservations which made agreement on a loan impossible. Great Britain did not have the support of the Bank of England, which made a loan impossible. The Federal Reserve Banks lacked not only willingness but the legal authority to participate, which made the loan impossible. Why, then, should others endeavor, by intimating acquiescence through generalities "in principle" and avoiding details which would involve a certain impasse, to create the impression that the United States alone offered the obstacle? Specific instructions were given Stimson and Mellon to stand firm.

The London Conference should be immediately adjourned. Its continuance will be only a continuing futility creating public apprehension and distrust. While I am an accredited member of it, I hope to Heaven it will be dissolved long before I reach London.

The Germans have already taken steps to help themselves, just as Schacht did in the old reparations crisis, namely by control of exchange, the raising of the interest rate, rationing of discounts, and supervision of credit transactions. Without such measures, new loans would be futile. With them, additional and properly considered aid can be given in the future if necessary.

I leave tomorrow morning for New York, sailing from there at 5:00 P.M. My stay here with the President has been an experience, and I leave with an increased admiration for his executive genius.

Left the White House 9:00 A.M. Wednesday, and arrived in New York where General Harbord and Warren Fairbanks met me at the train at 1:45 P.M. Sailed at 5:00 P.M.

Journal as Ambassador to Great Britain

It is interesting this evening to read the condensed radiogram account of the meeting of the London Conference, after having sat by the side of the President at the White House for two days while his guiding hand was steering a dangerous situation to a safe conclusion. The President never lost sight of the fact that he was dealing primarily with a financial crisis in Germany, that such a crisis demands immediate decisions, and that delay to render them only intensified that crisis. The interjection of a loan discussion meant the interjection of political discussion and delay.

As hoped for, the Prime Minister and other dignitaries in their speeches, confining themselves to generalities, adopted the President's suggestions and adjourned.

Now there is time to work out plans for other help if such is feasible, since Germany's further financial pressure from abroad is stayed. I expressed my ideas of this accomplishment to the President in the following radiogram:

HERBERT HOOVER,
White House,
Washington, D.C.

Have just received word of the London outcome. Congratulations. By your recent statement from Washington you again assumed leadership, and announced in advance of the Conference the only way out in a way which re-assured the financial and business world and preserved confidence. Not only this, but the statement determined the nature of a prompt report of the Conference and compelled its speedy adjournment thus preventing an otherwise inevitable debate over vital national differences which would have undermined world business confidence and largely, if not entirely, destroyed the present value of anything the Conference would have reported. Your intervention was necessary to preserve the full benefits of your reparations moratorium arrangement. In financial crises nothing is more important than central leadership, with definite opinions, and which acts without delay. This Conference could not have furnished it, and you alone were in a position to do so.

CHARLES G. DAWES

368

Journal as Ambassador to Great Britain

I made a statement relative to the Chicago Exposition and its finances which appeared in the press the day I left for Washington. The following is a copy of it:

Of the $10,000,000 bonds of the Century of Progress, secured by a 40% first lien on the gate receipts, $6,555,000 have been sold without individual or corporation guarantee. The remaining $3,445,000 are secured by individual and corporation guarantees, said guarantees amount in the aggregate to $5,571,000, in addition to the lien on gate receipts.

Of these I have sold on this trip something over $1,000,000, leaving about $2,400,000 of guaranteed bonds to be sold as needed during the latter part of next year.

Owing to our contracts for sale of exhibit space, which have been made and are being made, much of which is being paid for in advance to save discount for cash, it will probably not be necessary in order to complete the Exposition to make any additional solicitation of funds from the public.

Among the large purchasers of space are the American Telephone & Telegraph Company, International Telephone and Telegraph Company, Western Union Telegraph Company, Radio Corporation of America, Baltimore & Ohio Railway Company, Pullman Company, Illinois Central Railway Company, Chicago, Rock Island & Pacific Railroad Company, Chicago & North Western Railroad Company, and the General American Tank Car Company.

As announced yesterday by Mr. W. S. Knudson, President of the Chevrolet Company, the contract has been signed by the General Motors Corporation to expend approximately $1,000,000 for the erection of a building to house the exhibits to be made by that Company during the Exposition.

We have had available of its own funds for this Exposition at this early date approximately within one and one half million dollars of the amount which was available for the Chicago World's Fair of 1893 until the opening of its gates.

The $11,000,000 for which we had provided before the beginning of construction work last year on the Century of Progress Exposition, is approximately double the amount which was contributed by the citizens of Chicago to the World's Fair of 1893, during the entire period of its construction, which was $5,617,154.23. Public appropriations and the premium on souvenir coins, in addition to this amount, made up the $13,063,834.76 which was the total amount available for the 1893 Fair up to the time it opened its gates. After its opening, the World's Fair had gate, concession and other receipts of $15,723,698.04.

The compact and efficient business organization which Mr. Rufus C. Dawes, President, and his associates have built up for the Century of Progress has operated from the very beginning under a strict executive control of expenditures and budget system, and the material reduction in present building costs, due to general conditions, has resulted in the letting of building contracts much below the original estimates of cost. It is these two facts and the expectation of an early demand by enterprising business concerns for exhibit space which are largely responsible for the healthy financial condition of the Exposition.

Journal as Ambassador to Great Britain

The Exposition is having splendid cooperation from the Mayor and the South Park Commissioners. As its steady progress is realized, the large business concerns of our great city and country are daily enlisting in its work and purposes.

CHARLES G. DAWES *

At Sea,
Friday, July 24, 1931.

The press reports on the Conference which I am receiving through my friend, Charles J. Pannill, of the Radio-Marine Company, indicate some disappointment that the Conference did not at this time enter upon the task of readjusting reparations and European differences in general. Some of the writers, however, properly sense the reasons for the adopted procedure.

The settlement of a German financial crisis and that of fundamental European differences could not have been attempted concurrently at this time with anything but failure. The discussion of political considerations would have delayed the taking of an immediate and united attitude by the nations in the financial emergency, and that might have been disastrous. Events have put

---

* The final figures on the Chicago Century of Progress as given in the report of its President Rufus C. Dawes are as follows:

The Chicago Fair which was known as A Century of Progress, ran for a period of 170 days in 1933 and 159 days in 1934. Total attendance for the two seasons was 48,769,227 and the paid admissions were 39,052,236, or a daily average of 118,681. Revenue from admissions was $16,632,840.19. Space Rentals, receipts from concessionaires, sale of Guide Books, Merchandise etc., brought the total Gross Operating Revenue to $31,762,685.00. This amount exceeded Administrative and Operating Expenses by $13,130,060.21. The Construction Costs amounted to $12,441,894.88 and there remained $688,165.33 for demolition and final liquidation. After settlement with the Chicago Park District for restoration of the grounds, a surplus of $160,000.00 remained which was distributed to various non-profit organizations.

The Fair operated without any subsidies and was originally financed by securing individual and corporation Guarantors for an issue of $10,000,000.00 Gold Notes. These guarantees amounted to over $12,000,000.00. The whole issue was repaid, together with $1,480,888.02 for interest including the normal 2% tax.

Total disbursements for all purposes during the two years were $100,200,989.16 as follows:

By A Century of Progress		$42,900,989.16
By Concessionaires	(estimated)	24,000,000.00
By Exhibitors	(estimated)	33,300,000.00
		$100,200,989.16

370

RUFUS C. DAWES

MAJOR L. R. LOHR

the Versailles Treaty on trial again, France senses that. Other questions, almost as difficult, confront the nations. What folly would it have been to have interjected a half-baked discussion of them into a financial situation which demanded not only immediate but a united action!

It was President Hoover who sensed this from the first, and it is fortunate for the world that he did so. The greater and more difficult problems of new European and world adjustment which must now be faced, have not been made even more complicated by an initial failure.

At Sea,
Saturday, July 25, 1931.

The press despatches, a digest of which is radioed to the ship, contain most disquieting accounts of the loss of gold by the Bank of England today and yesterday. If the drain is not checked, England may be forced to take the same course as Germany and clamp down stringent credit and exchange restrictions. This, if it occurs, will be a severe shock to the world business conditions.

It is claimed that France is abetting these gold withdrawals from England. I cannot believe this possible. It is evident that another week-end crisis is on. Last week it was in Germany, now it is in England. Will or will not an increase in the Bank of England's interest rate stop the flow of gold from England under present conditions of world-wide financial distrust? That is the question under discussion today at London and New York, in my judgment.

At Sea,
Sunday, July 26, 1931.

Press reports that London exchange is now at 4.85½, which is above the gold exporting mark, but that in the last eleven days, London has lost about $155,000,000 in gold. I hope that the present rate of exchange is maintained.

I am re-reading General Pershing's book carefully on this trip.

371

Journal as Ambassador to Great Britain

Every page is interesting to me and brings back recollections of strenuous and important days. Every library should have this book and along with it the book of General James G. Harbord which is soon to be republished. They supplement each other.

London,
July 29, 1931.

Arrived in London yesterday at noon, in time to attend luncheon for Secretary Stimson at the Embassy which Caro had arranged before she left for America. It was of an official nature, with the Government well represented, although MacDonald and Henderson were absent in Berlin. Lord Macmillan, Lord De La Warr, Sir John Simon, Lord Reading and Albert V. Alexander were among those present.

After lunch Stimson went over with me the whole situation as he had met it here. Realized from his talk something of the difficulties he has very successfully faced. He seems not to have joined in the criticism of France and its attitude which is so prevalent in England. This is a very wise course to have taken and one which I learned from Ambassador de Fleuriau, the French Ambassador, today, was much appreciated in France.

This morning Stimson called at the Chancery, and we continued discussions. He leaves for Scotland on Friday. Hugh Gibson called to say he wanted me to take his place as the United States unofficial observer on the so-called Committee of Experts convened to settle certain differences between Great Britain, France and other allied nations as to how "deliveries in kind" by Germany under the Young Plan were to be handled.

I told him that I would not willingly consent to serve, and I thought that this committee should be at once adjourned for a considerable period. Its sessions may only add to the prevalent financial unrest, and probably add to the practical difficulties of the situation.

Since "deliveries in kind" are going on, the Expert Committee can later pass on any questions relative to respective interests in them. The development of any present controversy in this con-

AMBASSADOR AIMÉ DE FLEURIAU

SIR ROBERT KINDERSLEY

nection should be avoided as contributing to public disquiet in the present financial emergency.

At 3:00 P.M., de Fleuriau called and fully and frankly stated the French attitude and what had occurred in the German financial negotiations up to this time. He emphatically stated that at no time had the French Government or its representatives made or even mentioned political considerations which must be taken into account before France would join in relief measures for Germany, and that this subject had been brought up, not by the French but by the English and Americans in the conversations with Brüning and Curtius and then outlined to the press through German sources as having come from France.

He complained about the misrepresentation of the French, by a leading financier of London which had been reported to them. He complained of the recent London Conference and opposed any early calling of another such gathering or until the financial situation was much clearer. He felt political or other discussions, at this time, of what should be done in the future only made more difficult the accomplishment of what should be done in the immediate present.

He fully agreed with me as to the desirability of adjourning the so-called Expert Committee for the present. He said the French Government and the Bank of France were willing to co-operate and aid England in the protection of its gold reserve in any way possible. He deprecated the reports that withdrawals of gold from England by French business were arranged officially by the French Government or by the Bank of France.

He spoke highly of Sir Robert Kindersley, of whom he said that he was respected and trusted by the Bank of France and the French Government. This evening, Sir Robert called on me at the Embassy and has just left. Sir Robert, who is a director of the Bank of England, went, as representing it, to Hungary, and just recently to Paris. He had spent most of the day at the Bank of England. The gold withdrawals there today were small. He hopes that the acute demand is over, and that things will quiet down. While he regretted the delay caused by France in the acceptance of the Hoover moratorium proposal of June 20th, he stated that he understood perfectly the French standpoint and apprehensions. Of their recent attitudes he had no criticisms.

He believes in mutually-trustful and close cooperation between the Bank of England and the Bank of France. He is assisting just now in preserving a proper and needed cooperation of the Bank of France with the Bank of England.

The many conversations of today could not but remind me of our old tri-party war-time negotiations in France in army supply matters with British and French representatives. Englishmen and Frenchmen were then dying together at the front for a common cause, while in supply negotiations in the rear they would fight like dogs and cats. They would finally always act together—and so they will now.

London,
Thursday, July 30, 1931.

My notes of yesterday need some amplification to indicate the importance of the statements of de Fleuriau and Kindersley, and their relation to each other.

Only a week ago at the White House the President, in my presence, was receiving through New York the substance of telephone conversations with certain bankers in England impugning the sincerity of the proffers by France of cooperation in the financial relief of Germany. Kindersley can testify better than anyone else as to the real attitude of the Bank of France.

Kindersley, as the head of the banking house of Lazard Frères, is the actual agent of the Bank of France in its present purchase of English exchange in France to assist the Bank of England in protecting its gold reserve. Besides that he is a director of the Bank of England, and, as one respected and trusted by both institutions, is the real liaison between them.

The reported intransigent attitude of Snowden toward France seems to be a dangerous factor in a delicate financial situation. With my knowledge of what the President was hearing of the alleged insincerity of the French last week, the conferences with de Fleuriau enabled me to give him the additional information needed to get the actual situation with its complications and its dangers.

Journal as Ambassador to Great Britain

Stimson's contacts here have been chiefly with the Governmental and not with the financial authorities. In this financial crisis it is the latter who count most, and they will probably work through it if only conferences of statesmen do not at this time try to help them. That can come later.

Ambassador de Fleuriau and Kindersley are both in accord with me that at the present juncture no other Governmental conferences should be called. They would inevitably discuss political considerations jointly with financial problems. This would add to public distrust, and tend to undermine financial confidence.

Confidence is already enough disturbed. Ambassador de Fleuriau tells me that beginning as far back as the Hitler political upheaval in Germany there has been a steady remittance of German funds to France by Germans themselves, whose apprehensions as to the stability of German finance and economy have been aroused. In fact, said de Fleuriau, from the most of the European countries, including England, money has been remitted to France because of a feeling of local insecurity in financial conditions.

It was not drafts by France on other countries but remittances largely of this kind to her which have so contributed to the impression that she is looking only to her own interests and declining to cooperate properly in German and other relief measures.

Today de Fleuriau called and said the Expert Committee should be able to adjust French and English differences over the Young Plan this week, leaving only minor questions affecting the smaller countries which can be disposed of soon without arousing public apprehensions. Gibson corroborated this.

Spent some time with Stimson this afternoon; and Gibson called at the Embassy in the early evening.

Have just returned from a small dinner given at the House of Commons by Mr. and Mrs. Arthur Henderson for Secretary and Mrs. Stimson. The other guests were the Prime Minister and Miss Ishbel MacDonald and Mr. and Mrs. Alexander. MacDonald and Henderson are just back from Germany. Stimson leaves tomorrow night for Scotland.

Journal as Ambassador to Great Britain

Last Thursday, Kindersley left for Paris. The successful result and purpose of his visit are indicated by the official announcement of the Federal Reserve Bank of New York as follows:

"The Federal Reserve Bank of New York, in association with other Federal Reserve Banks, has agreed to purchase from the Bank of England, if requested, up to the approximate equivalent of $125,000,000 of prime commercial bills. This agreement has been made in cooperation with the Bank of France as a part of a credit arrangement in favor of the Bank of England, aggregating in all about $250,000,000."

This was given out yesterday in New York, and similar announcements were made officially of the arrangement in England and France. The press states that this arrangement, resulting largely through negotiations conducted over the long distance telephone, was considerably delayed by English objections to a $3\frac{1}{2}$ per cent interest rate which was first proposed. The difference between $3\frac{1}{4}$ per cent and $3\frac{1}{2}$ per cent was finally split at $3\frac{3}{8}$ per cent.

From this statement may be inferred something of the difficulties which Kindersley must have confronted due to the attitude of certain of those in official relationship to the situation. Everybody informed, knows that England's credit situation was in a crisis, demanding the same kind of help and cooperation from other nations which England had always in the past extended to them in their similar difficulties.

But it was difficult for England, which had always extended help in the past, to ask for it now. I am afraid that while Kindersley was properly asking help from the American and French banks, and in this connection, outlining its absolute necessity, he was hindered in his negotiations by a certain English attitude, based largely upon pride, that after all, the help was not so necessary. The arrangement is referred to this morning in the English press as a tripartite arrangement between the United

States, England and France for mutual interest, of which England will be the first beneficiary.

It is in the mutual interest of all concerned, of course, and while England is primarily benefited, the United States and France act because of benefits to themselves as well. But the form of the press statement is an indication of how England repels the thought of assistance.

London,
Friday, August 14, 1931.

During the first week of this month, I received a letter from my old friend, General Pershing, again asking me to come to France.

I left for Paris on the 7th (last Friday) arriving in the evening. General Pershing and Theodore Marriner (counselor of the Embassy) met me at the depot. General Pershing and I took dinner together that same evening, and on Saturday morning started for a two-day motor trip over the American battlefields and cemeteries. Santini, the war-time chauffeur of General Pershing, was at the wheel. To my relief, the General forbade his war-time devilism in speed. We stopped Saturday night at the care house at Romagne Cemetery, where 14,000 of our soldiers are buried.

During the trip, we were at Château-Thierry, Belleau Wood, Verdun, Rheims, Fère-en-Tardenois, St. Mihiel, Mont Sec, Montfaucon, and elsewhere in the Argonne and Champagne regions, travelling as we estimated about 550 miles in the two days.

As we were together in the old familiar places, the fourteen years seemed to drop away and we felt as young as we did when our work in the A. E. F. commenced. Every minute of this trip was interesting to both of us.

On last Tuesday afternoon, General Pershing and I called on Marshal Lyautey, at his Paris apartment, and when John urged him to take a trip to America, the Marshal said that at 77 he was too old. Upon John's demurring, the Marshal said: "I am six years older than you. If you and I were in our thirties, six years

377

would not make much difference between us, but in the seventies, as you will soon find, each year will change one more than six years then."

We spent a full hour with the Marshal whom I had wished to see about the French Colonial Exposition, of which he was the originator, and is now, as before, its active head.

The Colonial Exposition is a fine success. In two months, the attendance has been over 12,000,000. Before its closing, probably, this number will be increased to 25,000,000. Both artistically and financially, it has exceeded all expectations. The Marshal has a justified pride in the outcome, for like our own exposition in Chicago, it has required steady pulling against a strong current of opposition and criticism.

During my stay in Paris, I visited the Exposition twice, going with Sir Henry Cole and Mr. Paddock. General Pershing is finishing his work as chairman of the American Battle Monuments Commission. In a second car on our trip to the battlefields, we were followed by Major Price, the engineer officer in charge of construction, and Captain Teale, his assistant. They were on hand to explain the progress and plans of the construction work and landscaping, most of which is now completed. No other battle memorials in France surpass our own in dignity, impressiveness, or beauty. To my regret we did not find time to go to Soissons, where I wanted to visit the place near there where with other companions I had once unwittingly stood quietly as a target for three pieces of German heavy artillery.

London,
Sunday, August 16, 1931.

Through the 50,000,000 pound loan to the Bank of England by the Federal Reserve Banks and the Bank of France, the pound has been stabilized for the time being, but confidence in British economy and financial solidity has been much shaken. As a result, funds are still being withdrawn for foreign account. It is evident that unless confidence is restored, the funds available to the Bank of England to maintain the market for sterling will be exhausted and sterling decline to a point where gold exports will re-commence.

As yet, I judge that local withdrawals from British banks, due to a feeling of distrust, have not been large, but there is so much talk about a "crisis" they may commence.

The May Report (by the special Committee on Economy) having estimated the prospective budget deficit at 120,000,000 pounds (nearly $600,000,000), the bankers have informed the Government that unless measures are taken which assure the world that the budget will be balanced, Britain will soon be in the same financial situation as Germany. The Cabinet therefore is considering emergency measures and this week it is said will announce a plan to which it is hoped all parties will agree. Mac-Donald has already consulted Baldwin and Neville Chamberlain, Conservatives, as well as Liberal party leaders like Sir Herbert Samuel and Sir Samuel Hoare, their cooperation being necessary. The Government leaders in these preliminary discussions are MacDonald, Snowden, Henderson, J. H. Thomas and William Graham.

The British people when they are convinced that a real emergency exists, have always bravely met it face to face. Whatever sacrifices must be made, they will make, and in the end will achieve their objectives. In the meanwhile, however, conditions here are most distressing, and since political decisions—always difficult and time consuming—must be reached and then made governmental policy before general confidence will have a proper basis for its restoration, they will probably become more serious before they are better.

London,
Saturday, August 22, 1931.

My friend MacDonald is at the parting of the ways and must meet the supreme test of statesmanship. After a week of continuous and arduous negotiations, not yet finished, the crucial necessity for a momentous decision becomes evident.

The Trade Union Council, the body which in 1924 engineered the general strike, refuses to sponsor the cut in government expenditures which the Government must make or fail to meet the national emergency. Snowden apparently stands against their policy. Henderson is said to stand with them. MacDonald with Conservative and Liberal aid must, therefore, force his economy measures through to adoption against the most powerful element of his own party, and in spite of the defection of the organization leaders of his party. If he does not attempt this, he will have failed to rise to the necessities of the situation.

No revenue tariff concessions will bridge the gap between the positions on government expenditures reductions held by the Trade Union Council on the one hand, and the Conservatives and Liberals on the other.

MacDonald must stand for the nation's interest against his party's position, or for his party's position against the nation's interest. He is still looking for alternatives, but there seem to be none. If he announces a plan to which the Opposition can agree —and he and they are discussing such a plan today—it is proposed immediately to summon Parliament for next week's consideration and ratification of it.

In thinking of MacDonald's position, I recall a true and notable statement of Rutherford B. Hayes, a former President of the United States: "He who serves his country best, serves his party best."

I have outlined the political situation as it appears today, but every day may change it. In the meantime the flight of the pound continues. It begins to look as if it cannot be saved from depreciation, more or less severe, whatever may be the immediate political course of things.

Great Britain now seems to face inflation and currency depreciation or the adoption of a partial moratorium similar to that already existing in Germany.

London,
Tuesday, August 25, 1931.

MacDonald has stood the test, and has won an enviable reputation and a high place as a patriot and statesman. In a situation during the last few days growing hourly more acute, one which brought the King hurrying down from Scotland on his own initiative, and in which confusion in the Cabinet became more confounded, MacDonald, with Baldwin, Snowden, Thomas, Samuel, Neville Chamberlain, Lord Reading, and others, have risen above party considerations and united in a supreme effort to save the credit of their country.

With the King's assistance, for which he is receiving full and deserved credit, MacDonald, Baldwin and Samuel, at Buckingham Palace, arrived at an agreement to form a National Government. The present Cabinet having failed to agree upon a plan, resigned yesterday, and the King then asked MacDonald to remain as Prime Minister.*

Henderson split with MacDonald after the Trade Union Council had delivered what was practically an ultimatum against any reduction in present unemployment payments. The majority of the Cabinet stood with him against MacDonald, Snowden and Thomas.

Parliament will now be convened, and a national plan for balancing the budget adopted. It seems agreed that after the adoption of the plan a general election will be held. Whether this getting together has come in time to save sterling is the question. It has been the great and continued pressure of the Bank of England which has been primarily responsible for it. The Bank passed on to the Government some of the enormous pressure which the situation has brought upon it, and brought about a realization that the financial crisis through which it is passing bears directly upon general welfare, both national and individual.

In the meantime, however, matters have come to such a pass that nothing can safely be predicted as to the immediate outcome. The Bank of England in sustaining in foreign markets the price of sterling exchange above the gold export point has about exhausted the 50,000,000 pounds credit from the Federal Reserve Banks of the United States and the Bank of France and associated French banks. Will the banks of the United States and

---

* The new Cabinet, composed of only ten members, formed within twenty-four hours, contains four members of the Labour Party, namely, MacDonald, Snowden, Thomas and Sankey; four Conservatives, namely, Baldwin, Neville Chamberlain, Hoare and Cunliffe-Lester; and two Liberals, namely, Reading and Samuel.

Journal as Ambassador to Great Britain

France extend further credits when this credit is fully exhausted and how much more credit is needed? The public reaction to the steps taken by the new National Government will determine this in part; but many other factors bear upon it as well.

Stamp, who has been called back from his vacation in Ireland for consultation with the Prime Minister and as a director of the Bank of England, reports to me that the word which comes from American bankers to the Bank of England is favorable. J. P. Morgan is here personally, and has been consulted. The Morgan firm, in the floating of the $500,000,000 Anglo-French loan in the United States during the War, showed what courage, ability and prestige can do in a similar great emergency.

London,
Sunday, August 30, 1931.

This past week a credit to the United Kingdom of $400,000,-000 has been arranged with the United States and France, the latter two countries participating equally in the grant. This has relieved the immediate danger to the par of sterling. It came just in time.

MacDonald, risen to the heights of statesmanship, has been repudiated by his political associates and Henderson has taken his place as Parliamentary leader of the Labour party. The new National Cabinet is at work on the plan for balancing the budget.

Snowden has announced his retirement from politics on the dissolution of the present Government after completion of its tasks. The general recognition of the greatness of MacDonald's contribution to the national good in this crisis, and of the personal sacrifice it involved, is growing here and abroad.

Britain has squared itself to its great task. Its magnitude is difficult to appraise. It is difficult to see, everything considered, how a lowering of the standard of living can be averted for a considerable time at least. While it is dangerous to prophesy as to the immediate future, this people will work out of the present mess when sound governmental policies are inaugurated.

Last Thursday, my old classmate Clayton W. DeLamatre and

Journal as Ambassador to Great Britain

I were at Kirkcudbright, Scotland, where I dedicated the gymnasium presented by Thomas Cochran, of New York, to that old burgh. I also received the freedom of the town at the Council Chamber; received a gold key from the architect and the builders of the gymnasium, and an embossed scroll in a handsome box from the Council; while I presented a flag from the American Society of Naval History to the Kirkcudbright Academy and made three speeches.

DeLamatre and I were entertained at the fine old seat of the Earl of Selkirk (a title now extinct), where the family is now represented by Sir Charles Hope-Dunbar. The estate still consists of some 15,000 acres.

Saturday at lunch we had our old friends Chief Justice and Mrs. Charles E. Hughes, and Sir Ronald and Lady Storrs. Much enjoyed a long talk with the Chief Justice.

Our visiting friends, Mr. and Mrs. DeLamatre, left yesterday, very much to our regret. For forty-six years "DeL" and I have kept up our friendship which began at the Cincinnati Law School in 1885. At law school at 25 years he seemed old to me—now at 71 he seems young. In other words, in reality he has not changed much—the change has been in me. My own 66th birthday occurred Thursday when I was at Kirkcudbright, Scotland.

Address of the American Ambassador, General Charles G. Dawes, at the Opening Ceremony of the Cochran Memorial Gymnasium at Kirkcudbright, on Thursday, August 27, 1931.

An occasion like this has its peculiar lesson bearing not only upon the relations of the people of Britain and America but, held at such a time, bearing as well upon the world-wide conditions of depression which they, with other peoples, confront.

We meet here to dedicate an important gift from Thomas Cochran, an American of Scottish descent, to the town from which over a century ago his forebear sailed for America. It is his method of paying a tribute of respect not simply to the sturdy Cochran pioneers from whom he inherited those qualities which make for character and success in life, but as well to this city and school, and to the rugged country whose natural conditions contributed to the development of energy, enterprise and strength of character in its people. In the first volume of his history of Civilization in England, Buckle in his great generalizations points out the effect upon the character of a people and the nature of its government which results from an abundance of cheap food and the lack of necessity for great effort in securing it. The Scot has always had a hard battle with nature for his sustenance. Other things being equal, in proportion as mankind has to battle with nature, for his life, so does he develop in individuality and in mental, moral and physical strength. Where life is easy, mankind becomes more inert and less jealous of those individual prerogatives and that comparative personal liberty which he must possess in a hard country in order to live. As some one has phrased it: "Where the snow flies, there is the home of liberty." In the life of America, the Scot has played a great part. Thirteen of the Presidents of the United States have been of Scotch-Irish descent. The first Scotch settlers in America were men accustomed to hardships, and their work and influence in the early days of our national life were among the most important of its formative elements. Mr. Charles A. Hanna, the author of the authoritative work, "The Scot in Scotland, Ireland and America," dedicates it to "the forgotten dead of that indomitable race whose pioneers in an unbroken chain from Champlain to Florida formed the advance guard of civilization in its progress to the Mississippi and first conquered, subdued, and planted the wilderness between."

The Scot has ever dealt successfully with adversity and hardship, and the achievements of the Scotch people evidence how hardship and adversity strengthen mankind and, under natural laws, are inseparably associated with its continued advance. I deem it appropriate before a Scotch audience in Kirkcudbright, one of the historic strongholds of a battling people, gathered in the halls of an educational institution which has been maintained in continuous existence for over three and a half turbulent centuries, to comment on the influence upon the continued progress of mankind of present adverse conditions and the world-wide business depression.

We are too prone to seek in man's higher nature the causes of his improving human relationships when, as a matter of fact, the foundation of these improved relationships has been the compromises reached in a bitter struggle for existence under the laws of human nature and the survival of the fittest. Man progresses because of inexorable laws, the most important of which is that "Self-preservation is the first law of nature." The greatest steps in the improvement of his conditions and relationships have had their inception in common conditions of adversity. Sympathy may induce aspirations among individuals and peoples, but it is the instinct of self-preservation and self-interest which impels their most constructive joint decisions and actions.

Today, practically all the peoples of the world are living, for the time being, in the midst of adverse conditions and business depression. It is not a pleasant way to live. But, irrespective of the fact that we deplore it, we must recognize the important benefits which will accrue from it eventually. It is not in times of adversity that mankind makes its mistakes. It makes its most egregious errors and commits its greatest follies in times of prosperity. It is alone when common hardship is being endured that the absolute interdependence under a natural law of individuals, of classes of individuals, and of separate peoples, is realized in such a way as to influence mass attitudes, which are always assumed through the feelings of men and not through their reason. When common prosperity exists among the peoples, a common cause of it is not always perceived by the masses; but they sense the cause of a common suffering.

CHARLES A. HANNA

Journal as Ambassador to Great Britain

The present economic distress which most nations are experiencing at this time, bringing home to the average man everywhere a sense of the interdependence not only of individuals but of classes of individuals, will tend in all countries to bring about delayed domestic reforms by making them politically practicable. Again, in proportion as there is a correct sensing by each nation of what is actually its own self-interest, the hope of constructive accomplishment in international negotiations is advanced. Whatever may be said currently and superficially to the contrary, the attitude of a nation in an international negotiation or conference is always determined primarily by its conception of its own self-interest.

The freedom of action and attitudes of the respective national delegates to international conferences is always restricted and generally determined by domestic public sentiments. In general, an international negotiation results in a compromise, the terms of which are in effect dictated chiefly by the balanced consideration of domestic public sentiments. It is, therefore, because of its peculiar effect upon respective domestic public sentiments that a general and world-wide economic crisis and depression produces such a favorable environment for quick common action by the nations. That the self-interest of any particular people at such a time as this rests in constructive domestic and international cooperation needs no involved explanation to them, for they sense it. Such a condition of public sentiment arising from mass feelings silences the demagogues who in normal times, by promoting international prejudices for internal political purposes, embarrass and delay, even if they do not actually prevent, sensible and constructive agreements of mutual self-interest among the nations. In prosperous times the outcries of a radical minority, as vociferous as it is unrepresentative, exercise their maximum influence upon the timid and irresolute in public place. But it is different in a time of real crisis, either domestic or international. Then, under the laws of human nature, the separate peoples are sensing their own national and international interest in terms of their own personal interest, and, as an inevitable result, not only their domestic but their international relationships improve.

The reasons for an improved international relationship do not primarily lie in any softening of national selfishness in international negotiations. If nations were not inherently selfish they would not long exist. The self-interest of every nation, and that of its citizens, however, lies in better international understandings and economic peace. This is true at any time. But in a great economic crisis like the one through which the world is passing, while the people of each nation may not think of it academically, it becomes a matter of feeling and therefore one which determines their attitude. The constructive actions of man in emergency are born primarily of his instincts and necessities, and not of his aspirations.

Whenever in a crisis or time of real adversity individuals, classes or nations, meet in negotiations with the determination on the part of each to act solely for his own self-interest, but where a common action and understanding by all is recognized by all as imperatively essential to their respective self-interest, then it is probable that important steps forwarding better human relationships will be taken. That such will be the nature of any international conferences which may be held during this world depression constitutes the only firm basis of hope for their favorable outcome. It may be remarked here that a characteristic of such conferences is the marked absence of ethical platitudes. It was not sympathy but national self-interest which forced international common action in the adoption of the expedients of the past few months. No voluntary individual, national or international understandings of great importance are ever permanent unless they are based upon a substantial mutual interest.

London,
Sunday, September 6, 1931.

Uncertainty, like a great pall, lies over a depressed world economy. If it was a mere matter of current adjustment of credits, I think the par of sterling could be maintained by the United Kingdom, but two additional essentials are required in the long run. The national budget must be balanced and British production costs so lowered as to regain for the country a greater share of international trade which alone will bring her a favorable balance of trade, even when invisible items are included.

The first essential—the balancing of the national budget—depending, as it does, upon British patriotism and capacity for self-denial, and being an agreed upon national policy, will be accomplished.

The second essential, if it depended upon British business enterprise alone, would be forthcoming. But business enterprise is handicapped by the absence of national agreement and uncertainty in tariff policy, as well as by the lack of confidence and credit.

At best, British international trade cannot be expected to revive except slowly. But local business will be immediately helped by a tariff policy which will prevent some of the present worldwide dumping into Britain of surplus products at prices below the cost of production.

How can the pound sterling be maintained unless the present drain of money out of the country is lessened by at least the amount the people now spend abroad for that which can be produced at home as cheaply as abroad; but is not so produced because of this "dumping?"

Time is a most essential element in this situation. How long will it take before a British business man can know just what he can depend upon as a settled basis of national economic and social policy. The question of the par of the pound sterling is involved in the answer.

Matters are quiet at the Chancery, possibly because for the moment each nation is so busy with its own troubles that it keeps its nose out of the troubles of others.

Mr. Klotz, a representative of the State Department, when in Berlin, had an interview with Dr. Schacht, who talked freely with him. Klotz told me of it the other day. Schacht maintained that a National Government was needed in Germany in order to get a real working understanding with France. He said Germany wanted an understanding with Poincaré not with Briand, and France wanted one with the Nationalists of Germany, not alone with the Socialists—and then the understandings would be more permanent. He said the German Nationalists would be satisfied with the present western frontier and France's retention of Alsace and Lorraine, that they would not raise the question of the Austria-German customs union, as within three years France would be found supporting it since it alone would save Austria, that they could not, nor could anyone else, prevent agitation over the Polish Corridor, which was racial in nature, and that they would also favor postponement of reparations discussions pending economic events which would control future policies.

London,
Sunday, September 13, 1931.

The world-wide demoralization of business deepens, if anything. Democracy is on trial, and in Britain it seems to rally finely to its task. Here, as in our own country, it must honestly face the results of its past errors, resolve not only to correct them but also resignedly to pay the cost of them.

Yielding to the urge of the crowd and the spirit of extravagance and reckless times, it has followed the easy path. It must now "rightabout-face" in certain essential governmental, fiscal and economic policies, and its parliamentary body must authorize and concur in them. The statesman must supplant in influence and power the demagogues and politicians at such a time or democracy will undermine itself.

History tells the story of what will inevitably happen if democracy falls. There will come despotism—constructive despotism like that of Mussolini or destructive and terrible like that of Soviet Russia—one or the other. This generation is living in fateful times.

As things are very quiet at the Chancery, have occupied my mind much of the week with archaeology and anthropology, stimulated by the presence of Dr. Henry Fairfield Osborne. Before we knew he was coming, Sir Josiah Stamp and I had planned a trip to Ightham, the home of Benjamin Harrison, the grocer-archaeologist, who, over fifty years ago, identified the first eoliths and proved the existence of man in the Tertiary era.

Together with Osborne we made the trip yesterday. It was of enthralling interest to us all. We stopped first at Down house where Charles Darwin "thought and worked for forty years and died 1882." We saw the room where he wrote his *Origin of Species* with its old furnishings intact.

In a house adjoining where he is staying for a while, we called upon the eminent scientist Sir Arthur Keith, formerly president of the British Association, the next meeting of which Osborne is here to attend. These two anthropologists differ as to the origin of man, Keith holding that he descends from the anthropoid apes, and Osborne from some distinct but related species. They are great friends and no debate ensued, much as all would have enjoyed it.

Sir Edward Harrison, the son of Benjamin Harrison, is a friend and former colleague of Stamp in the Treasury. With him, later in the afternoon, we examined the collection of artifacts from the surrounding district made first by his father, but amplified by the son.

We saw one of the two first eoliths with which Benjamin Harrison first dated man back to the Tertiary period. It was placed in the wall of the neighborhood church (14th century) just above a memorial plaque to Benjamin Harrison. We went also to Coldrum Stone Circle, from which came the Bronze Age bones (identified by Sir Arthur Keith) now in the local church. It was a most memorable day for me. We started in the morning and

A RAINY DAY AT DOWN HOUSE, SEPTEMBER 12, 1931
Left to right: General Dawes, Sir Arthur Keith, Mrs. Dawes,
Lady Stamp in background, and Prof. Henry Fairfield Osborn
(Sir Josiah Stamp at the camera).

AT COLDRUM STONES, SEPTEMBER 12, 1931

Left to right: Maxwell Stamp, Sir Edward Harrison, Prof. Henry Fairfield Osborn, General Dawes.

arrived home in the late evening. Lady Stamp and Caro went with us.

I have read and admired Dr. Osborne for many years and it was a great privilege to have this fine visit with him.

During the week have been reading *Harrison of Ightham* by Sir Edward R. Harrison, *The Races of Europe* by W. Z. Ripley, *The Antiquity of Man* by Sir Arthur Keith, *Fossil Man in Spain* by Hugo Obermaier, with an introduction by Dr. Osborne, and what I call my prehistoric archaeological text book *Human Origins* by my friend, Dr. MacCurdy. Osborne presented me with Obermaier's book.

London,
September 16, 1931.

An ominous thing happened yesterday. The sailors of the British Atlantic Fleet—16 ships—including the *Hood, Nelson* and *Rodney* being involved, "ceased work" or, in other words, mutinied at their proposed reduction in pay. This took place near Invergordon, Scotland, in Cromarty Firth. It is somewhat reassuring that before taking action the sailors sang the national anthem as indicating their loyalty, but the fact remains that there has been organized resistance to authority which sets a dangerous example to other classes of the military and civil services at this particular time.

The situation, financial, industrial and political, daily grows more acute, and were it elsewhere but in Britain one would feel that it was very dangerous.

Yesterday I had a long talk with J. H. Thomas, Minister for the Dominions. He had just come from a private conference with Prime Minister MacDonald and had told him that he (Thomas) favored a general election in October. Up to this time, Thomas was for the present Government "sticking it out" for a year. Thomas, like MacDonald and Snowden, in this crisis, has placed his country's interest above that of party, and his reasons for his changed ideas as to the wisdom of an immediate general election are wholly impersonal and patriotic. He recognized that a tariff policy must supplement the budget balancing legislation, and has become convinced that a tariff law, passed after the fight and after the Cabinet changes which its consideration in the present Parliament will involve, will be considered by the public here and abroad as expressing a fixed governmental policy justifying a restored public confidence. He feels that a public verdict must precede the passage of such a law. He gave me to understand that MacDonald agreed with him. The press, however, is divided upon the question of the advisability of a general election, some papers fearing the further unsettlement of financial conditions and the continued "flight from the pound" to which it will contribute. Uncertainty fills the air. A decision must be quickly taken. Fortunately for Britain its Parliament does not function under our Senate rules. It has not parted with its power to make quick decisions by a majority vote, less than two-thirds. Individuals cannot interminably delay emergency remedies.

The United Kingdom, already over-burdened by taxation, faces for the remainder of the fiscal year 1931–1932 and the year 1932–1933, an aggregate budget deficiency of around 246,000,000 pounds, and this enormous amount must be met both by radical economies and increased taxation. Added to this problem is that greater one of restoring the balance of foreign trade.

"Clouds and darkness" now surround this brave and devoted people in their national life, as often before, but again they are girding themselves for the supreme effort which the situation makes imperative.

London,
September 17, 1931.

Called on my friend, J. H. Thomas, Minister for the Dominions, this morning. He gave me the present phase of the Government program. Tonight he told me that the Cabinet meets to decide the question of the present National Government submitting itself to a general election to be called as soon as possible after October 15th. Personally he now favors this.

Snowden will retire and "go upstairs" (peerage) if this kind of an election is agreed upon. He feels that the naval mutiny is well adjusted, but realizes the adverse example to the other services of an adjustment reached by such methods. If the present Government, with a tariff program, enters a general election, he predicts a great victory.

In order to get a balanced view of a rapidly changing situation and to keep our Government properly advised, I called on Arthur Henderson at his office, as leader of the Opposition in the House of Commons. He evidently feels the difficulties of his present position. He emphasized the seriousness of the situation, and spoke at length of his reasons for his personal course. Knowing him as I do, I cannot but feel that as leader of the Opposition, he will cooperate in the maintenance of law and order to the best of his ability; and it may be that the future may have an important part for him to play in this connection.

I received a note from the Prime Minister that he had received an invitation from the two National Broadcasting chains of the United States urging him to broadcast next week to our country, but that he would not do this without my approval.

This I did not regard as wise and I so informed the State Department, saying that, left to myself, without negative word from it, I should inform MacDonald tomorrow. Receiving no reply, I wrote MacDonald and insert here the correspondence:

> 10 Downing Street, Whitehall,
> 17th September 1931.

My dear Dawes,

I ought to tell you that I am being urged to broadcast to America. I am offered one day next week between 11:00 and 11:30 p.m. I will not do this, however, unless you approve, and as arrangements have to be made without delay, I shall be glad if you will let me know quickly if there is any objection.

Yours very sincerely,

H. E. General C. G. Dawes, C.B.   J. Ramsay MacDonald

> London, September 18, 1931.

My dear Prime Minister:

I have your note relative to the invitation extended to you by the Broadcasting Companies for a broadcast in America next week.

There is in the United States an acute financial situation and considerable unrest among the depositing classes. In such circumstances, official reassurances, wise from a general standpoint, may have upon the depositing and investing classes an exactly contrary effect to that which is intended. However constructive from a political angle an address in the United States from the British Prime Minister might be, it is an unusual incident. Financial repercussions being different from political repercussions, reassurances may result in questionings as to why they are necessary, instead of an addition to public confidence.

In such sensitive conditions, and there being no specific objective for such an address important enough to justify any risks, I think it would be unwise to make it.

With best regards,

Your friend,
CHARLES G. DAWES

10 Downing Street, Whitehall,
September 20th, 1931.

MY DEAR DAWES,

Thank you so much for your letter about Broadcasting. I had those suspicions myself and that is why I insisted upon consulting you. We are in an awful state just now, and I can think of nothing but that. Still, I believe we could come out of it stronger than we were when we were thrust into it, but we shall all have to lay our heads together to stop the mad follies we have been committing in matters of international finance.

With kindest regards to Mrs. Dawes and yourself, I am,

Yours always sincerely,
J. RAMSAY MACDONALD

London,
Saturday, September 19, 1931.

My friend Thomas Cochran of J. P. Morgan & Company, who has been visiting in London, brought Mr. Morgan to lunch at the Embassy.

The fact that the pound sterling is in a critical situation has been increasingly evident, and yesterday the New York stock market reflected a panicky condition there.

Telephoned J. H. Thomas to come to lunch with us in order that the whole situation might be developed and the State Department be kept informed. Our conference was long. Despite every effort, including strenuous work by the Bank of England and the bankers of New York and Paris, the liquid resources of the Bank of England, including the gold reserve, are being rapidly depleted.

The pound sterling cannot be maintained at its present par of exchange probably longer than several days. Thomas had not realized, nor apparently have his colleagues of the Cabinet, the present crisis in exchange, for it has been precipitated almost

J. H. THOMAS, SECRETARY OF STATE
FOR THE COLONIES

over night. He was given the situation. What happened in sterling today and yesterday thrusts forward the question which the Bank of England must decide. Shall its remaining gold be used in what seems to be a hopeless effort to maintain exchange? If not, at what point in the lowering exchange value of the pound shall the remaining gold and foreign credits be used for stabilization?

The Cabinet, at its meeting yesterday, had not made its decision about the general election. This sterling crisis, however, should insure at the next Cabinet meeting next Monday, or soon thereafter, the formulation and wording of the platform upon which the present National Government will go before the people next month in a general election. It has been feared that any other election than such a one might degenerate into a contest of parties in which the opposition, especially if the pound remained at par, would maintain that an emergency did not exist, thus lessening the usefulness of the election, its helpful effect upon general confidence here and abroad, and the constructive power of any government which resulted from it.

Panic conditions in Amsterdam, Switzerland and Germany, to say nothing of Britain and the United States, added to the sterling crisis, create an emergency which only a united British people behind a strong National Government can meet. That Government will then have an enormous task on its hands, to make possible the revival of British foreign trade.

London,
Monday, September 21, 1931.

On Saturday the withdrawals from the Bank of England were no less than 15,000,000 pounds.

The Prime Minister sent two cables to the State Department through the British Ambassador at Washington apprizing it of the situation and of the imminence of a departure of the British currency from the gold standard. Stimson sent me a long cable repeating the Prime Minister's cables and giving a summary of a discussion between himself, Secretary Mellon and Secretary of Commerce Robert P. Lamont, with the President.

Journal as Ambassador to Great Britain

Of the facts stated in the Prime Minister's cables, I had already been informed through Tom Cochran, who had been in continuous contact with the Bank of England and by telephone with Tom Lamont of J. P. Morgan & Company, and George L. Harrison, of the Federal Reserve Bank of New York.

At 7:00 P.M., last (Sunday) evening, Sir Warren Fisher, Permanent Secretary to the Treasury, asked me by telephone to come to the Treasury. There he handed me the statement which the Prime Minister was giving to the press, announcing the necessity of suspending sub-section 2 of Section 1 of the Gold Standard Act of 1925. Fisher was worn out with work, and much depressed. He wanted me to assemble the representatives of the American banks with London branches later in the evening and urge them to cooperate with the British banks in restricting purchases by British citizens of foreign exchange, except that required for the actual needs of trade or for meeting existing contracts.

Ambassador de Fleuriau joined us, and Fisher made the same request of him as to the French banks with London branches.

I promised to do this immediately and with the aid of my staff assembled at the Embassy at 10:30 P.M. representatives of all American banks with London branches, except one who was out of the city. About twelve executives were present. At our meeting, Frederick Hyde, managing-director of the Midland Bank, was present to explain the details of the method of restricting foreign exchange purchases which the British banks were to adopt.

I read to the meeting the Prime Minister's statement, which I append hereto, and made the request for cooperation with the British banks. All present agreed and passed a resolution that they would do everything in their power to aid in the present situation.

During the evening Tom Cochran and another member of the Morgan firm, Walter K. Whigham, a director of the Bank of England, called. After arranging to have the American bankers meet some of the British bankers later in the night at the home of Sir Austin Harris, I went to the Chancery (about midnight) and cabled the State Department.

This afternoon (Monday) got a report from a Cabinet member regarding the Cabinet meeting this morning. They have now decided to let the question of a general election rest for the present in abeyance. Events constantly changing, attitudes change with them. The apparent inconsistencies in the attitude of the Cabinet at various times, as I note them in these pages, is a reflection of the great difficulties with which the Government finds itself confronted.

Many generalizations suggest themselves to me as events succeed events, but they change their form as generalizations do with one in that close contact with things happening, which lessens the perspective that time and distance alone properly give. The mosaic into which all these pieces from all over the world are fitting themselves, is too vast to be vizualized yet, and I will not attempt it. I will only record what I see in my small way.

I attach, however, a summary of the situation resulting in the break in sterling, handed me by a most competent authority.

The recent German collapse created acute domestic situations in many countries, for example, such as America, Switzerland, Holland, Sweden and others. All of these countries in consequence had enormous lock-ups in Germany and their local needs in consequence became pressing. For these reasons they have been impelled to withdraw their London balances, not necessarily because of their lack of faith in sterling but because they, as a matter of fact, needed their funds at home to restore a liquidity which was impaired by their frozen assets in Germany. This same reason actuated nationals of many foreign countries to sell their sterling securities on the London market and immediately repatriate the funds resulting from these sales. London has been fairly flooded with these selling orders for three weeks and it has been impossible to estimate to what extent these sales might eventually go, as the amount of such prospective sales is immeasurable. It is logical to assume that if the German collapse had not occurred, the present crisis here would have been averted.

Statement of the Prime Minister to the Press
September 20, 1931

His Majesty's Government have decided after consultation with the Bank of England that it has become necessary to suspend for the time being the operation of sub-section (2) of Section 1 of the Gold Standard Act of 1925 which requires the bank to sell gold at a fixed price. A Bill for this purpose will be introduced immediately and it is the intention of His Majesty's Government to ask Parliament to pass it through all its stages on Monday, September 21st. In the meantime the Bank of England has been authorized to proceed accordingly in anticipation of the action of Parliament.

The reasons which have led to this decision are as follows: Since the middle of July funds amounting to more than £200 millions have been withdrawn from the London market. The withdrawals have been met partly from gold and foreign currency held by the Bank of England, partly from the proceeds of a credit of £50 millions which shortly matures, secured by the Bank of England from New York and Paris and partly from the proceeds of the French and American credits amounting to £80 millions recently obtained by the Government. During the last few days the withdrawals of foreign balances have accelerated so sharply that His Majesty's Government have felt bound to take the decision mentioned above.

This decision will of course not affect obligations of His Majesty's Government or the Bank of England which are payable in foreign currencies.

The gold holdings of the Bank of England amount to some £130 millions and having regard to the contingencies which may have to be met, it is inadvisable to allow this reserve to be further reduced.

There will be no interruption of ordinary banking business. The banks will be open as usual for the convenience of their customers; and there is no reason why sterling transactions should be affected in any way.

It has been arranged that the Stock Exchange shall not be opened on Monday, the day on which Parliament is passing the necessary legislation. This will not, however, interfere with the business of the current settlement on the Stock Exchanges which will be carried through as usual.

His Majesty's Government have no reason to believe that the present difficulties are due to any substantial extent to the export of capital by British nationals. Undoubtedly the bulk of the withdrawals have been for foreign account. They desire, however, to repeat emphatically the warning given by the Chancellor of the Exchequer that any British citizen who increases the strain on the exchanges by purchasing foreign securities himself or assisting others to do so is deliberately adding to the country's difficulties. The banks have undertaken to cooperate in restricting purchases by British citizens of foreign exchange, except those required for the actual needs of trade or for meeting existing contracts, and should further measures prove to be advisable, His Majesty's Government will not hesitate to take them.

His Majesty's Government have arrived at their decision with the greatest reluctance. But during the last few days the international financial markets have become demoralized and have been liquidating their sterling assets regardless of their intrinsic worth. In the circumstances there was no alternative but to protect the financial position of this country by the only means at our disposal.

His Majesty's Government are securing a balanced budget and the internal position of the country is sound. This position must be maintained. It is one thing to go off the gold standard with an unbalanced budget and uncontrolled inflation. It is quite another thing to take this measure, not because of internal financial difficulties, but because of excessive withdrawals of borrowed capital. The ultimate resources of this country are enormous, but there is no doubt that the present exchange difficulties will prove only temporary.

Treasury Chambers,
Whitehall, S.W.1,
20th September, 1931.

Journal as Ambassador to Great Britain

London,
September 27, 1931.

It has been a momentous week in international finance and British national economy. The first repercussions of the drop of sterling from par resulted in far-reaching financial disturbances abroad—in a rising stock market in England and a falling one in America and elsewhere, and in a stimulus of a certain kind to business expectations here and discouragement elsewhere. From a broad standpoint, it would seem that since what has occurred is only due to the mandates of economic law enacted by human nature which have over-ridden inevitably the temporary barriers attempted to be interposed to their operation by fallible human judgment, it will eventually prove of benefit to mankind everywhere.

Wherever governments, or business, or classes have attempted to keep certain rates of exchangeability exempt from the operation of natural law during this world depression, such as sterling here and wheat and cotton in America as well as labor both here and there, they have failed. It is difficult, but wise, for us to recognize that this failure only accelerates under natural laws the healing process of wounds which mankind, in its folly, periodically inflicts upon itself.

During the week I have conferred a number of times with representatives of the Government—with Lord Reading about the serious clash between Japan and China in Manchuria, which, for the time, is less disquieting, and with J. H. Thomas, the Minister for the Dominions. I discussed with Thomas the question of an international conference on silver. He hopes to get Canada to initiate one. Our Government would much prefer such a conference to a meeting held in Europe or London. A conference held in Canada would be much more likely to "stick to its knitting" and not expand its discussions into general international finance, debts and other economic questions.

During the past week, the British Cabinet seems to have arrived at the conclusion that a general election must be quickly held. Thomas tells me that it will formally reach and announce this decision tomorrow (Monday).

Dr. MacCurdy and his wife are visiting us at the Embassy. With them I attended the lecture upon the origin of man given last night, by Sir Arthur Keith, at the meeting of the British Association. It was one of the most interesting and absorbing addresses I have heard.

At the suggestion of the Prime Minister, Sir Herbert Samuel, the Home Secretary, wrote asking for my opinion as to the advisability of his acceptance of an invitation to broadcast in America. I advised against it in such times as these.

Yesterday (Saturday) the pound sterling closed in the New York market at $3.84 which is about $1.02 below its gold par.

London,
Thursday, October 1, 1931.

The decision for a general election has not yet formally been taken. A member of the Cabinet says that the decision will be made by the Cabinet tonight. What has been going on is an effort to formulate a platform covering the tariff upon which the Government will go before the people in such words as will prevent loss of Liberal support.

The delay is dangerous to general confidence, and the decision has too long been held in abeyance. People demand aggressive leadership in troublous times. When aggressive leadership does not head the Right for that very reason they often follow the Left which seldom lacks it.

There is a serious under-current of general apprehension. When I went to Parliament Tuesday evening about 8:30, I passed through a great crowd of unemployed gathered in the neighborhood and hemmed in by police, both mounted and on foot. Some rioting took place. It is maintained that for these gatherings, and their apparent attitude, a comparatively small band of Communists is responsible and that the masses themselves are quiet.

But, nevertheless, the determination by a general election of the real attitude of the people, which is assumed to be conservative and in favor of law and order, grows more and more necessary to afford the basis of a stabilization of British confidence. One must not expect anything in these times but be ready for everything.

Today I took lunch at the Astors' with the Aga Khan, and Bernard Shaw. Went to the mat with Shaw on Russia.

Monday night we had an interesting group, mostly scientists, at dinner at the Embassy, including Dr. Henry Fairfield Osborne, of the American Museum of Natural History, his associate Dr. W. K. Gregory, Dr. C. G. Abbot (secretary of the Smithsonian Institution), Dr. George Grant MacCurdy (director of the American School of Prehistoric Research) and George Davison, of the Central Hanover Bank.

Last night, Wednesday, together with our house guests, the MacCurdys, we had at dinner Sir Josiah and Lady Stamp and Mr. and Mrs. Davison. Stamp is being currently consulted by the Prime Minister in finance matters. He discussed the gold standard problem with Davison and me and the question of a stable forward market on pounds without which the foreign trade of the world must be transacted in terms of dollars or francs.

If world banking headquarters are not to shift from London to New York, the pound must soon be stabilized and yet how can it be for a long time to come? If foreign business is to be transacted in pounds, buyers and sellers of merchandise and commodities, etc., must have a forward market on pounds in order to protect themselves from its inevitable fluctuations. Otherwise, seeking a stable medium of exchange, they will use dollars or francs which are both on a stable gold basis.

London,
October 4, 1931.

The outward political situation has not much changed. A general election is settled actually but not formally. Its announcement on Wednesday is apparently inevitable, but in the meantime the efforts to satisfy the Liberals on the tariff plank of the

National platform continues with bitterness and internal Cabinet dissension increasing.

This delay in a time of national emergency, because of political differences of a comparatively minor nature, is disorganizing and dangerous in its general effects. In a crisis, leadership which hesitates too long is lost. But if the matter is settled by Wednesday, one hopes for the best.

In the business situation, this interesting thing is worth noting. A section of the press and the City is emphasizing every incident which by any manner of treatment can be made to reflect upon the soundness of American and French finance, in order to frighten and deter those who are trying to transfer funds to the United States and France. In a word, the cry is not simply "Buy British" but as well "Sell America and France." If they are succeeding in frightening the English as thoroughly as the Americans here who call on me at the Chancery, they will live greatly to regret it, for in the long run such methods only accelerate panic withdrawals.

I am sending several cables daily to the State Department and keeping our Government authoritatively advised to the moment.

London,
Tuesday, October 6, 1931.

My dear and faithful friend Dwight W. Morrow died suddenly yesterday at his home in Englewood, New Jersey. I loved him as a brother and mourn his loss. Among all the leading men of our country, of whom I have known some intimately in my public and private life during the last forty years, I regard Dwight Morrow as the ablest. My deep affection for him has not prompted this judgment, for there were several among these leaders whom I loved not more but as well. In my opinion none excelled him in balanced judgment, none in industry, none in character, none in kindliness and generosity, none in companionability, none in initiative and none equalled him in sheer intellectuality.

Dwight was unique. We shall not know his like again. That he cared for and trusted me has always been to me a precious

400

thought. It is difficult for me to write of his untimely death except in terms of personal bereavement, but I am deeply sensible that it is a national and world loss as well.

He died full of accomplishment, but even so only at the threshold of a great career of public usefulness. The words on General Gordon's tomb in St. Paul's apply to Dwight as well: "At all times and everywhere he gave his strength to the weak, his substance to the poor, his sympathy to the suffering, his heart to God." I feel desolated. A great man has fallen in the thick of the conflict and at the height of his powers.

The British Cabinet has agreed at last. The present Government will go before the electorate on October 27th. MacDonald will ask for a full mandate to do what is necessary without defining it.

Today when I was at the Bank of England, Governor Norman came to me to pay a tribute to Dwight. Dwight is universally mourned. The Prime Minister telephoned asking if there was objection to his national broadcast tomorrow evening to this nation being relayed also to the United States. I saw none and told him so.

London,
Sunday, October 11, 1931.

Have arranged for a memorial meeting of the London friends of Dwight Morrow at the Embassy next Wednesday afternoon.

The President's plan, recently announced, for the mobilization of a reserve by American banks for the rediscount of paper not eligible for rediscount at the Federal Reserve Banks, has had a beneficial effect upon impaired confidence at home and here. The investment houses and the City here have been full of panic talk and irresponsible statements about French and American banks. I think it is growing somewhat less.

The campaign for the general election is in progress. Lord Reading, the Secretary of State for Foreign Affairs in the MacDonald Cabinet, called me to the Foreign Office during the week, and reported upon his trip to Paris to see Laval, the French Prime Minister, before Laval leaves for his American visit on October

16. He arrived at no definite impression of any plans the French may have in mind. He is convinced that, as yet, they have no idea of relinquishing any claim to the "unconditional" portion of the reparations fixed by the Young Plan.

The present general election is one of the most important appeals to the country in Britain's political history. If the Socialists win, it will prove disastrous to the country and to Europe; nor will we be unaffected. All expect a victory for the present Government, backed as it is solidly by the Conservatives and a portion of both Liberals and Labour followers.

The war situation in Manchuria is most disturbing.

The financial situation in Austria, Switzerland, Holland and Germany continues critical.

London,
Tuesday, October 13, 1931.

Large gold shipments to Europe are being currently made from the United States. As a consequence of the withdrawals and as a measure to check them, the Federal Reserve Bank of New York has raised its interest rate from $1\frac{1}{2}$ to $2\frac{1}{2}$ per cent.

It would seem that if gold shipments continue in substantial amounts, the policy of a progressive weekly raising of the rates by $\frac{1}{2}$ per cent for a time should be inaugurated. Our gold position is very strong, and the confidence of New York in it would seem quite justified. If it is justified, however, the progressive raising of the interest rate (as would be done as a matter of course in normal times when over-large gold shipments are continuing) should not hurt us.

On the contrary, if we underestimate the drawing power of the Continent when stimulated to action by an unjustified but real loss of confidence in the dollar, and do not attempt to check withdrawals, now, by the first means in our power—the interest rate—we may regret it later. Such a course might result in a greater unnecessary loss of liquid resources in the early stages of a situation which may become more troublesome later.

As a matter of fact, reports indicate that the European countries are seriously alarmed over disturbing reports from America and the present rate of gold shipments. Even in our strong gold position, we should not minimize the possible suction power of the Continent in the sale of American securities and withdrawal of balances if it becomes increasingly panic-stricken.

I cabled the State Department my feelings along these lines. There is danger of miscalculating both the extent of possible Continental fears and its repercussions upon us.

These are momentous times. In this general election in Britain, democracy is undergoing a supreme and decisive test on this side of the ocean. What will be the outcome? In Germany, today, there is a governmental crisis. What will happen? In Manchuria, Japan and China today are on the brink of war. What if war comes? In all the countries of the world economic crisis exists. To what will it lead? Fear and continuing uncertainty—of those alone we are certain.

In the break-up of old conditions, many old controversies may be settled. That at least seems probable. If the Nationalists come into power in Germany, for instance, reparations will be wiped out. Germany will then settle that question for herself, and the world will accept it, for it cannot secure reparations by going to war for them. But speculation is useless. Events are in the saddle.

London,
October 14, 1931.

The memorial meeting for Dwight was held at the Embassy this afternoon. The distinguished company almost without exception were his personal friends, known to me as such and to whom I had sent invitations. About fifty were present. Six nations and two Dominions were represented by their diplomatic heads in London, France, Italy, Japan, Mexico, New Zealand, the Union of South Africa, besides the United States. Those who paid their tributes—some of them most impressive, especially that of Montagu Norman, Governor of the Bank of England—spoke largely in terms of personal bereavement. They were the French Ambassador, the Italian Ambassador, the Japanese Ambassador, the

Mexican Minister, Montagu Norman, Sir Robert L. Craigie, Charles A. Selden, of *The New York Times*, representing the American correspondents, and myself.

The occasion was worthy of our dear friend who has passed away, mourned by the world. The meeting was something less than an hour in length. I sent a cable of sympathy to Mrs. Morrow and her family as representing those present.

London,
October 18, 1931.

Brüning has won in the Reichstag by a small majority and his ministry stands. The bank rate in the United States has been increased by one per cent and is standing now at 3½ per cent. The export of gold from America still continues. The net amount exported in the last two months is around $700,000,000.

The critical situation in Manchuria is maintained. The general election campaign is on here and the indications favor a pronounced majority for the National Government.

Arrangements had been concluded with the B. B. C. (British Broadcasting Corporation) for broadcasting to America not only the recent speech of Lloyd George but also of the campaign speeches of Snowden, Henderson, Samuel and of some from more radical leaders. Fortunately, I heard of this a few hours before the first speech—that of Lloyd George. I entered a strong protest against all this broadcasting, stating, however, that I did so personally and not officially.

As a result, the British Broadcasting Corporation, without public explanation, cancelled it. My reason given was that the disturbed condition of public feeling, especially among the depositing classes in the United States, was such that no risks of increasing it by the broadcasting of exciting speeches from here should be taken. My intervention was fortunate for quite a part of Lloyd George's speech was to the effect that the United States was in a most dangerous banking and industrial crisis, inferentially brought upon it by its tariff policy. To be sure, his speech was published in the United States, but that is a very different kind of distribution than one to millions of radio sets, many of them in smaller communities where the smaller banks of the country, which are having the hardest fight to survive, are located.

The sudden cancellation of this broadcasting provoked widespread press inquiries as to its cause, but the British Broadcasting Corporation, while it deals in a miscellaneous and variegated vocal output of enormous amount, kept its own tongue under strict and wise restraint.

London,
October 25, 1931.

Hoover has shown fine qualities of leadership in this crisis. It is a fortunate thing for our nation that he is our President at this particular time. He has never stopped "trying" no matter how this or that effort disappointed both him and the public, and recently the beneficial outcome of his courage and initiative is plainly evident.

Today, President Hoover transmits to me through the State Department a line of thought on the subject of the possible establishment of a stable future market on a gold basis for sterling, stating that it is for my own consideration and unofficial inquiry if I deem it wise. This is a subject which I have been discussing from time to time in my official cables.

In these anxious times I have been declining all current invitations but have fulfilled on Friday and Saturday (yesterday) three engagements made several months ago.

On Friday, Caro and I went to Leamington, leaving on the morning train. We were entertained at lunch by the Countess of Warwick at the historic Castle of Warwick, together with a few others concerned with the school which I later addressed in the afternoon.

Reaching home in the evening I attended the first annual banquet of a new medical college.

Last night I was the guest at their 18th Annual Dinner of the Royal Marines Old Comrades Association (London). I have seldom in my life had such a reception as here. The speech of Colonel William P. Drury, the president, deeply impressed me,

Journal as Ambassador to Great Britain

and when, after his introduction, I arose I threw away the speech I had been formulating in my mind and spoke on British law and order—a subject subconsciously in the minds of everyone there at this particular time.

London,
Thursday, October 29, 1931.

The general election on Tuesday resulted in an overwhelming victory for MacDonald and the National Government. All except a few scattering returns are now in and the next Parliament will stand about 552 for and only 56 against the Government. Mac-Donald's splendid fight in Seaham, his constituency which he represented in the last Parliament as a Labour member, resulted in his election as a National Labour member by nearly six thousand majority over the Labour candidate. He could have run in a safe district but, like a thoroughbred, he chose the high hurdle with its greater risk. By so doing, this personal victory adds both to his prestige and power as head of the new National Government.

Britain has now made a splendid start in the long and difficult work of financial, industrial and trade reconstruction.

As a guest of Ambassador de Fleuriau, with him and de Cartier, the Belgian Ambassador, I heard the returns at the Savoy Hotel where great enthusiasm prevailed.

This afternoon, having received a cable from the State Department, asking for information as to the British attitude toward an international monetary conference, and knowing that MacDonald would go to Scotland tomorrow for a time, I made an engagement to meet him at 10 Downing Street at 5:30 this afternoon. When I met him there he told me that at his desk this morning he had just written on a sheet of paper "General and Mrs. Dawes" when the door opened and his Secretary told him I had telephoned that I wished to come and see him. This looked like telepathy. He said he had made the notation so as to save an early evening for him and Ishbel to come to the Embassy where, before the fire and in the midst of tobacco smoke, he and I could foregather and talk over his recent experience.

Photo by Navana, Ltd., London

BARON DE CARTIER DE MARCHIENNE

Journal as Ambassador to Great Britain

His old friend, Sir Alexander Grant, was with him. MacDonald was at the end of a strenuous day. He had called on the King in the morning and except for a short Cabinet meeting, had spent most of the day trying to select his new Cabinet. He says he is having a hard time of it. For Baldwin he has words of highest praise. The latter is cooperating to the last degree. But the Conservative pressure upon Baldwin in making his selections for Conservative representation in the new Cabinet is so embarrassingly great that MacDonald told me he had said to Baldwin that possibly his only practicable way out might be to let MacDonald make them.

MacDonald has been through a great strain but looks well. As Grant said, he will have his reaction a day or so later and must take a few days' rest.

The purpose of my call was to inquire about the international monetary conference which Laval had told the President that Lord Reading, on his recent visit to Paris, had requested be called. MacDonald said that Reading had made no such request, and that evidently Laval had misunderstood him. He also said that the British Government in this matter will proceed only after we both have discussed it and after we have mutually agreed to the wisdom, purpose and plan of such a conference.

Last Sunday night, Sir Josiah Stamp and his family took dinner with us. As he is a director of the Bank of England and daily consulted in its important matters, I gave him some questions for answer about the prospects of the establishment of a forward market for sterling. This paper I handed to him and he wrote his answer on its back. I attach it hereto.

Memorandum to Stamp

Sterling must be revalued on a gold basis and a stable pound future market must be established if Britain is to hold its position in the financing of world trade.

In the ordinary course, the continental countries which have devalued currency have allowed the matter to drift an indefinite time until values had settled under natural conditions at a point considered safe to stabilize. Would it contribute to the shortening of the time necessary to determine the safe point of valuation if a future market were established now in sterling dealings as far as six months?

In the present situation is not this possible: that as soon as such a market

407

was opened, six months' forward sales would be at somewhat less rate than current, but at the same moment present values would stabilize at a point equal to the six months quotation, less interest charges, and the tendency of the time factor on 30, 60, 90 and 180 day sales would be to minimize immediate fluctuations in sterling transactions?

Again, would not the innumerable hedging and arbitrage transactions over six months act as a sort of mattress stabilizing every point and would soon indicate the natural point of valuation?

The obvious major purpose of such future market would be to allow stabilization of commercial bills in foreign trade, which are now being seriously damaged by the unknown value of sterling at the time of payment.

Britain is performing a large world service in financing foreign trade bills, but how can it be continued unless some sort of futures' market is established?

Reply of Sir Josiah C. Stamp

1. The London earnings from the sterling bill are so important an item in the balance of trade and so irreplaceable (it would take 60 millions of new exports to make good 10 millions of loss) that every effort must be made to defend the London position.

2. Some think our position should be narrowed by cutting down our range. I would cut out the speculative and finance bills, but try to keep all the genuine trade bills.

3. If we do not succeed in holding sterling bills, they cannot be immediately replaced by dollars and francs, and world trade will suffer badly—this will hurt us all.

4. To keep the bill, sterling must be found to be reasonably stable for a minimum of three months. Apart from this, slow variation to a new equilibrium does not matter much.

5. The chief lack is a forward market for sterling dollars, 3 to 6 months. This existed in 1920–25, and should be deliberately formed and backed until individual risk takers support naturally. Not much more is wanted.

6. It is no use attempting it until the Government is stable.

7. We should not attempt a *de jure* stabilization on a fixed gold devaluation until we are quite sure of our position and until we have had an international gold conference, because the pound at $4.20 or $4.00 can get us into just as serious trouble as at $4.86 if gold movements go on as badly as before. We ought not to tie ourselves to gold at all until it has promised to behave itself and not wobble. This may be too much for France, and possibly U.S.A.

8. Possibly a new kind of link with gold, not at a fixed point, but within a range, will be invented.

9. This larger range problem need not get in the way of a 90 day stability—the trader doesn't mind sterling being at a different point for trade bills so much if it doesn't change during the currency of this bill.

10. It may be that the risks of a future market at the outset can be shared between the two countries.

Journal as Ambassador to Great Britain

London,
November 8, 1931.

MacDonald has chosen a strong cabinet. Eleven of the twenty members are Conservatives, as should be, since the majority of the new House is overwhelmingly Conservative. The leading members of the Cabinet besides MacDonald are Stanley Baldwin (Lord President of the Council), Neville Chamberlain (Chancellor of the Exchequer), Sir John Simon (Secretary of State for Foreign Affairs), Walter Runciman (President of the Board of Trade), Sir Herbert Samuel (Secretary of State for Home Affairs), Sir Samuel Hoare (Secretary for India), and J. H. Thomas (Secretary for Dominion Affairs). Snowden stays in the Cabinet as Lord Privy Seal, a place less exacting in its work than his former position as Chancellor of the Exchequer.

I do not regard an international monetary conference as wise at this particular time, and have so advised our Government. If it were called before the stabilization of the pound sterling in relation to gold, it would surely resolve itself into a committee of the whole on this particular subject which would be a procedure both unnecessary and unwise.

France and ourselves are both interested in sustaining our respective international trade, and do not want to lose that part of our trade which, owing to Great Britain's long established international banking system, must be carried on in terms of the pound sterling and not in dollars or francs. We both, therefore, want to see the pound stabilized and a pound future market provided for. Until this is done, general international business cannot to any great extent be done in terms of pound sterling and will suffer severely in volume.

Now, this stabilization of the pound is primarily Great Britain's problem. It is a business question, and will be largely settled by events and conditions which will determine hereafter the natural point at which sterling can be safely stabilized in its relation to gold. Therefore events should now be awaited. Otherwise, any conference called would be confronted necessarily by hypothetical questions. A conference called by the Government nominally as a monetary conference, but which would certainly concern itself with the question of pound stabilization, should not be called in any event unless agreement in principle on this question has already been reached in preliminary negotiations. In such cases, if preliminary agreement is reached, the conference is unnecessary; if not so reached, the conference would be foredoomed to failure.

If such a conference was called at this particular time, an extreme difference of opinion might develop as to what should be the nature of the cooperation, if any, of the United States and France in the stabilization of the pound. There would be no valid ground for the United States and France to extend anything but a moral help to the pound unless help additional to that is plainly and unmistakably justified by their self-interest.

If this self-interest exists, our individual banks and merchants concerned must be relied upon for the really constructive and practical contributions in the situation. In the determination of their attitude from a business standpoint, these parties would only be embarrassed and handicapped by any pronouncement of a conference called by the Governments. The fact is that the pound stabilization question is primarily a trade and financial, and not a political, matter.

For the present, at least, if Governments discuss it, they should do so through diplomatic channels, not in an international conference. The effect of the inevitable failure of a conference from the calling of which the public will have expected a definite settlement, will only tend to unsettle the gradually reviving state of confidence in our own country and elsewhere. It will introduce a business question into politics with a naturally adverse effect.

> On Train for Paris,
> November 13, 1931.

On last Monday evening, when I was attending the annual Lord Mayor's dinner at Guildhall and during the Prime Minister's speech, a note was handed me saying that our Secretary of

SIR JOHN SIMON

State wished me to speak with him by telephone on an urgent matter.

He notified me that our Government desired me to go to Paris and represent it during the meetings of the Council of the League of Nations commencing Monday, the 16th, to consider and act upon the Manchurian situation in a continuation of the endeavor to avert the threatened war between Japan and China. The Secretary talked with me for a considerable time, explaining the situation as he viewed it. He sent me the announcement of my detail to this duty which he gave the press as follows:

I have asked General Dawes, the Ambassador in London, to go to Paris during the coming meeting of the statesmen who compose the Council of the League of Nations, inasmuch as this meeting will consider the present situation in Manchuria and questions may arise which will affect the interests or treaty obligations of the United States. I desire to have at hand in Paris a man of General Dawes' standing particularly as the American Ambassador to Paris is at home on leave. It is not anticipated that General Dawes will find it necessary to take part in the meeting of the League Council, but he will be in a position to confer with the representatives of the other nations present in Paris in case such conference should seem desirable.

I got busy at once and have been ever since. I first saw my friend, Matsudaira, the Japanese Ambassador to Great Britain. Our personal friendship facilitated the frankest kind of a discussion between us. I then saw Sir John Simon, the new Foreign Secretary, with whom also I have had for some time the most friendly relations. After we had gone over the situation, I suggested that he meet Matsudaira and me together, as we all seemed to be united in purpose with about the same views as to the procedure the situation required.

Yesterday the three of us met for a long conference. In the light of possible events, all attitudes and plans are, of course, tentative. Last night at the Embassy, Matsudaira and I had another conference. Both he and Simon will be in Paris by Monday.

Through the Chinese Legation, I got in touch with Alfred Sao-ke Sze, the Chinese representative on the League Council at Geneva, and will meet him at my hotel in Paris at noon on Sunday. Through the French Ambassador, I made an appointment to meet Briand at 11:30 tomorrow at the Quai D'Orsay.

Journal as Ambassador to Great Britain

In my first talk with Matsudaira, we both felt that the League should withdraw its time limit for the evacuation of Japanese troops. To have made it was a serious error, in my judgment. We agreed that the immediate objective should be the cessation of hostilities under an armistice, pending discussion of the best agencies and methods for final settlement. In my talk with Simon, immediately afterward, he agreed that while the League might have the better juridical argument, Japan, notwithstanding, seemed to have the argument in its favor as to the necessary location of troops. His idea was the same as that of Matsudaira and myself, independently formed, namely that the League had best propose a cessation of hostilities without suggesting any change at present in the location of Japanese troops, pending an agreement upon the agencies and methods of securing final settlement. This, he said, seemed to be the Prime Minister's view of the matter in the short talk he had had with him. Simon had instinctively realized, as had Stimson, the unwisdom of the time limit clause for Japanese troop evacuation in the League proposition.

All this was before the meeting yesterday of Simon, Matsudaira and myself.

I am finishing these notes on the Channel boat.

> Dictated on my return from
> Paris, December 11, 1931.

The Manchurian situation on the evening of November 13, 1931, when I arrived in Paris, was well epitomized in an editorial by Walter Lippmann in the Paris edition of the *New York Herald* of December 6, as follows:

The known and undisputed facts are that since September 18, Japan has occupied all the railroads in southern Manchuria in which Japanese capital is invested; that she has occupied many Chinese cities including the capitals of the three Manchurian provinces; that she has driven out the local Chinese authority in the occupied region; that she refuses to evacuate it until China agrees to accept her interpretation of the treaties, and that she has thus far refused to state what her treaty demands are or to have them discussed in the presence of any neutral witness.

It is known, too, that the matter was first brought to the attention of the

Journal as Ambassador to Great Britain

Council of the League on Saturday, September 19, by the Japanese delegate, Mr. Yoshizawa, who assured it that his Government had taken all possible measures to prevent the local incident at Mukden from leading to undesirable complications; that by Monday, September 21, the Japanese had occupied the railway up to Changchun, and that on that day, Mr. Sze, the Chinese delegate, invoked Article XI of the Covenant. It is known that the Council addressed several appeals to both sides not to aggravate matters, and that on October 24, it adopted a resolution by a vote of 13 to 1, Japan dissenting, calling upon Japan to evacuate by November 16 and upon China to make arrangements for the safety of the Japanese in evacuated territories. It is known, finally, that Japan refused to comply and, in fact, greatly extended the area of military occupation.

I also append a copy of the resolution adopted by the Council of the League of Nations, sitting in Geneva, on October 24, 1931, which read as follows:

The League Council, in pursuance of the Resolution passed on September 30, and noting, in addition, the invocation by the Chinese Government of Article XI of the League Covenant; and that Article II of the Pact of Paris has also been invoked by several Governments, recalls:

(1) The undertaking given the Council by the signatories of the Governments in that Resolution; and particularly the statement of the Japanese representative that the Japanese Government would continue, as rapidly as possible, the withdrawal of troops into the railway zone, proportionately as the safety of the lives and property of the Chinese nationals is effectively assured; and the statement of the Chinese representative that his Government will assume responsibility for the safety of the lives and property of the Chinese nationals outside that zone, and the pledge which implies the effective protection of Chinese subjects residing in Manchuria;

(2) The Council recalls further that both Governments had given assurances that they would refrain from any measures which might aggravate the situation and are therefore bound not to resort to any aggressive policy or action, and to take measures to suppress hostile action;

(3) The Council recalls the Japanese statement that Japan has no territorial designs in Manchuria, and notes that this statement is in accordance with the terms of the League Covenant and the Nine-Power Treaty, the signatories of which are pledged to respect the sovereignty, independence and administrative integrity of China;

Being convinced that the fulfillment of these assurances and undertakings is essential for the restoration of normal relations between the two parties, the Council:

(a) Calls on the Japanese Government immediately to proceed progressively with the withdrawal of their troops into the railway zone so that total withdrawal may be effected before the next meeting of the Council;

(b) Calls on the Chinese Government in the execution of their general pledge to assume responsibility for the safety of the lives and property of all Chinese subjects in Manchuria, to make such arrangements for taking

413

over the territory thus affected as will insure the safety of the lives and property of Japanese subjects there, and requests the Chinese Government to associate with the Chinese authorities designated for the above purpose, the representatives of other powers, in order that such representatives may follow the execution of such arrangement;

(4) The Council recommends that the Chinese and Japanese Governments should immediately appoint representatives to arrange the details of the execution of all points relating to evacuation and to take over all evacuated territory so that they may proceed smoothly and without delay;

(5) The Council recommends that the Japanese and Chinese Governments as soon as evacuation is completed begin direct negotiations on questions outstanding between them, particularly on those arising out of the recent incidents, as well as those relating to existing difficulties due to the railway situation in Manchuria;

For this purpose, the Council suggests that the two parties should establish a conciliation committee or some such permanent machine.

The Council decides to adjourn until November 16th, on which date it will again examine the situation, but authorizes the President to convene a meeting at any earlier date should such, in his opinion, be desirable.

On my arrival at Paris, I gave to the press immediately the following statement:

The views of my Government correspond in general with those of the Council of the League in the Manchurian situation and in the endeavor to prevent war and forward a peaceful settlement.

The Council of the League in this connection is considering matters which presumably affect not only the treaty rights and general interests of the United States under the Nine-Power Pact but relate to the Kellogg Pact as well. I will be in Paris therefore to confer with the members of the Council individually with regard to a problem which is of common concern and involves mutual treaty interests. I shall hope to make every contact which is essential to the exercise of any influence we may have in properly supporting this effort to avert war and to make effective the Kellogg Pact.

The United States is not a member of the League and the methods which have been followed on occasions when a matter of mutual concern and self-interest to the League and ourselves is under consideration, have varied. On this occasion there is no anticipation on the part of my Government or myself that it will be found necessary for me to attend the meeting of the Council.

It was the feeling of our State Department that the present objective of the United States and that of the Council of the League of Nations, in principle, was the same in that they were both seeking to prevent war and to bring about a peaceful settlement of the difficulties between Japan and China.

Journal as Ambassador to Great Britain

The United States desired to associate itself with the League in this effort, but did not wish that the association should become an alliance. Our Government left it largely to my discretion to contribute in any proper way towards finding ways and means by which China and Japan might be brought to agree upon some method which would achieve the prevention of war between them and result in a peaceful settlement. I was in Paris as the representative of the United States to confer with the Council of the League in regard to a difficult problem which was of common concern.

I had long had the firm conviction that the United States could exert a more powerful influence for peace in the world by a rigid maintenance of the independent right of judgment and action at all times in a matter of mutual concern to the United States and the League.

Our Government had stated in the announcement of my assignment to this work on the Manchurian situation that it was not anticipated I would find it necessary to attend the meetings of the Council of the League and, by this intimation, as well as in its communications to me during the month I was in Paris, the matter of my attendance was left to my discretion. I fully realized, however, that in view of the importance of the critical situation in Manchuria, my unexplained declination of a general invitation of the Council to attend its meetings would be regarded by many as lessening the influence of the United States toward a peaceful settlement, and my right course, therefore, was to hold a decision on this matter of attendance in abeyance until I could know better from contact with the situation where my duty lay.

I called upon M. Briand, the President of the Council of the League, at the Quai D'Orsay on the next day, November 14. In its resolution of October 24, the Council, by a vote of thirteen to one, had called upon Japan to evacuate by November 16 the Manchurian territory outside the railroad zone where it was not allowed by treaty to maintain troops. Secretary Stimson had realized the unwisdom of the Council in setting a time limit for evacuation, and in his communications to the Chinese and Japanese Governments had not associated our Government in the Council's suggestion to this effect.

415

Journal as Ambassador to Great Britain

In my conversation with Briand, he inferentially admitted that the time limit suggestion of the Council was an error by his statement to me that it seemed necessary for the time being that no League recommendation as to immediate change in troop location be made, nor, indeed, any reference to troop movements as necessarily indicating any general policy of Japan other than the protection of Japanese life and property. We discussed the necessity of a continuing recognition of the fact that any pronouncement by the League or ourselves must take into consideration the importance of preserving, as far as possible, the prestige of the Governments of both Japan and China, in order that any adverse domestic public opinions might not be aroused, making more difficult a peaceable settlement. Briand inquired as to the probable attitude of the United States if, instead of proceeding under Article XI as at present, the Council hereafter came to consider possible action under Articles XV and XVI of the Covenant, which provide for sanctions.

My reply was that I had been informed that the United States would not join in the consideration of the question of sanctions or in the enforcing of them if hereafter imposed by the League, acting under Articles XV and XVI. Briand then brought up the question of my personal attendance at the sessions of the Council of the League, which question had confronted me at every meeting I had had with the press, and indeed with nearly everybody else. Briand maintained that if I did not attend the sessions it would be considered generally as an indication of an attitude on the part of our Government of less cooperation than heretofore in the purposes of the League in this situation, and therefore be a decided injury to its prestige and influence.

In answer, I told him that in my present judgment, if I did attend the Council meetings, it would lessen the helpfulness of the United States in the situation, and that a parallel cooperation of the United States, reserving its independence of action and decision, would be more effective in securing peace than if, by attendance at the meetings, to the curiosity of the world press and the justified apprehension of my Government, I became involved in the discussions of methods to be adopted by a body of which the United States was not even a member. I told him, however, that I was holding in abeyance any final decision in this matter of attendance until contact with the situation in Paris for a time would better enable me to settle the question wisely.

I said further that if in the future I came to believe that the greatest influence of the United States for the common objective of peace could be exercised by my attendance at the meetings of the Council, I would not hesitate to attend them.

It is difficult for one who has not engaged in them to realize how strenuous these protracted international negotiations become where continuing emergency is involved in a continually changing situation, and where the negotiations must be conducted between a large number of individuals. To cover these particular negotiations required cables during the month between the State Department at Washington and myself aggregating over 100,000 words, besides numbers of telephonic consultations between the President and the Secretary of State and myself. Obviously I cannot adequately cover them here.

The fact, however, that what occurred constitutes to some extent at least a precedent for the useful cooperation of the United States and the League, acting independently in matters of mutual concern and interest, leads me to comment more particularly upon my own activities.

It was not the desire of the American Government that, as its representative, I be put in the position of an arbitrator or initiator of League action, but to use my discretion in contributing by advice and counsel toward the finding of ways and means whereby China and Japan might be brought to agreement under a proper settlement. This implied on my part a recognition of League leadership in the devising of methods and formulas where those methods and formulas appealed to our individual judgment as wise.

I do not wish the fact that I am emphasizing in these notes the details of the relationship of the efforts of the United States to those of the League and such acts of cooperation as we took on lines parallel to those of the League, to create an impression that I regard our part in the negotiations as not conducted under League leadership. This would be unfair and unjustified. Reserving independence of judgment, most of what I did was supplementary to the plan of the Council, upon which chiefly devolved the responsibility of initiation.

The negotiations on the succeeding days, November 15, 16, 17, 18, 19 and 20, were critical and to me highly educational as to the proper course which, as the representative of the United States, I must continue to pursue. I found the attitude of the United States in this situation seemed one of first importance in the minds of the representatives of both China and Japan and was also necessarily a prime consideration by the Council itself in the determination of its own policy. As a consequence, the recurring crises in the negotiations during these days, and indeed generally until the Council had published its tentative Resolution on November 25 first crystallized at my office in the Ritz Hotel.

Upon receiving messages from their Governments which, if presented to the League, would create an impasse and tend to bring about the failure of the negotiations, both Matsudaira and Sze would first bring the situation to my attention. Kenkichi Yoshizawa, the Japanese representative on the Council, had called upon me to say that he had asked Matsudaira to represent him in his contacts with me. During those days also, Sir Eric Drummond, the Secretary-General of the League and thus representative of the Council, would call for a preliminary discussion of the different situations, and the course which seemed wise to take from the standpoint of the Council. Sir John Simon and I would also exchange calls. This made it possible for me on several critical occasions to exercise an influence in preventing impasses which might have occurred if the representatives of China and Japan had first gone directly to the Council, where the nature of the difficulty was sure to have become public before it was settled. It was evident, during these negotiations, that whenever a matter was given to the League Council for confidential discussion at a "closed" meeting, it became public property in the press the next day.

The fact that the Japanese and Chinese representatives both notified me first at my separate office of the instructions of their Governments as to the representations which they were about to make before the Council, also enabled me at times to assist in the delaying of presentation of dangerous ultimatums to the Council until our own Government could exert a conciliatory influence through our Ambassadors at Tokyo and Nanking in an effort to resolve them. It also led me at times to advise the Council of the League, through Sir Eric Drummond, to postpone a public meeting of the Council where such dangerous ultimatums might be made public. An instance of the latter occurred on November 15, the day before the first meeting of the Council, when the preliminary statement which I had received of the then attitude of the Japanese Government made it certain that if that should be stated in a public meeting of the League, it would create an immediate impasse. I promptly brought this situation to the attention of Sir John Simon, who had just arrived in Paris, of Sir Eric Drummond of the Council, and of Massigli, who represented Briand. It was then arranged that at the first meeting of the Council there would be no speeches except the opening speech of Briand, followed by an adjournment subject to the call of the president. No opportunity was, therefore, given for a premature public precipitation of the serious impasse then existing between China and Japan.

Sir John Simon left early November 19th for London, after having given extremely useful cooperation and advice in the general situation. He did not again return, but Great Britain was still represented on the Council by Lord Cecil. During all this time, the question of my attendance at the meetings of the Council of the League kept interjecting itself among the members of the Council and of the press. Mr. Arthur Sweetser, of the League Secretariat, assigned to the American cooperation with the League, was present at all meetings of the League Council, both closed and open, for the purpose of reporting its proceedings to me. These reports showed that the question of my attendance was under considerable discussion at the meetings of the Council.

My experience, by this time, having demonstrated beyond question that the greatest influence which our Government could exert in the Paris negotiations, would be subserved by my nonattendance at the Council meetings, I determined to close once and for all such discussions and announce publicly that I would not attend the meetings, giving the reasons therefor.

I therefore, on November 19, called up Secretary Stimson by

telephone to secure approval of this action. I suggested that he might make the statement of this decision from Washington. He replied the next morning to the suggestion made over the telephone, giving me a suggested press statement to be given out if it seemed to be helpful. He said that the President and he both thought that any such statement had better come from me in Paris rather than from Washington, since the limitations of our action with the League seemed to be better understood at Washington than it was by the members of the League themselves. He also sent me a statement of the general position of the United States, suggesting that I might use it as an explanation of my position to Briand, if it seemed advisable.

I saw Briand on November 20 and explained to him the general attitude of the United States, of which he expressed approval. I also told him that the eventual public reaction upon the cooperation of the League and the United States in the interests of peace would be based upon their respective acts and not upon press discussions of the methods by which we achieved cooperation, and informed him that I had decided not to attend the meetings of the Council. It was a friendly discussion. I said that I was sure he now realized, as well as I did, that my present method of conferring individually with the members of the Council as to matters of mutual interest and concern to the United States and the League was, in fact, the only useful and constructive method of procedure on my part, since it did not result, among other things, in premature press discussion of tentative opinions.

After this interview, on the same day, I gave out textually to the Press the following statement of my position:

I have been directed to come to Paris for the purpose of discussing with the representatives of the different nations assembled here the crisis which is taking place in Manchuria. As a signatory of the Pact of Paris and of the so-called Nine-Power Treaty, the United States is deeply interested with its fellow signatories in seeing that the lofty purpose of those treaties is fulfilled. It has been the hope of my Government that a settlement in accordance with the principles of those treaties would be arrived at through discussion and conciliation during the conference in Paris and that the presence here of a representative of the United States would contribute to bring about a solution through this method. The United States is, of course, not a member of the League of Nations, and it, therefore, cannot take part in the discussions bearing upon the application of the machinery of the League Covenant. Since, in the present crisis, it may be possible that such discussions may arise, it is obvious that my presence at the meetings of the Council would not only be inappropriate, but might even embarrass the efforts of the Council itself. But the position thus necessarily assumed by the United States in no way indicates that the United States is not wholly sympathetic with the efforts being made by the League to support the objective of peace in Manchuria. The United States must, however, preserve its full freedom of judgment as to its course.

During the period between November 14 and November 24, as the result of its deliberations and negotiations, the Council of the League developed a tentative draft of a resolution to be presented for final adoption by the Council of the League which had been agreed to in effect by all members of the Council except Japan and China. On November 24, this proposed draft had reached a form practically the same as that finally adopted by the League on December 9. I determined that this was the appropriate occasion to let the attitude of the United States be known upon the proposal. Briand stated before the Council that morning that it would be a useful contribution if the United States would let its attitude be known and, if it approved, would so inform China and Japan.

The text of this resolution as finally adopted on December 9 was as follows:

(1) The Council reaffirms the resolution passed unanimously by it September 30, 1931, by which the parties declare that they are solemnly bound, and it therefore calls on the Chinese and Japanese Governments to take all steps necessary to assure its execution so that the withdrawal of the Japanese troops within the railway zone may be effected as speedily as possible.

(2) Considering events have assumed more serious aspects since the meeting of the Council on October 24, the Council notes that the two parties will undertake to adopt all measures necessary to avoid any further aggravation of the situation and refrain from any initiative which may lead to further fighting or loss of life.

(3) The Council invites the two parties to continue to keep the Council informed regarding the developments of the situation.

(4) The Council invites other members of the Council to furnish the Council with any information received from their representatives on the spot.

(5) Without prejudice to carrying out the above-mentioned measures, and desiring, in view of the special circumstances of the case to contribute towards the final and fundamental solution by the two Governments of the questions at issue between them, the Council decides to appoint a Commis-

sion of five members to study on the subject and report to the Council on any circumstances which may affect international relations and threaten to destroy the peace between Japan and China or the good understanding between them on which peace depends.

The Chinese and Japanese Governments will each have the right of nominating one assessor to assist the Commission, and the two Governments will furnish the Commission all facilities to obtain on the spot whatever information it may require.

It is understood that should the two parties initiate any negotiations, these would not fall within the scope of the Commission nor would it be within the Commission's competence to interfere with the military arrangements of either party.

The appointment and the deliberations of the Commission shall not prejudice in any way the undertakings given by the Chinese Government in the resolution of September 30, as regards the withdrawal of the Chinese troops within the railway zone.

(6) Between now and its next ordinary session which is to be held on January 25, 1932, the Council, which retains charge of the matter, invites the President to follow up the questions and to assume it afresh, if necessary.

The text of this resolution had not, however, been made public, and it was vitally important that with the publication of the text of the tentative resolution, there be published simultaneously a statement on the part of our Government approving the general plan of settlement embodied in the resolution. By this method would best be indicated, not only the joint attitude of the Council of the League and the United States, but the parallel efforts and cooperation which had led to it.

I then sent by Sweetser the following suggestions to Briand, confidentially:

(1) The United States is active with the Parties.

(2) Will gladly come to see Briand when answer to Sze's despatch is received by the Council, which will be some time tomorrow. (Parenthetically, Sze has informed the League that he has sent cables to his Government on the situation to which he expects an answer tomorrow.)

(3) Mr. Dawes feels that the United States cannot express any opinion on Council's negotiations until at least the text of Resolution is published.

I regarded it as particularly important that no public reference should be made to this cooperative and parallel attitude of the United States until the proposed resolution of the League was published. Under the normal procedure of the League, the reso-

ARISTIDE BRIAND

lution could not be valid until presented at a meeting of the Council and there agreed to by China and Japan. I wanted to be sure, however, that the Council, in connection with the presentation of this particular tentative resolution, was agreed between themselves, excepting Japan and China, regarding its publication and presentation. I wired the State Department, that what was in my mind was to ask Briand, as president of the Council, to give to the press, well in advance of the public Council meeting, the text of the agreed-upon resolution which he would present for consideration, and that then, as we might decide, we could make a statement of the favorable attitude of the United States in principle toward the method recommended in the resolution. Our Government wired me approving this program, to be used at my discretion.

On November 25, having learned that this method appealed to Briand, I sent him confidentially, through Sir Eric Drummond, a copy of the statement I proposed to make after the publication by the Council of the tentative Resolution, as follows:

The United States Government approves the general plan of settlement embodied in the proposed Resolution of the Council and has so informed both China and Japan. It has urged upon them acquiescence in the general plan embodied in the proposed Resolution.

I gave this statement to Drummond with the understanding, that, as representing the United States, I would make it public when notified by Briand that the conditions we agreed upon had been complied with. On November 25, therefore, following immediately the publication of the communiqué of the Council giving the text of the tentative resolution, I gave the statement to the press. Thus was the United States associated with the League before the world in this effort for a peaceful settlement between Japan and China.

The conferences after this time were largely devoted toward getting the Japanese and Chinese to agree to support the resolution in the Council. If they complied, the vote on the resolution would be unanimous, and this would keep the procedure under Article XI. During this time the various troop movements and military clashes in Manchuria and the question of the creation of a neutral zone, including Chinchow, were the subject of constant discussion. By December 1, there were a few remaining points of difference between Japan and China, the principal ones being the manner in which the declaration and resolution of the League would cover the point of protection of Japanese nationals against bandits. The draft of the resolution, together with the declarations and reservations made by China and Japan after its passage, will indicate the nature of the discussions at this period, and they need no recapitulation. It may be said that not until a day or so before the resolution was finally passed by the Council, was it at all certain that either the Japanese or the Chinese would agree to it at the last public meeting of the Council.

The news from China as I am dictating this morning (December 16, 1931) to the effect that President Chiang Kai-shek and Wellington Koo have resigned and that Nanking, the seat of Government, is at present filled with a mob of Chinese students and in a state of disorder, leads me to digress into a statement of those broad considerations which the United States and certain nations represented on the Council of the League had necessarily in mind from the beginning of the negotiations. In this way will be better explained the difficulties which constantly confronted us in the Paris negotiations because of the continuing instability of the then existing Chinese Government and the fact that the internal conflict upon policy between the military and civil elements in the Japanese Cabinet resulted in occasional and unexpected changes in the attitude in Paris of the representatives of the Japanese Government acting under instructions from Tokyo.

In fact, during much of the time it seemed as if we were dealing with two separate Governments in Japan and no Government at all in China, representing real power of decision. The inflamed condition of Chinese and Japanese domestic public sentiment endangered the existence of the respective Governments whenever they submitted constructive suggestions to the Council in the interests of a peaceful settlement.

In this situation, as Sir John Simon had said, from the juridical standpoint, China had the best of the argument, but from the standpoint of realities, the argument seemed to be with Japan. This was so from the first. Every advance of Japanese troops outside of the railroad zone, in which it had the right under treaty to maintain troops, constituted on the part of Japan, not only a disregard of the Kellogg Pact and of that somewhat indefinite set of precedents which is called international law, but as well an infraction of the Nine-Power Pact guaranteeing the integrity of China and the "Open Door", to which, among the nations then represented, the United States, Great Britain, France and Italy were signatories. On the other hand, Manchuria was in a state of disorder, with the Chinese authorities in many localities unable to protect the lives and property of Japanese nationals from bandits and other hostile elements in the Chinese population in Manchuria.

The occasional movements of Japanese troops to protect the lives and property of resident Japanese, whatever laws and treaties provided, was however, recognized generally as inevitable and unavoidable. It was evident that no Japanese Government could stand which, under these circumstances, would not move its troops to protect Japanese residents in Manchuria from massacre. Civilized nations employ their marines constantly in similar efforts, and it will be remembered that our own Government, when we were at peace with Mexico, sent General Pershing into that country in command of 10,000 troops on a bandit chasing expedition after Villa.

During these negotiations, it seemed to us a question of doubt whether either the Japanese Government at Tokyo, or the Chinese Government at Nanking, could completely control the movements of their soldiers on the field.

From the juridical standpoint, the outside nations could move under the Kellogg Pact, the Covenant of the League of Nations, or the Nine-Power Pact. At the time the Paris negotiations commenced, they had moved only under the Kellogg Pact and under Article XI of the League Pact, and not under the Nine-Power Pact which had been equally infracted. The reason for this action is obvious. Under the Kellogg Pact and Article XI of the Covenant of the League of Nations, only settlements by peaceful methods are envisaged. Any resolution of the League of Nations under Article XI would become valid only by unanimous vote of the fourteen members of the Council of the League, including those of Japan and China. It was extremely important to secure the agreement of Japan and China to a resolution under Article XI of the League Covenant, not simply because it would bind them to an agreement for peaceful settlement of the present difficulties, but because it would constitute a formula for the relationship of those two nations in the future, behind which might be mobilized the moral sentiment of the world.

From the beginning this was in the mind of our Government. It fully realized, as did the members of the Council of the League, that if there was a failure in reaching unanimous agreement to a League resolution of this kind, the next step, if taken, would inevitably be a convocation of the Powers signatory to the Nine-Power Pact. Such a convocation, bringing together for a discussion of the situation, the signatory powers of the Nine-Power Pact, would inevitably involve them in the consideration of the use of force. Of the infraction of the treaty there would be no question. The nations would convene to discuss the matter of broken treaty obligations. In the event a settlement was not then reached with Japan, the other signatory nations would be confronted with the alternative of a humiliating acceptance of the status quo or a resort either to war or some form of sanctions. The League itself, under Articles XV and XVI of the League Covenant—which would not, of course, bind the United States—could proceed to sanctions by economic boycott.

The United States, as well as the members of the Council, had reason to make every possible effort for the settlement of the present impasse between China and Japan under Article XI of the Covenant of the League and the Kellogg Pact rather than under Articles XV and XVI of the Covenant or the Nine-Power Pact, although, to be sure, the resolution finally adopted by the League Council and approved in principle by the United States, has not settled the fundamental issues involved in the Manchurian situation.

While no one now can be safe in prediction, it would seem, nevertheless, that this resolution has at least brought about the prevention of a general war between China and Japan at this time, making possible a comparatively peaceful stabilization of

LORD ROBERT CECIL

the Manchurian situation and ensuring further peaceful discussion of the unsettled and fundamental issues involved.

Again, if the resolution had not been adopted, the prestige of the League of Nations would have been greatly damaged. In large part, due to the able leadership of Briand and Cecil, during these negotiations, the Council in several instances sacrificed juridical consistency to practical duty. By so doing, it saved to the world the prestige of the League which still can be used to mobilize the moral force of the world in time of emergency.

For the League and its work, these four weeks of parallel endeavor and cooperation have given me much respect. While fully recognizing its world usefulness, my contact with its work and methods, as representing the United States, likewise convinces me that for us to become an ally of the League instead of an associate in certain of its constructive efforts from time to time, would not materially aid to its influence, while it would be most destructive of our own.

It is manifestly improper for me to comment in detail upon the nature of the several prospective impasses between China and Japan which, precipitated publicly before the Council, might have caused the breaking off of negotiations and the delaying of the final resolution of which the independent intervention of our Government was a most important, if not the determining, influence. The respective representations made to me by the Chinese and Japanese which, presented, would have caused an impasse, were confidential and must be respected as such. At the time when one of these impasses was pending, Sir John Simon and Sir Eric Drummond called on me for a discussion of the situation, and presented a resolution of the Council for our consideration, which, in its form, was practically the one finally adopted. Simon and Drummond desired me to ask our Government to consider suggesting to both China and Japan that they be satisfied with the substance of what was suggested in the purely tentative declaration presented. Upon my presenting and recommending this suggestion to our Government by telephone, it acted upon it.

We again intervened directly between China and Japan during this period, making representations to them parallel to those of the League against any military measures which would further aggravate the Chinchow situation. This occurred about December 7.

The last public meeting of the Council which adopted unanimously the resolution, was held December 10. On December 9, at a session, Briand read the draft resolution, and Yoshizawa, the Japanese member of the Council, immediately thereafter requested an adjournment until the next afternoon. Yoshizawa's request for a delay was based upon a desire to receive instructions which he expected from Tokyo that evening as to whether Japan would prefer the Council text in reference to police measures, which was not entirely satisfactory to her, to be inserted in the declaration preceding the resolution, or to make a unilateral declaration of her own.

During the last few days, the question that engrossed all parties to the negotiations, including the Governments they represented at home, was the critical military situation around Chinchow. A misunderstanding had arisen between Japan and China in relation to the establishment of a neutral zone. This misunderstanding was such that it created a reaction in the respective domestic public sentiments of Japan and China. In the form the Japanese position had been stated, the lack of information as to the factors involved had created on the League Council and on the part of our own Government a strong resentment against Japan. The limits of the zone which Japan proposed were considered as designed by her to be unacceptable to the Chinese. This misunderstanding was serious and yet, as a matter of fact, there was no real ground for it.

On the night of December 9, Secretary Stimson called me up asking for information as to whether the resolution was likely to be passed, and at that time told me that from messages received from W. Cameron Forbes, our Ambassador at Tokyo, it was now plain to him that the limits of the neutral zone proposed by Japan had been determined by geographical considerations, as was fully recognized by China and Japan, and that our Government, in pressing Japan upon this point of the definition of the zone, had just discovered this fact, which he thought should be brought to the attention of the Council as clearing up the matter. This telephone call from the Secretary was received about 2:00 A.M.

This new statement of fact by telephone, which I immediately transmitted to the Council, induced some reflection on my part, and on the next day, preceding the meeting of the Council at 5:00 P.M., considerable activity. It nearly led to my making an appearance before the Council, after the resolution had been passed, in order to make a statement, with this important background, which I deemed might be of value in its effect not only upon public sentiment in China and Japan, but generally.

To make a long story short, in five or six hours of quite strenuous activity, and having altered the statement in minor details after submitting it to Briand, to Robert E. Olds (representing Sze), to Matsudaira and to Drummond, all of whom were agreed, I completed it.

In such an important international negotiation as this, it was necessary to give each party consulted some little time for consideration of the many possible repercussions involved. The parties I have named had had that opportunity. The matter of my appearance before the Council and of making necessary statements had been left to my discretion by our Government. However, about half an hour before I expected to go to the meeting of the Council, coming into the meeting after the resolution had been passed and its actual business concluded but before its adjournment in order to make a statement, I received another telephone call from Secretary Stimson, asking me how matters were going.

I then informed him of my intention in a short time to make the statement, which I read to him. He recognized its importance, but his time for its consideration was of necessity limited to our short telephone conversation. The Secretary suggested that Briand read the statement, which I told him was impracticable. He felt that he did not have sufficient time to consider the matter and, without argument, I told him that I would not make it. And, as matters have eventuated, it was perhaps well enough. However, I am quite sure that the statement would have done no harm, and it might have done some good. I append it hereto as an interesting recollection.

Journal as Ambassador to Great Britain

Proposed statement by me at close of Council session but not used

The patient labor of the Council has now resulted in an agreement of China and Japan to refrain from future aggression and for the appointment of a Commission. This agreement, if faithfully observed by both parties, may well lead to a final and peaceful solution of this difficult problem.

For the moment, through a misunderstanding alone, the discussion of a most promising effort of bringing about a cessation of hostilities between China and Japan is in abeyance. The misunderstanding arose as follows: Dr. Wellington Koo discussed tentatively with certain foreign Ministers at Nanking the cessation of hostilities between the armies and the mutual withdrawal of forces around Chinchow. This suggestion was not intended as a proposal to the Japanese Government but was made merely for the purpose of sounding out on the subject the Powers represented by the Ministers. This tentative suggestion of Dr. Koo, which he did not intend should be made to the Japanese Government, was conveyed to it in such a way that Japan regarded it as a definite proposition. The Japanese Government then made a definite proposition embodying the idea, agreeing to be responsible to the League for its observance of the arrangements, if made, and this was a chief factor in causing orders to be given for a retreat of its troops which were already advancing. As matters stand at present, therefore, the Japanese public have the impression that Japan has been misled into troop withdrawal, and China, having made its suggestion only for discussion, is in a position where if she orders her troops to withdraw, the public impression in China is created that China has been coerced. The situation is this:

China, in good faith, made a constructive suggestion for discussion, which, having been presented to Japan as a proposition instead of a suggestion, Japan then, in good faith, ordered a troop withdrawal.

An understanding of this situation by the public of both nations should make possible the further exploration of the original idea of Dr. Wellington Koo and the consequent proposition of Japan for a mutually satisfactory arrangement for a cessation of hostilities around Chinchow and a redisposition of the respective forces to avoid the risk of conflict. The continuance of such a discussion involves no humiliating concessions by either of the nations and will only emphasize the earnest desire of both for honorable peace.

On December 11th I received the following cable from Secretary Stimson:

The President and I are highly gratified by the manner in which you handled a most difficult job while in Paris. Your success in cooperating with the League materially assisted in obtaining a successful conclusion to the negotiations and your ability in the situation in upholding American prestige was skillful.

I join the President in extending my sincerest congratulations. Please felicitate Dooman on my behalf for his highly efficient and competent service.

STIMSON.

Journal as Ambassador to Great Britain

London,
December 20, 1931.

I arrived in London from Paris December 11th, exactly four weeks from my arrival in Paris on the Manchurian assignment. During this last week I have dictated a summary of my experience and work in Paris which I have inserted as a part of these notes.

During my stay in Paris I had little time to leave my office which I established in the Ritz Hotel. Between calls from my fellow negotiators, the preparation of cables, telephones from the President and Secretary Stimson at Washington, and calls from the journalists, not to speak of representatives from those time wasters—the self-appointed guardians of the peace of the world, whose numbers multiply in times of business depression—I was virtually a prisoner at my office.

Caro joined me after the first week.

In Paris we only went out in the evening twice, to the Thanksgiving dinner of The American Legion, and to a family dinner at the home of my old war-time friend, General de Chambrun, now in command of the French troops in Tunisia. At the dinner of General de Chambrun, the guests included Marshal Petain and Captain de Marenches. The latter was the liaison officer during the war between Pershing and Foch and Petain, and during that time we became staunch friends. He was a very able man. He was wounded in the war, and belonged, like de Chambrun, to the old French nobility. During the evening he spoke to me of his heart trouble, and within a week he died.

London,
December 21, 1931.

Secretary Stimson called me by telephone from Washington this afternoon and said that the President and he desired me to be chairman of the United States delegation to the Disarmament Conference at Geneva in February.

I told him that I did not feel competent to engage in the technical negotiations which, to such an extent, this convention will involve. My suggestion was that Gibson would be better qualified. The discussion indicated, however, that he and the President were fully resolved in the matter.

Upon inquiry as to whether my appointment was satisfactory to Senator Swanson, who will be a member of the Delegation, he replied that it was. I told him under the circumstances that I would accept. This is certainly a difficult assignment. If I had not had some experience in international negotiations and did not know what I was taking on, I would feel highly honored. As it is, the appointment leaves me cold. However, I will do the best I can.

NOTE: A few days after this last journal entry I was called to Washington by Secretary Stimson for a consultation in connection with my prospective duties as chairman of the American Delegation to the Disarmament Conference to be held in Geneva. After arriving I presided in the State Department at the first meeting of the Delegation, but shortly thereafter President Hoover asked me to serve as President of the Reconstruction Finance Corporation and in order to accept that appointment February 2, 1932, I resigned as Ambassador to Great Britain and as chairman of the Disarmament Delegation.

The following letter was received from the Prime Minister after my resignation:

10 Downing Street,
Whitehall.
20th January, 1932.

MY DEAR DAWES:

Whilst of course I am delighted to hear of any news that tells me you are moving onwards and upwards and that new opportunities come to you to help your country, I grieve much that the announcement which appears in to-day's paper means that you are going to leave us. We have had a very good time together, which I think has been completely undisturbed by disagreements or misunderstandings. How happy the world would be if every country's relations with the others had been conducted in the spirit in which you and we have managed as regards our own.

When you wander back here to be lazy, or for any other purposes, do remember that as long as I am above ground there will be somebody who will expect to see you and will greet you with gladness. All the friendly sentiments I am trying to express are to be shared by your wife, and I can only conclude by sending you my very best wishes for the success of the great undertaking to which you have put your hand.

Believe me to be,

Yours always sincerely,

J. RAMSAY MACDONALD

INDEX

Abbot, Dr. C. G., 399
Abercorn, Duke of, 242
Adams, Charles F., 105, 123, 132, 138, 140, 161, 165, 193
Afghanistan, 228
Aga Khan, 272, 399
Alexander, A. V., 36, 42, 61, 168, 308, 372
Alfonso, Infante Don, 236, 333, 339
Allenby, Lord, 202
Ames, Knowlton, 10
Ancient and Honourable Artillery Co., 179
Archbishop of Canterbury, 158
Armstrong, Sir Henry, 306
Ashfield, Lord, 227
Asquith, Lady, 306
Astor, John Jacob, 29
Astor, Lord and Lady, 26, 74, 115, 192, 266, 314, 399
Atherton, Ray, 12, 14, 35, 41, 44, 49, 83, 123, 342, 358
Austro-German Customs Union, 331, 334, 387

Baker, Newton D., 270
Baldwin, Stanley, 35, 83, 206, 214, 260, 307, 379, 407
Balfour, Arthur James, 104, 170
Barons' Court, 242
Bartley, E. Ross, 218
Baruch, Bernard M., 227
Beach, Mr. and Mrs. Arthur, 221
Beauchamp, Lord, 306
Belin, F. L., 54
Bennett, James O'Donnell, 52
Bennett, Richard B., 245, 254
Birkenhead, Lord, 228
Blackitt, Sir Basil, 255
Blake, Tiffany, 195, 200, 202, 203
Boggs, Col. F. C., 10
Bordonaro, A. Chiaramonte, 250, 262
Bosworth, C. H., 342

Boyd, Dr. W. W., 342
Boys Brigade, Glasgow, 200
Bracken, Brendan, 192, 227, 266, 274
Branch and Chain Banking, 93
Brancker, Sir Sefton, 243
Briand, Aristide, 67, 113, 130, 161, 170, 308, 344, 415, 427
Bridgeman, Lord, 29
British tariff, 245, 253, 260, 337, 380, 386, 389
British Treasury Control System, 55, 277, 284; Dawes monograph, 287, 306, 308, 311; Stamp's memo, 316; Royal Commission report, 325, 334
Brüning, Dr. H., 256, 259, 363, 373, 404
Buckingham, Earl of, 140
Bunau-Varilla, Philippe, 106
Bureau of the Budget, U. S., 4, 56, 265, 277, 289, 299
Burke, Edmund, 140
Business depression, world wide, 252, 260, 274, 336, 349, 355, 388
Butler, Pierce, 55

Campbell, Malcolm, 306, 308
Carmania, S.S., 212
Carnegie Foundation, 203
Cartier, Baron de, 406
Castle, William R., 360, 365
Cecil, Lord, 29, 60, 107, 427
Century of Progress, Chicago, financing, 5; guarantees, 6, 8; Trustees' resolution, 10, 84, 93, 98, 204, 218; London office, 238, 259, 348; statement on sale of bonds, 93, 218, 369; report after closing, 370
Cermak, Anton, 359
Chamberlain, Sir Austen, 17, 92, 257
Chamberlain, Neville, 379, 409
Chambrun, General Adalbert de, 431
Charles, Sir James, 212, 215
Chatterjee, Sir Atul C., 256
Chelmsford, Viscount, 27

Index

Index

Index

Index

Locarno, 119, 159, 172
Logie House, 118
Lohr, Major L. R., 10, 94, 97, 347
London *Observer*, 89
London *Times*, 70, 85-8, 150, 163, 171, 197, 222
Longworth, Alice Roosevelt, 30
Loomis, Frank B., 266
Lord Bishop of London, 34, 43, 262
Lord Mayor of London, 129
Lord Provost of Elgin, 58
Lossiemouth, 13, 44, 48, 56, 58, 229
Lothian, Earl of, 192
Luther, Dr. Hans, 366
Lyautey, Marshal, 47, 377-8

MacCurdy, Dr. George Grant, 223-6, 232, 389, 398
MacDonald, Ishbel, 56, 58, 82, 101, 108, 375
MacDonald, J. Ramsay, 14, 36, 41, 45, 49, 53, 55, 65, 69, 93, 99, 118, 163, 245, 375, 433; General election, 398, 406; Gold Purchase Discontinued, 395; Naval disarmament, cruiser requirements, 60; letter to Hoover, 79-82; security pact with France, 161, 164, 171, 176; speech on Hoover conference, 167; statement to Parliament on policy, 38; to press, 15, 105, 125, 139, 145, 165, 248; new Cabinet, 409; Tariff question, 246, 380; visit to America, 16, 23, 32, 44, 71, 83, 101, 105, 108, 121, 164
MacDonald, Malcolm, 42, 60, 229
Macmillan, Lord, 372
McCarl, John R., 4
McCormick, Col. R. R., 6, 8, 10, 213, 352
McCormick, Ruth Hanna, 30, 254
McCutcheon, John T., 195, 199, 202-3
McElroy, Dr. Robert, 221
McHardy, General A. A., 48
McKeever, Mr., 179
McKenna, Sir Reginald, 42, 247
McKinley, William, 192
McLennan, D. R., 10
Madden, Sir Charles, 82
Magdalen College, 27
Magoffin, Ralph V., 219
Maharajah of Alwar, 31, 263
Malkin, Herbert, 315, 326, 329
Manchurian crisis, 35, 108, 397, 402, 411, 414-420, 423, 430
Marconi, Marchese, 255

Marenches, Captain de, 106, 431
Marfield, C. Howard, 6
Marietta College, 342
Marriner, J. Theodore, 2, 192, 377
Marshall, John, 216
Marston Moor, 33
Masaryk, Thomas G., 162, 170
Massigli, René, 106, 110, 178, 308, 328, 419
Matsudaira, Tsuneo, 17, 23, 24, 26, 28, 33, 43; ratio of capital ships, 52, 67, 72, 84, 90, 105, 117; Japanese position, 120, 122, 157, 163, 177, 197, 225, 246, 315, 326, 345, 411, 418
Meath, Earl of, 47
Mellon, Andrew W., 27, 349, 360-366, 393
Merrille, Mr. and Mrs., 138
Merry del Val, Alfonso, 336
Meyer, Eugene, 366
Middle Temple, 122, 129, 162, 203, 254, 343
Military Board of Allied Supply, 48; motor transport, 106, 121, 140, 286
Mill, Dr. John Hubert, 206
Mills, Ogden, 361, 363, 366
Mills, W. W., 54, 56, 220
Miranda, Duke of, 333, 335
Mitchell, Mr. and Mrs. William D., 237
Morgan, J. P., 50, 52, 255, 382, 392
Morrow, Dwight W., 97, 105, 123, 125, 129, 130, 140, 154, 157, 160; appeal to Briand, 164, 168, 174, 182; conflicting duties, 191, 193, 219; Senate campaign, 204, 216, 254; Senate rules, 313, 326, 328, 330, 338, 347, 357, 360, 366, 400, 403
Mosley, Lady Cynthia, 37
Mount Ephraim, 179
Mussolini, Benito, 157, 167, 211, 388

Naval Board, U. S., 96
Naval Conference of 1930, consultative pact, 171, 174, 177, 181; delegates for U. S., 97; drafting treaty, 180, 187; escalator clause, 247, 341; experts, 131, 150; French cabinet crisis, 155, 157, 159; French-Italian negotiations, 212, 248, 253, 278, 305, 307, 312, 327, 330, 336, 346; French security, 161, 164, 171, 174, 177, 181; Impasse, 157, 162; Invitation to conference, 90; methods of procedure, 102, 109, 126, 128, 139, 151, 165, 168; Quantitative

439

Index

differences, 146, 151; public opinion, 150, 157; safeguarding clause, 187; Senate foreign relations committee, 222; tentative plan of U. S., 134-8; three-power pact, 155, 165, 170, 178, 185; treaty ratified, 224, 249; treaty signed by U. S., 193

Navy Memorial for U. S., 82

New York Herald, 412

New York Times, 167, 202, 226, 235, 349, 404

Niebla, 223, 234

Nielson, Carston, 256

Norfolk, Duchess of, 161

Norman, Montagu, 50, 62, 366, 401, 403

North Berwick, 50

Obermaier, Hugo, 389

Ochs, Adolph, 202

Olds, Robert E., 429

O'Leary, John W., 6, 8, 84

Oliphant, Lancelot, 83

Ortiz, Rubio, 191

Osborne, Dr. Henry F., 388, 399

Oxford University, 27

Page, Arthur W., 166, 192

Page, Thomas Nelson, 192

Palestine, protection for Americans, 61, 63, 65

Palmstierna, Erik K., 263

Pannill, Charles J., 370

Parker, Rev. Sir William H., 86

Parmentier, Jean, 106; reparations, 354

Payot, General, 106

Peabody, Stuyvesant, 9

Peabody Donation Fund, 158, 255

Peel, Earl, 279

Pembroke, Lord, 121

Penn, William, 140

Pershing, General J. J., 54, 70, 92, 106; war book, 268, 343, 371, 377, 425, 431

Pesson-Didion, 106

Petain, Marshal, 106, 431

Petrie, Sir Flinders, 31, 41, 225

Pettifer, Arthur, 111

Pick, George, 10

Pilgrims Society, 13, 17, 105, 131, 154, 157, 160, 181, 310

Pinckney, Mr. and Mrs., 158

Pirelli, Alberto, 50, 53, 62, 157

Plumer, Field Marshal, 111, 210

Poincaré, Raymond, 52

Pole, Sir Felix, 259

Polish Corridor, 387

Pollard, H. M., 242

Powell, Francis, 259

Pratt, Admiral William V., 105, 124, 127, 140, 181

Press Club, 88

Price, Major, 54, 378

Princeton University, 30

Queen Mary of England, 13, 31, 38, 204

Queen's Hall, 205

Quesnay, Pierre, 54

Ralston, James L., 182

Ramsay, Dr. Arthur S., 214

Rawson, Frederick, 10

Reading, Lady, 141

Reading, Lord, 30, 247, 338, 372, 397, 401, 407

Reconstruction Finance Corporation, 432

Reed, David A., 97, 105, 123; agreement with Japan, 127, 129, 163; technical knowledge, 132, 140, 168, 174, 177, 182, 217

Reed College, 342

Reichsbank, 350-366

Reid, Mrs. Whitelaw, 29, 213

Reparation Commission, 26, 43, 151

Reuters, Ltd., 163

Riddell, Lord, 88

Rio Tinto Mine, 223, 234

Ripley, W. Z., 389

Ritchey, Lawrence, 354

Robertson, Andrew W., 98

Robinson, Sir Harry Perry, 26

Robinson, Joseph T., 97, 105, 123, 129, 138, 161, 172, 174, 187, 192, 205, 217

Rockefeller Institute, 170

Rogeri, Signor, 17

Rogers, Will, 115, 124, 129

R-101, airship, 243

Roop, J. Clawson, 4, 114, 265

Roosevelt, Franklin D., 254, 346

Rosenwald, Julius, 8, 10, 94

Rothwell, W. E., 242

Royal Free Hospital, 174

Royal Scot train, 204

Royal Society, 261

Royal Treasury Commission, 326

Runciman, Walter, 409

Rutherford, Sir Ernest, 261

Salisbury, Lord, 132

Samuel, Sir Herbert, 379, 398, 404

Sarnoff, David, 98

440

Index

Index

45246